The Russian Revolution and the Unfinished Twentieth Century

David North

Mehring Books
Oak Park, Michigan
2014

Published by Mehring Books
P.O. Box 48377
Oak Park, MI 48237
Printed in the United States of America
© 2014 Mehring Books

Library of Congress Cataloging-in-Publication Data

North, David, 1950–
The Russian Revolution and the Unfinished Twentieth Century / David North.
    pages cm
Includes index.
ISBN 978-1-893638-40-2 (paperback : alkaline paper)
ISBN 978-1-893638-43-3 (ebook)
1. Soviet Union—History—Revolution, 1917-1921. 2. Soviet Union—Politics
and government. 3. Soviet Union—Historiography. 4. Socialism—History—20th
century. 5. Capitalism—History—20th century. 6. Revolutions—History—20th
century. 7. History, Modern—20th century. 8. World politics—20th century. I.
Title. II. Title: Russian Revolution and the Unfinished Twentieth Century.
  DK265.N625 2014
  947.084'1--dc23

                                             2014025277

About the Author

David North has played a leading role in the international socialist movement for more than forty years, and is presently the chairperson of the International Editorial Board of the *World Socialist Web Site* and the Socialist Equality Party (US). His many published works include *The Heritage We Defend*; *The Crisis of American Democracy*; *Marxism, History and Socialist Consciousness*; and *In Defense of Leon Trotsky*.

Contents

Foreword

There is broad agreement among historians that the twentieth century — as a distinct epoch in politics and culture — began in August 1914 with the outbreak of World War I. But the question of when the century ended — or whether it has ended at all — is the subject of intense controversy. The dispute is not over the formal dating of a given 100-year span of time. Clearly, the 1900s are over and we live in the twenty-first century. And yet, though halfway through the second decade of the new century, our world remains well within the gravitational field of the twentieth. If historians still look back in anger on the last century, it is because mankind is still fighting — in the spheres of politics, economics, philosophy, and even art — its undecided battles.

Until recently, historians were fairly confident that the twentieth century had been successfully laid to rest. The collapse of the Stalinist regimes in Eastern Europe in 1989 and the dissolution of the Soviet Union in December 1991 set into motion a tidal wave of capitalist triumphalism that engulfed, with little resistance, academic institutions all over the world. The professoriat proceeded rapidly to bring its theories of history into alignment with the latest newspaper headlines and editorials.

Prior to the events of 1989–91, the vast majority of the academic specialists assumed that the Soviet Union, which they more or less equated with socialism, would last forever. Even those who were familiar with Leon Trotsky's critique of Stalinism viewed his prediction that the regime of the

Kremlin bureaucracy would lead, unless overthrown by the Soviet working class, to the dissolution of the workers' state and the restoration of capitalism, as the unrealistic and self-justifying jeremiad of Stalin's vanquished foe.

As the Stalinist regimes dissolved themselves, however, the professors and think-tank analysts hastened to proclaim that not only had the United States achieved an irreversible victory over its Cold War adversary, but capitalism had expunged its socialist nemesis from the realm of historical possibilities. The spirit of the moment found its consummate expression in an essay by the Rand analyst, Francis Fukuyama, entitled "The End of History?" published in the journal *The National Interest*. He wrote:

> What we may be witnessing is not just the end of the Cold War, or the passing of a particular period of post-war history, but the end of history as such: that is, the end point of mankind's ideological evolution and the universalization of Western liberal democracy as the final form of human government.[1]

To be fair to Fukuyama, he did not argue that the future would be placid and trouble free. However, he claimed that there could no longer be any doubt that liberal capitalist democracy, however imperfectly practiced in the United States and Western Europe, represented, in terms of mankind's political and economic evolution, an unsurpassable ideal. History had "ended" in the sense that there was no credible intellectual and political alternative to liberal democracy based on capitalist market economics. In a book published in 1992 that developed his argument, Fukuyama wrote:

> In our grandparents' time, many reasonable people could foresee a radiant socialist future in which private property and capitalism had been abolished, and in which politics itself was somehow overcome. Today, by contrast, we have trouble imagining a world that is radically better than our own, or a future that is not essentially democratic and capitalist. Within that framework, of course, many things could be improved: we could house the homeless, guarantee opportunity for minorities and women, improve competitiveness, and create new jobs. We can also imagine future worlds that are significantly worse than what we know

---

[1] *The National Interest* 19 (Summer 1989), p. 3.

now, in which national, racial, or religious intolerance makes a comeback, or in which we are overwhelmed by war or environmental collapse. But we cannot picture to ourselves a world that is *essentially* different from the present one, and at the same time better. Other, less reflective ages also thought of themselves as the best, but we arrive at this conclusion exhausted, as it were, from the pursuit of alternatives we felt *had* to be better than liberal democracy.[2]

Fukuyama's analysis combined bourgeois political triumphalism with extreme philosophical pessimism. It might have been appropriate for the publisher to insert in every copy of Fukuyama's book a prescription for Prozac. If the existing capitalist reality was, for all intents and purposes, as good as it could get, mankind's future was very bleak. But how realistic was Fukuyama's hypothesis? Though he claimed to draw inspiration from Hegel, Fukuyama's grasp of dialectics was extremely limited. The claim that history had ended could make sense only if it could be demonstrated that capitalism had somehow solved and overcome the internal and systemic contradictions that generated conflict and crisis. But even Fukuyama avoided such a categorical conclusion. He acknowledged that capitalism would be plagued by social inequality and the discontent that it engendered. He went so far as to admit the possibility that the dissatisfaction with the "imperfect reciprocity of recognition [i.e., social inequality] will be the source of future attempts to find alternatives to liberal democracy and to capitalism from the Left."[3] But what, then, was left of Fukuyama's proclamation of history's end?

The American historian Martin Malia (1924–2004) understood that Fukuyama's theory was untenable. He cautioned against "triumphalist talk that History, after having overcome the illusions of both fascism and Communism, had at last arrived at a safe harbor in market democracy." Malia expressed doubts about the viability of "a post-Marxist vision of the end of history..."[4] Capitalism, he feared, would never free itself from the specter of its historical antagonist. "The socialist idea will surely be with us as long as inequality is, and that will be a very long time indeed."[5] Thus, Malia argued,

---

[2] Francis Fukuyama, *The End of History and the Last Man* (New York: The Free Press, 1992), p. 46.

[3] Ibid., p. 299.

[4] Martin Malia, *The Soviet Tragedy* (New York: The Free Press, 1994), p. 514.

[5] Ibid.

the only way to combat the persistence of socialist aspirations was to insist, on the basis of the Soviet experience, that socialism could not work. This was the thesis of *The Soviet Tragedy*. The dissolution of the Soviet Union in 1991 was the inevitable outcome of the October 1917 Revolution. The Bolshevik Party had attempted the impossible: the creation of a non-capitalist system. This was the fatal historical error of Lenin and Trotsky.

> The failure of integral socialism stems not from its having been tried out first in the wrong place, Russia, but from the socialist idea per se. And the reason for this failure is that socialism as full noncapitalism is intrinsically impossible.[6]

This argument was hardly substantiated, and Malia ended his book on a strangely ambivalent and troubled note. He foresaw the possibility of a renewed upsurge of a mass revolutionary movement for socialism.

> The unprecedented Leninist phenomenon appeared because of the unprecedented world crisis of 1914–1918. Any analogous global crisis could drive dormant socialist programs once again toward maximalism, and consequently towards the temptation of seeking absolute power in order to achieve absolute ends.[7]

While Fukuyama had argued that the "End of History" signified the end of socialism, Malia mournfully acknowledged that socialism would continue to attract adherents, even though the goal of a noncapitalist society was impossible to realize. The British historian, Eric Hobsbawm (1917–2012), who had been a devoted member of the Stalinist British Communist Party for more than a half-century, borrowed and modified the arguments of both Fukuyama and Malia in the formulation of a theory of twentieth century history that struck a chord among a broad layer of moderately left and ex-left academics. Hobsbawm was too knowledgeable a historian, and too steeped in empiricist methodology, to accept the metaphysical speculations of Fukuyama. He trimmed Fukuyama's conception to more manageable proportions. The dissolution of the Soviet Union signified, if not the end of history, the end of the twentieth century. In *The Age of Extremes*, Hobsbawm argued that the

---

[6] Ibid., p. 225.
[7] Ibid., p. 520.

years between the outbreak of World War I in 1914 and the dissolution of the Soviet Union in 1991 comprised the "Short Twentieth Century"

> which, as we can now see in retrospect, forms a coherent histori-
> cal period that has now ended ... there can be no serious doubt
> that in the late 1980s and early 1990s an era in world history
> ended and a new one began. That is the essential information for
> historians of the century...[8]

Hobsbawm's periodization of the twentieth century as a "short" seventy-seven year time span between 1914 and 1991 reformulated, in a less strident form, Malia's rejection of the revolutionary project of the Bolsheviks. By bringing the curtain down on the drama of the twentieth century with the dissolution of the Soviet Union in 1991, Hobsbawm proclaimed the end of the revolutionary epoch that had begun with the outbreak of World War I. Between 1914 and 1991, socialism — in one form or another — had been seen as an alternative to capitalism. That period ended, for all time, in 1991. Hobsbawm left little doubt that the revolutionary socialist project as conceived by Lenin and Trotsky probably had been an illusion from the start. In the light of 1991, the Bolshevik seizure of power, *three quarters of a century earlier*, could be seen to have been a tragic error. Even if one could find, in the circumstances that existed in 1917, political justification for the decisions of the Bolshevik leaders, Hobsbawm insisted that the October Revolution was a one of a kind, absolutely unique and unrepeatable event — the outcome of circumstances so peculiar as to be without any contemporary political relevance.

Fukuyama and Hobsbawm placed the fate of the Soviet Union at the center of their periodization of the historical process. For Fukuyama the dissolution signified the "End of History." For Hobsbawm it marked the end of the "Short Twentieth Century." The vast historical significance they attributed to the dissolution of the Soviet Union was a somewhat backhanded acknowledgment that the October Revolution was the central political event of the twentieth century. However, both the "End of History" and "Short Twentieth Century" theses were based on a fundamentally false conception of the historical foundations of the October Revolution and the nature of the Soviet state as it evolved in the decades following the Bolshevik seizure of state power in 1917. While Fukuyama engaged in abstract theorizing that

---

[8] Eric Hobsbawm, *The Age of Extremes* (New York: Pantheon Books, 1994), p. 5.

paid little attention to specific problems of historical causality, Hobsbawm accepted the conventional and superficial view that the socialist revolution in Russia would never have taken place had it not been for the primal disaster of World War I. "Without the breakdown of nineteenth-century bourgeois society in the Age of Catastrophe," he wrote, "there would have been no October revolution and no USSR."[9]

This is a tautology, not an explanation. The real intellectual challenge, evaded by Hobsbawm, was to identify the deep-rooted contradictions, of a global character, that finally erupted in world war *and* social revolution. After all, World War I was preceded by years of intensifying Great Power conflicts. And in the decades that preceded the October Revolution, socialism had emerged as an international mass movement of the working class. Prior to 1914 socialists had not only expected the breakdown of bourgeois society, but had also warned that the breakdown might assume the form of a devastating European-wide and even global war. Far from welcoming such a war as an essential precondition for socialist revolution, the great Marxists of the pre-1914 era placed the struggle against imperialist militarism at the center of their political work.

Only as it became increasingly evident that a major imperialist war was imminent did socialists begin to consider the strategic implications, from the standpoint of revolutionary struggle, of such an event. The critical point is that even before 1914, Marxian socialists had recognized the common origin of war and revolution in the historical crisis of the capitalist system. Ignoring the pre-1914 debates within the socialist movement, Hobsbawm's superficial treatment of the problem of historical causality portrayed the October Revolution as a merely contingent and accidental outcome of the war.

A serious flaw in the arguments of Fukuyama, Hobsbawm and, we should add, Malia, was their uncritical identification of the Soviet Union, at all stages of its history, with socialism. The Stalinist regime was accepted as the inevitable outcome of the original sin of the October Revolution. This fatalistic and ultra-deterministic view of Soviet history refused to consider the possibility of a non-Stalinist course of development. Hobsbawm expressed complete indifference to the struggle of oppositional tendencies within the Soviet Communist Party — especially that led by Leon Trotsky — to the emerging bureaucratic dictatorship headed by Stalin. He dismissed discussion about alternatives to Stalin's rule as an illegitimate exercise in counterfactual history.

---

[9] Ibid., p. 8.

However intense the conflict within the Communist Party, Stalin's faction eventually prevailed; and, from that point on, Stalinism was — to cite the cynical phrase of the historian — "the only game in town." What Trotsky and the Left Opposition said and wrote in the struggle that raged within the Communist Party between 1923 and 1927 was beside the point. For Hobsbawm, the issue was rather straightforward. Stalin won. Trotsky lost. That's all there was to it. Historians should not concern themselves with what might have been.

Hobsbawm's peremptory dismissal of alternatives to Stalinism was far less the expression of an uncompromising historical objectivity than an exercise in political apologetics. He was hardly a detached and impartial commentator. During his long membership in the British Stalinist movement, Hobsbawm had never objected to the Soviet bureaucracy's falsification of the history of the Russian Revolution and the role of Leon Trotsky. Hobsbawm went to his grave in 2012, at the age of ninety-five, without ever acknowledging forthrightly that he had upheld for decades the official Stalinist history of the USSR that had been based on lies.

The dissolution of the Soviet Union, according to Hobsbawm, had brought the "Age of Extremes" to an end. Capitalism was once again, as it had been before 1917, "the only game in town." And while it was not unlikely that society would experience violent upheavals at some point in the future, there existed no prospect that a mass revolutionary socialist movement would re-emerge.

Hobsbawm's narrative led the reader to conclude that mankind had arrived at an impasse and that its situation was hopeless. "We do not know where we are going," he wrote at the end of *The Age of Extremes*. Hobsbawm saw nothing in the experience of the past that might serve as a positive guide for the future. He was certain of only one thing: the socialist revolution of October 1917 neither could nor should serve as an example or guide for the struggles of the future. "If we try to build the third millennium on that basis," he wrote, "we shall fail." And "the price of failure," Hobsbawm intoned in the final sentence of his long book, "is darkness."[10]

The lectures and essays published in this volume were, for the most part, developed in opposition to the claim that the dissolution of the Soviet Union had brought to a conclusive end the epoch of world socialist revolution. In opposition to Fukuyama's "End of History" and Hobsbawm's "Short

---

[10] Ibid., p. 585.

Twentieth Century," I argued that the dissolution of the Soviet Union, while certainly an event of great importance, did not mark the traumatic end of socialism. History would continue. And, to the extent that the twentieth century is defined as an epoch of intense capitalist crisis, giving rise to wars and revolutions, it is most appropriately characterized as "unfinished." That is, the central economic, social and political contradictions that confront mankind at the start of the twenty-first century are, in the main, the same as those it confronted at the beginning of the twentieth. For all the scientific advances, technological innovations, political upheavals and social transformations, the twentieth century ended on a strangely inconclusive note. None of the great social, economic and political issues that underlay the struggles of the century had been conclusively settled. The First World War was preceded and actually triggered by conflicts over the borders of states in the Balkans. Nearly eighty years later, the dissolution of Yugoslavia — instigated by the United States and Germany — set into motion a decade of bloody conflict over state sovereignty and the location of borders. World War I began in 1914 with the decision of the Austro-Hungarian Empire to punish the nationalist regime in Serbia for its obstruction of imperial interests. Eighty-five years later, in the twilight of the twentieth century, the United States bombed Serbia mercilessly to compel it to accept the imperialist rearrangement of borders in the Balkans.

This is not merely a case of *plus ça change, plus c'est la même chose* (the more things change, the more they remain the same). It is, rather, an example of the long-term persistence of fundamental socioeconomic and political issues that connect the world of 2014 with that of 1914 and endow the twentieth century with its "unfinished" character.

By way of comparison, let us consider how the world of 1800 would have appeared to those who celebrated New Year's Eve at the dawn of the twentieth century. As the 1800s came to a close, the Napoleonic Wars had clearly receded into the realm of history. The French Revolution and the battles of Austerlitz and Waterloo appeared to those alive in 1900 as the epic struggles of a very different age. The personalities of Robespierre, Danton and Napoleon continued to fascinate. But they were figures of another time and historical place, distant from the world of 1900. Of course, their impact on world history endured. But the political world in which they lived had been fundamentally and dramatically transformed in the course of the nineteenth century. In Western Europe and North America the processes of bourgeois-democratic and national-state consolidation precipitated by the American and French

Revolutions of the late eighteenth century had been largely completed. The industrial revolution had changed the economic and social structures of the advanced countries. The old conflict between the feudal aristocracies and rising bourgeoisie was transcended by the new form of class struggle arising out of the rapid development of industrial capitalism and the emergence of the proletariat. The inadequacy of the general democratic phrases that guided the great struggles of the late eighteenth century was made painfully obvious by the revolutions of 1848. *The Rights of Man* was written in the language of the old bourgeois-democratic revolutions. *The Communist Manifesto* was written in the language of the new proletarian socialist revolution.

By the turn of the twentieth century, politics had acquired a thoroughly global character, based on the development of a highly interconnected world economy. The system of national states, consolidated in the course of the nineteenth century, came under terrific strain, which assumed the form of an increasingly bitter struggle among the most powerful capitalist states for world domination. During the first decade of the twentieth century, the term "imperialism" entered into common usage. In the years leading up to the outbreak of World War I, the economic foundations of this new phenomenon and its social and political consequences were carefully analyzed. In 1902 the British economist J.A. Hobson wrote a book, entitled *Imperialism*, in which he argued, "The economic root of Imperialism is the desire of strong organized industrial and financial interests to secure and develop at the public expense and by public force private markets for their surplus goods and their surplus capital."[11] In 1910, the Austrian Social Democratic theoretician Rudolf Hilferding, in his work *Finance Capital*, called attention not only to the inherently antidemocratic and violent character of imperialism, but also to its revolutionary implications:

> The action of the capitalist class itself, as revealed in the policy of imperialism, necessarily directs the proletariat into the path of independent class politics, which can only end in the final overthrow of capitalism. As long as the principles of *laissez-faire* were dominant, and state intervention in economic affairs, as well as the character of the state as an organization of class domination, were concealed, it required a comparatively mature level of understanding to appreciate the necessity for political struggle,

---

[11] J.A. Hobson, *Imperialism: A Study* (Cambridge: Cambridge University Press, 2010), p. 113.

and above all the necessity for the ultimate political goal, the conquest of state power. It is no accident, then, that in England, the classical country of non-intervention, the emergence of independent working class political action was so difficult. But this is now changing. The capitalist class seizes possession of the state apparatus in a direct, undisguised and palpable way, and makes it the instrument of its exploitative interests in a manner which is apparent to every worker, who must now recognize that the conquest of political power by the proletariat is his own most immediate personal interest. The blatant seizure of the state by the capitalist class directly compels every proletarian to strive for the conquest of political power as the only means of putting an end to his own exploitation.[12]

In 1916, with the world war entering its third year, Lenin provided a succinct characterization of imperialism:

The supplanting of free competition by monopoly is the fundamental economic feature, the *quintessence* of imperialism.

... Imperialism, as the highest stage of capitalism in America and Europe, and later in Asia, took final shape in the period 1898–1914. The Spanish-American War (1898), the Anglo-Boer War (1899–1902), the Russo-Japanese War (1904–05) and the economic crisis in Europe in 1900 are the chief historical landmarks in the new era of world history.

... the decay of capitalism is manifested in the creation of a huge stratum of *rentiers*, capitalists who live by "clipping coupons." ... export of capital is parasitism raised to a high pitch. ... Political reaction *all along* the line is a characteristic feature of imperialism. Corruption, bribery on a huge scale and all kinds of fraud. ... the exploitation of oppressed nations ... by a handful of "Great" Powers ...[13]

In *War and the International*, written in 1915, Trotsky identified the conflict as

---

[12] Rudolf Hilferding, *Finance Capital* (London: Routledge & Kegan Paul, 1981), p. 368.

[13] V.I. Lenin, *Collected Works*, Volume 23 (Moscow: Progress Publishers, 1964), pp. 105–106.

a revolt of the forces of production against the political form of nation and state. It means the collapse of the national state as an independent economic unit.

... The War proclaims the downfall of the national state. Yet at the same time it proclaims the downfall of the capitalist system of economy. By means of the national state, capitalism has revolutionized the whole economic system of the world. It has divided the whole earth among the oligarchies of the great powers, around which were grouped the satellites, the small nations, who lived off the rivalry between the great ones. The future development of world economy on the capitalistic basis means a ceaseless struggle for new and ever new fields of capitalist exploitation, which must be obtained from one and the same source, the earth. The economic rivalry under the banner of militarism is accompanied by robbery and destruction which violate the elementary principles of human economy. World production revolts not only against the confusion produced by national and state divisions but also against the capitalist economic organizations, which has now turned into barbarous disorganization and chaos.[14]

In these writings we encounter the vocabulary and terminology of contemporary international geopolitics. The world described in them is one that we can still recognize as our own. It is the world of capitalism, of oligarchic elites, of massive conglomerates that pursue their global interests, and of authoritarian regimes. These works were written at the dawn of an epoch — of wars and revolutions — in which we still live. The conflicting conceptions of the twentieth century have far reaching implications for our understanding of the present and our expectations for the future. The "End of History" thesis legitimizes resignation and complacency. The "Short Twentieth Century," with its narrative of inevitable defeat and the ultimate futility of the revolutionary struggle for socialism, promotes a mood of existential hopelessness in a capitalist world which — even as it moves inexorably toward a catastrophe that threatens the extinction of civilization — will always possess sufficient power to crush whatever mass opposition may arise.

---

[14] Leon Trotsky, *The War and the International* (Colombo: A Young Socialist Publication, June 1971), pp. vii-viii.

The conception of the "Unfinished Twentieth Century" rejects the ahistorical pessimism of the petty-bourgeois intelligentsia. The "Unfinished Twentieth Century" locates humanity in the midst of a continuing and unresolved conflict. The outcome of the global crisis that began in August 1914 has yet to be decided. The historical alternatives confronting mankind are those identified by Rosa Luxemburg, in the midst of World War I, nearly a century ago: "Either the triumph of imperialism and the destruction of all culture, and, as in ancient Rome, depopulation, desolation, degeneration, a vast cemetery; or, the victory of Socialism, that is, the conscious struggle of the international proletariat against imperialism."[15] For Marxists, the existential category of *hopelessness* has no place in a scientific appraisal of historical possibilities. We understand existing conditions, in all their complexity, as the transitional manifestations of law-governed socioeconomic contradictions that can (and must) be comprehended and acted upon. The understanding of the "unfinished" character of the twentieth century places immense importance on the study of its history. The upheavals and struggles of the past are seen as vital strategic experiences whose lessons must be thoroughly assimilated by the international socialist movement.

More than twenty years have passed since the formulation of these conflicting interpretations of the significance of the dissolution of the Soviet Union. Which of them have stood the test of time? Contrary to Fukuyama's expectation, history, in the aftermath of the dissolution of the USSR, shows no sign of abating. One of his central claims was that the "End of History" would be characterized by a decline in the frequency of wars. With learned references to Hume, Kant and Schumpeter, Fukuyama argued that liberal democracy was peaceful. "The argument then," he prophesied, "is not so much that liberal democracy constrains man's natural instincts for aggression and violence, but that it has fundamentally transformed the instincts themselves and eliminated the motive for imperialism."[16]

Mr. Fukuyama was gazing into a faulty crystal ball. Just as the Rand scholar was imagining a post-Soviet world of universal peace, the US was proclaiming that it would not permit the emergence of a new competitor to its position as the world's hegemonic power. This new strategic doctrine required the virtual institutionalization of war as the *essential* instrument of US geopolitics. Accordingly, the 1990s witnessed a steady escalation of US military

---

[15] Rosa Luxemburg, *The Junius Pamphlet* (Colombo: Young Socialist Pamphlet, undated), p. 17.

[16] *The End of History and the Last Man*, p. 263.

operations. The decade began with the first invasion of Iraq and ended with the savage bombing campaign against Serbia.

The tragedy of 9/11, whose murky origins and execution have never been adequately explained, was seized upon by the Bush administration to declare a never-ending and constantly expanding "War on Terror." Under Obama, the crazed hunt for "terrorists" has merged with unrestrained geopolitical appetites that have made the entire planet — and outer space as well — a potential theater for US military operations. The terrible human cost of the chaos generated by the post-Soviet eruption of imperialist militarism is indicated by the fact that the number of refugees in the world today (July 2014) exceeds fifty million, the highest number since the end of World War II.[17] Afghanistan and Pakistan — the prime target of Washington's homicidal rampage through Central Asia — account for more than four million of the total number of refugees.

Since Fukuyama announced the triumph of liberal democracy, it has become more and more apparent that it is in crisis everywhere, above all, in the United States. The American state assumes ever more ruthlessly the character of an uncontrollable Leviathan. The Bill of Rights is being eviscerated. The US government asserts authority over its citizens — not only to spy upon them and gather data about the most private aspects of their lives, but also to kill them without due process of law — that would have been virtually inconceivable less than a generation ago. As for Eric Hobsbawm's "Short Twentieth Century," its intellectual shelf life proved shorter than its author could have possibly imagined. The new twenty-first century had hardly started before it became apparent that it would be preoccupied with the historical problems of the 1900s. Far from receding into an ever more distant past, the twentieth century has acquired the character of a massive debt which no one knows how to pay off.

* * *

This unpaid debt exacts interest in the form of continuous demands for the revision of history in accordance with present-day political agendas. The practice of history — or, to call things by their right name, "pseudo-history" — is being ever more crassly subordinated to the financial and political interests of the ruling elites. The distinction between history and propaganda is being systematically obliterated.

---

[17] Available: http://www.bbc.com/news/world-27921938

The outcome of the degradation of history into propaganda has been the creation of yet another approach to the twentieth century. The "End of History" and the "Short Twentieth Century" is giving way to the "Fabricated Twentieth Century." The creation of this school involves the suppression, distortion and outright falsification of the historical record. The aim of this project is to whitewash and legitimize the worst crimes of twentieth century capitalist imperialism and, conversely, to criminalize and render morally illegitimate the entire struggle of the international socialist movement.

In this exercise in right-wing historical revisionism, the socialist revolution of October 1917 is portrayed as the primal crime of the twentieth century, from which all subsequent horrors — including and in particular, Hitler's Nazi regime and the Holocaust — inevitably, and even legitimately, followed. Prior to the dissolution of the Soviet Union, such a grotesque perversion of twentieth-century history would have been considered, especially in Germany, as intellectually illegitimate and deserving of contempt.

In the mid-1980s and early 1990s, Germany was the scene of a famous *Historikerstreit* — a "Conflict of Historians" — that was provoked by the publication of an essay by the historian Ernst Nolte. He argued that the crimes of the Nazi regime should be seen as an understandable response to the October Revolution, the Russian Civil War of 1918–21 and the barbarism of Soviet Bolshevism. Calling for a sympathetic reassessment of the Third Reich, Nolte wrote that Nazi actions were "the fear-borne reaction to the acts of annihilation that took place during the Russian Revolution." Nolte continued: "The demonization of the Third Reich is unacceptable. We may speak of demonization when the Third Reich is denied all humanity, a word that simply means that all that is human is finite and thus can neither be all good nor all bad, neither all light nor all dark."[18]

Nolte's writings represented the most explicit attempt by a member of the German academic establishment, since the end of World War II, to mount a defense of Hitler and the Third Reich. He even justified the brutal treatment of European Jewry on the grounds that Chaim Weizmann, the leader of the Zionist World Congress, had declared in 1939 that Jews should fight with Britain against Germany.[19] In a grossly tendentious biography of

[18] "Between Historical Legend and Revisionism? The Third Reich in the Perspective of 1980," by Ernst Nolte in *Forever In the Shadow of Hitler?*, James Knowlton, ed., Truett Cates, tr. (Amherst, NY: Humanity Books, 1993), pp. 14–15.

[19] Cited by Geoffrey Eley in "Nazism, Politics and the Image of the Past: Thoughts on the West German *Historikerstreit* 1986–1987," *Past and Present*, No. 121, November, 1988, p. 175.

Martin Heidegger written in 1992, Nolte defended the philosopher's anti-Semitism and embrace of Nazism. "In comparison [with communism] the German revolution of National Socialism was modest, even meager in its ... goals — the restoration of Germany's honor and equality of right — and moderate in its methods." [20]

Nolte's writings encountered principled opposition in the German and American academic community. He was accused of engaging in historical apologetics on behalf of Nazism, and his reputation as a scholar was shattered. Today, however, Nolte's star is on the rise. Now ninety-one years old, he is being hailed as a prophet whose time has finally come. In its issue of February 14, 2014, *Der Spiegel*, the most widely circulated news magazine in Germany, featured a cover story in which it was claimed that Nolte's views have been vindicated. *Der Spiegel* asserted that when compared to the crimes of Stalin, the scale of Hitler's crimes appears diminished. Among the historians interviewed by *Der Spiegel* was Professor Jörg Baberowski, who is chairman of the department of East European Studies at the prestigious Humboldt University in Berlin. Defending Nolte, with whose views he has always agreed, Baberowski declared, "Hitler was no psychopath, and he wasn't vicious. He didn't want people to talk about the extermination of the Jews at his table."[21] Justifying Nolte's efforts to downplay the scale and unique character of the crimes of the Third Reich, Baberowski stated: "Historically speaking, he was right."[22]

About what was Nolte right? Interviewed by *Der Spiegel*, Nolte claimed that Hitler was forced into war by the intransigence of Britain and Poland. But that is not all. *Der Spiegel* reported that Nolte "insisted on ascribing to the Jews their 'own share of the "gulag,"'" because some Bolsheviks were Jews. Based on this logic, the Jews were at least partly responsible for Auschwitz. Somewhat taken aback by Nolte's bluntness, *Der Spiegel* acknowledged that his position "has long been an argument of anti-Semites."[23] But that was the extent of *Der Spiegel*'s criticism, and the statements of Nolte and Baberowski encountered virtually no public protest. The fact that the arguments of Nolte and Baberowski went largely unchallenged is an expression of not only intellectual but also political processes. During the past year, there has

---

[20] *Martin Heidegger: Politik und Geschichte im Leben und Denken* by Ernst Nolte, cited in a review by Richard Wolin, *The American Historical Review* Volume 98, No. 4, Oct. 1993, p. 1278.

[21] Available: http://www.spiegel.de/international/world/questions-of-culpability-in-wwi-still-divide-german-historians-a-953173.html

[22] Ibid.

[23] Ibid.

been a determined political campaign to build public support for a revival of German militarism. Spearheaded by Joachim Gauck, the country's president, the leading newspapers demand that the German people overcome their post-World War II pacifism and accept that Germany has legitimate great power interests that require military operations beyond its borders.

Significantly, the revival of calls for Germany to seek, once again, its "place in the sun" has been accompanied by efforts to discredit the long-established historical consensus — dating back to the publication in 1961 of historian Fritz Fischer's ground-breaking and magisterial study *Germany's Aims in the First World War* (*Griff nach der Weltmacht*) — that the Imperial regime of Kaiser Wilhelm II bore major responsibility for the outbreak of the war in 1914. Fischer, who died in 1999, is now the target of relentless attacks that are aimed at destroying his posthumous reputation as a scholar.

The ongoing crisis in Ukraine exemplifies the subordination of history to contemporary geopolitical agendas. The political marketing by the United States and Germany of the right-wing putsch of February 2014, in which fascist organizations played a major role, as a democratic revolution has been facilitated by the flagrant falsification of the historical record. This process is the subject of the penultimate essay in this volume.

* * *

This volume constitutes a portion of the record of the struggle waged by the International Committee of the Fourth International over the past twenty years to defend historical truth against the distortions and falsifications that followed the dissolution of the Soviet Union. This was a struggle for which the Trotskyist movement was well prepared. Since the formation of the Left Opposition in 1923, the Trotskyists had been compelled to defend the historical record and legacy of the October Revolution against the lies of the Stalinist bureaucracy. The bureaucratic reaction against the program and principles of the October Revolution began in the early 1920s with the distortion of the pre-1917 factional struggles inside the Russian social democratic movement, with the aim of casting Trotsky as an inveterate opponent of Lenin. Then, the political positions of Trotsky were misrepresented to portray him as the brutal enemy of the Russian peasantry. In the aftermath of Trotsky's expulsion from the Russian Communist Party in 1927 and his exile from the USSR in 1929, every event in Soviet history was falsified in accordance with the political interests of the Stalinist regime. Even Sergei Eisenstein had to recut his 1927 cinematic masterpiece, *Ten Days that Shook the World*, so that there would be no image of Trotsky, the man who had actually organized and led the October 1917 insurrection in Petrograd.

The lies and falsifications of the 1920s — which were employed to remove Trotsky from power and to repudiate the program of socialist internationalism upon which the October Revolution was based — metastasized in the 1930s into the frame-ups of the Moscow Trials that were staged by Stalin as a pseudo-legal smokescreen for the mass extermination of the generation of Marxists that had led the working class to power, formed the Communist International and created the Soviet Union. Lies about history, as Trotsky explained, serve a vital role as the ideological cement of political reaction. Whether in the form of judicial frame-ups, state and media propaganda, or the distortion of the historical record by unscrupulous petty-bourgeois academics, their purpose is to legitimize the crimes of the ruling elites, disorient public opinion, and deprive the great mass of the people of the information and knowledge they require in order to mount an effective and revolutionary struggle against the capitalist system. Thus, the struggle against the falsification of history is not a secondary, let alone optional component of political work. The defense of historical truth — especially that pertaining to the October Revolution and the strategic experiences of the international socialist movement in the twentieth century — is necessary for a renaissance of socialist consciousness in the working class.

In the final years of the Soviet Union, there was an upsurge of popular interest throughout the country in the history of the Russian Revolution. After decades of suppression, articles about Trotsky and, more importantly, works by Trotsky, became widely available. This development aroused anxiety within the Soviet leadership. In contrast to the persistent pro-capitalist orientation of the Stalinist bureaucracy, which sought to convince the public that a reversion to market economics was the only way forward, Trotsky's writings and the record of the Fourth International's struggle against Stalinism made clear that a socialist alternative to the bureaucratic regime was possible.

Among the Kremlin's central aims in carrying through the dissolution of the USSR was to preempt the resurgence of a socialist perspective in the working class. Thus, the dissolution was accompanied by a new campaign of historical falsification, centered on the claim that the Soviet Union was, from the start, a doomed enterprise. The emergence of this new "Post-Soviet School of Historical Falsification" moved along the same trajectory as the writings of Fukuyama, Malia and Hobsbawm. All these works conveyed the basic message that the dissolution of the USSR followed inexorably from the October Revolution, and that no other outcome was possible. Stalinism was not a perversion of the October Revolution, but rather its necessary consequence. There was no alternative.

In the development of the conception of the "Unfinished Twentieth Century," the lectures and essays in this book insisted that the historical record proved conclusively that there did exist an alternative to Stalinism. I challenged Hobsbawm's claim that any consideration of alternatives to Stalinism was a pointless and intellectually illegitimate exercise in counterfactual history. "History must start from what happened," he wrote. "The rest is speculation."[24]

I call attention to this particular passage because it typifies an approach to the history of the Soviet Union that is widespread and insidious. Hobsbawm does not resort to outright falsification of historical material. But he sins against historical truth by withholding important facts and presenting an incomplete record. Hobsbawm's omissions contribute to the distortion of history.

Unfortunately, in many of the lectures and essays, I was compelled to deal not only with omissions but also with blatant distortions of historical facts. There were times when I could not help but be amazed at the brazenness with which some individuals, who call themselves historians, can put down on paper statements that are demonstrably untrue, and thereby leave to posterity evidence of their intellectual dishonesty.

The practice of falsification has been abetted by the influence of various schools of postmodernism, whose cumulative impact on the study and writing of history has been nothing short of catastrophic. The connection between this regression in philosophy and the falsification of history cannot be overstated. Let us refer again to the work of Professor Baberowski, a disciple of Michel Foucault, who described in his *Der Sinn der Geschichte* (*The Meaning of History*) the methodology that guides his work:

> In reality the historian has nothing to do with the past, but only with its interpretation. He cannot separate what he calls reality from the utterances of people who lived in the past. *For there exists no reality apart from the consciousness that produces it.* We must liberate ourselves from the conception that we can

---

[24]   Eric Hobsbawm, *On History* (London: Weidenfeld & Nicolson, 1997), p. 249.

understand, through the reconstruction of events transmitted to us through documents, what the Russian Revolution really was. *There is no reality without its representation.* To be a historian means, to use the words of Roger Chartier, to examine the realm of representations.[25] (Emphasis added)

Baberowski invokes the most extreme proposition of idealist solipsism — there exists no reality outside of and apart from thought — to legitimize the repudiation of historiography as the truthful reconstruction of a past that objectively existed. History, he tells us, exists only as a subjective construction. There is no objective historical truth that accurately depicts social, economic and political conditions as they once really existed. That sort of historical reality is of no interest to Baberowski. "A history is true," Baberowski declares, "if it serves the premises set up by the historian."[26] This debasement of history condones the writing of fraudulent narratives to serve subjectively contrived agendas — for example, the rehabilitation of Hitler's criminal regime. It is not an accident that Professor Baberowski has joined forces with the likes of Ernst Nolte.

Future generations will struggle to understand how philosophical reactionaries such as Jean-François Lyotard, Richard Rorty and Foucault, working with concepts rummaged from the "basement of bourgeois thought,"[27] came to exert such an unwarranted and dangerous influence in the last decades of the twentieth century and the first decade of the twenty-first. I would be very pleased if the lectures and essays in this volume that deal with philosophical issues help future scholars understand the political and social pathology of the postmodernist pandemic.

The polemical approach taken in this book is, I believe, appropriate to both the subject matter and the times in which we live. History has become a battleground. "The tradition of all the dead generations weighs like a nightmare on the brain of the living," wrote Marx.[28] Fifteen years into the new century, neither politicians nor historians can free themselves from the nightmares of the last one. The ever-mounting conflicts and crises of the twenty-first

---

[25] Jörg Baberowski, *Der Sinn der Geschichte: Geschichtstheorien von Hegel bis Foucault* (Munchen: C.H. Beck, 2005), (translation by D. North), p. 22.

[26] Ibid., p. 9.

[27] The phrase was coined by G.V. Plekhanov.

[28] Karl Marx and Frederick Engels, *Collected Works*, Volume 11 (New York: International Publishers, 1979), p. 103.

century are invariably entangled in disputes over twentieth-century history. As contemporary political struggles evoke historical issues, the treatment of these issues is more and more openly determined by political considerations. The past is falsified in the interest of present-day political reaction. By exposing at least some of the most glaring falsifications of the history of the twentieth century, it is the author's hope that this book may prove to be a weapon in the revolutionary struggles of the future.

* * *

The material in this book is presented, with only few exceptions, chronologically. This allows the reader to follow the evolution of the International Committee of the Fourth International's work on historical issues over a period of two decades. As part of the normal editing process, I have made stylistic changes where necessary to facilitate the often bumpy passage of lectures from the auditorium where they are heard to the printed page where they are read.

The lectures and essays reflect the benefits of the intense collaboration that I have enjoyed with comrades and co-thinkers in the Trotskyist movement internationally and within the United States. I have been discussing and working over the tragic and tortured history of the German workers movement with Ulrich Rippert, the national secretary of the Partei für Soziale Gleichheit, for close to forty years. I gratefully acknowledge the assistance I have received from Frederick S. Choate, whose knowledge of Russian and Soviet history is an intellectual resource that I have drawn upon for many years. I am grateful to the indefatigable editorial team of Mehring Books, Jeannie Cooper and Heather Jowsey, who have managed to assemble a coherent and properly referenced volume out of the disparate parts. I also wish to thank Linda Tenenbaum of the Socialist Equality Party in Australia for the care with which she has reviewed so many of the lectures and essays in this volume as they progressed from rough draft to final form.

Finally, I must call attention to the role played by the late Soviet-Russian historian and sociologist Vadim Rogovin in the development of the historical work of the International Committee of the Fourth International. In February 1993 we met for the first time in Kiev. He had recently completed a study, entitled *Was There an Alternative?*, of the struggle waged by the Left Opposition against the Stalinist regime between 1923 and 1927. As a result of our discussions there and in Moscow, Vadim resolved to work with the

International Committee in the development of an "International Counter-offensive Against the Post-Soviet School of Historical Falsification." Despite being stricken with terminal cancer in 1994, he lectured at meetings sponsored by the International Committee all over the world. Vadim's study of Leon Trotsky's struggle against Stalinism grew to seven volumes. To this day, there is not another work on the Soviet Union written after 1991 that is remotely equal — in style and substance — to this masterpiece of historical literature.

In January 1998 I shared a platform with Vadim for the last time. He traveled with his wife Galya to Sydney, Australia, to lecture at the International School sponsored by the Socialist Equality Party. At the conclusion of his lecture, Vadim announced the dedication of the final volume of his historical work to the International Committee. Eight months later, on September 18, 1998, Vadim died in Moscow at the age of sixty-one. It is to the memory of this fighter for historical truth that I dedicate this volume.

David North
July 12, 2014

1

The Bolshevik Seizure of Power
in October 1917: Coup d'État or Revolution?[1]

One of the staples of anti-Marxist literature is that the Russian Revolution was a putsch, or coup d'état, engineered by a handful of ruthless malcontents who were determined to impose a totalitarian dictatorship upon the people. According to this argument, the Bolshevik Party was nothing more than a tiny sect prior to 1917, and it came to power only because it was able to exploit the mass confusion created by the revolution. But where did the revolution that caused all the confusion come from? Harvard University historian Richard Pipes insists that the revolution was entirely the work of a crazed intelligentsia "which we have defined as intellectuals craving power. ... They were revolutionaries not for the sake of improving the conditions of the people but for the sake of gaining domination over the people and remaking them in their own image."[2]

Since the 1980s a number of historians have attempted to provide a more detailed picture of the Russian working class and its political life prior to 1917. The best of these works give readers a sense of what was going on among the masses, and show that the Bolsheviks had established, well before 1917, a commanding political presence within the working class. By 1914 the

---

[1] Lecture delivered at the University of Michigan in Ann Arbor on April 18, 1995.
[2] Richard Pipes, *Russia Under the Bolshevik Regime* (New York: Vintage Books, 1995), p. 495.

1

Mensheviks, who once had held strong positions within the popular organizations of the working class, were in headlong retreat before the surging
Bolsheviks. It should come as no surprise that Professor Richard Pipes has
denounced empirically-grounded research into the development of the pre-
1917 Russian workers movement.

> Hordes of graduate students, steered by their professors, in the
> Soviet Union as well as the West, especially the United States,
> have assiduously combed historical sources in the hope of
> unearthing evidence of worker radicalism in prerevolutionary
> Russia. The results are weighty tomes, filled with mostly mean-
> ingless events and statistics, that prove only that while history is
> always interesting, history books can be both vacuous and dull.[3]

I will make use of some of these "weighty tomes" and cite their "meaning-
less events and statistics" to give a brief overview of the political development
of the Russian working class in the decade that preceded the conquest of
power by the Bolsheviks. The defeat of the 1905 revolution resulted in a staggering decline in the numerical strength and political influence of the revolutionary organizations. In the years of revolutionary upsurge, between 1905
and 1907, both the Bolsheviks and Mensheviks — the two antagonistic factions of the Russian Social Democratic Labor Party (RSDLP) — had grown
by tens of thousands. After June 1907 their mass membership faded away. The
impact of defeat produced widespread demoralization. Revolutionary politics and aspirations were abandoned even by activists who had devoted years
to the struggle. The drift among broad sections of the Russian intelligentsia
back to religion and the flourishing of all sorts of backward attitudes, including a fascination with pornography, found its reflection within the membership of the revolutionary movement. By 1910, according to Trotsky, Lenin's
loyal and active contacts within Russia numbered about ten people.

However, this was not an unproductive period. Lenin and Trotsky,
despite their disagreements, were analyzing the events of 1905 and drawing
strategic lessons that laid the foundations for the victory of the socialist revolution in 1917. For Trotsky, the 1905 revolution demonstrated that the democratic revolution in Russia could be led only by the working class, and that
the democratic revolution would assume an increasingly socialistic direction.

---

[3] Ibid., p. 494.

This insight into the sociopolitical dynamics of the Russian Revolution laid the basis for the theory of permanent revolution.

For Lenin, the experiences of 1905 led to a deepening of his analysis of the differences between Bolshevism and Menshevism. They shed new light on the significance of the split in the socialist workers movement. The tactics employed by the Mensheviks throughout the 1905 revolution confirmed Lenin's belief that Menshevism represented an opportunist current that reflected the influence of the liberal bourgeoisie on the working class. The development of a revolutionary movement, Lenin insisted, required the persistent deepening of the struggle to expose before the working class this political characteristic of Menshevism.

Under the leadership of the shrewd Prime Minister, Stolypin, the tsarist regime enjoyed, after the close call of 1905, a revival of its political fortunes. However, Stolypin's assassination in 1911, which was organized by the secret police, removed the tsar's most capable minister just as the workers movement entered into a new phase of radical activity. The mass strikes in 1912 created a new political climate favorable to a rapid growth in Bolshevik influence.

The period of reaction, from 1907 to 1912, produced a sharp turn to the right among the Mensheviks. Drawing their inspiration from what was, in fact, the weakest side of German Social Democracy — that is, the domination of the German party by the reformist trade unions — the Mensheviks moved into the political orbit of the bourgeois liberals, and their aspirations assumed a definite reformist coloration. During the period of reaction, the Mensheviks benefited from their ties with the bourgeois liberal Cadets. But with the upsurge of the working class from 1912 on, the Bolsheviks began to overtake them, even in the trade unions once dominated by the Mensheviks.

An indication of the political radicalization of the working class came in April 1913, at a meeting of the Petersburg metalworkers union. This organization had been dominated by the Mensheviks for several years. However, with 700 to 800 workers present, the meeting elected a Bolshevik majority to the union's interim directing board.[4]

In late August 1913, a second election was held for a permanent directing board. It was attended by between 1,800 to 3,000 workers out of a total union membership of 5,600. A Bolshevik directing board was elected, and the Mensheviks managed to obtain only about 150 votes. The class-conscious workers of St. Petersburg discerned the differences in the positions of the

---

[4] Victoria Bonnell, *Roots of Rebellion* (Berkeley: University of California Press, 1983), p. 394.

Bolsheviks and Mensheviks. The latter opposed the involvement of the trade unions in struggles of an overtly political and revolutionary character. The Bolsheviks, on the other hand, sought openly to utilize the unions for precisely such a purpose.

Throughout the remainder of 1913 and into 1914, the Bolsheviks continued to oust the Mensheviks from their dominant positions in the unions. Among the organized tailors, for example, the Bolsheviks achieved an overwhelming majority in the leadership by July 1914. Out of eleven board members, ten were Bolsheviks and one was a Socialist-Revolutionary. The Mensheviks had lost all their support.

The printers, who were among the most skilled and educated workers, elected Bolshevik candidates in April 1914 to nine of the eighteen full seats on their board of directors and to eight of the twelve candidate seats.

Another indication of the growth of the Bolsheviks' support at the expense of the Mensheviks comes from the respective sizes of their press circulation. The Menshevik newspaper, *Luch*, had a press run of about 16,000 per issue. But *Pravda*, the Bolshevik daily, had a press run of 40,000.

By July 1914, on the eve of the war, the class struggle in the major industrial centers of Russia had assumed revolutionary dimensions. Incidents of street fighting between workers and police were reported in St. Petersburg. For the tsarist regime the war came at an opportune moment. While the pressure of war led, over a period of three years, to a sharpening of social conflict, its initial impact was to douse the revolutionary workers movement with a tidal wave of chauvinist fervor. The highly developed Bolshevik organization, which had been operating under conditions of borderline legality, was shattered and again driven underground.

Trotsky was to write later that had it not been for the war, the eruption of revolution in late 1914 or 1915 would have meant a mass proletarian movement unfolding, from the beginning, under the leadership of the Bolsheviks. The revolution began in February 1917 under conditions that were far less favorable to the Bolsheviks than they had been in July 1914. First, their organization was barely functioning in Russia. A great number of their working class factory cadre had been drafted into the army and were dispersed along a wide front. The factories were populated by far less politically experienced workers. Finally, the mass mobilization of the peasantry inside the army meant that when the revolution erupted, the proletarian character of the social movement, at least in its beginning stages, was far less pronounced than it had been in 1914. That is why the Socialist-Revolutionary Party, based largely on the peasantry, emerged out of the first weeks of the revolution as the largest political party.

Despite the unfavorable relation of forces the Bolsheviks were not entirely without influence in the revolutionary events that brought about the collapse of the tsarist regime in February–March 1917. As Trotsky explained in *The History of the Russian Revolution*, the uprising of February 1917 was not purely "spontaneous," i.e., without any trace of political leadership. Years of political agitation and education by the Bolsheviks, and even the Mensheviks, at least to the extent that the general conceptions of Marxism found expression in the activities of the latter, had left their residue on the consciousness of St. Petersburg workers.

Every mass movement possesses a certain type or level of consciousness, which has been formed over an extended period of time. The collective social and political consciousness of the working class was not a blank slate. The events of 1905 had not been simply forgotten. A generation of more conscious workers had followed and been influenced by the theoretical and political conflicts between the Bolsheviks and Mensheviks. There is a reason why the eruption of February 1917 led to the creation of soviets (workers councils) and assumed the form of a political struggle against tsarism, rather than of apolitical rioting and looting. Insofar as the war had not entirely destroyed the underground organization and eliminated their cadre from the factories, the Bolsheviks were still in a position to impart a more militant consciousness to the mass uprising of February 1917. Taking all this into account, we agree with — and contemporary historical research substantiates — Trotsky's assertion that the February Revolution was led by "conscious and tempered workers educated for the most part by the party of Lenin."[5]

Lenin's "secrets"

The most common assertion of the reactionary historians is that the seizure of power by the Bolsheviks was the outcome of a sinister conspiracy organized and carried out behind the backs of the Russian people, including the working class in whose name the revolution was made. To fathom how the greatest revolution in history arose as the product of such a conspiracy, one must refer once again to Richard Pipes:

---

[5] Leon Trotsky, *History of the Russian Revolution* (New York: Pathfinder Press, 1980), p. 199.

> Lenin was a very secretive man: although he spoke and wrote voluminously, enough to fill fifty-five volumes of collected works, his speeches and writings are overwhelmingly propaganda and agitation, meant to persuade potential followers and destroy known opponents rather than reveal his thoughts. He rarely disclosed what was on his mind, even to close associates. As supreme commander in the global war between classes, he kept his plans private. To reconstruct his thinking, it is necessary, therefore, to proceed retroactively, from known deeds to concealed intentions.[6]

Consider this: To produce fifty-five volumes of political literature, each volume between 300 and 500 pages, means that Lenin, in the course of his thirty-year political career, had an average annual written output of between 600 and 1,000 pages (in printed form). This output included economic studies, philosophical tracts, political treatises, resolutions, newspaper commentaries and articles, extensive professional and personal correspondence, innumerable memoranda and private notes, such as the *Philosophical Notebooks,* which enable us to follow the intellectual development of Lenin's conceptions. Much of Lenin's working day, for years on end, was spent at the writing desk. And yet all this writing, according to Pipes, was nothing more than the means by which Lenin skillfully concealed what he was really thinking!

It must be pointed out that Pipes' indictment of Lenin utilizes the very reasoning employed by Stalin in the organization of the frame-up of Leon Trotsky and the Old Bolsheviks during the Moscow Trials of the 1930s. Stalin and his accomplices claimed that the public writings and statements of Trotsky over a period of several decades, including the years when he stood at the leadership of the Red Army, were a cover for his secret decades-long conspiracy to destroy the Soviet Union. The "investigative methods" of Stalin and the celebrated Harvard historian — described by Pipes himself as the retroactive movement "from known deeds to concealed intentions" — calls to mind the juridical procedures of a medieval witch trial.

As for the specific allegation that Lenin kept his thoughts to himself as he "plotted" the secret overturn of the Provisional Government, it is hard to take this argument seriously. One must bear in mind that throughout 1917 Lenin exercised his influence upon the Bolshevik Party and the working class

---

[6] Richard Pipes, *The Russian Revolution* (New York: Vintage Books, 1991), p. 394.

principally through the written word. Indeed, it was a written document, known unpretentiously as the "April Theses," that decisively changed party policy following Lenin's return from exile, and set the Bolsheviks on the road to power. Later, between July and October 1917, he was in hiding and depended on the force of his written arguments to influence the Bolshevik Party. Lenin could hardly have overcome the resistance inside the Bolshevik Party leadership to his call for the overthrow of the Provisional Government had it not been for the influence he exerted upon the party's mass membership through the medium of his writings. John Reed recognized the unique character of Lenin's authority when he wrote in his famous *Ten Days That Shook the World* that Lenin was one of the very few political leaders in world history who had become the leader of masses because of his intellectual powers.

The conspiracy theory favored by Pipes and so many others is most convincingly refuted by historical research carried out by scholars who have unearthed a wealth of information about the scope of the mass working class movement upon which the Bolshevik bid for power was based. A study of this material leads one to the conclusion that the conquest of power by the Bolshevik Party was anything but the outcome of a putsch prepared in the back room of a safe house in Petrograd. The Bolshevik Party spent much of the year trying to keep pace with a mass movement that possessed a dynamic momentum whose equal had not been seen since the French Revolution.

Bolshevism and the working class

On the eve of the February Revolution, according to *The Blackwell Encyclopedia of the Russian Revolution*, there were approximately 3.5 million workers in the factories and mines of Russia. There were another million and a quarter workers located in transport and construction. The actual number of people who might be classified as wage workers comprised 10 percent of the population, or about 18.5 million.[7] Petrograd was a great industrial center whose environs were the home of 417,000 industrial workers. Of these, about 270,000 were metalworkers. Fifty thousand workers were employed in the textile industry and 50,000 in the chemical industry. The other major industrial center of Russia was Moscow, with about 420,000 workers, one-third of whom were textile workers and one-quarter metalworkers.

---

[7] Harold Shukman, ed., *The Blackwell Encyclopedia of the Russian Revolution* (Oxford: Basil Blackwell, Ltd., 1994), p. 19.

There were also large concentrations of industrial workers in the Urals, Ukraine— whose Donbass region employed approximately 280,000 workers — as well as in the Baltic region, Transcaucasia and Siberia. Relative to the size of the entire population, the working class was numerically small. But it was highly concentrated. Over 70 percent of the workers in Petrograd were employed in enterprises consisting of more than 1,000 workers. Two-thirds of Ukrainian workers were in enterprises that employed more than 500 workers. It was the same in the Urals.[8]

Before Lenin's return to Russia in April 1917, the Bolshevik Party leadership in the capital had adopted a policy of giving conditional support to the bourgeois Provisional Government, including its continuation of the war against Germany and Austria-Hungary, on the grounds that the revolution could not leap over the bourgeois democratic stage of its development. Lenin opposed this policy, but he was still in Switzerland and unable to intervene directly in the deliberations of the party leadership in Petrograd. The editorial board of *Pravda*, led by Stalin, refused to publish statements by Lenin which took strong exception to the conciliatory policies of the Bolshevik Party. Not until Lenin returned to Russia was he able, in the course of several weeks of factional struggle, to change the party's orientation. The divisions in the Bolshevik Party arose from the fact that Lenin was fighting to change a programmatic position that he had developed and defended for many years. To the Old Bolsheviks whom he now attacked, Lenin's new line — calling for the preparation of the overthrow of the Provisional Government and the assumption of power by the working class — was a heretical capitulation to the theory of permanent revolution that had been propounded by Leon Trotsky, in opposition to the Bolsheviks, for a decade.

Lenin had come, by his own route, to the perspective with which Leon Trotsky had been so prominently identified. The experience of the World War, refracted through his own study of modern imperialism, had led Lenin to conclude that the Russian Revolution was the beginning of a world socialist revolution; that the international crisis of capitalism, interacting with the weakness of the Russian bourgeoisie and its subordination to international capital, left open no possibility of a progressive bourgeois democratic stage of Russian development; and that the only class capable of breaking Russia's subordination to imperialism and carrying through the democratic tasks of the revolution was the proletariat. These conclusions formed the basis of Lenin's

---

[8] Ibid.

"April Theses," which called for the transfer of state power to the workers' soviet.

The debate at the April conference was not that of a small circle of underground revolutionaries. As the membership of the party grew rapidly, the inner-party struggle involved and was followed by significant strata of the working class. The British historian Steve Smith has argued that Lenin's "April Theses" had a direct and powerful impact on the consciousness of the most advanced sections of the Petrograd working class, particularly in the Vyborg district and on Vasil'evskii Island. Smith offers as evidence a resolution passed by general assemblies of workers at the Puzyrev and Ekval' factories during the "April Days" — that is, the first great working class demonstrations against the Provisional Government:

> The government cannot and does not want to represent the wishes of the whole toiling people, and so we demand its immediate abolition and the arrest of its members, in order to neutralize their assault on liberty. We recognize that power must belong only to the people itself, i.e., to the Soviet of Workers' and Soldiers' Deputies as the sole institution of authority enjoying the confidence of the people.[9]

Leon Trotsky wrote in his *History of the Russian Revolution* that the principal feature of a revolution is "the direct intervention of the masses in historic events." Despite the efforts of the representatives of the bourgeoisie, such as Milyukov, and the moderate leaders of the Soviet to establish the authority of the Provisional Government, the events of February unleashed a burst of popular democratic creativity. The factory and work committees that were formed in Petrograd and throughout Russia were the practical expression of the determination of the proletariat to assert its power and reorganize society along anticapitalist lines. Factory committees evolved into complex structures involved in virtually every aspect of daily life. They formed subcommittees that were responsible for the security of their factories, food supply, culture, health and safety, the improvement of working conditions, and the maintenance of labor discipline through the discouragement of drunkenness.

---

[9] Steve A. Smith, "Petrograd in 1917: the view from below," in *The Workers' Revolution in Russia, 1917: The View From Below,* ed. Daniel H. Kaiser (Cambridge: Cambridge University Press, 1987), p. 66.

As the revolution deepened, the committees became increasingly pre-occupied with the organization and control of production. *The Blackwell Encyclopedia* cites the work of a Soviet historian, Z.V. Stepanov, who "counted 4,266 acts by 124 factory committees in Petrograd between 1 March and 25 October and calculates that 1,141 acts related to workers control of production and distribution; 882 concerned organization questions; 347 concerned political questions; 299 concerned wages; 241 concerned hiring and firing and the monitoring of conscription."[10]

By the late summer and autumn of 1917, the factory committees began to demand that the employers provide them with access to order books and financial accounts. By October some form of workers control was in effect in 573 factories and mines, with a combined work force of 1.4 million workers.

Throughout 1917 the Bolsheviks developed enormous strength within the factory committees. Well before the Bolsheviks obtained a majority inside the Petrograd Soviet, they were in the leadership of the most important factory committees. A study of the resolutions passed by local assemblies shows that there was an enthusiastic response to the slogans and principal demands of the Bolshevik Party. In Moscow, which was less developed politically than Petrograd, the month of October 1917 saw more than 50,000 workers pass resolutions in support of the Bolshevik demand for the transfer of power to the soviets; and there is overwhelming evidence that the Bolshevik seizure of power was welcomed by a large majority of the working class.

We are given an idea of the mood of the working class in October 1917 in the study of developments at the textile center of Ivanovo-Kineshma, 250 miles northeast of Moscow, by the historian David Mandel. Strong support for the Bolsheviks predated the outbreak of revolution. By October 1917 it had become overwhelming. If anything, workers in Ivanovo-Kineshma expressed impatience with the slow pace of Bolshevik activity in Petrograd. When a Bolshevik orator, in a speech to the Kineshma Soviet in late September 1917, posed the rhetorical question: "History calls on us to take power ... Are we ready?" a voice from the audience replied, "We have been ready for a long time now, but we don't know why they are still asleep in the center."[11]

Even if one is inclined to treat such historical anecdotes skeptically, there is no doubt about the reality of the objective process they are

---

[10] *The Blackwell Encyclopedia of the Russian Revolution*, p. 22.

[11] David Mandel, "October in the Ivanovo-Kineshma industrial region," ed. Frankel, Frankel and Knei-paz, *Revolution in Russia: Reassessments of 1917* (Cambridge: Cambridge University Press, 1992), p. 160.

intended to illustrate. Between April and October, the Bolshevik Party experienced a phenomenal growth. In April 1917 the Petrograd organization of the Bolsheviks consisted of about 16,000 workers. By October its membership had risen to 43,000, of whom two-thirds were workers. In June 1917 the elections to the First All-Russian Congress of Soviets produced 283 Socialist-Revolutionary delegates, 248 Menshevik delegates and only 105 Bolshevik delegates. The elections to the Second All-Russian Congress, which assembled on the eve of the October Revolution four months later, produced an astonishing transformation: the Bolsheviks' share of the delegates rose to 390, the Socialist-Revolutionaries' share fell to 160 and the Mensheviks to seventy-two.

Workers repeatedly changed their political affiliations in the course of the revolution, generally moving to the left as they became increasingly disgusted with the Provisional Government and the refusal of the moderate socialist parties to break with it. As the historian Tim McDaniel has pointed out:

> Economic crisis, the continuation of war, the acceleration of class conflict, and the Kornilov putsch transformed the vast majority of politically active workers into enemies of the Provisional Government in its various incarnations. ... They came to see no essential distinction between the new government and the old tsarist regime, except that the Provisional Government was now more clearly a "bourgeois dictatorship."[12]

The letter of a worker who had been a member of the Socialist-Revolutionary Party to a Bolshevik newspaper reflects the shifts in the political mood during 1917:

> Because of profound misunderstanding I joined the SR party, which has now passed to the side of the bourgeoisie and lent a hand to our exploiters. So that I shall not be nailed to this mast of shame, I am quitting the ranks of the chauvinists. As a conscious proletarian, I am joining the Bolshevik comrades who alone are the genuine defenders of the oppressed people.[13]

---

[12] Tim McDaniel, *Autocracy, Capitalism and Revolution in Russia* (Berkeley: University of California Press, 1988), p. 355.

[13] *The Workers' Revolution in Russia, 1917: The View from Below*, pp. 73–74.

Of course, the radicalization of the working class in 1917 was not a homogeneous process without its own complex contradictions. Even in areas where the strength of the Bolsheviks grew rapidly, as among the Donbass miners, they also encountered opposition. There were times when they were the victims of sharp shifts in the moods of workers. And yet, for all its contradictions, the October Revolution was the outcome of a massive and politically-conscious movement of the working class.[14]

Summing up the results of his research into the causes of the Bolshevik victory, Professor Steve Smith has written:

> [T]he Bolsheviks themselves did not create popular discontent or revolutionary feeling. This grew out of the masses' own experiences of complex economic and social upheavals and political events. The contribution of the Bolsheviks was rather to shape workers' understanding of the social dynamic of the revolution and to foster an awareness of how the urgent problems of daily life related to the broader social and political order. The Bolsheviks won support because their analysis and proposed solutions seemed to make sense. A worker from the Orudiinyi

---

[14] This conclusion has been substantiated by the outstanding scholarship of Alexander Rabinowitch, professor emeritus of the University of Indiana. In the preface to *The Bolsheviks in Power*, the third volume of his monumental study of the Russian Revolution, Rabinowitch — summing up the conclusions of the antecedent volumes — writes:

> *The Bolsheviks Come to Power*, together with *Prelude to Revolution*, challenged prevailing Western notions of the October revolution as no more than a military coup by a small, united band of revolutionary fanatics brilliantly led by Lenin. I found that, in 1917, the Bolshevik party in Petrograd transformed itself into a mass political party and that, rather than being a monolithic movement marching in lock step behind Lenin, its leadership was divided into left, centrist, and moderate right wings, each of which helped shape revolutionary strategy and tactics. I also found that the party's success in the struggle for power after the overthrow of the tsar in February 1917 was due, in critically important ways, to its organizational flexibility, openness, and responsiveness to popular aspirations, as well as to its extensive, carefully nurtured connections to factory workers, soldiers of the Petrograd garrison, and Baltic Fleet sailors. [Bloomington and Indianapolis: 2007, pp. ix–x]

Professor Rabinowitch's conclusions carry exceptional weight, and not only because of the authority he has earned in the course of a half-century as a master of the historian's craft. Rabinowitch has explained that — having grown up in a family of Russian emigrés with strong Menshevik sympathies — he began his research into the Russian Revolution firmly believing that the Bolshevik seizure of power lacked mass support. The weight of the evidence that he uncovered as he combed the archives of Leningrad-St. Petersburg compelled him to revise his conceptions. Professor Rabinowitch's work exemplifies an intellectual integrity and devotion to truth that should serve as an example to a new generation of scholars.

works, formerly a bastion of defensism where Bolsheviks were not even allowed to speak, stated in September that "the Bolsheviks have always said: 'It is not we who will persuade you, but life itself.' And now the Bolsheviks have triumphed because life has proved their tactics right."[15]

More than a half-century ago, when there still existed an American intelligentsia that believed in the possibility of human progress and was capable of reflecting intelligently, even if not entirely sympathetically, on the meaning of the Russian Revolution, there appeared an influential book by the literary critic Edmund Wilson entitled *To the Finland Station*. Wilson, notwithstanding his own patrician distrust of the masses in revolution and his pragmatic disdain for dialectics, argued that Lenin's arrival at the Finland Station in April 1917 marked a high point in man's struggle to make himself the unfettered master of his own social development.

"The point is," wrote Wilson, "that western man at this moment can be seen to have made some definite progress in mastering the greeds and the fears, the bewilderments, in which he has lived."[16]

We heartily agree with this assessment, from which Wilson was later to retreat under the pressure of McCarthyism. The Russian Revolution still represents the highest point in the conscious efforts of humanity to assume control of its own destiny, to consciously master all that represents, in one form or another, the domination of the uncomprehended forces of nature over human development.

Marxism did not introduce into the world a new set of utopian conceptions. It recognized the potential for changing history within existing social forces. It discovered a social force, the working class, capable of ending the historically-evolved forms of class oppression. The oppression of the proletariat by the capitalist class had to be ended not simply because it was, in the conventional sense of the term, morally wrong; but because this oppression had become a fetter on the progressive development of human society itself. Precisely therein lay the immorality of capitalist oppression.

Marxism introduced into the working class an understanding of the historical process of which it was a part; and thereby transformed this class from an object of history into its conscious subject. The Marxist education of the

---

[15] Ibid., p. 77.
[16] Edmund Wilson, *To The Finland Station* (London: Macmillan Publishers, 1983), p. 472.

working class began in 1847. The October Revolution, seventy years later, was the outcome of this great process of socialist enlightenment.

For reasons which must be studied and assimilated, the Russian Revolution suffered a tremendous setback. But this fact by no means invalidates the enduring significance and relevance of the events of 1917.

2

Was There an Alternative to Stalinism?[1]

Permit me first of all to thank the Institute of Russian and East European Studies for this invitation to speak here at Glasgow University. I am not a professional historian. But the study of history is an inescapable requirement of membership in the Fourth International. Indeed, within the Fourth International there has never been a clear line of demarcation between history and politics. This has left Trotskyists open to criticism from all sides. Political opponents resent our introduction of historical questions into discussions of contemporary politics, while professional historians often dismiss as mere politics what we have to say about the Russian Revolution and its aftermath.

With our political opponents I see no possibility of a rapprochement. Our differences on innumerable questions of program reflect, in general, very different conceptions of the relation of the historical experiences of the international workers movement to the present problems and tasks of the socialist movement. But I think there is a great need for a renewed dialogue and, to the extent that this is possible, an active intellectual alliance between Marxists who trace their political heritage to the October Revolution and historians who are committed, whatever their personal political positions, to the scientific study of Russian and Soviet history.

The collapse of the Soviet Union has been followed by an outpouring of pseudohistorical literature intent on demonstrating that the October

---

[1] Lecture delivered on October 25, 1995 at Glasgow University in Scotland.

Revolution and the Soviet Union were the outcome of a criminal conspiracy that imposed an alien and unworkable dogma upon an unwary population. These tendentious works — usually described as magisterial in the admiring reviews of the establishment press — are, for the most part, the products of two closely related ideological schools. The first is that of the old Cold War anticommunists, represented by people like Richard Pipes of Harvard University and Martin Malia of the University of California. The second is that of the reconstructed Stalinists, i.e., former defenders and even high-ranking officials of the old Soviet regime, who have recently discovered, after it became profitable to do so, that they were the victims of Bolshevism. The most notorious representative of this school is General Dmitri Volkogonov.

In his recent biography of Lenin, Volkogonov devotes several pages to the dispersal of the Constituent Assembly in January 1918, an act which the general cites as one of the prime examples of Bolshevik criminality. In the shutting down of the Constituent Assembly, writes Volkogonov, Lenin, "revealed himself as the new intellectual of the Marxist type, a utopian fanatic, believing himself to have the right to perform any experiment so long as the goal of power was served."[2]

However one may wish to interpret this event, no one actually was killed in the dispersal of the Constituent Assembly. But not too long after he had written this severe indictment of Lenin's morality, Volkogonov, in his capacity as President Boris Yeltsin's chief military adviser, oversaw the October 1993 bombardment of the Russian parliament building, the White House, which resulted in the deaths of over 1,000 people. It would appear that notwithstanding his objections to Lenin, Volkogonov firmly believes in his own right to perform experiments. It all depends, in the final analysis, on the particular class interests of the power that is being served.

The post-Soviet school of historical falsification

Pipes, Malia and Volkogonov represent different trends of what can best be described as a new post-Soviet school of historical falsification, and its refutation is an urgent task of all serious scholars. The aim of this school is not only to discredit the Russian Revolution, but also to promote an environment of ideological intimidation that actively discourages all genuinely scientific examination of the complex economic, social, political and cultural

---

[2] Dmitri Volkogonov, *Lenin: A New Biography* (New York: The Free Press, 1994), p. 178.

processes which, in the totality of their interaction, determined the course of the Russian Revolution. The implications of this attack are far reaching. In the final analysis, the target of this school of historical falsification is the entire heritage of progressive and revolutionary thought and struggle, spanning centuries, out of which Marxism arose.

Lest I be accused of overdramatizing the issue, allow me to refer to the contribution made by Professor Alexander Tchoudinov, a member of the Russian Academy of Sciences in Moscow, at the 18th International Congress of Historical Sciences, held in late August–early September 1995 in Montreal. Quoting from St. Matthew and St. Augustine, Tchoudinov bitterly denounced all and sundry representatives of utopian thought who held up the possibility of a secular solution to the sufferings of man. "Only God," thundered Tchoudinov, "can eliminate the vices and defects of this life, but He will do so only at the end of the world." Yes, this was actually said at an International Congress of Historical Sciences. "Christianity," Tchoudinov proclaimed, "delivered people from the illusion of possibility to eliminate all social evil and, consequently, to establish the government free of vices."

Tchoudinov bemoaned the "dechristianization of social and political thought in the age of the Renaissance [which] revived the utopic tradition of ancient philosophy." He angrily scolded More and Campanella, before moving on to the Age of Enlightenment, where so much evil work was accomplished by Rousseau, Mably, Diderot and, to quote Tchoudinov, "many others, less eminent ones." The terrible work of the rationalists gave rise to Robespierre, then to Marx and, of course, Lenin. Finally, Tchoudinov arrived at his conclusion:

> It is important to notice, in the end, the totalitarian regimes of the twentieth century were the result of dechristianization of public consciousness in previous epochs.[3]

All of this was said in the presence of dozens of professors, many of whom were squirming in embarrassment. And they had good reason to be embarrassed. The proper venue for Tchoudinov-Rasputin's rantings was not a Congress of Historical Sciences, but a synod of Russian Orthodox metropolitans. It is a reflection of the shocking decline in intellectual standards that

---

[3] "Utopias in History," in Acts/Proceedings, 18th International Congress of Historical Sciences (Montreal, 1995), pp. 487–489.

the podium of a scholarly conference was made available for such theological drivel, and, even worse, that not a single historian rose from his seat to challenge Tchoudinov.

There is an unexplained contradiction in the analysis offered by both the old Cold War anticommunists and the reconstructed Stalinists. On the one hand, they ascribe to Marxism a rigid determinism, which, they claim, is the theoretical source of the attempt of the Bolsheviks to impose an unworkable antimarket utopia upon Russian society. But then, these bitter opponents of "determinism" resort to the most extreme determinism in their interpretation of post-1917 Soviet history, which they explain as the inexorable outcome of the unfolding of Bolshevik ideology. Every episode of Soviet history, we are told, arose inevitably out of the October Revolution. After depositing Lenin at the Finland Station in April 1917, the train of history, commandeered by ruthless Marxists, moved along a single track that led to the debacle of 1991, with preprogrammed stops at the Lubyanka and the Gulag Archipelago.

Stalin's fear of Trotsky

The fact that this interpretation has found widespread acceptance is even indicated in the title of this lecture: "Was there an alternative to Stalinism?" The very posing of the question suggests that, at best, only a speculative answer is possible. However, that is not the case. The study of the history of the Soviet Union demonstrates that there was an alternative to Stalinism. The growth of the bureaucracy and its usurpation of political power were consciously and systematically opposed from within the Bolshevik Party. The most significant opposition was that which arose in 1923 under the leadership of Leon Trotsky. One answer to the question "Was there an alternative to Stalinism?" is that Stalin and the Soviet bureaucracy certainly thought there was. Trotsky and the Left Opposition were subjected to a degree of repression that was as brutal as it was relentless. Always conscious of the dubious character of his own claim to the continuity of Bolshevism, Stalin himself believed that Trotsky represented the most dangerous political opposition to his regime.

A vivid portrayal of Stalin's fear of Trotsky is to be found in, of all places, the 1987 biography of the Soviet dictator by Dmitri Volkogonov. Basing himself on materials he found in Stalin's personal library, Volkogonov draws a picture of an omnipotent dictator who lived in fear of an isolated and stateless exile. He reports that everything written by or about Trotsky was kept by

Stalin in a special cupboard in his study. Stalin's copies of these writings were heavily underlined and filled with vituperative comments.

> Trotsky was no longer present, yet Stalin grew to hate him even more in his absence, and Trotsky's spectre frequently returned to haunt the usurper. Stalin came to curse himself for agreeing to let Trotsky go into exile abroad. He would not admit even to himself that he had feared Trotsky at the time, but he certainly feared the thought of him. The feeling that he would never be able to solve the "problem" of Leib Davidovich (as he tended to address Trotsky in his mind, using the Yiddish form of Lev) boiled over into violent hatred.[4]

Volkogonov continues:

> the main reason Stalin feared the spectre of Trotsky was because Trotsky had created his own organization, the Fourth International ... The spectre was wreaking a revenge more painful than Stalin himself could have devised. ...
>
> The thought that Trotsky was speaking not only for himself, but for all his silent supporters and the oppositionists inside the USSR, was particularly painful to Stalin. When he read Trotsky's works, such as *The Stalin School of Falsification*, *An Open Letter to Members of the Bolshevik Party*, or *The Stalinist Thermidor*, the Leader almost lost his self-control. ...
>
> ... Trotsky's collected works were published in dozens of countries, and it was from these that world opinion formed its image of Stalin, not from books by the likes of Feuchtwanger and Barbusse.[5]

Volkogonov has absolutely no sympathy for Trotsky's personality or political ideas. The notion that Trotsky might be viewed as an alternative to Stalin is abhorrent to Volkogonov. He does everything he can to present Trotsky's actions and writings in the very worst light. But this makes his account of

---

[4] Dmitri Volkogonov, *Stalin: Triumph and Tragedy* (New York: Grove Weidenfeld, 1988), p. 254.
[5] Ibid., pp. 255–259.

Stalin's fixation with the activities of his exiled opponent all the more significant. In its own way, even if unintentionally, this account underscores the glaring weakness of so many volumes on Soviet history, in which the treatment of Trotsky and the Left Opposition is of the most cursory character.

The personality and political role of Leon Trotsky, as a leader of the October Revolution and as the most important Marxist opponent of the Stalinist regime, looms over all discussions of Soviet history. He remains, even to this day, "the great unmentionable." How to deal with Trotsky always has been a difficult problem, both for the Stalinists and the anti-Marxist bourgeois historians. Within the Soviet Union, even after the death of Stalin and the Khrushchev revelations, the regime could not permit an honest accounting of his activities and ideas. Of all the Bolshevik leaders murdered by Stalin, Trotsky was the only one who was never formally rehabilitated by the Soviet regime. As late as November 1987, the heyday of *glasnost*, when Gorbachev delivered his long-awaited review of Soviet history on the occasion of the seventieth anniversary of the October Revolution, the Soviet leader vehemently denounced Trotsky, even as he found some kind words to say about Stalin's contributions to the socialist cause.

It is not hard to understand why the historical role of Trotsky presented such difficulties to the Soviet bureaucracy. The record of his work constituted an unanswerable indictment of the entire Stalinist regime, summed up in the title of his political masterpiece, *The Revolution Betrayed*.

Among anti-Marxist historians, the struggle waged by Trotsky against Stalin implicitly challenges the thesis that the totalitarian regime was the necessary and genuine expression of Bolshevism. If the anti-Marxist historians have not been able to ignore Trotsky, they have generally done their best to trivialize the significance of the political struggle he waged against Stalinism. One of the better known anti-Marxist historians has gone even further. Allow me to refer to the influential three-volume work by Professor Leszek Kolakowski, *The Main Currents of Marxism*. He writes:

> Many observers, including the present author, believe that the Soviet system as it developed under Stalin was a continuation of Leninism, and that the state founded on Lenin's political and ideological principles could only have maintained itself in a Stalinist form.[6]

---

[6] Leszek Kolakowski, *Main Currents of Marxism*, Volume 3, "The Breakdown" (New York: Oxford University Press, 1978), p. 2.

If Stalinism did, indeed, represent the legitimate and necessary apotheosis of "Lenin's political and ideological principles," how is one to explain the struggle waged by Trotsky and the Left Opposition? Kolakowski anticipated this question and offers the following explanation:

> The Trotskyists, and of course, Trotsky himself, regarded his removal from power as a historical turning point; but there is no reason to agree with them and, as we shall see, it can well be maintained that "Trotskyism" never existed, but was a figment invented by Stalin. The disagreements between Stalin and Trotsky were real to a certain extent, but they were grossly inflated by the struggle for personal power and never amounted to two independent and coherent theories. ... In reality, however, there was no basic political opposition between the two men, let alone any theoretical disagreement.[7]

Kolakowski's assertion testifies to the intellectual bankruptcy and cynical indifference to historical facts that underlies the claim that there existed no alternative to Stalinism. What credibility can be attached to a thesis that requires that one accept the incredible: that the struggle that split the Bolshevik Party and the international Communist movement in the 1920s and 1930s signified, in essence, nothing? The mass killings ordered by Stalin, the destruction of all those within Soviet society who were suspected, because of their political biography or intellectual interests, of even the most remote connection to Trotskyism — all this supposedly was done even though the Soviet dictator had no basic political or theoretical differences with Trotsky. And, at the same time, we are expected to believe that Trotsky wrote thousands of articles denouncing the Soviet regime and worked tirelessly to build an international movement dedicated to its overthrow only to conceal his agreement with Stalin's policies!

Was Stalinism inevitable?

Taking as their point of departure an ideologically-motivated conclusion — that the regime of Stalinist totalitarianism was the predetermined outcome of Bolshevik theory and politics — the adherents of the post-Soviet

---

[7] Ibid., pp. 8–9 and p. 22.

school of falsification ignore facts that indicate otherwise. The professional standards of these authors are deplorably low. And yet, the underlying argument retains a certain seductive attraction, even for many students who are by no means sympathetic to the ideological prejudices of the post-Soviet school of falsification. After all, how is one to explain the transition from Lenin to Stalin? Is it not true that within only a few years of having conquered power, the Bolshevik regime had been transformed into a ruthless dictatorship? Is it not reasonable to look for the seeds of this transformation within the Bolshevik Party, and especially its ideology?

This argument is not new. Back in the 1930s, at the high point of the Stalinist terror, even as his old comrades were being slaughtered and he himself was being pursued by GPU assassins, Trotsky was repeatedly confronted with the accusation that he, as a leader of the October Revolution, shared responsibility for the enormities of the Soviet regime.

He replied to these attacks by pointing to the basic flaw in the historical methodology of these critics. In seeking to discover the source of Stalinism in the ideology of Bolshevism — that is, by transferring the concept of original sin to the study of Soviet politics — the anti-Marxists examined Bolshevism as if it had evolved inside a sterile laboratory. They overlooked the fact that the Bolshevik Party, for all its dynamism, was only one element in the vast social panorama of the Russian Revolution. Though it was certainly the decisive political factor in the development of the Russian Revolution, the Bolshevik Party did not create it out of nothing. And even after it had conquered state power, the Bolshevik Party did not thereby become the sole determinant of social reality. The limits of its power were conditioned by a mass of antecedent historical factors, not to mention a complex interaction of international political and economic variables.

The party not only influenced; it was also influenced by the social conditions that it confronted upon taking power. The Bolshevik Party could, through decrees, abolish private ownership of the means of production, but it could not abolish a thousand years of Russian history. It could not abolish all the different forms of social, economic, cultural and political backwardness that were the legacy of Russia's historical development over those many centuries.

All human beings carry within their DNA the genetic matter that determines the general pattern of their biological development. But even in this natural process the influence of conditions external to the human body, such as an atmosphere altered by the effects of industry, plays a not unimportant role. And if the fate of every man and woman is considered from the standpoint of their existence as social animals, we know that the historical circumstances in which they live may exert a very decisive influence on even the purely physical aspects of their development.

If anthropologists cannot ignore the decisive influence of external, socially-conditioned factors in the development of humans, historians should not attempt to deal with a complex political phenomenon such as the Bolshevik Party as if its political evolution proceeded in accordance with instructions encoded invisibly within its general theoretical outlook.

Our refutation of the ideological metaphysicians of the post-Soviet school of falsification does not require that we attribute perfection to the Bolshevik Party, or deny the possibility that political errors made by Lenin and Trotsky following the October Revolution — such as the ban on inner-party factions at the Tenth Party Congress in 1921 — contributed in some way to the growth of bureaucracy and the eventual consolidation of the Stalinist dictatorship. One might even conclude that there were elements in the organizational conceptions and forms of Bolshevism that could be and were, under certain conditions, utilized by Stalin to build up a dictatorial regime. But the critical phrase is *under certain conditions*. Bolshevism contained within itself conflicting tendencies. But their development can only be understood within the context of the development of the economic and social contradictions confronting Soviet society as a whole.

Even in considering the roles played by the most crucial individuals, it is necessary to recognize the primacy of objective conditions and circumstances.

Stalin's political evolution

Several years ago I had a discussion in Moscow with Ivan Vrachev, one of the few individuals who had been a member of the Left Opposition in the 1920s — he signed the oppositionist Declaration of the 84 — and had managed to survive Stalin. He knew Trotsky and most other leaders in the Bolshevik Party, including Stalin, very well. I asked Vrachev whether there was anything about Stalin that would have led him to believe that he was a man capable of ordering the extermination of comrades with whom he had worked so closely for many years.

Vrachev replied that he had asked himself this question many times, but he could recall nothing that would have led him to believe that Stalin would be capable of such crimes. Vrachev then related the following story.

In 1922, he was about to leave Moscow for an important assignment in the provinces. He had been experiencing pains in his side, but did not care to ask for a postponement of his trip. Before his departure, Vrachev was obligated to meet with Stalin, who was in charge of the party organization. He went to the Kremlin, where he reviewed with Stalin the details of his impending trip.

At some point in the discussion, Stalin seemed to become aware of Vrachev's physical discomfort. Stalin became quite alarmed, and his entire demeanor seemed to express genuine concern. He told Vrachev that it was impermissible to take such risks with his health, ordered him to postpone his departure, and telephoned personally to make the arrangements for a physical examination of Vrachev by the best Kremlin doctors. As it turned out, Vrachev required an operation. Recalling this event, Vrachev conceded that it was possible Stalin was merely concerned with building his apparatus. But his impression remained that Stalin was then still capable of feeling and expressing genuine human emotions.

Stalin committed monstrous crimes. It is difficult to believe that there did not reside within his personality latent psychological elements that made him capable of mass murder. But even in the case of Stalin, these pathological and criminal tendencies were brought to the surface and molded into a particularly hideous form by a certain set of objective conditions. In this regard, it is worth noting an observation made by Trotsky in the late 1930s. He wrote that if Stalin had foreseen the outcome of his battle with the Left Opposition, and even knowing in advance that he would attain absolute power, he would not have embarked upon it.

Ironically, one of Stalin's political advantages in the struggle against his opponents was that he foresaw so little. Comfortable in his own pragmatism, Stalin was unencumbered by the type of principled considerations, based on serious theoretical analysis, that played such a fundamental role in Trotsky's selection of political alternatives. The Opposition's urgent warnings that his policies, domestic and international, would lead to disaster were dismissed by Stalin as panic-mongering. We find in a recently published letter from Stalin to Molotov, dated June 15, 1926, a passage which reveals a great deal about Stalin: "I am not alarmed by economic matters," he wrote. "Rykov will be able to take care of them. The opposition wins absolutely zero points on economic matters."[8]

---

[8] Lars T. Lih, Oleg V. Naumov and Oleg V. Khlevniuk, ed., *Stalin's Letters to Molotov* (New Haven: Yale University Press, 1995), p. 114.

This was Stalin's private assessment of the overall importance of an issue upon which the fate of the Soviet Union rested. It was worth "zero points." Stalin could not imagine that the accumulating contradictions of the Soviet economy under the regime of the NEP would eventually explode in his face and drive him to adopt, only a few years later, the desperate, reckless and murderous policies of mass collectivization.

The international context of the October Revolution

Central to both Trotsky's perspective of permanent revolution and Lenin's "April Theses" was the inextricable link between the struggles of the Russian working class and the international, especially the European, proletariat. Neither Lenin nor Trotsky conceived of the October Revolution in primarily national terms. They understood and justified the overthrow of the Provisional Government as the beginning of an international proletarian resolution of the global capitalist contradictions that were exemplified by the First World War. This perspective had nothing in common with the goal of establishing a self-sufficient socialist system within the boundaries of an economically backward Russia. It was not until the autumn of 1924, several months after Lenin's death, that Bukharin and Stalin introduced the idea that socialism could be established on a national basis, in one country.

Before that time it was an axiomatic premise of Marxism that the survival of the Bolshevik government, let alone the development of a socialist economy, depended upon the victory of socialist revolutions in Western Europe. It was fervently believed that the conquest of power by the working class in the advanced capitalist countries would provide Soviet Russia with the political, financial, industrial and technological resources vital for its survival.

It might be argued — and it was at the time by the Mensheviks and their allies among the European social democrats — that the Bolsheviks were mad to base the struggle for power on such far-flung international revolutionary calculations. It should be noted, however, that Rosa Luxemburg, whose attitude toward Lenin was by no means uncritical, found precisely that aspect of Bolshevism worthy of the most unstinting praise. She wrote in 1918:

> The fate of the revolution in Russia depended fully upon international events. That the Bolsheviks have based their policy entirely upon the world proletarian revolution is the clearest

proof of their political farsightedness and firmness of principle and of the bold scope of their policies.[9]

Luxemburg was not optimistic about the prospects for the Bolshevik regime. Nor did she agree with many elements of the policies pursued by the Bolsheviks after coming to power. But it never occurred to her to suggest that the Bolsheviks should not have taken power or that their political errors were the expression of some sort of utopian fanaticism. Even as she criticized the suppression of democracy and the excessive use of terror, Luxemburg directed her moral condemnations not at the Bolsheviks, but at the German social democrats, whose betrayal of revolutionary principles and support for the war policies of the German government, which included the occupation of large portions of Russia, had placed the Soviet government in such a desperate situation.

> It would be demanding something superhuman from Lenin and his comrades if we should expect of them that under such circumstances they should conjure forth the finest democracy, the most exemplary dictatorship of the proletariat and a flourishing socialist economy. ...
> ... All of us are subject to the laws of history, and it is only internationally that the socialist order of society can be realized. The Bolsheviks have shown that they are capable of everything that a genuine revolutionary party can contribute within the limits of the historical possibilities. They are not supposed to perform miracles. For a model and faultless proletarian revolution in an isolated land, exhausted by world war, strangled by imperialism, betrayed by the international proletariat, would be a miracle.[10]

And she concluded:

What is in order is to distinguish the essential from the nonessential, the kernel from the accidental excrescences in the

[9] Rosa Luxemburg, *The Russian Revolution and Leninism or Marxism?* (Ann Arbor: The University of Michigan Press, 1961), p. 28.
[10] Ibid., pp. 78–80.

> policies of the Bolsheviks. ... It is not a matter of this or that
> secondary question of tactics, but of the capacity for action of
> the proletariat, the strength to act, the will to power of socialism
> as such. In this, Lenin and Trotsky and their friends were the
> *first*, those who went ahead as an example to the proletariat of
> the world; they are still the *only ones* up to now who can cry with
> Hutten: "I have dared!"[11]

How refreshing these words sound today, even after the passage of nearly eighty years! They bear witness to the fact that the most conscious socialists of that period were well aware that the isolation of the Russian Revolution represented the greatest danger to its survival.

The defeats suffered by the European working class in the aftermath of World War I, above all in Germany, were the principal cause of the political degeneration of the Soviet regime. The isolation of Soviet Russia altered drastically the relation of class forces that had made possible the Bolshevik conquest of power. We are speaking here not of a purely theoretical problem, but a physical reality. The principal social base of the October Revolution was a very small but strategically positioned working class. The crisis of Bolshevism cannot be understood apart from the impact of the civil war on the working class.

The costs of civil war

In his writings on the causes of the degeneration of the Bolshevik Party, Trotsky frequently referred to the physical and spiritual exhaustion of the working class by the end of the civil war in 1921. Recently-published studies by conscientious historians — whose works, as one might expect, are far less known to the general public — provide important factual information that sheds critical light on the scale of the social catastrophe confronting the Soviet government.

In the valuable study, *Soviet State and Society Between Revolutions, 1918–1929*, Professor Lewis Siegelbaum of Michigan State University cites statistical data on the shrinkage of the industrial working class in the course of the civil war. At the time of the revolution, there was a total of 3.5 million workers in factories employing more than sixteen workers. That figure dropped to two million in 1918 and to 1.5 million by the end of 1920.

---

[11] Ibid., p. 80.

The worst losses were in the big industrial centers. The number of industrial workers in Petrograd numbered 406,000 in January 1917. By mid-1920 that figure had fallen to 123,000. In addition to this absolute numerical decline, the size of the proletariat as a percentage of the city's total population also declined significantly.

Moscow lost about 100,000 workers between 1918 and 1920, and during the same period the number of factory and mine workers in the Urals dropped from 340,000 to 155,000.

The major industrial and manufacturing sectors of the Soviet economy suffered staggering losses. The textile industry lost 72 percent of its workforce. The machine and metalworking industry lost 57 percent.

The decline of the proletariat was part of a general process of urban depopulation. From a population of 2.5 million in 1917, only 722,000 people were left in Petrograd by 1920, the same number as had lived in the city a half-century earlier. Moscow's population fell between February 1917 and late 1920 from two million to just over one million, somewhat less than the number recorded in the census of 1897.

Many factors contributed to this disastrous process, of which disease was among the most important. Tens of thousands of people succumbed during epidemics of cholera, influenza, typhus and diphtheria. The Moscow death rate rose from 23.7 per thousand in 1917 to 45.4 in 1920.

Another major factor in depopulation and deindustrialization was the desperate need of the newly-created Red Army for troops to fight the imperialist-backed White armies. Mobilizations by the Red Army removed well over a half-million workers from the factories between 1918 and 1920.

The impact of this demographic catastrophe was felt not only economically, but also politically. The Red Army depended for its successes, to a great extent, on the devotion and initiative of the most class-conscious sections of the working class. The depletion of the industrial proletariat involved the loss of precisely those workers who had played important roles in the revolutionary struggles of 1917, in factory committees or in other party-led organizations. There is no question that a statistically-significant section of workers who had, at the very least, voted for the Bolsheviks in elections to the soviets and then to the Constituent Assembly were drawn away from the industrial locations by the demands of the civil war.

The losses suffered by the Communist Party were staggering. It has been estimated that 200,000 out of 500,000 Communists who served in the Red Army were killed during the civil war. The political implications of such devastating mortality rates among the revolutionary cadres can be better appreciated by drawing attention to the influx of new members into the Communist Party, particularly after the military position of the Soviet government improved as a result of major victories in the autumn of 1919. Between August 1919 and March 1920, the membership of the party grew from 150,000 to 600,000. The caliber of this new intake was, in general, very much lower than that of those who had been lost.

By the end of the civil war, the social and political base of the Soviet government and the ruling party had been significantly altered. The "dictatorship of the proletariat" had lost a significant section of the proletariat upon which it had been based. And the "vanguard party" had suffered the loss of a large section of those who, by dint of long experience, had constituted a genuine political vanguard within the working class. Moreover, the actual social composition of the Bolshevik Party had undergone a fundamental change. The percentage of members who described their social origin as white collar, as opposed to proletarian, had increased significantly. Siegelbaum draws attention to the growing importance of this "lower middle strata," or petty bourgeoisie, in the affairs of the party and state organizations.

> The lower middle strata thus successfully grafted themselves onto the workers' and peasants' revolution. The result was that the social composition of the revolutionary state was more heterogeneous and less proletarian than generally has been acknowledged. What impact these "alien elements" had on the day-to-day functioning of the state, whether they possessed a specific psychology that was itself alien to the original revolutionary project, is not entirely clear.[12]

The character of the Bolshevik Party was changed not only by the loss of seasoned working class cadres and the influx of tens of thousands of inexperienced and politically-questionable recruits. Among the older cadres who had survived the years of revolution and civil war, the "professional demands of power" (to borrow a phrase used by Christian Rakovsky, Trotsky's closest political ally in the Opposition) took an unforeseen and serious toll. In a backward country where a vast portion of the population was illiterate

---

[12] Lewis Siegelbaum, *Soviet State and Society Between Revolutions*, 1918–1929 (Cambridge: Cambridge University Press, 1992), pp. 62–63.

and technical skills were in limited supply, party members were invariably dragged into management and administrative positions. The innumerable and ever expanding state agencies and party organizations vied with each other to obtain the services of cadres who possessed some sort of managerial skills. In this way a significant section of the party cadre was swept up in a process of bureaucratization.

Amidst economic chaos and desperate poverty, positions within the organizations and agencies of the state and party provided some small measure of personal security. The possibility of obtaining one passable meal a day at the workplace canteen constituted a not insignificant privilege. In all sorts of small but important ways, a bureaucratic caste, with specific social interests, gradually took shape.

The impact of the NEP

The Soviet government introduced the New Economic Policy (NEP) in 1921. It encouraged the revival of a capitalist market in order to restore the foundations of organized economic activity in Russia. Although a necessary response to the ruinous economic situation confronting the isolated Soviet state, the NEP accelerated the process of political degeneration within the ruling party. Given the fact that the proletarian base of the state and party had been drastically weakened, the impetus given by the NEP to the growth of capitalist tendencies within Soviet Russia was bound to have dangerous political consequences.

The NEP breathed new life into social elements that had viewed the Bolshevik Revolution as the apocalypse. Businessmen and traders re-emerged, and by 1922 a stock exchange was once again functioning in Moscow. The social climate became far more tolerant of inequality, and moods which reflected a certain moral and political decline found expression within the party membership, particularly those who were active in the upper echelons of the bureaucracy.

The NEP contributed to a revival of distinctly nationalist sentiments. The October Revolution was a great event in the history of the international workers movement. But it was also a transformative episode in Russian history. The revolution roused into action millions of people, both workers and peasants, in an epochal project of social reconstruction. The upheaval altered countless aspects of daily life. For many members of the party — especially the new recruits from the lower middle strata for whom the Bolshevik regime had opened new opportunities — the October Revolution appeared as the beginning of a great national revival. Against the background of defeats of the European working class, the practical tasks of building the national Soviet economy appeared to these forces far more realistic than the vision of world socialist revolution.

The caliber of political life within the party deteriorated. From 1920 on leading Bolsheviks frequently voiced their anxiety over the bureaucratization of the state apparatus. Lenin actually referred to Soviet Russia as a "workers state with a bureaucratic twist." But despite the concerns, the process of bureaucratization was nourished by deep-rooted objective tendencies related to the backwardness of Russia, and the party itself could not remain immune from the intrusion of bureaucracy into all spheres of social life. In the absence of a politically active working class, the methods of bureaucratic management and administration migrated rapidly into the affairs of the party. The most pronounced expression of this process was the growing influence of Stalin, whose principal responsibility as general secretary consisted of selecting the personnel required for the staffing of critical party and state positions. More and more, the power of appointment, which Stalin used to build up a network of supporters, invalidated and replaced the traditional forms of party democracy.

In March 1922, at the Eleventh Party Congress, Lenin warned that the party was in danger of being overwhelmed by the bureaucracy that administered the state. Shortly afterwards he was incapacitated by a stroke that removed him from political activity for several months. When he returned to work in the autumn of 1922, Lenin was stunned by the degree to which the situation within the party had deteriorated. He identified Stalin as the key figure in the process of bureaucratic degeneration. It is clear from the notes and documents prepared by Lenin during the last months of his politically-active life that he was preparing for a decisive confrontation with Stalin at the Twelfth Party Congress scheduled for April 1923. The famous testament written by Lenin calling for Stalin's removal from the post of general secretary, as well as the letter Lenin sent to Stalin threatening to break all personal relations with him, were part of a political dossier that Lenin intended to present to the party congress. The massive stroke suffered by Lenin in March 1923 saved Stalin's political career.

In the months that followed Lenin's final incapacitation, opposition grew to the bureaucratic methods employed by the "triumvirate" of Stalin, Zinoviev and Kamenev. The political tensions were exacerbated by deepening anxiety over the consequences of the NEP, expressed particularly, as Trotsky explained in the spring of 1923, in the worsening disparity between industrial and agricultural prices and the continuing deterioration in the conditions of the working class.

The Left Opposition

As it became clear that Lenin would not return to political activity, Trotsky came under pressure to speak out against the suppression of inner-party democracy. On October 8, 1923, Trotsky addressed a letter to the Central Committee that called attention to serious weaknesses in economic policy and also criticized the bureaucratization of party life. One week later, his criticisms were endorsed in a "Declaration" signed by forty-six prominent party members. These events marked the beginning of the political struggle of the Left Opposition.

The myth that Stalinism grew organically out of Marxist and Bolshevik ideology is contradicted by the historical record. There exist tens of thousands of documents, most of which were hidden from the Soviet people for decades, in which the development of Marxism found expression in the struggle waged against the Stalinist bureaucracy.

The far-sightedness of the Opposition found expression in the "Declaration of the 46," which warned that unless there was a radical change in the policies and methods of the leadership, "the economic crisis in Soviet Russia and the crisis of the factional dictatorship in the party will deal heavy blows at the workers' dictatorship in Russia and the Russian Communist Party. With such a load on its shoulders, the dictatorship of the proletariat in Russia and its leader the RCP cannot enter the phase of impending new worldwide disturbances except with the prospect of defeats on the whole front of the proletarian struggle."[13]

The issues that brought the Opposition into existence in 1923 were the growth of bureaucratism within the party and differences over economic policy. But it was only after the struggle was engaged within the party that the full depth of the programmatic differences of the conflicting tendencies, and, more critically, the antagonistic social forces upon which they were based, emerged into the open. At first, the criticisms of Trotsky and the Platform

---

[13] Leon Trotsky, *The Challenge of the Left Opposition 1923–25* (New York: Pathfinder Press, 1975), p. 450.

of the 46 threw the triumvirate into disarray, and it offered a few insincere political concessions. But then it recovered its nerve, counterattacked, and appealed to the social forces that, within the framework of NEP, had become the new constituency of the Soviet regime. This was the significance of Stalin's unveiling in late 1924 of the theory of "socialism in one country."

It is doubtful that Stalin anticipated the response that would be evoked by this revision of the international perspective upon which the Bolshevik Revolution had been based, or that he even understood why Trotsky invested his new theory with such far-reaching significance. But Stalin must have already sensed that there existed within the party, not to mention the broader population, a constituency that would welcome such a nationalist reformulation of the party's perspective. In declaring that socialism could be built in one country, Stalin was validating the practices and outlook that had become fairly common among tens of thousands of party bureaucrats.

Socialism in One Country

The theory of "socialism in one country" appealed especially to the growing bureaucratic strata which were tending with increasing consciousness to identify their own material interests with the development of the "national" Soviet economy. But it was not only bureaucrats who responded to this perspective. Within broad layers of the working class, the general political exhaustion expressed itself in a retreat from the internationalist aspirations of the October Revolution. Especially after the debacle suffered by the German Communist Party in October 1923, the promise of a national solution to the crisis of Soviet society seemed to offer a new lifeline for the besieged revolution.

In one of his more candid moments, Stalin suggested that the theory of "socialism in one country" served the valuable function of offering the Soviet masses a reason to believe that the October Revolution had not been made in vain, and that those who denied the possibility of building socialism in Russia, regardless of the fate of the international revolutionary movement, were dampening the faith and enthusiasm of the working class. It was necessary to assure the workers that they were, through their own efforts, achieving socialism. To arguments of this sort Trotsky replied in 1928:

> The theory of socialism in one country inexorably leads to an underestimation of the difficulties which must be overcome and to an exaggeration of the achievements gained. One could not

find a more antisocialist and antirevolutionary assertion than Stalin's statement to the effect that "socialism has already been 90 percent realized in the USSR."... Harsh truth and not sugary falsehood is needed to fortify the worker, the agricultural laborer, and the poor peasant, who see that in the eleventh year of the revolution, poverty, misery, unemployment, bread lines, illiteracy, homeless children, drunkenness, and prostitution have not abated around them. Instead of telling them fibs about having realized 90 percent socialism, we must say to them that our economic level, our social and cultural conditions, approximate today much closer to capitalism, and a backward and uncultured capitalism at that, than to socialism. We must tell them that we will enter on the path of *real* socialist construction only when the proletariat of the most advanced countries will have captured power; that it is necessary to work unremittingly for this, using both levers — the short lever of our internal economic efforts and the long lever of the international proletarian struggle.[14]

The insistence on the inextricable dependence of the Soviet Union upon the development of world socialist revolution and, conversely, the impossibility of constructing socialism in a single country, constituted the theoretical and programmatic foundation of the struggle waged by Trotsky and the Left Opposition against the Stalinist bureaucracy. It is not possible to understand the program of the Left Opposition if its separate elements — such as the reestablishment of party democracy, the development of planning, the strengthening of industry — are detached from this central unifying conception.

Most historians, including those not entirely unsympathetic to Trotsky, are inclined to see in his commitment to world revolution the weakest element of his overall program. And, therefore, even the sympathetic historians tend to treat his opposition to Stalinism as if it were quixotic. By pursuing the chimera of world revolution, they suggest, Trotsky failed to anchor his opposition to Stalinism to a secure foundation.

This criticism gravely underestimates the revolutionary potential that existed in the international workers movement of the 1920s and 1930s, and fails to appreciate the really dreadful impact of Stalinism on the development

---

[14] Leon Trotsky, *The Third International After Lenin* (New York: Pathfinder Press, 1996), pp. 84–85.

of world revolution. The political destruction of the Comintern by the Stalinists — that is, its transformation into an appendage of the Soviet bureaucracy — was the major cause of the calamitous defeats suffered by the working class, above all in Britain in 1926, China in 1927, Germany in 1933 and Spain in 1936–37. These defeats, in turn, profoundly affected the course of developments within the Soviet Union.

What accounts for this failure, even among conscientious contemporary historians, to study the international revolutionary strategy of Trotsky and the Left Opposition with the seriousness that it deserves? The reactionary political environment and the stagnant intellectual culture exerts an insidious influence on academics. Little remains of their youthful optimism. The skepticism toward, if not outright rejection of, the very possibility of socialist revolution is a response to the horrendous decline in the political and theoretical level of the international workers movement. Contemporary historians, even those who once considered themselves sympathetic to socialism — and were drawn, for that very reason, to study the Russian Revolution — now find it impossible to imagine a mass labor movement led by Marxists and animated by revolutionary internationalist aspirations. Their present-day pessimism has acquired a retroactive character. They project their current sense of hopelessness about the future onto their estimations of past revolutions.

This brings us, in conclusion, to the present-day significance of the Left Opposition as a subject of contemporary historical study. This, I am convinced, is one of the richest and most important areas for serious researchers. Until recently there existed no possibility of undertaking a systematic study of the Left Opposition. Comparatively little is known about this extraordinary movement of political opposition to the totalitarian dictatorship. This terrible void in our knowledge of one of the most important political struggles of twentieth century history is the legacy of Stalinism. The Soviet bureaucracy's consolidation of power was accompanied by the discrediting, criminalization and physical destruction of its political opponents. The terror was supplemented by a campaign of historical falsification that had as its aim the obliteration from the consciousness of the Soviet and international working class of all traces of the great Marxist tradition and culture represented by Trotsky and the Left Opposition. Only in this way could the Soviet bureaucracy establish the false identification of Stalinism and Marxism.

The conditions for destroying the vast edifice of lies are now emerging. The opening of the archives in Russia, notwithstanding the political circumstances that made this possible, marks the beginning of a new era in Soviet studies — and one with the most profound intellectual and political implications for the future of Marxism.

Slowly but surely, the discovery, publication and critical assimilation of documents and long-lost manuscripts will reshape public consciousness of the historical development of the Russian Revolution. There will be growing recognition of the Marxist alternative to Stalinism advanced by Trotsky and the Left Opposition. Brilliant political figures like Rakovsky, Preobrazhensky, Piatakov, Joffe, Sosnovsky, Eltsin, Ter-Vaganian, Boguslavsky, Vilensky and Voronsky, to name only a few of the leading Oppositionists, will be the subject of major biographies; and, the life of Trotsky — one of the greatest political and intellectual figures of the twentieth century — will be reexamined in the light of new and vital information. Marxism and the cause of international socialism can only gain from this vital process of intellectual renewal.

3

The Long Shadow of History: The Moscow
Trials, American Liberalism and the Crisis of
Political Thought in the United States[1]

Just about one month ago, *The New York Times* published a review of
the new biography of Leon Trotsky by the late Russian historian General
Dmitri Volkogonov. The reviewer was Richard Pipes, a professor of history
at Harvard University. Being familiar with the writings of both Pipes and
Volkogonov, I hardly expected the review to be anything other than a diatribe
against Leon Trotsky. After all, if the *Times* had been interested in producing
a critical review of Volkogonov's book it would not have given the assignment
to a man whose academic work, like that of so many other members of the
Harvard faculty, has been merely an extension of his services to the US government as a Cold War strategist and ideologist.

The review proceeded along predictable lines. Pipes examined
Volkogonov's biographical indictment of Trotsky not as a conscientious his-
torian, but rather as a witness for the prosecution. Even less than Volkogonov,
Pipes does not care to examine Trotsky's life in the context of history.
Instead, he seeks to blame Trotsky for everything in this history of which
Professor Pipes does not approve. Whether or not Volkogonov's — or his

---

[1] Lecture delivered on April 23, 1996 at Michigan State University in East Lansing.

own — judgments are supported by facts is of no importance to Pipes. Rather than drawing attention to the many crude mistakes contained in Volkogonov's biography, Pipes adds a fair number of his own, including lies taken directly from the old Stalinist school of historical falsification.

For example, Pipes' review depicts Trotsky as "Inordinately vain, arrogant, often rude..." This hostile caricature of Trotsky's personality was standard fare in Soviet textbooks for over sixty years. Pipes denounces Trotsky's inability to accept "the kind of disciplined teamwork that the Bolshevik Party required of its members."[2] Trotsky's unyielding opposition to the bureaucratic discipline imposed by Stalinism is presented as if it were the expression of a serious personal and political failing.

In the same review — it is amazing how many lies appear in a review of less than one thousand words — Pipes asserts that Lenin "had a very low opinion" of Trotsky's political and administrative abilities.[3] This false statement corresponds entirely to the version of history that was retailed in the Soviet Union during the years of Stalin's totalitarian dictatorship. This lie is refuted by Lenin's political testament of December 1922, in which he wrote that Trotsky "is distinguished not only by outstanding ability. He is personally perhaps the most capable man in the present C.C. [Central Committee]..."[4]

Finally, Pipes refers to Stalin as "Lenin's true disciple and legitimate successor."[5] This is precisely what Stalin wanted, or, to put it more accurately, demanded that everyone believe during his years in power. Those who are familiar with Soviet history know that Lenin, in the final period of his politically-active life, called for Stalin's removal from the post of general secretary and then threatened to break off all personal relations with him. Not even Volkogonov attempted to deny these well-known facts.

Cold War ideology and Stalinist lies intersect

Before proceeding any further, I should attempt to clarify what must appear to be a paradox. Why would Pipes, a Cold War anti-Soviet ideologue, make use of lies that were concocted by the Stalinist regime to defend itself

[2] Available: http://www.nytimes.com/1996/03/24/books/the-seeds-of-his-own-destruction.html?pagewanted=all&src=pm
[3] Ibid.
[4] V.I. Lenin, *Collected Works*, Volume 36 (Moscow: Progress Publishers, 1966) p. 595.
[5] Available: http://www.nytimes.com/1996/03/24/books/the-seeds-of-his-own-destruction.html?pagewanted=all&src=pm

against its political opponents? This paradox can only be understood by examining the political interests that were disguised for so many years by the ideological clichés of the Cold War era.

Notwithstanding the conflicts between them, the ideologists of the Soviet bureaucracy on the one hand and American capitalism on the other shared a common and politically indispensable lie: that the Soviet leaders were dedicated Marxists and that the Soviet Union was, more or less, a socialist society. The leaders of the Soviet state used this lie to preserve the legitimacy of the bureaucratic regime. Even when Khrushchev denounced Stalin's crimes in the "secret speech" of February 1956, he was at pains to absolve the bureaucratic regime of the atrocities that were committed in its interests. The "cult of personality" theory — which portrayed the Great Terror as merely the consequence of one leader's excesses — preempted an examination of the relation between Stalin's crimes and the consolidation of political power by the ruling bureaucracy.

As for the Cold War ideologists in the United States, the identification of Stalinism with Marxism and socialism was necessary to discredit all left-wing opposition to capitalism. That the rise of Stalinism was opposed from the left by tens of thousands of socialists within the Soviet Union was a historical fact which Cold War ideologists found rather inconvenient. After all, what would become of the thesis that forms the basis of 98 percent of everything ever written in the United States about the Soviet Union — that Stalinism was the unavoidable outcome of both Marxist theory and the 1917 October Revolution — if American historians and journalists acknowledged that the consolidation of the Stalinist regime was achieved through the physical extermination of virtually the entire socialist working class and intelligentsia in the Soviet Union?

The physical elimination of Soviet Marxists took place in the course of the Great Terror that swept the Soviet Union between 1936 and 1939. The central events of this terror were three horrifying show trials, in which the principal defendants were leaders of the October Revolution and former members of the Central Committee that ruled Soviet Russia in the days of Lenin. They stood accused of crimes ranging from sabotage to plotting the assassination of Stalin. In the course of these trials, all the defendants abjectly confessed to the crimes of which they were accused. Only Trotsky, who was living in exile and was charged in absentia, denounced the trials as a frame-up.

This brings me back to Pipes' review of Volkogonov. Had the Harvard professor confined himself to the standard collection of falsehoods that are found so commonly in the field of American Sovietology, his review might not have merited any special comment. But Pipes included one passage which made it impossible to ignore: "Trotsky and Lev Sedov, his son and closest aide, frequently said and wrote that Stalin's regime had to be overthrown and Stalin himself assassinated."[6]

The Moscow Trials

If ever a passage evoked the ghosts of the unquiet dead, it is Pipes' assertion that Trotsky and his son called for the assassination of Stalin. This is the allegation that provided the legal pretext for the Moscow Trials, the death sentences pronounced upon dozens of innocent defendants, and the campaign of politically directed antisocialist genocide that took place against the backdrop of the trials.[7]

By the time the trials began, Stalin had exercised virtually unlimited political power in the Soviet Union for nearly a decade. The Left Opposition, formed in 1923 to fight the growing power of the bureaucracy, was finally defeated in 1927. The leaders of the opposition were expelled from the Soviet Communist Party and exiled to the far reaches of the USSR. Trotsky was exiled to Alma Ata in Kazakhstan, which borders China. Despite the organizational defeat of the Left Opposition, Trotsky continued to wield considerable political and moral influence as the greatest Marxist critic of Stalin's policies. In 1929 the Politburo, dominated by Stalin, ordered Trotsky deported from the Soviet Union. Trotsky was exiled first to the island of Prinkipo, off the coast of Turkey; later, in 1933, to France; and then, in 1935, to Norway.

The decision to deport Trotsky was the most serious political error that Stalin ever made. As a man whose power was based exclusively upon his control of the bureaucratic machinery of the Soviet state and the Communist Party, Stalin had underestimated the power that Trotsky could wield, even as an exile, through his mastery in the sphere of ideas.

In the early 1930s, political opposition to the Stalinist regime grew steadily within the USSR, even within the ranks of the Communist Party. The catastrophic results of Stalin's collectivization policies, the general chaos that prevailed in Soviet industry as the result of adventuristic "Five Year Plans," and the suppression of every manifestation of independent political thought

---

[6] Ibid.
[7] See Appendices 1 and 2 beginning on page 363.

stimulated opposition to Stalin. Many historical works have already cited as a sign of widespread opposition the surprising results of the Seventeenth Party Congress in 1934, in which a large number of votes were cast against Stalin's reelection to the post of general secretary. More recent political studies, particularly those by the Marxist historian Vadim Rogovin, have shed new light on the depth of political hostility to Stalin and the growing influence of Trotsky.

Following the victory of fascism in Germany in January 1933, for which he held Stalin principally responsible, Trotsky called for the construction of a new International and the overthrow of the Stalinist regime in a political revolution. His writings commanded the attention of an international audience and made their way into the Soviet Union through the *Bulletin of the Left Opposition*. In the mid-1930s, even after years of repression, the traditions, principles and political culture of the October Revolution and the old Bolshevik Party remained powerful factors in the consciousness of broad sections of the Soviet population. A sudden change of events, especially in the volatile international situation, could strengthen revolutionary elements within the Soviet working class and produce a revival of mass support for genuine Bolshevism, that is, for the political line represented by Trotsky.

That is why Stalin decided to destroy Trotsky, his known supporters and all those who represented in any way the program and traditions of the October Revolution. The assassination of Leningrad party leader Kirov in December 1934 was the pretext for mass arrests of former oppositionists. During the next year Zinoviev and Kamenev, the closest political associates of Lenin in the old Bolshevik Party, were tried *in camera* on trumped up charges and sentenced to lengthy prison terms. Many articles written by Trotsky in 1935 warned that Stalin was exploiting Kirov's mysterious assassination to create the pretext for an all-out assault on the surviving representatives of Bolshevism. Trotsky's warnings were vindicated. The arrests and trials of 1935 set the stage for the first of the Moscow show trials of the principal leaders of the October Revolution in August 1936.

Once again Zinoviev and Kamenev were placed on trial, but this time on capital charges. Other defendants of the first Moscow show trial included such famous Old Bolsheviks and former leaders of the Left Opposition as Mrachkovsky, Ter-Vaganian and Smirnov.

But the chief accused was Leon Trotsky, who was charged in absentia with having masterminded a vast conspiracy against the Soviet Union and its leaders. The indictment claimed that Trotsky had entered into an alliance with Nazi Germany and Japan for the purpose of dismembering the Soviet Union and restoring capitalism to its former territories. Stalin and other leading members of the Soviet Communist Party were, according to the indictment, to be assassinated. Somehow, Trotsky had communicated this plot to his confederates inside the Soviet Union, who supposedly enthusiastically agreed to implement it. Under his supposed direction, the plot had been set into motion through numerous acts of industrial sabotage that had resulted in the deaths of scores of people.

There was no evidence to support these allegations other than the personal confessions of the accused. All the defendants placed on trial proclaimed, in response to questions put to them by the prosecutor Vyshinsky, that they were guilty of all the charges leveled against them. There existed absolutely no other corroborating evidence. An attempt by Stalin to endow the testimony with an element of realism went disastrously awry. A lesser-known defendant, E.S. Goltsman, testified that he had traveled to Copenhagen in 1932, where he supposedly met with Sedov, who then arranged for a conspiratorial rendezvous with his father. According to Goltsman, the first encounter with Sedov took place in the lobby of the Hotel Bristol. But it was soon established by Danish journalists that the Hotel Bristol had been torn down in 1917. This devastating exposure had no impact on the outcome of the trial. On August 24, 1936 all the defendants were sentenced to death. They were shot within twenty-four hours.

When the trial began, Trotsky was living in Norway. He had just completed his comprehensive analysis of the Soviet Union and the Stalinist regime entitled *The Revolution Betrayed*. He immediately denounced the trial as a frame-up and set about to expose it. But his first efforts were interrupted by the Norwegian government, which feared that Trotsky's exposure of the trial and denunciations of Stalin might harm relations between the Soviet Union and Norway. The Social Democratic government placed Trotsky and his wife under house arrest, where he was held under conditions resembling solitary confinement for the next four months. Finally, in December 1936, Trotsky and his wife were placed aboard a freighter bound for Mexico, where he had been granted asylum by the radical nationalist government of Lazaro Cardenas.

Trotsky arrived in Mexico on January 9, 1937, less than two weeks before the start of the second show trial in Moscow. Among the new defendants were world famous Bolsheviks such as Yuri Piatakov, former head of Soviet industry; Grigory Sokolnikov, who had been among the first leaders of Soviet finance; Muralov, the hero of the civil war; Mikhail Boguslavsky, another Old

Bolshevik; and the renowned Marxist journalist, Karl Radek. The accusations were as astonishing as those presented at the first trial, and once again the entire case rested on the confessions of the accused.

The credibility of the second trial suffered a devastating blow when another attempt to support the confessions of the accused with a bit of local color blew up in Stalin's face. Piatakov testified that he had flown from Berlin to Oslo in December 1935 to meet Trotsky and receive directives for the conduct of terrorist activities against the Soviet regime. Unfortunately for the organizers of the trial, the official records of the authorities at Oslo airport established that due to bad weather not a single aircraft had landed at that facility in the month of December 1935. Piatakov's "phantom flight," as Trotsky referred to the episode, never took place. Commenting on this dramatic exposure, Trotsky wrote:

> Stalin's misfortune is that the GPU cannot dispose of the Norwegian climate, the international movement of airplanes, or even the movement of my thought, the character of my affiliations, and the progress of my activities. That is why the elaborate frame-up, imprudently raised to great heights, has fallen from the nonexistent airplane and has been smashed to bits. But if the accusation against me — the principal defendant, inspirer, organizer, director of the plot — is built upon grossly false testimony, what is the rest of the business worth?[8]

By any objective standard the credibility of the indictments and the legitimacy of the proceedings in Moscow were dealt a shattering blow. Despite this, all but two of the defendants were sentenced to death. The two spared men, Radek and Sokolnikov, were sentenced to terms of ten years imprisonment, but were murdered shortly thereafter in prison.

From Mexico, Trotsky issued an appeal for the establishment of an international tribunal to conduct an independent investigation into the allegations made by the Stalinist prosecutors. In a speech delivered in English before newsreel cameras, Trotsky stated:

> Stalin's trial against me is built upon false confessions, extorted by modern Inquisitorial methods, in the interests of the ruling

---

[8] *Writings of Leon Trotsky 1936–37* (New York: Pathfinder Press, 1978), pp. 173–174.

clique. *There are no crimes in history more terrible in intention or execution than the Moscow trials of Zinoviev-Kamenev and of Piatakov-Radek.* These trials develop not from communism, not from socialism, but from Stalinism, that is, from the unaccountable despotism of the bureaucracy over the people!

What is my principal task now? To reveal the *truth*. To show and to demonstrate that the true criminals hide under the cloak of the accusers. What will be the next step in this direction? The creation of an American, a European and subsequently, an *international commission of inquiry*, composed of people who incontestably enjoy authority and public confidence. I will undertake to present to such a commission all my files, thousands of personal and open letters in which the development of my *thought* and my action is reflected day by day, without any gaps. I have nothing to hide! Dozens of witnesses who are abroad possess invaluable facts and documents which will shed light on the Moscow frame-ups. The work of the commission of inquiry must terminate in a great *countertrial*. A countertrial is necessary to cleanse the atmosphere of the germs of deceit, slander, falsification and frame-ups, whose source is Stalin's police, the GPU, which has fallen to the level of the Nazi Gestapo.

Esteemed audience! You may have many varying attitudes toward my ideas and my political activity over the past forty years. But an impartial inquiry will confirm that there is *no stain on my honor, either personal or political.* Profoundly convinced that right is on my side, I wholeheartedly salute the citizens of the New World.[9]

The Moscow Trials produced a stunned reaction throughout the world. The spectacle of old and internationally-renowned revolutionaries, the founders of the Soviet Union, confessing to having entered into an alliance with Nazi Germany for the purpose of murdering Stalin and restoring capitalism staggered public opinion. Could the accused be guilty of such crimes? Were the proceedings in Moscow a legitimate exercise of justice? But despite the widespread skepticism toward the trials, Trotsky's call for an international commission of inquiry encountered serious political obstacles.

---

[9] Ibid., pp.179–80. Also available: http://www.youtube.com/watch?v=b3nD5bFm3Jg

The Communist parties throughout the world, acting under the supervision of the Soviet secret police, mounted an international campaign to build support for these trials, particularly among the radical and substantial left-liberal sections of the European and American intelligentsia.

In the United States the efforts of the Stalinists were boosted by *The New York Times*, whose Moscow correspondent Walter Duranty declared his confidence in the legitimacy of the trials and the confessions. He suggested that those who had doubts about the reliability of the confessions would profit by reading Dostoevsky and learning more about the mysteries of the "Slavic soul." Another prominent defender of the trials was the United States ambassador to the Soviet Union, Joseph Davies, who declared that he was convinced of the guilt of the accused.

To a far greater degree than has been generally appreciated, the Moscow Trials were a critical episode in American political life, particularly for one of its most important constituent elements, liberalism. To understand this, one must review the political context, both domestic and international, within which the Moscow Trials took place.

American liberals and the Moscow Trials

The extent to which the Great Depression, which began in late 1929, transformed the intellectual and political climate within the United States has been largely forgotten. But not since the Civil War had the United States confronted such a fundamental crisis. The secession crisis of 1860–61 had called into question the survival of the Union. The Wall Street crash and the Great Depression called into question the viability and moral legitimacy of the capitalist system. Nowadays, when successful Wall Street speculators and the titans of big business are glorified in the popular media as the human embodiment of all that America holds dear, it is hard to imagine a time when such individuals were denounced publicly by President Franklin Delano Roosevelt as "the malefactors of great wealth." Capitalism had become something of a dirty word in the United States.

The liberalism of the American intelligentsia was not based on clearly defined political and economic conceptions. It was as amorphous as the term itself, which generally meant nothing more than a vague commitment to the gradual improvement of social conditions and the curtailment of corruption in urban politics. The Depression produced within this social milieu a certain sense of urgency, a heightened interest in social problems and even a degree of sympathy for radical politics.

The prestige of the Soviet Union grew considerably among sections of the American liberal intelligentsia. With 25 percent of the workforce unemployed, the gospel of self-regulating markets, unfettered competition and rough individualism was less convincing than it had been before October 1929. The conditions that developed after the Wall Street crash undermined old assumptions about the compatibility of market economics with social progress. Against the backdrop of the American crisis, the apparent successes of the Soviet economy, the "excesses" of collectivization notwithstanding, generated respect and even admiration for the concept of economic planning. It appeared to many liberal intellectuals that the world had something to learn from the Soviet Union.

The growing sympathy for the USSR was accelerated by a critical change in Soviet foreign policy. The rise of fascism in Germany and the growing strength of reactionary movements throughout Europe were seen by many liberals as the harbingers of a general collapse of bourgeois democracy. At this critical point, from the standpoint of democratic liberalism, the significance of the Soviet Union in world politics changed dramatically. In 1935, at the Seventh Congress of the Communist International, the Soviet Union unveiled the policy of "popular frontism." Frightened by the danger posed by Nazi Germany, the Soviet bureaucracy henceforth would direct its energies toward the establishment of alliances with the democratic imperialist powers: Britain, France and the United States. As a necessary corollary of this policy, local Communist parties were to ally themselves with, and support in every way possible, the liberal and progressive parties of what they referred to as the "democratic" bourgeoisie. Parties, politicians and governments were no longer to be defined and analyzed according to the class interests they served. Rather, they were to be evaluated as either "fascist" or "antifascist." The political independence of the working class and the goal of socialism were to be sacrificed by the Communist parties in the interest of what was really an imperative of Soviet foreign policy.

In order to implement this policy, the Soviet Union and the national Communist parties began to aggressively court the liberal and radical intelligentsia of Europe and the United States. The day-to-day politics of the Communist Party assumed an increasingly liberal coloration, most notably in the American Stalinists' endorsement of Roosevelt and the New Deal. Many liberal intellectuals were flattered by the new attention devoted to them by the Stalinists, and were pleased to find that their opinions and concerns were taken so seriously. Their personal identification with the Soviet Union seemed, at least in their own eyes, to make up for the fact that they lacked any substantial program for radical action in the United States.

The liberals' uncritical admiration for Soviet accomplishments did not signify an endorsement of revolutionary change within the United States. Far from it. Most liberal intellectuals were inclined to view an alliance with the USSR as a means of strengthening their own timid agenda for social reform in the United States, and of keeping fascism at bay in Europe. The Soviet Union was no longer feared as a spearhead of revolutionary upheavals. The liberals understood that the defeat of Trotsky had signified the Soviet Union's abandonment of international revolutionary aspirations. By the mid-1930s the Stalinist regime had acquired an aura of political respectability.

In examining the liberal response to the Moscow Trials, one more important political fact must be kept in mind. Just one month before the beginning of the first trial, the Spanish Civil War erupted in July 1936. Spain was threatened with fascism, whose victory would certainly lead to the outbreak of World War II. Soviet Russia was seen as the most important ally of the Republican, antifascist forces. Few liberal intellectuals were inclined to examine too carefully the real significance of Stalinist politics in Spain. For the most part, they ignored the manner in which the Stalinists were destroying, through political terror, the revolutionary movement of the working class and ultimately guaranteeing the victory of Franco. On the surface — and few liberals cared to look beyond it — the Soviet Union seemed to be the rock upon which all the hopes of "progressive forces" depended for the defeat of fascism in Spain.

This is why Trotsky's call for an international commission of inquiry to investigate the Moscow Trials encountered, especially within the United States, widespread hostility among the liberal intelligentsia. Two of the most prominent journals which represented the views of this milieu, *The New Republic* and *The Nation*, endorsed the trials and opposed the call for an independent investigation. *The Nation* bent over backwards to support the trials, suggesting that those who expressed doubts simply were not familiar with the criminal justice system in the USSR. It was necessary to understand, *The Nation* wrote, that "Soviet public law differs from ours in several essential respects."[10]

Malcolm Cowley, the editor of *The New Republic*, exemplified the intellectual laziness and somewhat frightening political stupidity of American liberals. He was a prominent figure in American letters. Even today you will come across numerous anthologies or still current editions of major American

---

[10] *The Nation*, February 2, 1937.

novels whose introductions were written by Cowley. This sophisticated and urbane liberal offered his considered opinion on the proceedings in Moscow in an essay entitled, "The Record of a Trial," published in the April 7, 1937 issue of *The New Republic*:

> By all odds the most exciting book I have read this year is the stenographic record of the recent trial in Moscow, as translated into English by the People's Commissariat of Justice. I started reading it from a sense of duty: having heard so many arguments about the trial, and having read so many attacks on the good faith of the Soviet courts, I wanted to learn as much as I could from original sources. I learned a great deal, but chiefly I continued out of pure fascination with the material. Judged as literature, "The Case of the Anti-Soviet Trotskyite Center" is an extraordinary combination of true detective story and high Elizabethan tragedy with comic touches. I could accept it as a fabricated performance only on the assumption that Marlowe and Webster had a hand in staging it. Judged as information, it answers most of the questions raised in my own mind by the brief newspaper accounts of the trial.
>
> But before discussing the testimony, I had better explain my attitude toward Russian affairs as it has developed during the last few years. I am not a "Stalinist" except insofar as I deeply sympathize with the aims of the Soviet Union, and insofar as I believe that Stalin and his Political Bureau have in general followed wiser policies than those advocated by his enemies. ... But without paying allegiance to Stalin I am certainly against Trotsky. My opposition is partly a question of temperament: I have never liked the big-city intellectuals of his type, with their reduction of every human question to a bald syllogism in which they are always right at every point, miraculously right, and their opponents always stupid and beneath contempt. I have never liked Trotsky's books ... But most of all I am against Trotsky on political grounds. It has seemed to me for several years that hatred of Stalin is his deciding principle, and that his slogan of "the permanent revolution" is likely to destroy the revolution permanently, by attacking and weakening socialism in the one country where it now exists.

... Stalin, with all his faults and virtues, represents the Communist revolution. Trotsky has come to represent the "second revolution" that is trying to weaken it in the face of attacks from the fascist powers.[11]

With its insufferable smugness and pomposity, this essay was a sorry illustration of all that was corrupt and rotten in modern American liberalism. Old revolutionaries were being publicly humiliated and then murdered in Moscow. But people like Cowley found ways to rationalize the horrors and keep a smile on their faces. They evaluated the greatest historical and moral issues on the basis of their own narrow social interests and petty individual concerns. To the extent that the international policy of the Stalinist regime coincided with their own political agenda, liberals such as Cowley resented and opposed what they considered to be the "disruptive" activity of Trotsky. His analysis of the contradictions of Soviet society produced in these layers a feeling of annoyance. As far as people like Cowley were concerned, Trotsky, by insisting on the counterrevolutionary character of the Stalinist regime, was introducing into their lives unnecessary political and moral complications.

John Dewey and the Committee for the Defense of Leon Trotsky

Despite Stalinist opposition and the hostility of broad sections of the liberal intelligentsia, the Trotskyist movement established a defense committee. It found support among a small section of liberals and left radicals. Among the most prominent defenders of Trotsky was the writer James T. Farrell, the author of the *Studs Lonigan* trilogy. The committee achieved its greatest success when it persuaded John Dewey, then seventy-eight years old and the foremost American philosopher, to serve as its chairman. Dewey agreed to travel to Mexico and preside over a subcommission of inquiry that was to take Trotsky's testimony regarding the charges brought against him in the Moscow trials.

John Dewey (1859–1952) was, for many decades, the foremost representative of a genuinely democratic and idealistic tendency within American liberalism. He towered intellectually over the liberal community to which he addressed his essays and lectures. In contrast to the vast majority of those who

---

[11] *The New Republic*, April 7, 1937, pp. 267–269.

called themselves liberals, Dewey took his democratic convictions very seriously. His decision to associate himself with the Committee for the Defense of Leon Trotsky, indeed to become its chairman, expressed the depth of the democratic idealism that permeated his thought.

Dewey joined the Committee for the Defense of Leon Trotsky because, in the first place, he believed that Trotsky should not be denied the right to answer the charges against him. Dewey did not have the type of opportunistic, fifty-fifty attitude to democracy and truth that was characteristic of so many popular front liberals. For people like Malcolm Cowley, truth was in general an excellent thing. It was, especially when expedient, to be defended with all due eloquence. Their problem with truth only arose when it got in the way of more pressing personal and political concerns — like their professional status, their standard of living and the fate of the Democratic Party.

But Dewey's concern with the issues raised by the Moscow Trials was not merely that of a sincere civil libertarian. Or, to put it somewhat differently, his concern with civil liberties was bound up with his preoccupation with more profound problems of social and economic life. Dewey spoke for a strain of American liberal thought that believed deeply in social progress and did not presume the identity of democracy and market economics. It believed that a democracy without social equality was a hollow shell. Dewey opposed the New Deal on the grounds that it provided nothing more than reformist palliatives that would leave capitalism intact. In the early 1930s Dewey worked strenuously, though rather ineffectively, for the formation of a third political party opposed to the existing capitalist parties. He viewed the Depression as an irrefutable demonstration of capitalism's failure.

Dewey argued — with a certain naïveté — that nothing that was essential to liberalism, as he understood it, required that its fate be tied to that of the capitalist system. He insisted that the democratic principles espoused by American liberalism, above all a commitment to social equality, were in irreconcilable conflict with the contemporary development of capitalist society. Dewey acknowledged that in its historical development, liberalism was an expression of bourgeois economic interests and its general world outlook. But the democratic ideals that had been championed by liberalism in the nineteenth century had come into conflict with the social and political realities of twentieth century capitalism. Those who failed to recognize the change in historical conditions had become, in Dewey's eyes, "pseudoliberals," paying a purely verbal homage to democracy, while legitimizing market economics and all the social injustice and misery it produced.

Dewey was not a Marxist or a revolutionary. He explicitly rejected the class struggle as a means through which socialism should or could be realized. He was never able to answer to either his own or anyone else's satisfaction how socialism could be realized. But that is not the issue here. What strikes one in the political and social writings of old Mr. Dewey is how much further he was prepared to go in his criticisms of American capitalism than any representative of our contemporary "liberal intelligentsia," to the extent that one can even speak at the present time of such a social grouping.

As he assumed the chairmanship of the commission, Dewey denounced the intellectual dishonesty of those liberals who opposed Trotsky's right to defend himself. He stated that it was impossible to separate the cause of historical progress from the struggle for historical truth, and that the questions that confronted liberals who sympathized with the Soviet Union could not be evaded. In a speech delivered shortly before his departure to Mexico, Dewey declared:

> Either Leon Trotsky is guilty of plotting wholesale assassination, systematic wreckage with destruction of life and property; of treason of the basest sort in conspiring with political and economic enemies of the USSR in order to destroy Socialism; or he is innocent. If he is guilty, no condemnation can be too severe. If he is innocent, there is no way in which the existing regime in Soviet Russia can be acquitted of deliberate, systematic persecution and falsification. These are unpleasant alternatives for those to face who are sympathetic with the efforts to build a Socialist State in Russia. The easier and lazier course is to avoid facing the alternatives. But unwillingness to face the unpleasant is the standing weakness of liberals. They are only too likely to be brave when affairs are going smoothly and then to shirk when unpleasant conditions demand decision and action. I cannot believe that a single genuine liberal would, if he once faced the alternatives, hold that persecution and falsification are a sound basis upon which to build an enduring Socialist society.[12]

---

[12] Jo Ann Boydston, ed., *The Later Works of John Dewey, 1925–1953*, Volume 11, (Carbondale: Southern Illinois University Press, 1987) p. 318.

Dewey concluded this speech by quoting words written by Zola in the era of the Dreyfus case: "Truth is on the march and nothing will stop it."

Dewey traveled to Mexico in April 1937. He could not be dissuaded from undertaking this mission, despite appeals from his family and friends, who were frightened by the denunciations and even physical threats that were being orchestrated by the American Communist Party. The questioning of Trotsky spanned more than a week, from April 10 to 17, 1937. The transcript of Trotsky's testimony runs to nearly 600 printed pages. It offered a detailed account of Trotsky's political life and convictions.

Trotsky and Dewey presented a fascinating contrast. The former was the very embodiment of revolutionary passion and energy, a man who had stood at the center of the most tumultuous events in modern history, a master dialectician who employed striking metaphors to illuminate the political and social complexities that had given rise to the proceedings in Moscow. Dewey was a very different man: an old Yankee from Vermont, ponderous and sparing with his comments, a man of the college lecture hall, not mass rallies and battlefields. And yet, for all their differences in temperament and political conceptions, they shared a passionate commitment to the truth, which they considered the intellectual and moral mainspring of progress.

In his own way Trotsky paid a rare and poignant tribute to Dewey. In the final session of the hearing in Mexico, Trotsky delivered a four-hour defense of his life, beliefs and reputation. His speech, whose eloquence was accentuated by the fact that it was delivered in English and required of the great orator the most intense intellectual concentration, was followed in rapt silence.

"Esteemed Commissioners," Trotsky declared as he came to the end of his speech:

> The experience of my life, in which there has been no lack of either successes or of failures, has not only not destroyed my faith in the clear, bright future of mankind, but, on the contrary, has given it an indestructible temper. This faith in reason, in truth, in human solidarity, which, at the age of eighteen I took with me into the workers' quarters of the provincial Russian town of Nikolaiev — this faith I have preserved fully and completely. It has become more mature, but not less ardent. In the very fact of your Commission's formation — in the fact that, at its head, is a man of unshakable moral authority, a man who by virtue of his age should have the right to remain outside of the

skirmishes in the political arena — in this fact I see a new and truly magnificent reinforcement of the revolutionary optimism which constitutes the fundamental element of my life.

Ladies and gentlemen of the Commission! Mr. Attorney Finerty! And you, my defender and friend, Goldman! Allow me to express to all of you my warm gratitude, which in this case does not bear a personal character. And allow me, in conclusion, to express my profound respect to the educator, philosopher and personification of genuine American idealism, the scholar who heads the work of your Commission.[13]

To this Dewey replied, "Anything I can say will be an anticlimax," and he quickly brought the hearing to a dignified conclusion.

The findings of the Dewey Commission

The commissioners returned to the United States. Nine months later they issued detailed findings which refuted every aspect of the case that had been presented by the Stalinist regime at the trials in Moscow. Permit me to cite the most important of the findings:

- Finding Number 16: "We are convinced that the alleged letters in which Trotsky conveyed alleged conspiratorial instructions to the various defendants in the Moscow trials never existed; and that the testimony concerning them is sheer fabrication."
- Finding Number 17: "We find that Trotsky throughout his whole career has always been a consistent opponent of individual terror. The Commission further finds that Trotsky never instructed any of the defendants or witnesses in the Moscow Trials to assassinate any political opponent."
- Finding Number 18: "We find that Trotsky never instructed the defendants or witnesses in the Moscow trials to engage in sabotage, wrecking, and diversion. On the contrary, he has always been a consistent advocate of the building up of socialist industry and agriculture in the Soviet Union and has criticized the present regime on the basis that its activities

---

[13] *The Case of Leon Trotsky: Report of Hearings on the Charges Made Against Him in the Moscow Trials* (New York: Merit Publishers, 1968), pp. 584–585.

were harmful to the building up of socialist economy in Russia. He is not in favor of sabotage as a method of opposition to any political regime."

- Finding Number 19: "We find that Trotsky never instructed any of the accused or witnesses in the Moscow trials to enter into agreements with foreign powers against the Soviet Union. On the contrary, he has always uncompromisingly advocated the defense of the U.S.S.R. He has also been a most forthright ideological opponent of the fascism represented by the foreign powers with which he is accused of having conspired."

- Finding Number 20: "On the basis of all the evidence we find that Trotsky never recommended, plotted, or attempted the restoration of capitalism in the U.S.S.R. On the contrary, he has always uncompromisingly opposed the restoration of capitalism in the Soviet Union and its existence anywhere else."

The commission summed up its findings with the following conclusion: "We therefore find the Moscow trials to be frame-ups. We therefore find Trotsky and Sedov not guilty."[14]

Trotsky made the point that the commission could have limited itself to a finding that he was not guilty of the charges. It went beyond that, stating unequivocally that the Moscow trials were a frame-up. In effect, the commission found that the organizers of the trials, principally Stalin, were among the worst criminals in world history. Stalin and his accomplices had orchestrated a state frame-up in order to provide a legal cover for the murder of not only the trial defendants, but also of hundreds of thousands of other innocent victims.

By now I hope that you will understand why the Socialist Equality Party has publicly protested Richard Pipes' gratuitous rehabilitation of the Moscow Trials. Stalin's criminal proceedings legitimized the Terror that claimed hundreds of thousands of lives and dealt a staggering blow to the cause of international socialism. The fight to expose the trials consumed the final years of Trotsky's life. The Moscow Trials were finally discredited. Even the Soviet bureaucracy, shortly before its downfall in 1991, was compelled to admit that the proceedings were a legal travesty. More than fifty years after their execution, all of the victims of the trials were officially rehabilitated.

In light of this history, we could not observe with passive equanimity the attempt by Pipes, in the interests of his own reactionary political agenda, to

---

[14] *The Later Works of John Dewey,* Volume 11, pp. 322–323.

rehabilitate the Moscow Trials. When lies are told about such events, a blow is struck against the historical consciousness of mankind. Every one of us is outraged when we read or hear of attempts to deny the fact of the Holocaust. Behind the denial that six million Jews were murdered by fascism is the preparation of future acts of genocide. The event in modern history that bears the closest comparison to the Holocaust is the Stalinist terror against the socialist working class and intelligentsia of the Soviet Union.

Both the Holocaust organized by the Nazis and the Great Terror organized by the Stalinists were criminal products of a counterrevolutionary reaction to the mass political movement of the socialist working class throughout Europe. It is true that the economic and social bases of the Nazi and Stalinist regimes were very different. But in their political orientation, both Russian Stalinism and German fascism embodied a reactionary nationalistic response to socialist internationalism which, under the influence of Marxism, had become such a powerful force in the European working class during the first decades of the twentieth century. Hitler and Stalin, each in his own way, sought to destroy the political, intellectual, cultural and ethical foundation built up in the working class movement by Marxism over generations. Hitler used the methods of ethnic genocide. Stalin was more precise: his genocide based itself on a process of political selection. He identified those who, through their politics or intellectual achievements, reflected the influence of the socialist traditions that had inspired the October Revolution, and he ordered their destruction.

Let us now return more directly to the issue raised in the title of this lecture: the relation of the Moscow Trials to the present-day crisis of political life in the United States. The trials produced a deep and lasting effect on the development of political life in this country. The opportunistic flirtation of a section of popular front liberals with Stalinism left a bitter political aftertaste. In a fundamental sense, many liberal intellectuals were deeply embarrassed, if not thoroughly discredited, by the Moscow Trials. By the third trial in March 1938 — this time Bukharin was the chief defendant — it was all but impossible to maintain the pretense that all was well with the Soviet system of justice. However, the erstwhile liberal defenders of Stalinism were not inclined to admit honestly that they had made a mistake or examine why their judgment had been so faulty. A new mood began to emerge within these circles. The liberal admirers of Stalinism now began to acknowledge that the trials were, perhaps, a travesty of justice. But the unfortunate events in Moscow, they claimed, showed what happened when social change was sought through revolutionary methods. "Violence begets violence!" "The Moscow Trials arose out of the amoralism, if not immoralism, of Bolshevism." "What occurred in 1937 began in 1917!" "Stalin may be bad, but Trotsky would have been worse!"

To a great extent, the very arguments which have become the clichés repeated endlessly over the years to discredit socialism have their origins in the defensive justification by American liberalism for its complicity in the horrifying events of the late 1930s. Liberal disillusionment with Stalinism proceeded along the line of least resistance — not to a revolutionary Marxist critique of the Soviet bureaucracy, but toward a general abandonment of any sort of active interest in and support for socialism. This trend became especially pronounced after the signing of the Stalin-Hitler pact in August 1939, which the former friends of the USSR interpreted not as a betrayal of the working class and international socialism — that they could have forgiven — but as a betrayal of the foreign policy of the Roosevelt administration.

Following the Nazi invasion of the Soviet Union in June 1941 and the entrance of the United States into the Second World War the following December, there was a temporary, opportunistic rapprochement between the liberal intelligentsia and Stalinism. Liberals could, without any risk to their reputations and careers, combine patriotism with the expression of friendly sentiments toward the USSR. But this happy situation lasted only until the end of the war, or more precisely, until Churchill formulated his "iron curtain" metaphor in a speech at Fulton, Missouri in March 1946.

Liberalism and the Cold War

With the onset of the Cold War, public opinion shifted rapidly to the right. A ferocious anticommunism swept the ranks of American liberalism, and it contributed decisively to the reactionary environment without which the witch hunts of the late 1940s and early 1950s could not have taken place.

There are many reasons for the disgraceful role played by American liberalism in contributing to the wave of political reaction that was to have such a devastating effect upon the intellectual level and political climate of the United States. Certainly, the economic upturn that followed the war was a decisive material factor in the weakening of radical political tendencies. The return of prosperity and the new dominance of the United States in world affairs produced a revival of confidence in the prospects for capitalism. The so-called American Century had begun. The amelioration of social conditions, or at least the sense that American capitalism possessed the material resources to deal with its ongoing domestic problems, contributed to the increasing conservatism and complacency of liberalism.

But the peculiar ferocity of American anticommunism, especially the fact that it encountered so little organized resistance, cannot be attributed exclusively to the material environment of postwar prosperity. Other political and ideological factors must be considered. First of all, one cannot underestimate the degree to which the dishonesty and cynicism of American Stalinists had succeeded in making them utterly loathsome to broad sections of the working class. The term "Stalinist hack" became part of the everyday vocabulary of the American labor movement, and it conjured up the image of a two-faced petty labor bureaucrat who simply "toed a line" without any real concern for its effect upon the welfare of the working class.

The American Stalinists were directly involved in the GPU conspiracy that led to the assassination of Trotsky in August 1940, and they supported the prosecution of leaders of the Trotskyist Socialist Workers Party on trumped-up charges of sedition in 1941. They endorsed the utilization against their political opponents in the workers movement of the very laws that were to be used against them several years later. Unlike the Stalinist parties in Western Europe, which managed to salvage their reputations on the basis of their role in the anti-Nazi resistance movements, the Communist Party in the United States opposed all manifestations of industrial militancy or political radicalism during World War II. Thus by the end of the war, the Stalinists had lost virtually all credibility among the most militant sections of the working class. Only an organization as unprincipled, cynical and deceitful as the American Communist Party could have enabled its right-wing opponents in the CIO bureaucracy to pose as dedicated champions of the rights of the American working class.

But neither the activities of the American Stalinists nor, for that matter, the policies of the Soviet Union provide an adequate explanation for the liberal intelligentsia's postwar lurch to the right. The question that must be answered is why their opposition to Stalinism found its principal mode of expression in support for the Cold War policies of American imperialism. An important part of the answer to this question must be found in a basic failure of their understanding, both theoretical and political, of the origins and nature of the Stalinist regime in the Soviet Union. There was a dramatic change in the attitude of the liberal intelligentsia to the Soviet Union between 1936 and 1946. And yet, there was a definite political and theoretical continuity between the pro- and anti-Soviet positions. When they supported Stalin against Trotsky, and then Truman against Stalin, the liberal intelligentsia proceeded from the identity of Stalinism and Marxism.

This placed the liberal intelligentsia in a politically and intellectually untenable position. On the basis of the facile formula that Stalinism equals Marxism and socialism, the liberals left themselves only two alternatives: The first was to oppose Stalinism from the right as supporters of American imperialism; the second, to serve as apologists of Stalinism. *The New Republic* wound up in the first camp; *The Nation*, in the second.

The fate of the liberal and democratic intelligentsia in the United States demonstrated the impossibility of combining a principled radical opposition to both Stalinism and imperialism without understanding the nature of the Soviet regime. In the 1930s the liberal intelligentsia had, with few exceptions, accepted the identification of Stalinism with Marxism. Ten and fifteen years later, it was still proceeding on the basis of this false and reactionary identity. Those who simply reversed their assessment of the Soviet Union, converting the positives that had been attributed to Stalinism in the 1930s into negatives a decade later, inevitably fell into line behind the political and cultural witch hunters.

In the final analysis, the evolution of the liberal intelligentsia in the late 1940s was rooted in the material interests of the petty-bourgeois social strata from which its membership was largely recruited. The personal characteristics that are found so commonly within these social strata — egotism, selfishness, cowardice, etc. — were contributing factors in determining the part played by different individuals in this process. But the intellectual factor — that is, the absence of a general theoretical comprehension of the October Revolution and, in particular, the political origins and significance of Stalinism — must not be discounted. It was not only the scoundrels and cowards among the liberal intelligentsia who fell into line behind American imperialism in the 1940s. Even John Dewey, notwithstanding his intelligence, integrity and courage, stumbled badly following the trials. He exposed the trials, but he could not explain them. Dewey took refuge in empty platitudes about Bolshevik methods leading inevitably to the crimes of Stalinism. On this basis, in the final years of his life, Dewey shared the Cold War conceptions of so many of his inferiors in the liberal camp. If Dewey left behind no real successor, it was because American liberalism no longer had anything to say that was remotely progressive.

We have tried to show how the tangled relationship between the liberal intelligentsia and Stalinism contributed to the stagnation of political and intellectual life in the United States. The paralysis of social thought is mired in its false identification of Stalinism with Marxism. The lies of pseudo-scholars like Pipes, amplified to the nth degree by the mind-numbing media, serve to reinforce the reactionary and conformist politics in the United States. Without an understanding of the rise, decline and fall of the October Revolution — which cannot be achieved except on the basis of the careful study of the struggle waged by the Trotskyist movement against Stalinism — no way can be found out of this blind alley.

Intellectual conformism and the crisis of US society

The need to come to grips with this problem is demonstrated by the condition of contemporary political life. The United States is passing through a social crisis, the signs of which are apparent to all who wish to open up their eyes and be honest with themselves. Yet it is virtually impossible to find any serious questioning of the prevailing economic system. Of course, nothing of the sort is to be expected of the mass media. But even in the more selective journals one comes across virtually nothing except vulgar, mundane and hackneyed ideas. Rarely is there even a suggestion that an alternative to capitalism must be found. And even when, almost by accident, one comes across a writer or lecturer who appears to be attempting to say something intelligent, one senses that this individual is engaged in self-censorship, taking care not to go beyond the bounds of what is possible and permissible within the framework of capitalism.

This intellectual stagnation has continued for so long, it is hardly recalled that serious doubts in the viability of capitalism as a social system were not unusual within a broad layer of liberal intellectuals up until the postwar period. For students who have been kept on a diet of intellectual and political conformity, it may come as quite a surprise to pick up a volume of the political writings of John Dewey from the early 1930s. Dewey was not a Marxist. He was not a revolutionary. Indeed, one could only with extreme reservations consider him a socialist. But when read within the context of today's stagnation and conformity, this venerable dean of the old liberal tradition appears far more radical than he did in his own day, and certainly more courageous and far to the left of any tendency that defines itself as liberal or even radical today.

If one goes to the library and leafs through a volume of Dewey's political and social writings, one finds passages which, were he alive and writing such things today, would likely bar him from employment at any major American university or, at the very least, consign him to obscurity.

Let me cite one characteristic passage, written during the Depression:

> When the present crisis is over in its outward sensational features, when things have returned to a comparatively more comfortable state called "normalcy," will they forget? Will they even complacently congratulate themselves on the generosity with which society relieved distress? Or will they locate the causes of the distress of unemployment and modify the social system? If they do the former, the time of depression will recur sooner or later with renewed violence until the social system is changed by force. The alternative is such a recognition of society's responsibility for the evil as will by planned foresight and deliberate choice change the economic and financial structure of society itself.
>
> Only a change in the system will ensure the right of every person to work and enable everyone to live in security.[15]

Such obvious truths are hardly spoken today. Discussion of all social and political questions is blighted by one great lie: the identification of Marxism with Stalinism. Especially today, the collapse of the Soviet Union is proclaimed to be the ultimate proof that socialism is not viable and that there can be no alternative to capitalism. The political effect of this lie is to block any serious attempt to come to grips with the deepening social crisis. Even where the existence of this crisis is acknowledged and described, no serious solution is offered. Take, for example, the recently-published book by the MIT economist Lester Thurow, *The Future of Capitalism*. This book is full of striking economic data which clearly demonstrate the failure of capitalism as a social system.

Thurow, however, does not draw that conclusion. He is one of those who is careful to censor himself. Nevertheless, Thurow provides shocking documentation of the growth of inequality and general poverty. He points out that all gains in male earnings during the 1980s went to the top 20 percent of the workforce. Sixty-four percent of that gain went to the top 1 percent. The pay of the Fortune 500 executives rose from 35 to 157 times that of the average production worker. Thurow notes the dramatic decline of real wages for males

---

[15] Jo Ann Boydston, ed., *The Later Works of John Dewey, 1925–1953*, Volume 6 (Carbondale: Southern Illinois University Press, 1985), p. 155.

over the last quarter-century. Even though the Gross Domestic Product has risen 29 percent since 1973, average median wages have fallen by 11 percent. Only those in the upper-middle class and higher have seen, in real income terms, any genuine improvement in their living standards over this extended period. Those on the lower rungs, on the other hand, have suffered terribly. Real wages for workers between the ages of twenty-five and thirty-four have dropped by a quarter since the early 1970s. For young workers under the age of twenty-four, the proportion earning less than the official poverty level for a family of four rose from 18 percent in 1979 to 40 percent in 1989.

Perhaps the most remarkable fact presented by Thurow is the following: he points out that the period between 1950 and the year 2000, if present trends continue to the end of this decade, will mark the first half-century in American history when living standards actually declined in real terms. Thurow states that there really is no precedent for the massive wave of corporate downsizing and restructuring that has had such a disastrous impact upon living standards across a very broad spectrum of the working population.

The impact of downsizing and restructuring has been severe and long-lasting. Of those who lost their jobs in the first wave of downsizing in the 1980s, 12 percent never reentered the workforce and 17 percent remained unemployed for at least two years. Of the 71 percent who were reemployed, 31 percent took a wage reduction of 25 percent or more. Thurow also writes about an expanding "lumpenproletariat" of homeless people and chronically unemployed. Forty percent of homeless unmarried men have been in jail.

He sums up the growth of social distress and inequality as follows:

> No country not experiencing a revolution or a military defeat with a subsequent occupation has probably ever had as rapid or as widespread an increase in inequality as has occurred in the United States in the past two decades. Never before have Americans seen the current pattern of real-wage reductions in the face of rising per capita GDP.[16]

And, finally, Thurow concludes:

> In the absence of any vision that could generate the enormous restructuring efforts that would be necessary to begin reducing

---

[16] Lester C. Thurow, *The Future of Capitalism* (New York: William Morrow, 1996), p. 42.

inequality and to cause real wages to rise, what happens? How far can inequality widen and real wages fall before something snaps in a democracy? No one knows, since it has never before happened. The experiment has never been tried.[17]

The question that arises is precisely why there is no "vision" to guide the type of massive social restructuring that is so obviously necessary. The answer given by Thurow illustrates the very point that I have sought to make in this lecture. "Capitalism," he writes, "has a current advantage in that with the death of communism and socialism, it has no plausible social system as an active competitor. It is impossible to have a revolution against anything unless there is an alternative ideology."[18]

Thurow's conclusion illustrates the impact of the identification of Stalinism and socialism. The rebuilding of a revolutionary workers movement on the basis of Marxist principles and genuine socialist traditions requires an implacable struggle against the falsifiers of history. This fight will be won, for if history proves anything, it is that, in the long run, truth is more powerful than lies.

---

[17] Ibid., p. 261.
[18] Ibid., p. 310.

4

Leon Trotsky and the Fate of Socialism
in the Twentieth Century:
A Reply to Professor Eric Hobsbawm[1]

Dedication

A year and a half ago, I was privileged to attend the lectures given by Professor Vadim Rogovin in Australia. At the conclusion of the second lecture in Melbourne, I had a very interesting discussion with a great friend and supporter of the movement on the role of Leon Trotsky. In the course of that discussion a number of ideas occurred to me which I discussed with her. She said she hoped that one day I would have a chance to elaborate these ideas in a lecture of my own. I said that I looked forward to that opportunity.

Unfortunately, that friend, Judy Tenenbaum, the mother of Linda Tenenbaum who is chairing this International Summer School, died early last year. It was, for all of us who knew her, a great loss. I would therefore like to dedicate this lecture to her memory. It is, from my standpoint, a responsibility and a debt that I very gladly repay to someone who always welcomed me with great warmth when I came to Australia and had a chance to visit her.

* * *

The loss of optimism

In 1899, Franz Mehring, the great Marxist theoretician of German Social Democracy, wrote that while the nineteenth century had been one of hope,

---

[1] Lecture delivered January 3, 1998 at the International School on Marxism and the Fundamental Problems of the Twentieth Century, held in Sydney Australia.

the twentieth would be that of revolutionary fulfillment. Mehring allowed that the march of historical progress might proceed along paths more complex than expected, and that there existed no prophet who could predict the future with absolute certainty. "But," he proclaimed, "with a joyous courage and proud self-confidence the class-conscious proletariat crosses over the threshold of the twentieth century."

Mehring's words expressed the widespread optimism that was felt throughout the socialist movement on the eve of the twentieth century. He spoke for a movement that believed passionately in the historical mission of socialism. Hardly more than fifty years had passed since Marx and Engels had written the *Communist Manifesto*. Only forty years before, Marx had lived in London as an impoverished and isolated revolutionary exile. And just twenty years before, Bismarck had illegalized most socialist activity in Germany. But as the nineteenth century drew to a close, the Social Democratic Party had survived the anti-Socialist laws to become the largest political party in the country. Moreover, beyond the borders of Germany, socialism had become a mighty international movement, among whose followers were to be found innumerable men and women of extraordinary courage, vision and, not infrequently, real genius.

The optimism to which the socialists gave revolutionary expression was felt throughout society, including among the bourgeoisie and cultured layers of the middle class. In his memoirs written after the outbreak of World War II, the Austrian writer Stefan Zweig recalled, as one might a dear departed friend, the confidence which prevailed at the turn of the century:

> In its liberal idealism the nineteenth century had been truly convinced that it was on the straight and unmistakable path to the best of all possible worlds. One looked with contempt upon earlier epochs — with their wars, famines and revolts — as a time when people were immature and insufficiently enlightened ... this belief in an uninterrupted, unstoppable "progress" had for this Age the power of a religion; one believed in "progress" more than one did in the Bible, and this gospel seemed to be utterly substantiated by the daily wonders produced by science and technology.[2]

[2] Stefan Zweig, *Die Welt von Gestern: Erinnerungen eines Europäers* (Frankfurt am Main: Fischer Taschenbuch Verlag, 1997), (translation by D. North), p. 17.

Very little of this faith has survived the traumas of the twentieth century, which at times has seemed to be the graveyard of all man's hopes. In the terrible light of all that has occurred — the two world wars, the innumerable regional bloodbaths, failed revolutions, and the Holocaust — the optimism of the last years of the nineteenth century has come to be seen as an expression of a naïve faith in human reason and an unjustified belief in progress.

There is little sense, as we approach the new millennium, that the future will see radical improvements in the human condition. At most, there is an uneasy and fragile hope that in the twenty-first century man will be spared the horrors of the last one. It is a sad fact that this century's imminent demise arouses, more than anything else, a sense of relief, as if a particularly rough and unpleasant journey is finally coming to an end.

It is not hard to imagine the themes that will predominate in the *fin-de-siècle* retrospectives which will soon bombard us: the twentieth century as the century of unimaginable horrors, of mass murder and of totalitarian bestiality. It is undeniable that these descriptions are, to a certain degree, appropriate. But they can, through misuse and overuse, assume the character of platitudes. In the hands of the media these phrases are transformed into sound bites that serve to deaden consciousness, rather than enlighten it. Judging from what has already appeared on the subject, one can predict that the violence and tragedies of the twentieth century will be invoked to demonstrate the destructive role of all "ideology" — especially Marxism — and thereby substantiate the futility of any revolutionary critique of the existing social order.

This century has witnessed the most gigantic upheavals in world history. Never before had the masses been active on such a dramatic scale, and with such a high degree of consciousness. Conversely, never had force and violence been employed with such ruthlessness to suppress revolutionary mass movements. The moralists of the bourgeois media generally fail to note that the worst crimes were those committed directly (as in Germany and Spain) or indirectly (as in the Soviet Union) in defense of the world capitalist system.

There has been no shortage of tragedy in the twentieth century. But the tragedies are an expression of the immensity of the historical tasks undertaken. For the first time humanity placed on its agenda, as a practical task, the abolition of class society. Man sought to bring the prehistory of the human race to an end. The Bolshevik Revolution of October 1917 represented, notwithstanding the subsequent fate of the Soviet Union, an ineradicable milestone in man's historical progress. However unfashionable such "deterministic" conceptions may be at the present time, we believe that the most powerful tendencies of the law-governed development of man as a social being found a necessary, if only anticipatory, expression in the October Revolution. A renewed effort to complete what was begun in 1917 is, we are convinced, *inevitable*.

The paramount political and intellectual task of our time must be a study of October 1917 — the first proletarian socialist revolution — and its aftermath, not only in Soviet Russia, but throughout the world. This, in its totality, represents the most critical element within the corpus of strategic historical experiences from which Marxists must extract the theoretical and practical lessons that will guide the working class in the twenty-first century. A serious discussion of the prospects for socialism — and, therefore, of the future of mankind — must involve an examination of the October Revolution. This revolution can be supported or opposed, but it cannot be ignored. The answers one gives to the problems of the present day are inseparably linked to one's assessment of the October Revolution, its aftermath, fate, and legacy.

If the October Revolution was doomed to failure; if the Bolshevik seizure of power was, virtually from the start, a fatal enterprise; if Stalinism was the unavoidable outcome of Bolshevism; if the crimes of the Stalinist era flowed from the very concept of the "dictatorship of the proletariat"; if the final breakdown of the Soviet Union testifies to the bankruptcy of socialist economics, then Marxism, it must be confessed, has suffered a devastating political, intellectual and moral shipwreck. This is, at the present time, the dominant view among university academicians. If, on the other hand, the October Revolution realistically contained within it other possibilities; if Stalinism was not the outcome of Bolshevism, but its antithesis; and if the rise of Stalinism was, in fact, opposed by Marxists, then the historical situation of revolutionary socialism is very different.

The International Committee of the Fourth International upholds the second position. This necessarily brings us into conflict not only with the outright and unabashed defenders of reaction, but also with the mood of skepticism, demoralization and political renunciation that is commonly found among so many who, at least until recently, considered themselves socialists.

Among those who were influenced by Stalinism, the collapse of the Soviet Union — an event they had utterly failed to foresee — has radically changed their attitude toward the October Revolution and its place in history. Reaction, as Leon Trotsky once noted, not only conquers, it also convinces. Many long-time friends of the Soviet Union, or, perhaps more precisely, of the Soviet bureaucracy, who professed great admiration for Lenin and the "Great October Revolution" — and thought of themselves as very progressive people for doing so — now look upon the October Revolution as a disaster that should not have happened. The seizure of power was a terrible mistake. If there is any lesson to be drawn from October 1917 and its aftermath, it is that the entire revolutionary socialist project, as envisaged by Marx and implemented by Lenin, has been tragically and irrevocably refuted.

This is the perspective that emerges from a book by the British historian, Eric Hobsbawm, who was for many years a member of the Communist Party. Entitled *On History*, it consists of various essays and lectures he has written over the last quarter century. While the writings cover a wide range of topics, the dominant theme of this volume is the historical significance of the October Revolution.

As I will have many harsh things to say about Professor Hobsbawm's book, allow me to preface my remarks by stating quite clearly that in the course of his long professional career as a historian he has written many valuable scholarly works. The volumes he devoted to the French Revolution and the development of capitalism in the nineteenth century were thoughtful and sensitive studies. A more recent book, a critical analysis of the role of nationalism and the nation state, offered many worthwhile and timely insights.

However, the subject of the Russian Revolution is dangerous territory for Professor Hobsbawm, for in this field his scholarship is compromised by his politics. Hobsbawm once confessed that as a member of the CPGB he had avoided writing about the Russian Revolution and the twentieth century, because the political line of his party would have prevented him from being entirely truthful. Why he chose to remain a member of a party that would have compelled him to tell lies is a question to which he has never given a convincing answer. It would have been best for him, and no loss to the writing of history, had he continued to limit himself to events before 1900.

Counterfactual history

The most important document in Hobsbawm's book is a lecture that he delivered in December 1996, entitled "Can We Write the History of the Russian Revolution?"

In opening the lecture, Professor Hobsbawm makes a valid point: "[T]he most burning debates about twentieth-century Russian history have not been about what happened, but about what might have happened."[3] Discussion of

---

[3] Eric J. Hobsbawm, *On History* (London: Weidenfeld & Nicolson, 1997), p. 243.

the Soviet Union, he notes, thus raises the problem of "counterfactual" history — that is, in considering a particular historical situation, to what extent is it possible to make credible judgments about what did not happen, or about what might have happened. Hobsbawm is correct when he observes that discussion of Soviet history raises innumerable counterfactual questions. Of all the counterfactual questions that might be asked about it, the most important is whether the Russian Revolution could have followed a substantially different path from that which led to the Stalinist dictatorship.

Though writing as one who is sympathetic to the Revolution, who maintains that the policies of Lenin and the Bolshevik Party proceeded from what they perceived to be the hard realities of the existing political situation in 1917, and that they rose to power on a powerful, even irresistible wave of popular support, Hobsbawm ultimately concludes that there is no basis for arguing that the Revolution could have turned out substantially different than it actually did.

In contrast to Richard Pipes, for whom the October Revolution was a sinister conspiracy imposed upon the Russian people by ruthless socialist ideologues, Hobsbawm recognizes the historical processes that were at work in the Revolution. However, he fails to offer any substantial assessment of the role of the subjective factor — of parties, policies, political leaders, mass consciousness, etc. — in the historical process. Hobsbawm, as a serious historian, does know that the subjective factor exists and exerts an influence on the outcome of events. But what he has to say about the relation between the objective and subjective factors is confused, inconsistent, inexact and vague. He acknowledges, in writing about Lenin and Stalin, that "Without the personal input of these single men, the history of the Russian Revolution would certainly have been very different."[4] Yet he fails to say anything very definite about what in that history would have been different.

Hobsbawm would not deny that Lenin played an important role in the Russian Revolution. But he is very reluctant to consider counterfactuals — alternatives — in a historical scenario where Lenin is not included. Had Lenin not made it back to Russia from Switzerland in 1917, there is not much more one can say, writes Hobsbawm, other than that things might have, or might not have, turned out very differently. "And you can't get any further, except into fiction."[5]

---

[4] Ibid., p. 245.
[5] Ibid., p. 246.

In another passage in his lecture, referring to the historical role of Stalin, Hobsbawm states that one

> can argue quite plausibly that there was room for more or less harshness in the project of very rapid industrialization by Soviet state planning, but if the USSR was committed to such a project then, however great the genuine commitment of millions to it, it was going to require a good deal of coercion, even if the USSR had been led by someone less utterly ruthless and cruel than Stalin.[6]

In both passages, the underlying conception is that the subjective element cannot assume any decisive significance. This line of argument, in a lecture devoted to the consideration of historical alternatives for the Russian Revolution, becomes an outright apology for Stalinism. Hobsbawm argues as follows: the Bolshevik Party seized power in 1917 in the hope that a revolution in Germany, which Lenin believed to be imminent, would come to the rescue of Soviet Russia. This was a disastrous political miscalculation. Whatever Lenin's beliefs to the contrary, there were no serious prospects for a German revolution at the end of the World War. As for the claim that the German working class was betrayed by the Social Democratic leaders in 1918, Hobsbawm dismisses that as a myth. "A German October revolution, or anything like it, was not seriously on and therefore didn't have to be betrayed."[7]

This judgment tells us more about Hobsbawm's historical pessimism than it does about the conditions that existed in Germany in 1923. He simply discounts the possibility that a revolution might have succeeded in Germany without offering any examination of the actual political situation that existed in that country. There are valuable studies of the "German October" that argue persuasively that the outcome of the extreme crisis existing in Germany in the autumn of 1923 depended on the actions of the Communist Party. This was the argument made by Trotsky in 1924 in the aftermath of the political fiasco caused by the CP's decision, at the last minute, to call off a planned insurrection.[8]

---

[6] Ibid., p. 245.

[7] Ibid., p. 247.

[8] For a detailed account of the events of 1923, see Pierre Broué, *The German Revolution 1917–1923,* translated by John Archer (Chicago: Haymarket Books, 2006). Trotsky's assessment of the errors of the German Communist Party is cited on p. 822.

At a theoretical level, Hobsbawm's mistake flows from a fatalistic indifference to the impact of subjective politics on the course of events. I will cite a passage that sums up Hobsbawm's argument and which shows how his one-sided approach turns into an apology for Stalinism. As there was no chance for a German version of October 1917, "*The Russian Revolution was destined to build socialism in one backward and soon utterly ruined country...*" (emphasis added).[9] Thus, the Bolsheviks had seized political power in 1917 "with an obviously unrealistic programme of socialist revolution..."[10] Here, by the way, Hobsbawm appears to contradict himself by acknowledging the decisive role of the subjective factor. That is, he assigns devastating historical consequences to Lenin's mistake. Lenin, however sincere his beliefs and honorable his intentions, gambled and failed. Socialism in one country was the result. "History must start from what happened," declares Hobsbawm. "The rest is speculation."[11]

This is a simplistic conception, for "what happened" — if taken as nothing more than what was reported in the newspapers of the day — is certainly only a small part of the historical process. After all, history must concern itself not simply with "what happened," but also — and this is far more important — *why* one or another thing happened or did not happen, and what might have happened. The moment one considers an event — i.e. "what happened" — one is compelled to consider process and context. Yes, in 1924 the Soviet Union adopted the policy of "socialism in one country." That "happened." But the opposition to "socialism in one country" also "happened." The conflict between the Stalinist bureaucracy and the Left Opposition, about which Hobsbawm says not one word, "happened." Inasmuch as he deliberately excludes, or dismisses as unimportant, the forces of opposition which sought to impart to the policies of the Soviet Union a different direction, his definition of "what happened" consists of nothing more than a one-sided, one-dimensional, pragmatic and vulgar simplification of a very complex historical reality. For Hobsbawm, starting from "what happened" simply means starting, and ending, with "who won."

But even the most conscientious narrator of historical events can only deal with a small portion of "what happened." The study and writing of history always involves a significant degree of selection and specialization. This

---

[9] *On History*, p. 248.
[10] Ibid., p. 243.
[11] Ibid., p. 249.

selection and specialization, however, should at least be true to the historical process. It should draw together the main threads from which the historical process was woven. After all, "what happened" may be just as well defined in terms of the policy options that were rejected as by those that were implemented. Hobsbawm proceeds, however, as if the policies advanced by Trotsky ceased to be of real historical interest once they were rejected by the Communist Party and he was expelled and exiled.

If one delves beneath the academician's elegant prose, one is left with a mundane and unidirectional approach to history. "Stalin won," Hobsbawm is telling us, "and there is really no point considering what might have happened if he hadn't." To go beyond "what happened" — that is, to examine the historical process in the full range of its concrete possibilities — is mere speculation, a departure from historical reality and a flight toward insupportable judgments and self-satisfying illusions.

But if we include in "what happened" the contradictory and conflicting elements in the historical process, the gulf between "what happened" and "what did not happen" is not quite the speculative abyss suggested by Hobsbawm. After all, a fuller and more complete study of the historical process would convert at least a portion of "what did not happen" into "what might have happened."

To consider "what might have happened" on the basis of a study of the alternatives available to those making decisions is not merely empty speculation. If we exclude "what might have happened" from a consideration of history, then there would really be no reason to study history at all. History should, after all, teach us something.

During the first half of the twentieth century the international bourgeoisie experienced not a few major catastrophes. It made a careful study of these experiences and learned something from them. John Maynard Keynes was a bitter critic of the peace treaties that followed the First World War. Chastened by the disasters which flowed from Versailles, the bourgeoisie made the conceptions of Keynes the basis of its post–World War II policies.

Of course, there is a limit beyond which the consideration of historical alternatives — "the road not taken" — becomes unacceptably speculative. Also, from a methodological standpoint, the consideration of alternatives may underestimate, or even ignore, other factors that may have significantly reduced the possibility of historical evolution assuming a form substantially different from what actually occurred. Marxists, certainly, have made valid criticisms of precisely such illegitimate speculative approaches to the study of history.

Objective and subjective factors in history

This is not the sort of cautionary and valid objection that Hobsbawm is making. Rather, in his consideration of the history of the Russian Revolution and the Soviet Union, he adopts an ultra-deterministic, super-objectivist and fatalistic approach: there were no plausible alternatives to "what happened." This is justified on the basis of a simplistic identification of the processes of social revolution with those of nature.

> But at this stage we must leave speculation and return to the actual situation of a Russia in revolution. Great mass revolutions erupting from below — and Russia in 1917 was probably the most awesome example of such a revolution in history — are in some sense "natural phenomena." They are like earthquakes and giant floods, especially when, as in Russia, the superstructure of state and national institutions has virtually disintegrated. They are to a large extent uncontrollable.[12]

There is one basic difference between earthquakes and floods, on the one hand, and revolutions, on the other. In neither the movement of tectonic plates nor rivers is thought involved. The earth does not decide to rumble nor does a river weigh the consequences of overflowing its banks. In social revolutions, however, consciousness is an immense factor.[13] Revolution involves the action of thinking human beings. From the revolutionary who has devoted his entire life to its preparation, to the simple worker who has decided that the conditions of life have become so intolerable that he must fight the existing order, social revolution is a conscious act. However powerful the "purely" objective, i.e. economic, technological, etc., forces that underlie the social eruption — and in society there are no phenomena that are "purely objective," because every event involves the activity of human subjects — a revolutionary situation must signify that the objective impulses have gained access to the human mind and have been translated into complex forms of political

---

[12] Ibid.

[13] This is not to say that the conscious factor plays no role in natural events. The scale of the damage caused by an earthquake or flood will depend on the extent of conscious preparation in advance, and the speed with which conscious coutermeasures are implemented after the disaster strikes. The New Orleans hurricane of 2005 illustrates the role played by the conscious factor in a natural disaster, or the lack thereof.

thought. The comparison of social revolutions to various destructive natural phenomena, while valid in a certain limited sense, is among the most misused of metaphors. Unless the difference between the acts of nature and the acts of man is indicated, the metaphor serves only to mystify, distort and falsify the historical process.

Hobsbawm writes:

> We must stop thinking of the Russian Revolution in terms of the Bolsheviks' or anyone else's aims and intentions, their long-term strategy, and other Marxists' critiques of their practice.[14]

If one were to accept Hobsbawm's instructions, it would be simply impossible to provide a coherent narrative of, let alone understand, the Russian Revolution. They betray his inability to comprehend precisely that which comprises the most significant feature of historical development in the twentieth century: the unprecedented role of consciousness in the making of history. The emergence of mass socialist parties expressed a new historical phenomenon that only became possible through the interaction of two interrelated processes — the rise of the working class and the development of Marxism.

Even by the late nineteenth century, the program of social revolution was inscribed on the banner of political parties. Armed intellectually by Marx and Engels with an insight into the laws of social development, the leaders of the new socialist parties set out to prepare the working class for the anti-capitalist revolution in which it was destined to play the leading and decisive role.

Having acquired a scientifically-grounded insight into the laws of social development — and thus being able to interpret contemporaneously, to a degree hitherto impossible, the significance and implications of political events as they unfolded — the analyses, perspectives, strategies and programs of political organizations assumed an altogether unprecedented role in the historical process. History ceased to simply happen. *It was anticipated, prepared for and, to an extent hitherto impossible, consciously directed.* The generation of Marxists that entered into political activity in the closing years of the nineteenth century or the first years of the twentieth expected revolution as the consequence of socioeconomic contradictions that had been identified and analyzed. They conceived of their own, or their opponents', political work

---

[14] Ibid.

in terms of its ultimate consequences for the revolution. Only in this context is it possible to understand why such overriding importance was attached in Marxist polemics to uncovering the class interests served by different policies and identifying the "class nature" of political tendencies.

The Russian Revolution revealed the objective significance of the aims, intentions, strategies and critiques of all the political parties and tendencies that were, in one way or another, active in Russia in the years before 1917. What the principal political actors did between April and October 1917, where they lined up in the decisive battles, was anticipated in the great theoretical and political struggles that took place during the previous two decades.

It sounds plausible to describe the Revolution as an uncontrollable catastrophe that rendered the plans of mice and men irrelevant. But if consciousness counts for so little, if the element of theoretical foresight is insignificant amidst the chaos of a revolutionary epoch, then how should one evaluate the work of Lenin and Trotsky, both prior to, during and especially after 1917?

In the aftermath of the 1905 Revolution, the various factions of Russian Social Democracy sought to define the tasks of the working class in light of the experiences of that event. The answers they gave were to determine not only their own role in subsequent events, but also the future course of the Russian Revolution. Hobsbawm insists that "What Lenin aimed at — and in the last analysis Lenin got his way in the Party — was irrelevant."[15]

But this claim is belied by the simple fact that without the reorientation of the Bolshevik Party in the spring of 1917 on the basis of Lenin's "April Theses" — that is, the adoption of the strategic line previously formulated by Leon Trotsky — there would have been no seizure of power by the Bolsheviks. Revolutions are, indeed, mighty events; but policy and program — the products of consciousness — play within them a decisive role.

Hobsbawm seeks to minimize, to the very point of denying, the role of consciousness in the revolutionary process. Lenin, he writes, "could have no strategy or perspective beyond choosing, day by day, between the decisions needed for immediate survival and the ones which risked immediate disaster. Who could afford to consider the possible long-term consequences for the revolution of decisions which had to be taken *now* or else there would be an end to the revolution and no further consequences to consider?"[16]

---

[15] Ibid.
[16] Ibid.

This portrayal of Lenin as a vulgar *realpolitiker*, reacting pragmatically and intuitively to events as they arose, hardly makes sense even within the terms presented by Hobsbawm. The defense of the revolution required a comprehensive strategic conception, and its achievement depended upon a conscious insight into the class structure and dynamics of Russian society. Lenin and Trotsky were, quite obviously, very busy men during the period of revolution and civil war. But they did not stop thinking. A study of their writings — above all, Trotsky's great manifestos and speeches prepared for the congresses of the Communist International — still provoke astonishment at the depth and breadth of their strategic vision. Of all the political forces operating in the maelstrom of revolution and civil war, only the Bolsheviks were able to formulate a strategic line that provided a unifying banner for tens of millions of people in a vast and culturally disparate country. As E.H. Carr has aptly noted, the success of the Bolsheviks in the civil war depended to no small extent upon the fact that Lenin's genius was of a profoundly creative, rather than negatively destructive, character.

Hobsbawm's belittling of the significance of the elements of political consciousness makes it all but impossible to understand how the Bolsheviks came to power and why they triumphed in the civil war. If political parties are merely at the mercy of history's volcanic eruptions, it follows that the victory of the Bolsheviks was due either to their luck or their opponents' misfortunes — depending on your point of view.

Hobsbawm's fatalism

When applied to the post-revolutionary period, Hobsbawm's position serves as an apology for Stalinism. Buffeted by uncontrollable historical forces to which it could respond only with desperate improvisations, the fate of Bolshevism was sealed by 1921. As Hobsbawm writes, "By this time its future course was more or less prescribed..."[17] In another essay which appears in the same volume, Hobsbawm expresses this view even more emphatically: "Unfortunately I can think of no realistic forecast which ought to have envisaged the long-term future of the USSR as very different from what it has actually become."[18]

Thus, while the course of Soviet history might have developed along lines less cruel, the outcome of the historical process was basically decided by

---

[17] Ibid.

[18] Ibid., p. 48.

1921. Stalin simply played out, though with excessive violence, the hand he had been dealt by the preceding course of development. Hobsbawm leaves us with a "left" variation of the standard reactionary thesis: that there could not have been an alternative to Stalinism. He does not agree that Stalinist totalitarianism was the inevitable product of Marxism itself. Rather, he argues that Stalinism arose inevitably and inexorably out of the conditions that confronted the Soviet Union after 1917. To speak of an alternative to what actually happened is to engage in mere speculation. Objective conditions did not permit an alternative. The policies of the regime might have been somewhat less cruel, but this would have only been a difference of degree, not of kind.

What are our differences with this assessment? After all, the Trotskyists have always insisted that the Stalinist degeneration of the Bolshevik Party and the Soviet state was, in the final analysis, the product of unfavorable conditions. These were, principally, the historic backwardness of Russia; the economic devastation produced by seven uninterrupted years of world war; revolution and civil war; and the protracted isolation of the Soviet state that resulted from the defeats suffered by the European, and especially the German, working class after World War I.

However, there is a critical difference between recognizing the material foundations of Stalinism and declaring that from those foundations there could only be one political outcome — the irreversible bureaucratic degeneration of the USSR and its ultimate collapse in 1991. One little thing is missing from this conception of Soviet history: the role of politics, of program, of the struggle of tendencies, of consciousness, and the significance of the decisions made by individuals, motivated by a greater or lesser degree of political insight into the historical process. History is transformed into an entirely abstract and super-deterministic process: everything is determined by blind and uncontrollable forces. History swept the Bolsheviks into power; and then swept them, if not out of power, then at least into a blind alley.

Hobsbawm has already told us that "We must stop thinking of the Russian Revolution in terms of the Bolsheviks' or anyone else's aims and intentions, their long-term strategy, and other Marxists' critiques of their practice."[19] What this really means is that there is no reason to pay any attention to the political struggles that raged within the Bolshevik Party during the 1920s. What Trotsky wrote about Stalinism, the criticisms he made of Soviet policy, the conflict between the long-term strategy he advanced and that of the

---

[19] Ibid., p. 249.

Stalinist leadership is, as far as Hobsbawm is concerned, of very little importance. The fate of the USSR was already set in stone by 1921, and there was nothing that the Communist regime could do — regardless of who was in power — that would have made any fundamental difference. One suspects Hobsbawm believes that arguments to the contrary amount to little more than the pointless speculation of die-hard Trotskyists. It is therefore not surprising that his lecture makes absolutely no reference to the struggle of Trotsky and the Left Opposition against Stalinism. Indeed, in a 300-page book of essays and lectures whose central theme is the place of the October Revolution in the history of the twentieth century, Trotsky's name appears only once.

Hobsbawm does not hold Marxism responsible for Stalinism. But if the Stalinist dictatorship was the only plausible outcome of the October Revolution, it would be hard to make the case that the Bolshevik seizure of power served the interests of the working class and the cause of historical progress. One is left with the conclusion — at which Hobsbawm strongly hints — that October 1917 was a dreadful mistake and it would probably have been far better if Kamenev, the opponent of the insurrection, rather than Lenin, had prevailed in the deliberations of the Bolshevik Party.

Hobsbawm's argument not only calls into question the political legitimacy of the October Revolution; the validity of the entire socialist project is placed under a very dark cloud. It is hard to imagine that any social revolution would occur under conditions so perfect that its ultimate success was guaranteed. By its very nature, revolution — which is inconceivable without a massive dislocation and breakdown of the political and economic mechanisms of the existing order — is a leap into the unknown. The situation will be fraught with danger. It would be foolhardy, if not criminally irresponsible, for a political organization to summon the working class to a revolutionary insurrection if it did not believe in the possibility of mastering the situation, influencing its further development and subordinating it to the aims of its revolutionary program.

What reasonable basis is there, however, for such confidence if the lesson of October 1917 and its aftermath is that revolutionary parties are simply at the mercy of objective conditions; that they are merely hapless instruments of a historical process which compels them to carry out whatever orders they are given, no matter how terrible?

Thus, Hobsbawm provides not only an apology for Stalin — "objective conditions made him do it" — but also vindicates the classical liberal bourgeois democratic argument against revolution as an instrument of social change. But Hobsbawm's position is based, first, on a false method, and, second, on a rather slipshod — I would like to avoid the word dishonest — treatment of facts. His fatalism has nothing in common with the method of historical materialism. Hobsbawm invokes objective conditions as if they were a set of marching orders, which leave parties and people no choice but to do as they are told. Such a conception is simplistic in the extreme.

The divisions which opened up in the Russian Communist Party after 1921 testify to the fact that the objective conditions generated a wide range of responses. How leaders of the party responded to the problems, and the tendencies that developed around these responses, reflected not only their different evaluations of the objective conditions, but also their relation to different and even mutually hostile social forces.

Stalin's response to "objective conditions" tended more and more openly to reflect the social position and articulate the material interests of the growing state bureaucracy, whose personnel were recruited from the urban lower middle class. The policies of Trotsky and the Left Opposition, on the other hand, articulated in a highly conscious form the interests of the industrial proletariat. To the extent that the economic and social dislocation produced by the civil war seriously weakened this social force, which was the principal constituency for Marxist politics in the USSR, conditions for the development and implementation of socialist policies grew unfavorable.

These "unfavorable conditions" however, must not be considered as analogous to an uncontrollable meteorological phenomenon, but in concrete political terms — that is, as the expression of the struggle of antagonistic social forces. As the position of the industrial proletariat — decimated by the civil war — weakened, the Marxist leaders of the working class encountered increasingly ruthless and violent opposition from those elements within the party and state bureaucracy who considered the policies advanced by the Left Opposition threatening to what they perceived to be their material interests.

This was the substance of the political struggle that raged within the Communist Party and Communist International throughout the 1920s.

What if the Left Opposition had prevailed?

At this point I will make a series of statements that Professor Hobsbawm would regard as impermissibly speculative and beyond the pale of proper historical analysis:

First, had the Left Opposition prevailed in the struggle within the Russian Communist Party, the cause of international socialism would have been immeasurably strengthened. At the very least, the counterrevolutionary catastrophes of the 1930s — above all, the victory of German fascism — would probably have been avoided.

Second, with the victory of the Opposition the entire character of Soviet economic and political life would have developed along incomparably more progressive lines. The argument that the downward spiral of the USSR toward the totalitarian bestiality of the 1930s was pre-determined by uncontrollable "objective conditions" simply does not hold water. The very fact that "objective conditions" became increasingly unfavorable for the development of the USSR along socialist lines was, above all else, the political consequence of the defeat of Trotsky and the Left Opposition.

Third, and this point flows from the first two, the defeat of Trotsky and the Left Opposition set the stage for all the subsequent tragedies that were to befall the Soviet Union, the international working class and the socialist movement, and beneath whose shadow we still live today. I wish to add a further point: No discussion on the fate of socialism in the twentieth century deserves to be taken seriously unless it considers, with the necessary care, the consequences of Trotsky's defeat. It is necessary to consider not only "what happened" under Stalin; but also "what well might have happened" had Trotsky prevailed.

Is this an impossibly speculative venture? One must acknowledge that it is reasonable to ask whether such an enterprise is intellectually legitimate. Certainly, there is a danger that in dealing with counterfactuals we may find ourselves engaged in unjustified speculation and outright wishful thinking. In imagining alternative paths of historical development, we must not go beyond the range of possibilities that were actually available at the time. Also, we must retain a firm sense — based on a thorough study and comprehension of the economic foundations, technological level and class structure of the given society — of the limits within which the subjective activity of man, itself the product and expression of specific historically-formed conditions, could influence and alter that objectively-given environment.

Two historical digressions:
England in 1529 and France in 1794

For example, a historian of the Tudor Age could — if he cared to — consider what might have happened had Catherine of Aragon, the first wife of Henry VIII, given birth to a male heir. What effect would that have had on the development of England? Certain educated guesses are possible, but we would be unable to proceed very far before finding ourselves in terrain that is clearly of a highly speculative character. It is probably true that Catherine, had she produced a boy, and had that boy survived childhood, would not have found herself being sued for divorce by her libidinous husband. It is therefore possible, but by no means certain, that the remaining years of Henry's reign would not have been, at least in terms of his personal life, quite as colorful as they turned out to be.

However, could we go on from there to conclude that England, having avoided a royal marital crisis, would have remained a Catholic country? That would certainly be a highly speculative and questionable proposition. The struggle over the divorce only brought to a head a political crisis that was deeply rooted in socioeconomic processes that were sweeping across Europe. The really interesting and critical question that must be answered when studying the reign of Henry VIII is precisely why what began as a not particularly unusual crisis of dynastic succession turned into a struggle between church and state with revolutionary consequences. Against this backdrop, the motivations of individuals — who were largely unaware of the historical dimensions and consequences of their actions — do not appear to be all that decisive.

Even if we move forward several centuries, to the epoch of the French Revolution, historical personalities are still responding with only a limited consciousness of the weight of the historical forces bearing down on them. There is, of course, a great difference between the historical consciousness of a Robespierre and that of a Henry VIII or even an Oliver Cromwell. By the late eighteenth century the conscious awareness of social forces and interests was certainly more acute than it could have been a century or two earlier. But the force of historical necessity had not yet been translated into the appropriate forms of scientific thought — an achievement that only became possible with the development of modern capitalism and the emergence of the working class. Thus, in each of the stages of the French Revolution, notwithstanding the brilliance of its leading personalities, events were shaped by the overwhelming force of historical necessity.

This does not mean that things might not have worked out differently. One can imagine any number of "counterfactuals" that might have altered the course of events. But given the level of social development and the still limited range of man's insight into the underlying laws of historical development, those changes in the course of events would not have been introduced by the political actors themselves with anything approaching a clear understanding of the historical consequences of their actions.

In the France of 1794, there existed neither the objective means, nor, flowing from that, the corresponding level of scientific insight, to consciously determine — that is, to act with an understanding of the logic of socioeconomic processes — the course of historical development. Undoubtedly, the members of the Committee of Public Safety acted consciously, and with a not altogether unsubtle sense of the social forces active in the Revolution. Robespierre, for example, was certainly aware that Danton had powerful supporters among sections of the bourgeoisie. He sensed the danger that might flow from a confrontation with the Indulgents. But Robespierre could not be aware, in a modern sense, of the historical implications of his actions. The preconditions for the development of historical materialism had not yet matured, and the real forces which motivated historical behavior were still perceived and interpreted in various mystified ideological forms (i.e., Reason, the Rights of Man, Virtue, Fraternity).

The emergence of historical self-consciousness

Thus, any discussion of alternative historical outcomes for the French Revolution tends to veer rapidly toward hypotheses of a highly speculative character. Inasmuch as the leading personages could not foresee the historical consequences of their own actions, we can hardly claim with any degree of certainty that the victory of one faction of the Jacobins rather than another would have fundamentally changed the subsequent course of history, let alone state precisely how it would have been altered.

With the advent of Marxism the relation of man to his own history underwent a profound transformation. Man acquired the capacity to consciously interpret his thought and actions in socioeconomic terms, and, thereby, to precisely locate his own activity within a chain of historical causality.

This is why a consideration of alternative outcomes to the struggle inside the Russian Communist Party and the Communist International is not a hopelessly speculative enterprise. Here it is not the case, as it was in France 130 years earlier, of political factions groping in the dark, moved by socioeconomic forces of which they were unaware, defining and justifying their actions in largely idealistic terms.

Rather, Leon Trotsky and the Left Opposition entered into struggle with an extraordinarily far-reaching understanding of the historical implications of the issues confronting the Soviet Union and the international socialist movement. In both his analysis of the domestic and international contradictions of the USSR and the warnings he directed to the Stalinists, Trotsky left no doubt as to the ultimate consequences of the growing authority of the bureaucracy and the false policies of the Soviet leadership.

"Does bureaucratism bear within it a danger of degeneration, or doesn't it?" Trotsky asked in December 1923. "Anyone who denied it would be blind."[20]

This was written in the opening round of the struggle against the emerging Stalinist regime. Even at that early stage Trotsky had already raised the possibility that "the progressive degeneration" of the Communist Party could become one of "the *political* paths by which the victory of the counterrevolution might come about..."[21]

However serious the danger, Trotsky argued that conscious political foresight based on a Marxist analysis provided the party with the possibility of overcoming the crisis:

> If we set forth these hypotheses bluntly, it is of course not because we consider them historically probable (on the contrary, their probability is at a minimum), but because only such a way of putting the question makes possible a more correct and all-sided historical orientation and, consequently, the adoption of all possible preventive measures. The superiority of us Marxists is in distinguishing and grasping new tendencies and new dangers even when they are still only in an embryonic stage.[22]

In considering whether the victory of the Left Opposition would have significantly altered the course of Soviet and world history, we propose to deal concretely with three issues that were of fundamental significance in determining the fate of the USSR: 1) Soviet and inner-party democracy, 2) economic policy and 3) international policy.

It is noteworthy that virtually none of those political and intellectual tendencies that insist, in one form or another, that the Soviet Union was doomed from the outset — whether on account of the "fatal flaws" of Marxism or the impossible objective conditions confronting Bolshevism — ever attempt a concrete analysis of the policies advanced by the Left Opposition. Trotsky

---

[20] Leon Trotsky, "The New Course," *The Challenge of the Left Opposition 1923–25*, (New York: Pathfinder Press, 1975), p. 79.

[21] Ibid., p. 98.

[22] Ibid., pp. 98–99.

remains to this day "The Great Unmentionable" in Soviet history. On the rare occasions he is referred to, it is usually to misrepresent and falsify his work.

Both the silence and the lies represent in their own ways a form of tribute to the historical significance of Trotsky's struggle against Stalinism. All the claims that the demise of the USSR was inevitable, that the socialist revolution is by its very nature a utopian undertaking, that, therefore, the October Revolution led the Russian working class into a blind alley from which there could be no escape, that Marxism leads inevitably to totalitarianism, etc., are refuted by the historical record left by the Left Opposition. It clearly represented, in terms of the policies it advanced, a viable, theoretically acute and powerful political opposition to the Stalinist bureaucracy.

Inner-party democracy

Let us now proceed to the three issues that I have singled out. First of all, the question of Soviet and inner-party democracy: it is an historical fact, proven by the 1923 document that I have already cited, that Trotsky recognized at a very early stage of the struggle — even before the term Stalinism had entered into political usage — that the growth of bureaucratism and the demise of inner-party democracy posed a potentially mortal threat to Bolshevism and the survival of the Soviet regime. In countless documents, Trotsky and the Left Opposition insisted that the intelligent and correct formulation of Soviet policy, not to mention the political education of a Marxist cadre and the broadest layers of the working class, was inconceivable without a democratic regime within the Bolshevik Party. Trotsky wrote in 1923:

> It is in contradictions and differences of opinion that the working out of the party's public opinion inevitably takes place. To localize this process *only* within the apparatus, which is then charged to furnish the party with the fruit of its labors in the form of slogans, orders, etc., is to sterilize the party ideologically and politically. ... *the leading party bodies must heed the voices of the broad party masses and must not consider every criticism a manifestation of factionalism and thereby cause conscientious and disciplined party members to withdraw into closed circles and fall into factionalism.*[23]

---

[23] Ibid., p. 88.

Trotsky rejected the self-serving claims of the apparatus that opposition to the decisions of the ruling bodies of the party was invariably the expression of the interests of hostile class forces:

> It frequently happens that the party is able to resolve one and the same problem by different means, and differences arise as to which of these means is the better, the more expeditious, the more economical. These differences may, depending on the question, embrace considerable sections of the party, but that does not necessarily mean that you have there two class tendencies.
>
> There is no doubt that we shall have not one but dozens of disagreements in the future, for our path is difficult and the political tasks as well as the economic questions of socialist organization will unfailingly engender differences of opinion and temporary groupings of opinion. The political verification of all the nuances of opinion by Marxist analysis will always be one of the most efficacious preventive measures for our party. But it is this concrete Marxist verification that must be resorted to, and not the stereotyped phrases which are the defense mechanism of bureaucratism.[24]

The nature of the party regime impacted directly on the tasks of socialist construction. By its very nature, as Trotsky explained on innumerable occasions, efficient economic planning requires the interested and democratic participation of the masses in the decision-making process. It is incompatible with bureaucratic fiat. Thus, even as Trotsky offered a farsighted evaluation of the contradictions of the Soviet economy and concrete proposals for their amelioration, he stressed that both the formulation and implementation of a correct economic policy depended upon a democratic party regime.

The importance of inner-party democracy was not simply one of abstract principle, nor was its practical significance limited to its direct impact on the field of economic policy. What was ultimately at stake in the struggle waged by Trotsky in defense of Soviet democracy was the fate of the entire heritage of socialist culture and revolutionary thought as it had developed in the international workers' movement over the previous century. The bureaucracy dealt with Marxism as it did with Lenin's corpse: it was mummified and made the

---

[24] Ibid., p. 94.

object of ritualistic and semi-mystical incantations. After 1927 Marxism, for all intents and purposes, ceased to play any role whatsoever in the formulation of Soviet policy. The defeat of the Opposition sounded the death knell for the development of critical thought in virtually every sphere of intellectual and cultural activity.

Economic policy

I must at this point turn to the second issue — the economic policy of the Left Opposition. This is a vast subject that is not reducible to a few quotations. I will, however, offer several citations that at least indicate the profound difference between the Opposition's approach to problems of Soviet economic development and that of the Stalinist bureaucracy.

The conflict between the Opposition and the Stalinists over economic policy centered on the most fundamental question of historical perspective: Was it possible for the Soviet Union to build socialism on the basis of its own national resources, or was the socialist development of the USSR dependent, in the final analysis, upon the victory of the proletarian revolution in the advanced capitalist countries of Western Europe and North America? Until 1924 the unquestioned premise of Soviet policy — indeed, that which underlay the entire revolutionary project undertaken by the Bolsheviks in October 1917 — was that the seizure of power in Russia was only "the first shot" of the world socialist revolution. A nationally self-contained socialist state, especially one based on a country as economically and culturally backward as Russia, could not be viable. Stalin's introduction, in the autumn of 1924, of the "theory" of "socialism in one country" — which was not really a "theory" at all, but rather a crudely pragmatic response to the defeat of the German revolution during the previous year and the temporary decline of the revolutionary movement in Western Europe — ran counter to the internationalist orientation propounded by the Bolsheviks under the leadership of Lenin and Trotsky.

Professor Hobsbawm would not deny that the policy of "socialism in one country" was a major departure from the original vision of the October Revolution. However, he implies that this vision was not all too realistic inasmuch as the Russian Revolution was unavoidably "destined" to build, or at least attempt to build, socialism in one country. If pressed to defend this position, I suspect that Hobsbawm would be obliged to argue that while, in a general abstract sense, theoretical doctrine stood on the side of Trotsky, practical reality was firmly on Stalin's side. Trotsky's conception of world revolution made for compelling reading, but had little to offer in the actual context of the political and economic situation confronting the USSR in the mid-1920s. Thus, to claim that Trotskyist policies presented a real alternative to those adopted by Stalin is to indulge one's own revolutionary illusions.

I cannot be sure that Hobsbawm would argue in precisely this way. I am, to some degree, engaging in "speculation." But even if this is not quite the view of Hobsbawm, I have heard it expressed many times by bourgeois historians, not to mention out-and-out apologists for Stalinism.

The basic problem with this argument is that it proceeds from a deeply biased and stereotyped conception of Trotsky's views and the nature of his differences with Stalin. It is much easier to dismiss Trotsky's perspective if it is reduced to an impatient and romantic desire to storm the barricades of world capitalism, in contrast to Stalin's more astute and sober preoccupation with the development of the Soviet Union, based on a realistic appraisal of the national resources at its disposal.

We cannot compel those who write on Soviet history to actually read what Trotsky wrote. However, those who study his articles and books with the seriousness they require — and Trotsky was, in my opinion, among the very greatest political thinkers and writers of the twentieth century — will discover that it was especially in his analyses of the contradictions and problems of Soviet economic development that Trotsky's revolutionary internationalism found its most brilliant and subtle expression.

There is nothing in Trotsky's writings that would support the claim that he believed Soviet economic policy should consist simply of waiting for the working class in Western Europe or the United States to seize power. In fact, the main premise of his treatment of Soviet economic problems was that the USSR had to work out policies that would enable it to survive and develop in a more or less protracted transitional era — that is, a period whose duration could not be predicted — during which the Soviet Union would exist within an international economic environment dominated by the capitalist system.

Notwithstanding its program of "socialism in one country," the Stalinist bureaucracy through the 1920s still maintained, however inconsistently, the commitment of the USSR to international revolution. Trotsky's chief criticism of this program, considered from the standpoint of economic development, was not that it categorically denied the importance, at least in the long run, of world revolution for the fate of the Soviet Union. Rather, he stressed that the nationalist orientation that underlay "socialism in one country" led to autarchic policies that dangerously underestimated the impact — direct and indirect — of world economy on the Soviet Union.

It may seem paradoxical that Trotsky, the great protagonist of world revolution, placed greater emphasis than any other Soviet leader of his time on the overriding importance of close economic links between the USSR and the world capitalist market. Soviet economic development, he insisted, required both access to the resources of the world market and the intelligent utilization of the international division of labor. The development of economic planning required at minimum a knowledge of competitive advantage and efficiencies at the international level. It served no rational economic purpose for the USSR to make a virtue of frittering away its own limited resources in a vain effort to duplicate on Soviet soil what it could obtain at far less cost on the world capitalist market. Trotsky wrote in 1927:

> Resting our hope upon an isolated development of socialism and upon a rate of economic development independent of world economy distorts the whole outlook. It puts our planning leadership off the track, and offers no guiding threads for a correct regulation of our relations with world economy. We have no way of deciding what to manufacture ourselves and what to bring in from outside. A definite renunciation of the theory of an isolated socialist economy will mean, in the course of a few years, an incomparably more rational use of our resources, a swifter industrialization, and a more planful and powerful growth of our own machine construction. It will mean a swifter increase in the number of employed workers and a real lowering of prices — in a word, a genuine strengthening of the Soviet Union in the capitalist environment.[25]

Trotsky belonged to a generation of Russian Marxists who had utilized the opportunity provided by revolutionary exile to carefully observe and study the workings of the capitalist system in the advanced countries. They were familiar not only with the oft-described "horrors" of capitalism, but also with its positive achievements. The countless hours they had spent studying *Das Kapital* were enriched by many years of observing capital in action. Upon their return to Russia — and this applies especially to those who were among

---

[25] *The Platform of the Joint Opposition 1927* (London: New Park Publications, 1973), p. 41.

Trotsky's closest associates during the years of exile — they brought with them a keen understanding of the complexities of modern economic organization. If political struggles had not invested the issue with such profoundly tragic implications, they would have dismissed as simply laughable the idea that Russia could somehow leap into socialism merely by nationalizing its own paltry means of production. Trotsky argued that a precondition for the development of the Soviet economy along socialist lines was its assimilation of the basic techniques of capitalist management, organization, accounting and production.

In this very brief overview of the contrast between the economic policies of Trotsky and those of Stalin, it is necessary to touch on the question of collectivization. As is well known, Soviet agriculture never fully recovered from the traumatic consequences of Stalin's reckless and brutal collectivization of agriculture between 1929 and 1932. Clearly, a more rational approach to the problems of Soviet agriculture would have spared the USSR incalculable losses and endless agony. It is precisely in this area that the question of an alternative policy assumes historical significance, and that is why right-wing historians generally proceed as if none existed. Indeed, the claim is often made that collectivization arose out of Stalin's adoption, in the late 1920s, of the Left Opposition's program of rapid industrialization. In fact, Trotsky opposed and denounced the frenzied collectivization campaign launched by the Stalinists. Despite the pseudo-socialist demagogy that accompanied it, Trotsky warned that the policy, implemented with reckless disregard of the real productive capabilities of both industry and the countryside, proceeded from the same nationalistic and anti-Marxist conceptions of "socialism in one country" that underlay the previous failed economic programs of the Stalinist bureaucracy.

In a critique of Stalinist collectivization written in 1930, Trotsky acknowledged that he had previously advocated a more rapid tempo of industrialization, and the use of heavier taxation of wealthier sections of the peasantry (the kulaks) to provide resources for the development of heavy industry:

> But we never regarded the resources for industrialization as inexhaustible. We never thought that its tempo could be regulated by the administrative whip alone. We have always advanced, as a basic condition for industrialization, the necessity for systematic improvement in the conditions of the working class. We have always considered collectivization dependent upon

industrialization. We saw the socialist reconstruction of peasant economy only as a prospect of many years. We never closed our eyes to the inevitability of internal conflicts during the socialist reconstruction of a single nation. To remove contradictions in rural life is possible only by removing contradictions between the city and countryside. This can be realized only through the world revolution. We never demanded, therefore, the liquidation of classes within the scope of the five-year plan of Stalin and Krzhyzhanovsky.

... The question of the tempo of industrialization is not a matter of bureaucratic fancy, but of the life and culture of the masses.

Therefore the plan for building socialism cannot be issued as an a priori bureaucratic command. It must be worked out and corrected in the same way that the construction of socialism itself can only be realized, i.e., through broad soviet democracy.[26]

Trotsky reiterated the basis of his critique of Stalinist collectivization:

Again and again we decisively rejected the task of building a national socialist society "in the shortest possible time." Collectivization and industrialization we bind by an unbreakable tie to the world revolution. The problems of our economy are decided in the final analysis on the international arena.[27]

In attempting to conceptualize how the victory of the Left Opposition might have altered the history of the Soviet Union, we do not claim that it is possible to provide an exact picture of how it might have evolved. It is no more possible to present a detailed hypothetical reconstruction of the past than it is to predict the future. The implementation of different policies after 1924 would have introduced into the historical equation a vast quantity of new political, social and economic variables which, in the complexity of their mutual interaction, may have altered the course of events in a manner entirely unanticipated by those who are engaged in a retrospective evaluation of alternatives. But due consideration to the principle of historical "uncertainty" does not mean that it

---

[26] *Writings of Leon Trotsky 1930* (New York: Pathfinder Press, 1975), pp. 115–117.

[27] Ibid., p. 118.

is impossible to say anything convincing or intelligent about historical alternatives. There are very solid factual and theoretical grounds for concluding that the victory of the Left Opposition would have made highly probable a more rational, productive and humane evolution of the Soviet economy. Hobsbawm seeks to make light of this possibility by stating that industrialization was going to require "a good deal of coercion." The only question was how much. But that, as the history of the USSR amply proves, is not a small question. The dialectical relation between quantity and quality should not be forgotten. There is a profound difference between high rates of taxation on the wealthiest strata of the peasantry and the physical "liquidation of the kulaks as a class." Had the economic policy of the Opposition achieved nothing more than the avoidance of the horrors of Stalinist collectivization — and it is virtually inconceivable that it would have occurred had the Left Opposition triumphed — the USSR would have been spared a catastrophe, and all that flowed from it.

International strategy

Let us now turn to a consideration of the consequences of the defeat of Leon Trotsky and the Left Opposition on the fate of the international working class and the world socialist movement. This international dimension is not included in Hobsbawm's consideration of the counterfactual alternatives. Holding the position that the ultimate breakdown of the USSR flowed inexorably from the objective conditions with which it was confronted in 1921, Hobsbawm makes no effort to examine how the international policies pursued by the Stalinist regime actually impacted upon the evolution of the Soviet Union. He goes so far as to suggest that there existed little relation between the international and the domestic: "The Russian Revolution really has two interwoven histories: its impact on Russia and its impact on the world. We must not confuse the two."[28]

Yet such a separation would make incomprehensible the phenomenon of Stalinism. The Stalinist regime arose on the basis of a Russian nationalist reaction against the proletarian socialist internationalism that was embodied in the Bolshevik government under the leadership of Lenin and Trotsky. The program of socialism in one country provided a banner for all those elements within the bureaucracy who identified their own material interests with the development of the USSR as a powerful national state. The bureaucracy

---

[28] *On History*, p. 251.

obtained its privileges through the mechanism of state ownership of the means of production. The more it became conscious of the national-state foundations of its privileges, the less willing was the bureaucracy to place these at risk in the interest of world revolution. The program of socialism in one country legitimized the subordination of the interests of the international socialist movement to the national interests of the Soviet state, as they were conceived by the bureaucracy.

It was precisely at the level of the international class struggle that the consequences of the defeat of the Left Opposition were the most tragic and long-lasting, and where, therefore, the question of whether the USSR might have developed along different lines is posed most seriously and profoundly. In his own analysis of the growth of the Stalinist regime, Trotsky always stressed that the political reaction within the USSR against the program and traditions of October was greatly strengthened by the defeats suffered by the international working class. The initial setback suffered by the Left Opposition in the late autumn of 1923 was definitely bound up with the defeat of the German Revolution, which dimmed hopes that European workers would in the near future come to the aid of the USSR. This was the climate that created a broader audience for the nationalist perspective of socialism in one country. The political disorientation produced by the nationalist line of the Soviet leaders inside the Communist International led, in turn, to more defeats for the working class outside the USSR. Each of these defeats intensified the isolation of Soviet Russia, further eroded the confidence of Soviet workers in the perspective of world revolution, and undermined the political position of the Marxist and internationalist opposition to the Stalinist regime.

Being by nature highly skeptical of the possibility of revolution, which they tend to view as a violation of the normal course of historical development, professional historians find it easiest to dismiss as unrealistic and utopian the international perspective that animated the October Revolution. We have already seen how Hobsbawm considers Lenin's faith in the prospects for a German Revolution a fatal lapse in his political judgment. Though Hobsbawm says nothing at all about Trotsky's struggle against the political line of socialism in one country, I am sure that if he were asked to comment, he would reply that Trotsky's international perspective in the 1920s and 1930s was as unrealistic as Lenin's had been in 1918. Hobsbawm would argue that to consider Trotsky's international program as a viable alternative that, if followed, might have changed the course of Soviet history is just another exercise in counterfactual speculation that leads to a dead end.

How, then, can we demonstrate that the international policies of the Left Opposition, based on the theory of permanent revolution, would have greatly strengthened the Communist International and improved the international position of the Soviet Union? Of course, we cannot prove to a political and moral certainty that the victory of the Left Opposition would have guaranteed the success of revolutionary struggles outside the Soviet Union. We are perfectly prepared to admit that in the sphere of revolution, the outcome is decided not by logical proofs but by actual struggle. However, that does not mean that we cannot arrive at some plausible conclusions, based on historical evidence, about the probable consequences of an Opposition victory for the world revolutionary movement.

Let us consider, if only briefly, two critical episodes in the history of the international working class.

The Chinese Revolution

First, the catastrophic defeat of the Chinese Revolution in 1927. The cause of this defeat was the subordination of the Chinese Communist Party to the bourgeois Kuomintang, led by Chiang Kai-shek. The Chinese CP was instructed by Stalin to accept Chiang and the Kuomintang as the authoritative leadership of the democratic revolution. The political background of these instructions were the efforts of Stalin to establish closer relations between the Soviet Union and China via a political alliance with Chiang. Trotsky persistently warned that the subordination of the CCP to the bourgeois Kuomintang, a violation of the most basic lessons of Bolshevik strategy in 1917, would have disastrous consequences for the working class. Chiang was not an ally in whom the Communist Party and workers could place the slightest confidence. As soon as an opportunity presented itself, Chiang, responding to the pressures of his imperialist and bourgeois patrons, would turn savagely against the CCP and the revolutionary Shanghai workers. These warnings were ignored: even as the actions of Chiang grew more menacing, Stalin pressed the CCP to demonstrate its loyalty to the Kuomintang ever more ostentatiously. The CCP finally instructed revolutionary workers in Shanghai to disarm themselves before Chiang's troops entered the city. As Trotsky's condemnation of Stalin's policies echoed through the Communist International, events in China moved to a disastrous denouement. Chiang's troops entered Shanghai where, as Trotsky and the Left Opposition had warned, they proceeded to slaughter tens of thousands of Communist workers. The CCP was dealt a blow from which it never recovered.

It is not necessary to assert what is by the very nature of things unprovable: that the policies of the Left Opposition would have assured the victory of the Chinese Revolution in the 1920s — though I believe that such a victory would have been possible. But what can be said with a high degree of certainty is that the Chinese Communist Party would not have fallen victim to Chiang's coup of April 1927, and the position of the working class would not have been so disastrously weakened. As events turned out under the leadership of Stalin, the historical consequences of the defeat in China were of such a magnitude as to be incalculable. Aside from its immediate impact on the USSR — it deepened the Soviet Union's political isolation and, therefore, strengthened the bureaucratic regime — the 1927 defeat tragically altered the character of the revolutionary movement in China itself. With their position within the cities shattered by Chiang's counterrevolutionary blow, the confused remnants of the CCP retreated into the countryside and abandoned its historic orientation to the working class. Henceforth, the work of the CCP, under the leadership of Mao — who, by the way, had stood on the right wing of the shattered party — was to be based upon the peasantry. Thus, the party which came to power in 1949 had few serious links to the working class and bore little resemblance to the movement as it had existed prior to the catastrophe of 1927. Even to this day, as the heirs of Mao encourage and supervise the exploitation of the Chinese masses by transnational corporations, we are living with the direct consequences of the disastrous policies pursued by Stalin.

If the victory of the Left Opposition had done nothing more than avoid the catastrophe produced by Stalin's policies in China, that in itself would have profoundly altered the course of world history to the benefit of the Soviet Union and the international revolutionary movement.

Hitler's rise to power

Let us now consider the second episode: the rise of fascism to power in Germany. Prior to the victory of Hitler in January 1933, the two mass workers parties in Germany — the Social Democratic Party (SPD) and the Communist Party (KPD) — commanded the political allegiance of thirteen million voters. In the last German elections held prior to the appointment of Hitler as chancellor, the total vote of these two parties was greater than that received by the Nazis. The vote totals, however, do not fully express the relative strengths of the fascist and socialist movements. Even with its shock troops, Hitler's movement — based on the ruined petty bourgeoisie and lumpenized strata — was an amorphous and unstable mass. The two socialist parties, on the other hand, were based on a working class which, by virtue of its relation to the key productive forces, represented a powerful social and political force.

The one great advantage enjoyed by Hitler, however, was the political division of the workers' movement. The leaders of both the Social Democratic and Communist Parties refused to undertake any joint action to defend the working class against the fascist threat. The attitude of the Social Democrats flowed from their cowardly subservience to the rotting bourgeois Weimar regime and their fear of the potentially revolutionary consequences of a unified offensive of Social Democratic and Communist workers against the fascists.

The central problem facing the Communist Party was to overcome this debilitating division of the working class by offering to form a United Front with the Social Democrats to beat back the fascist threat. Notwithstanding the political opposition of the SPD leaders, official, direct and persistent appeals by the KPD for a United Front would have made, at the very least, a profound impression upon Social Democratic workers and demonstrated that the Communists were not responsible for the divisions with the ranks of the German proletariat. Even if the shifting of mass Social Democratic opinion had failed to overcome the resistance of SPD and trade union leaders to a serious struggle against Hitler, a persistent campaign by the Communist Party would have raised its stature in the eyes of millions of Social Democratic workers and drawn substantial sections of them over to its side.

But such a campaign was never waged by the KPD. Instead, in keeping with the ultra-leftist "Third Period" line imposed by the Stalinists at the Sixth Congress of the Communist International, the KPD declared that Social Democracy was a variety of fascism — "social fascism" to be precise. All agreements with this "social fascism" were deemed impermissible.

As early as 1930, Trotsky — who was, by then, in exile on the island of Prinkipo off the Turkish coast — warned that fascism represented a grave threat to the German and international working class, and that the failure of the KPD to fight for a united front was clearing the way for Hitler to come to power. On September 26, 1930, Trotsky wrote:

> *Fascism in Germany has become a real danger*, as an acute expression of the helpless position of the bourgeois regime, the

conservative role of Social Democracy in this regime, and the accumulated powerlessness of the Communist Party to abolish it. Whoever denies this is either blind or a braggart.[29]

A successful defensive struggle against fascism, he wrote, "means a policy of closing ranks with the majority of the German working class and forming a united front with the Social Democratic and non-party workers against the fascist threat."[30]

On November 26, 1931 Trotsky wrote:

> It is the duty of the Left Opposition to give the alarm: the leadership of the Comintern is driving the German proletariat towards an enormous catastrophe, the essence of which is a panicky capitulation before fascism.
>
> The coming to power of the National Socialists would mean first of all the extermination of the flower of the German proletariat, the destruction of its organizations, the eradication of its belief in itself and in its future. Considering the far greater maturity and acuteness of the social contradictions in Germany, the hellish work of Italian fascism would probably appear as a pale and almost humane experiment in comparison with the work of the German National Socialists.[31]

On January 27, 1932, replying to the pathetic claims of the Stalinist leaders that the victory of Hitler would merely pave the way for a Communist victory, Trotsky wrote:

> Fascism is not merely a system of reprisals, of brutal force, and of police terror. Fascism is a particular governmental system based on the uprooting of all elements of proletarian democracy within bourgeois society. The task of fascism lies not only in destroying the Communist vanguard but in holding the entire class in a state of forced disunity. To this end the physical annihilation of the most revolutionary section of workers does not suffice. It is

---

[29] Leon Trotsky, *The Struggle Against Fascism in Germany* (New York: Merit Publishers, 1971), p. 78.

[30] Ibid., p. 94.

[31] Ibid., p. 160.

also necessary to smash all independent and voluntary organizations, to demolish all the defensive bulwarks of the proletariat and to uproot whatever has been achieved during three-quarters of a century by the Social Democracy and the trade unions.[32]

I will cite just one more passage from the writings of Trotsky. In April 1932 Trotsky issued a statement warning that the victory of Hitler would make war between Germany and Soviet Russia inevitable. Choosing his words carefully, Trotsky explained how he would respond, were he in power, to a fascist victory in Germany:

> Upon receiving the telegraphic communication of this event, I would sign an order for the mobilization of the reserves. When you have a mortal enemy before you, and when war flows with necessity from the logic of the objective situation, it would be unpardonable light-mindedness to give that enemy time to establish and fortify himself, conclude the necessary alliances, receive the necessary help, work out a plan of concentric military actions, not only from the West but from the East, and thus grow up to the dimensions of a colossal danger.[33]

Possessing as we do knowledge of what was to come — the victory of the Nazis, the subsequent perfidy of Stalin's non-aggression pact with Hitler, the outbreak of World War II, Stalin's cowardly dismantling of Soviet defenses as Hitler prepared the launching of Operation Barbarossa, the loss of twenty-seven million Soviet soldiers and civilians in repelling the German invasion — one cannot read Trotsky's words without a sense of tragic loss and waste. How much human misery and suffering might have been avoided, how different the course of the twentieth century might have been, had the policies of Trotsky — of revolutionary Marxism — prevailed.

Our brief review of the defeats in China and Germany hardly qualifies even as a preliminary introduction to the subject of the counterrevolutionary role of Stalinism in the international workers movement and its impact on the evolution of the USSR. But we are already straining against the limits of what can reasonably be presented within the framework of one lecture. Yet

---

[32] Ibid., p. 186.
[33] *Writings of Leon Trotsky 1932* (New York: Pathfinder Press, 1973), p. 92.

there is one point that I must add for the sake of historical clarity. The defeat of the German working class marked a decisive turning point in the evolution of the Stalinist regime itself. Confronted with a serious threat from a powerful fascist regime for which his own policies were centrally responsible, Stalin moved to sever whatever tenuous connections still existed between the Soviet state and the goal of world socialist revolution. Henceforth, the defense of the USSR was to be based on the forging of political alliances with imperialist states — democratic or fascist, depending on the circumstances — at the expense of the interests of the international working class. The role of the Soviet Union in world affairs assumed a directly counterrevolutionary character, a transformation that found murderous expression in the betrayal of the Spanish Revolution, the massacre of Old Bolsheviks, the hunting down of revolutionary opponents of the Stalinist regime outside the borders of the USSR, and finally in the Stalin-Hitler Pact.

Hobsbawm is not merely blind to all this. His writing suggests that he has failed to subject to any critical review the political conceptions that allowed him to remain a member of the British Communist Party for many decades: "The terrible paradox of the Soviet era," Hobsbawm tells us with a straight face, "is that the Stalin experienced by the Soviet peoples and the Stalin seen as a liberating force outside were the same. And he was the liberator for the ones at least in part because he was the tyrant for the others."[34]

What Hobsbawm really should have written is that "the Stalin experienced by the Soviet people and the Stalin as he was deceitfully portrayed by the British Communist Party were not quite the same thing." Instead, unfortunately, Hobsbawm compromises himself as a historian by engaging in shabby pro-Stalinist apologetics, and thereby exposing what has been the tragic paradox of his own intellectual life.

In our review of the main differences between the Stalinist regime and the Left Opposition in the three areas of party regime, economic policy, and international strategy, we have attempted to demonstrate that the victory of Trotskyism — that is, of genuine Marxism — would have in all probability profoundly altered the course of Soviet history and that of the international socialist movement. We expect that this contention will be dismissed by those who interpret the history of the Soviet Union within the framework of a sort of absolute determinism of historical defeat. For these incorrigible sceptics and pessimists, who believe that the cause of socialism has been doomed from

---

[34] *On History*, p. 252.

the start, policies, programs and all other forms of subjective activity count for nothing.

The historical alternative to Stalinism must be studied

As we have already explained, it is impossible to state with certainty that Trotsky's victory would have guaranteed the survival of the USSR and the victory of socialism. But such a claim is hardly necessary to endow our consideration of historical alternatives with political and intellectual legitimacy. It is only necessary for us to establish that a real potential did exist for a course of historical development other than that which occurred; and that at certain critical points in its history the Soviet Union arrived, so to speak, at a fork in the road where the implementation of different, i.e. Marxist, policies would have made possible a far more favorable outcome of events.

We now anticipate another question, which is both serious and appropriate: Even if one were to grant that the positions of Trotsky and the Left Opposition represented, from the standpoint of theory, a genuine Marxist alternative to those of the Stalinist regime, did this Opposition ever represent a truly significant political force within the Soviet Union? After all, the consideration of alternatives, if it is not to be a fruitless speculative exercise, should limit itself to what was possible within the framework of the existing objective conditions.

In answering this important question, I would like to cite a valuable work entitled *The Birth of Stalinism* by the German historian Michal Reiman.

> The importance of the left opposition is often underestimated in the literature. ... many authors doubt that the opposition had any substantial influence on the mass of party members and even less on broader sections of the population. One can hardly agree with such views: they seem paradoxical indeed in light of the mountain of ammunition expended on the opposition by the party leadership in those years — the multitude of official declarations, reports, pamphlets, and books, not to mention the mass political campaigns that penetrated even the remotest parts of the USSR.
>
> In the spring of 1926 the united opposition, based on a cadre of old and experienced party leaders, conquered some fairly significant positions. It consolidated its influence in

Leningrad, the Ukraine, Transcaucasia, and the Urals region; in the universities; in some of the central government offices; in a number of factories of Moscow and the central industrial region; and among a section of the command staff of the army and navy, which had passed through the difficult years of the civil war under Trotsky's leadership. Repression by the party leadership prevented the opposition from growing, but its influence was still much greater than indicated by the various votes taken in the party cells.[35]

Trotsky and the other principal leaders of the Left Opposition were expelled from the Russian Communist Party at a plenum of the central committee held in July and August 1927. This failed to silence the Opposition. Reiman writes:

Even after the plenum, the party organizations continued to be flooded — especially in the large urban centers and the two capitals — with opposition literature and leaflets. Reports of heightened opposition activity came one after the other from various cities and from entire provinces — Leningrad, the Ukraine, Transcaucasia, Siberia, the Urals, and of course, Moscow, where the greater number of opposition political leaders were working. There was a steadily growing number of illegal and semi-legal meetings attended by industrial workers and young people. The influence of the opposition in a number of large party units became quite substantial. It hampered the former free functioning of the Stalinist party apparatus. The army was also strongly affected by opposition activity. Reports on a significant rise in the authority of the opposition came from the Leningrad military district and the garrison in Leningrad, from Kronstadt, and from troop units in the Ukraine and Byelorussia.

The main problem was not the increase in opposition activity, however, but the overall balance of power within the party. Quite a large number of famous political leaders were on the opposition side. The weakened authority of the party leadership,

---

[35] Michal Reiman, *The Birth of Stalinism: The USSR on the Eve of the "Second Revolution"*, trans. George Saunders (Bloomington: Indiana University Press, 1987), pp. 19–20.

especially of Stalin and Bukharin, was insufficient to turn the setbacks and failures of party policy into gains.[36]

How, then, did the Stalin faction overcome the challenge represented by the Left Opposition? Reiman explains: "The leadership could not cope with the situation without bringing the GPU into the fight."[37]

The subsequent history of the USSR and the international socialist movement is the record of the bloody consequences of the violence employed by the Stalinist bureaucracy to consolidate its power and privileges. It is impossible to conclude a discussion of historical alternatives without a consideration of the impact and costs of the Stalinist repression. Hobsbawm, as we have seen, skirts over this issue. Industrialization, he has told us, "was going to require a good deal of coercion, even if the USSR had been led by someone less utterly cruel than Stalin." Hobsbawm simply ignores the social basis and political purpose of the violence organized by the bureaucracy. Stalinist violence was not a matter of revolutionary excesses but of counterrevolutionary terror.

If Hobsbawm does not care to deal with this matter, it is because an honest treatment of the historical meaning and consequences of the purges, for the Soviet Union and the international socialist movement, cannot possibly be reconciled with his exercise in historical apologetics. There was an alternative to the Stalinist variant of Soviet development, and the Stalinist terror was the means by which it was annihilated. What was destroyed in the cellars of the Lubyanka and countless other execution chambers throughout the Soviet Union were hundreds of thousands of revolutionary socialists who had contributed to the victory of the October Revolution. Their influence upon the working class and Soviet society had not been limited to the propagation of specific political ideas, however important these ideas were. Stalin's victims were, in their collective activity, the representatives of an extraordinary socialist culture that imparted to the revolutionary movement of the Russian working class a world historical significance.

In Trotsky, this culture found its highest expression. As Victor Serge explained so brilliantly:

> For a man like Trotsky to arise, it was necessary that thousands and thousands of individuals should establish the type over a

---

[36] Ibid., pp. 27–28.
[37] Ibid., p. 28.

long historical period. It was a broad social phenomenon, not the sudden flashing of a comet...

... The formation of this great social type — the highest reach of modern man, I think — ceased after 1917, and most of its surviving representatives were massacred at Stalin's orders in 1936–7. As I write these lines, as names and faces crowd in on me, it occurs to me that this kind of man had to be extirpated, his whole tradition and generation, before the level of our time could be sufficiently lowered. Men like Trotsky suggest much too uncomfortably the human possibilities of the future to be allowed to survive in a time of sloth and reaction.[38]

Why have we devoted this lecture to a consideration of the possibility of alternatives in the historical outcome of the October Revolution? Certainly, the past cannot be changed and we must live with its consequences. But how we understand the past — and the process through which those consequences were formed — is the essential foundation of our comprehension of the present historical situation and the potential within it. Our assessment of the possibilities for socialism in the future is inextricably bound up with our interpretation of the causes of the defeats it suffered in the course of this century.

What lessons do we draw from the twentieth century? If all that has happened since the outbreak of World War I has merely been the expression of uncontrollable and incomprehensible forces, then there is little more one can do than hope or pray — depending on your preference and desperation — for better luck in the future.

But to those who have studied and assimilated the experiences of this century, the present historical situation and the prospects for the future appear entirely different. The events of this century acquire a broad historical context and meaning. No other period in history has been so rich in revolutionary and counterrevolutionary experience. The clash of conflicting social forces attained an unprecedented level of intensity. The working class, having achieved its first great revolutionary breakthrough in 1917, proved unable to withstand the terrific force of the counterrevolution that followed. However, through the work of Trotsky, the Left Opposition and the Fourth International, the nature of that counterrevolution and

---

[38] David Cotterill, ed., *The Serge-Trotsky Papers* (London: Pluto Press, 1994), p. 209.

the causes of the defeats were subjected to analysis and comprehended. And it is upon these theoretical and political foundations that the Fourth International prepares consciously, and with unrepentant revolutionary optimism, for the future.

5

Reform and Revolution
in the Epoch of Imperialism[1]

The twentieth century presents us with a striking paradox: there is not another epoch in human history during which the basic forms and rhythms of everyday life have been so profoundly changed. The scale and pace of scientific advances demand of us, almost continually, a revolution in our conception of the universe and the place of our planet within it. Even now, we are struggling to catch our breath after viewing the astonishing transmissions from the module that our technology has placed on Mars. Mankind is compelled to revise and expand, in accordance with scientific discoveries, its conceptions of time, space, and existence. These scientific advances have been achieved against the backdrop of this century's social catastrophes and cataclysms. The world map has been redrawn again and again; and the innumerable upheavals and their consequences have uprooted hundreds of millions of people and scattered them across the globe.

And yet, notwithstanding the upheavals and transformations in the conditions of life, in the domain of political concepts there has been nothing comparable to the advances in scientific thought. Man's knowledge of the universe has, since 1900, expanded exponentially; but his comprehension of the laws

---

[1] Lecture delivered on January 5, 1998, at the International School on Marxism and the Fundamental Problems of the Twentieth Century, held in Sydney Australia.

governing his own socioeconomic being is far lower than the level attained by the founders of modern socialism, Karl Marx and Frederick Engels.

If we consider the state of present-day bourgeois politics, there is not a single figure to whom one could point as a significant thinker or strategist. Nevertheless, the bourgeoisie has the advantage of possessing immense economic power and wealth. At least until the economic convulsions in Southeast Asia, the rising stock market and record profits did not make the need for a broad strategic vision appear all too urgent. Moreover, the long absence of any apparent political challenge to the domination of the capitalist class allowed it to concentrate its attention on the accumulation of wealth, rather than on the much more complex problem of defending it against the threat of social revolution.

As bad as the state of bourgeois politics, that of what is euphemistically called the "labor movement" is infinitely worse. The official labor movements are moribund, led by bureaucrats who are uninterested in, and hostile to, the interests of the workers they supposedly represent. The crisis of the labor movement is not merely the consequence of the dishonesty, corruption, ignorance and incompetence of the labor bureaucracy. Rather, these not very attractive qualities have their origins in social processes that have determined, over an entire historical period, the accommodationist and anti-socialist character of the labor movement. More than a half-century of opportunist policies — based on the systematic subordination of the working class to the post-war imperialist order — has shaped the social, political, intellectual and moral physiognomy of the labor movement.

For several decades, during the heyday of the post-war boom and the national welfare states that were based upon it, the long-term consequences of the theoretical stultification and political corruption of the workers' movement were not apparent. As long as social relations between the classes, at least in the major capitalist countries, proceeded along the lines of compromise within the framework of the welfare state, there was no place for great strategists of class war. The historical period demanded nothing more than pragmatic philistines, and such people were as abundant as mushrooms in all the imperialist countries.

Only since the relations of compromise and accommodation have been disrupted — that is, once the international bourgeoisie was no longer willing or able to play by the old and familiar rules — has the extent of the internal putrefaction of the post-war labor movement been exposed.

It would seem almost self-evident that the crisis confronting the working class has conclusively demonstrated the failure of reformism. However, the situation has been complicated by the fact that the downfall of social-democratic reformism has been overshadowed by the spectacular collapse of the Stalinist regimes in the Soviet Union and Eastern Europe. The masses are not naturally inclined to investigate the origins of the political phenomena with which they are confronted. Following the labels applied to these regimes, both by their leaders as well as their capitalist opponents, the masses of workers considered them to be "communist" and "socialist."

Between 1989 and 1991, the fall of the Stalinist regimes was presented by the propagandists of the bourgeoisie (and by a substantial segment of the Stalinists) as the failure of Marxism and socialism. To the extent that workers have accepted this explanation, they see no alternative to the capitalist market and its imperatives.

Of course, it is impossible to ignore the contradiction between the imperatives of the capitalist market and the needs of the working class. The unease of the masses finds an anticipatory reflection in segments of the professional middle classes who are themselves disquieted by the signs of increasing social polarization.

In the most recent period, a series of books has been published subjecting to criticism the unfettered operation of the capitalist market. Attention has been drawn to the impact of globalization on the conditions of the working class. Warnings have been made about increasing social polarization.

Eduard Bernstein and the revision of Marxism

In this climate of mounting anxiety, a renewed interest has emerged in one of the most important figures in the early history of European Social Democracy — the "father" of anti-Marxist revisionism, Eduard Bernstein. Within the last decade, Cambridge University Press has published a new edition of Bernstein's principal opus, *The Preconditions of Socialism*, an anthology of documents relating to the theoretical struggle over Bernstein's views, and, most recently, in 1997, a new biography of Eduard Bernstein, entitled *The Quest for Evolutionary Socialism: Eduard Bernstein and Social Democracy*, by the historian Manfred Steger. A companion volume of writings by Bernstein, translated and edited by Steger, has also been recently published by Humanities Press, which has been associated with the political endeavors of sections of the petty-bourgeois left.

Steger's biography is important, not for the level of its scholarship — which is nothing more than pedestrian — but for the political vision that inspires it. Bernstein's assault on Marxism, his attempt to disassociate socialism from working class revolution, and his proposal to redefine social-ism as nothing more than well-intentioned and ethically-motivated liber-alism — all this is seen by Steger as a beacon for our time. The relevance of Bernstein, according to Steger, is based, above all, on his recognition of the impossibility of a revolutionary alternative to capitalism.

> As the first prominent Marxist theorist of reform, Bernstein assumed that the increasing complexity of modern society made the large-scale revolutions of the old days obsolete. ...
>
> At the supposed "end of socialism," Bernstein's embryonic model of a "liberal socialism" represents the logical point of departure for the sole viable progressive project remaining in our post-Soviet and (perhaps) post-Keynesian era: a new focus on the role of civil society and a conception of democracy that favors the extension of personal rights over property rights.[2]

While proclaiming Bernstein as a hero for our times, Steger writes — with a combination of caution and cynicism — that he declines

> to evaluate Bernstein's political thought solely by applying philosophical standards. What makes his intellectual quest a worthwhile subject of academic inquiry is neither its degree of philosophical sophistication nor its lack of methodological purity. Rather, it is Bernstein's highly original attempt to for-mulate a coherent synthesis of two great political traditions that stand for individual self-realization and distributive justice.[3]

Bernstein, it must be recalled, claimed to have delivered a staggering the-oretical blow to the revolutionary conceptions of Marxism. Steger's admis-sion that he would prefer to avoid "philosophical standards" in evaluating the writings of Bernstein amounts to tacit acknowledgement that in the sphere of science and theory a direct confrontation between Bernstein and Marx would be something of an intellectual mismatch.

---

[2] Manfred B. Steger, *The Quest for Evolutionary Socialism: Eduard Bernstein and Social Democracy* (Cambridge: Cambridge University Press, 1997), pp. 14–15.

[3] Ibid., p.15.

But the theoretical shortcomings of Bernstein do not prevent Steger from embracing him as a prophet to whom we must turn. Today, no less than 100 years ago, the appeal of Bernstein is not derived from the intellectual force of his arguments, but from the yearnings of particular segments of the middle class, who find in his program, regardless of its underlying theoretical weakness, both an expression of their social interests and a response to their political moods. As an earlier and more intelligent biographer, Peter Gay, wrote some forty-five years ago, "If there had been no Bernstein, it would have been necessary to invent him. Political and economic conditions in Germany demanded a reformist doctrine around the turn of the century."[4]

A resurrection of Bernsteinism is hardly possible today. Indeed, it was, though this was not obvious at the time, "dated" from the moment of its birth. However, the renewed interest in Bernstein's life, and the controversies surrounding his work, does illustrate one very important point: even after the passage of 100 years, the political issues fought out at the very end of the nineteenth century remain extraordinarily relevant as we approach the end of the twentieth century.

It was, I believe, Mark Twain who said that although history does not repeat itself, it seems to rhyme. And, indeed, notwithstanding all the differences, one cannot help but be struck by the extent to which the political conditions and intellectual environment in which Bernsteinism emerged "rhyme" with the conditions that we confront today.

It is hard to fully appreciate now the extent to which Bernstein's proclamation of the "Death of Marxism" resonated with middle-class intellectuals in the closing years of the nineteenth century. In the midst of unprecedented capitalist prosperity and a vast expansion of its world-wide resources and influence, the Marxian conception of a capitalist system being driven to destruction through the development of its internal contradictions seemed to so many quite intelligent people to be completely at variance with the observable reality.

But there is one striking difference between the situation in 1898 and that which exists in 1998: Bernstein presented his critique of Marxism in a period in which the conditions of the working class were visibly improving. Reformism, however weak it appeared when it attempted to justify itself theoretically, seemed quite vigorous in practice. This fact must be understood to appreciate the appeal of Bernstein's message.

---

[4] Peter Gay, *The Dilemma of Democratic Socialism* (New York: Collier Books, 1970), p. 110.

Confidence in the possibility of the gradual and progressive reform of capitalism was the psychological ingredient of Bernsteinism at the end of the nineteenth century. No such optimism animates the perspective of those who suggest that today, a return to Bernsteinism is required. Rather, the milieu of the contemporary middle-class left is dominated by morbid pessimism. It has no confidence whatsoever in the role of the working class as an agent of social change. Its "reformism" amounts to little more than a vague and cowardly appeal to the financial elite to refrain from destroying what little is left of the welfare state. Bernstein, on the other hand, for all his weaknesses, was at least sincere in his illusion that capitalism, under the pressure and influence of socialists, would evolve peacefully into a just and humane society.

But despite this fundamental difference, there is one conceptual element that links the perspectives of today's demoralized reformists with that elaborated by Bernstein in the late 1890s: a haughty disdain for the materialist dialectic that constitutes the methodological foundation of Marxism. The inability to think and analyze phenomena dialectically — that is, as a unity of opposed determinations — rendered the reformists of the early twentieth century incapable of recognizing the internal contradictions that were, with the outbreak of World War I in 1914, to blow their entire world, and their complacent conceptions along with it, to smithereens.

The SPD: the first mass working class party

In the course of nearly a quarter of a century — from the end of the Anti-Socialist Laws in 1890 to the outbreak of World War I in 1914 — the SPD grew to become the largest political party in Germany. But a mere tally of the votes cannot by itself convey the extent and depth of the influence of the Social Democracy within the working class.

The SPD was, in its time, a unique historical phenomenon: it was the first truly mass party of the working class. Bernstein scandalized the leaders of the SPD when he declared, in 1898, that the movement embodied in the SPD was more important than its final goal. But the elemental force of his argument, notwithstanding the political apostasy that it implied, cannot be appreciated without having some sense of the scale of the movement led by the SPD.

The SPD presided over a massive publishing empire that produced books, newspapers, and periodicals that related to virtually every aspect of working class life. By 1895, the year of Engels' death, the SPD published seventy-five newspapers, of which thirty-nine appeared six times a week. By 1906, there were fifty-eight socialist daily newspapers.

In 1909, the circulation of Social Democratic newspapers reached one million, and stood at one and a half million on the eve of the war. The official circulation was less than the actual number of people who followed the socialist press, because many copies were circulated from worker to worker in factories, taverns, schools and neighborhoods. One very popular magazine, *Der Wahre Jakob*, reached a paid circulation of 380,000, but its actual readership approached one and a half million. It has been estimated that the total number of Social Democratic readers was about six million by 1914.

The circulation of *Vorwärts*, the principal political newspaper of the SPD, reached 165,000. The famous *Neue Zeit*, the theoretical journal edited by Karl Kautsky, had a circulation of 10,500. *Die Gleichheit*, a newspaper produced by the party for women workers, and which, under the editorship of Clara Zetkin, pursued an aggressively anti-militarist line, attained by 1914 a circulation of 125,000. The range of interests addressed by auxiliary newspapers published by the party can be gauged by their titles: *The Worker-Cyclist* (circulation 168,000), *The Singing German Workers Newspaper* (circulation 112,000), *The Workers Exercise Newspaper* (circulation 119,000), *The Free Innkeeper* (circulation 11,000), *The Abstinent Worker* (circulation 5,100), and *The Worker Stenographer* (circulation 3,000).

In addition to these regular publications, the SPD produced a mass of political literature, which assumed gigantic proportions during election campaigns: handbills, posters, special newspaper editions and pamphlets were printed in the millions. The party also ran several large printing houses that produced books dealing with history, politics and culture in editions which ran into the tens and even hundreds of thousands.

The SPD organized and coordinated a massive network of social activities that involved every section and age group of the working class. So profound was the identification of the SPD with the working class that the very word *Arbeiter* (German for worker) carried with it a political connotation.

By the turn of the century, the SPD was involved in at least twenty specific kinds of social activities, encompassing broad social and educational areas. It ran innumerable gymnastic clubs and singing societies. In just one city, Chemnitz, the SPD organized no less than 142 workers' singing societies, which gave a total of 123 concerts. In the region of Thuringia, the SPD sponsored 191 different gymnastic clubs.

For hundreds of thousands of German workers, the SPD was not simply a political organization: it was the axis around which they planned much of their lives. Whatever the particular interest of a worker — swimming, weight lifting, boxing, hiking, rowing and sailing, football, chess, bird watching, dramatics, health and conservation, temperance — the SPD had an organization in which he or she could enroll.

The SPD also devoted substantial resources to formal political education. From the 1890s on, it gave courses in history, law, political economy, natural sciences and oratory. Among those who lectured on these topics were Bebel, Liebknecht, Zetkin and Luxemburg. Three-month courses were offered three times a year. Enrollment grew from 540 in 1898 to 1,700 in 1907. An official Party school was established in 1906.

The role of the Party in the promotion of the cultural development of the working class is indicated by the growth of workers' libraries. Between 1900 and 1914, the party and the SPD-controlled trade unions helped to establish 1,100 libraries in 750 different localities. These libraries held over 800,000 volumes, and by 1914 there were over 365 librarians on the payroll of the SPD.

One final statistic deserves special mention. The SPD, in the first years of the century, undertook an aggressive campaign to recruit women workers into the party, and its efforts met with a powerful response. The number of female party members grew from 30,000 in 1905 to 175,000 in 1914. It should be noted that among the most popular of party publications was August Bebel's *Woman under Socialism*.

Before proceeding to an examination of Bernstein's position, consideration must be given to the international and national economic environment within which his conceptions developed. Bernstein denied the validity of the historical materialist dialectic, but his own intellectual and political evolution proceeded in accordance with its laws.

World economy between 1873 and 1893 presented a complex and highly contradictory picture. Both prices and profits were mired in a protracted depression. During those twenty years, the level of prices in Britain dropped by 40 percent. The price of iron fell by 50 percent. But this period of price and profit deflation was also one of booming industrial output and technological innovation. Indeed, these two aspects of world economic conditions were dialectically related. The pressure on the rate of profit provided the impulse for the development of new production and management techniques that led to a vast expansion of industrial output. Thus, even while the world economy was mired in a price and profit depression, industrial development, particularly in Germany and the United States, underwent an explosive growth.

Capital expanded into entirely new areas, such as Latin America, and the search for profitable investments led to the emergence of imperialist-style colonialism. The protracted price-profit recession came to a sudden conclusion toward the end of 1894, and capitalism entered into a period which was, from the standpoint of the bourgeoisie, so glorious that it received the name by which it is remembered to this day, *La Belle Époque*!

Germany was one of the most dynamic centers of this economic development, and this had profound and contradictory implications for the Marxist movement. A necessary condition for the expansion of the SPD was, quite obviously, the rapid growth of the working class. But this was itself conditioned by German industrial development. The unification of Germany, notwithstanding the reactionary political forms through which it had been achieved under Bismarck, laid the basis for the rapid growth of large-scale industry. Iron production increased from 2.7 million tons in 1880 to 8.5 million tons in 1900. Steel output grew during the same period from 625,000 to 6.6 million tons. Between 1873 and 1900, the number of ships arriving in German ports doubled. A central feature of German economic development was the concentration and cartelization of industry. Between 1882 and 1907, the number of small-scale enterprises rose by 8 percent while the number of large enterprises rose by 231 percent. By 1907, 548 industrial concerns employed nearly 1.3 million workers.

The official doctrine of the SPD was that of class war, but its own growth, if only indirectly, was bound up with the expansion of German national industry. The link between national industry and the development of the trade unions was even more direct. Until the mid-1890s, their growth lagged behind the party, upon which they were dependent for both political guidance and direct material-financial support. But the great economic boom which began in 1895, and lasted almost until the outbreak of the world war, fueled a vast expansion of the trade unions and radically changed the relations between the trade unions — whose leaders were generally individuals with only the most minimal interest in questions of Marxist theory and socialist principles — and the SPD. The more the size and economic resources of the trade unions expanded, the less willing were their leaders to accept the subordination of their practical concerns to broader problems of socialist policy and principles.

Bernstein's early years in the socialist movement

Bernstein was raised in a lower-middle-class Jewish family, the seventh of fifteen children. He became politically active in the socialist movement in 1872. He was attracted by Bebel's courageous defense of socialist and internationalist principles during the Franco-Prussian War. In 1875 he was a delegate to the unity congress of the Eisenachers and Lassalleans at Gotha.

Early in his political career, Bernstein had evinced an inclination toward various forms of petty-bourgeois democratic politics. For a time he came under the influence of Eugen Dühring, and somewhat later, while working as the secretary of Karl Hochberg, a left democrat who contributed financially to the SPD, Bernstein played a role in the drafting of a document that urged the party to abandon its exclusive orientation to the working class and to adopt a more conciliatory attitude toward the bourgeoisie. Marx and Engels were outraged by this document, and Bernstein was restored to their good graces only by traveling to London, in the company of Bebel himself, to apologize personally to the old revolutionaries for his violation of political principles.

Bernstein was compelled by the Anti-Socialist Laws to leave Germany in 1878, and his exile lasted for 23 years. He lived in Switzerland for several years, and then moved to England in the late 1880s. It was during his extended sojourn in England that he came into contact with the reformist Fabian society, and formed close friendships with its leading lights. He dined frequently with such people as Beatrice and Sidney Webb and George Bernard Shaw.

According to Steger, Bernstein was highly impressed by

> the social achievements made possible by the English workers' practical, utilitarian point of view. He spoke in glowing terms of the good relationship between British labor leaders and representatives of the liberal bourgeoisie, arguing that "such a marriage of convenience" had contributed to the success of English piecemeal reformism. For Bernstein, the evolving British model proved the possibility of mutually agreeable pacts between capital and labor, inspiring him to communicate his observations to his German party comrades.[5]

---

[5] *The Quest for Evolutionary Socialism*, p. 69.

The Fabians were only one element of the broader intellectual and political environment that was working upon Bernstein. The rapid growth of socialism in Germany and throughout Western Europe had made it clear to the bourgeoisie that its influence could not be contained simply through the use of state repression. It was necessary to respond to the intellectual challenge posed by Marxism. Thus, in the 1890s, the universities assumed a new and vital role — which they have not surrendered to this day — as ideological bulwarks against Marxism. The writings of Marx were now to be combed for inconsistencies and weaknesses that could be cited to disprove the claims of the socialist movement. The new academic "Slayers of Marxism" became figures of influence and authority, whose writings were widely praised and publicized. Figures such as Böhm-Bawerk, Tugan-Baranovsky, Benedetto Croce, Werner Sombart and Max Weber, not to mention dozens of lesser-known and far less gifted writers, maintained a steady barrage against virtually every aspect of Marxist theory.

In their own way, the works of these thinkers confirmed Marx's observation that "The mode of production of material life conditions the general process of social, political and intellectual life" and that social conflicts are reflected by and fought out in definite ideological forms.[6] The writings of these petty-bourgeois academic critics of Marx were reflected in the writings of Bernstein. Indeed, it is not an exaggeration to say that Bernstein added little, except his own political prestige, to the anti-Marxist arguments that were circulating in the universities of the day.

Engels began to sense a change in Bernstein's outlook, and complained that he was sounding more and more like a smug English shopkeeper. As long as Engels remained alive, he held Bernstein back. But after his death in August 1895, Bernstein's movement away from Marxism proceeded quite rapidly.

The Preconditions of Socialism

In 1898 Bernstein wrote a series of articles in which he repudiated the theoretical heritage and revolutionary program of the SPD. He elaborated these views at greater length in his book, *The Preconditions of Socialism*. The time had come, he insisted, to recognize that Marx's analysis of capitalism as a system torn by internal contradictions was a product of his Hegelian training

---

[6] Karl Marx and Frederick Engels: *Collected Works*, Volume 29 (New York: International Publishers, 1987), p. 263.

and bore no relation to the empirically observable reality. It was dangerously wrong for socialists to base their tactics upon the prospect of a major crisis of the capitalist system. All the available evidence suggested, rather, that capitalism possessed a virtually unlimited potential for progressive development; and that this would lead quite naturally, democratically and peacefully toward socialism. Those unfortunate Marxists who continued to argue that socialism would arise out of a major crisis generated by the internal contradictions of capitalism suffered from "catastrophitis," a disease that made them incapable of facing up to the facts of contemporary life.

Flowing from their mistaken fixation on non-existent economic contradictions, Marx and Engels were wrong in the belief that capitalism led to the impoverishment of the working class. The trade unions, Bernstein argued, had proven themselves capable of steadily raising the workers' share of the national income. As for Marx's emphasis on the labor theory of value and its supposedly scientific demonstration of the exploitation of the working class, this was another piece of the old theoretical baggage that needed to be junked. What need was there, Bernstein asked, to demonstrate the inherently exploitative character of the production of surplus value in the capitalist mode of production? This obsession with the problem of value formation had led the socialist movement to concentrate its fire against the capitalist mode of production, rather than formulating achievable demands, realizable through a combination of trade union activity and national legislation, for a more equitable distribution of the national income.

Bernstein maintained that the long-term interests of the working class would be secured not through revolution, but through the steady and incremental gains achieved by the trade unions. He castigated "some socialists" for whom "the trade unions are nothing more than an object-lesson demonstrating in a practical way the uselessness of any action other than revolutionary politics."[7] For Bernstein, trade unions were the means through which the unjust elements of capitalism were overcome: "By virtue of their socioeconomic position, the trade unions are the democratic element in industry. Their tendency is to erode the absolute power of capital and to give the worker a direct influence in the management of industry."[8] To the extent that Bernstein had misgivings about the role of trade unions, it was that they should not seek

[7] Eduard Bernstein, *The Preconditions of Socialism* (Cambridge: Cambridge University Press, 1993), p. 139.
[8] Ibid.

too much power. Their aim should be partnership with capital, not control over industry.

Another error of Marx and Engels, according to Bernstein, was their conception of the state as an instrument of class rule. The example of England, he argued, proved that in a democratic setup the state could function as the representative of the entire citizenry, working steadily for the general welfare. The aim of the working class must not be to replace the existing state, let alone smash it, but to make it an ever-more effective instrument of a supra-class democracy. Indeed, the working class had no need for, and should not pursue, the establishment of its own class rule. The "dictatorship of the proletariat" was a phrase that had no place in civilized political discourse:

> class dictatorship belongs to a lower civilization and, apart from the question of the expediency and practicability of the matter, it can only be regarded as a retrograde step, as political atavism, if it encourages the idea that the transition from capitalist to socialist society must necessarily be accomplished in the manner of an age which had no idea — or only a very imperfect idea — of the present methods of propagating and implementing legislation and which lacked organizations fit for the purpose.[9]

Democracy was a political form that guaranteed the rights of all citizens, and he spoke with boundless admiration for the civility that it had introduced into the affairs of mankind:

> in our times, there is an almost unconditional guarantee that the majority in a democratic community will make no law that does lasting injury to personal freedom. ... Indeed, experience has shown that the longer democratic arrangements persist in a modern state the more respect and consideration for minority rights increases and the more party conflicts lose their animosity. Those who cannot imagine the achievement of socialism without an act of violence will see this as an argument against democracy...[10]

---

[9] Ibid., p. 146.
[10] Ibid., p. 142.

... In a democracy, the parties and the classes supporting them soon learn to recognize the limits of their power and, on each occasion, to undertake only as much as they can reasonably hope to achieve under the circumstances. Even if they make their demands rather higher than they seriously intend in order to have room for concessions in the inevitable compromise — and democracy is the school of compromise — it is done with moderation.[11]

Bernstein did not believe that England was an exceptional case; democracy was no less likely to work its magic in Germany. The SPD, he claimed, was wrong to insist upon the unalterably reactionary character of the German bourgeoisie. "This might perhaps be true for the moment, although there is much evidence to the contrary. But even so, it cannot last long."[12] The German capitalist class would prove far more susceptible to appeals for democratic reform, if only the SPD stopped threatening it with social revolution. The task of the party was to reassure the bourgeoisie that "it has no enthusiasm for a violent revolution against the entire non-proletarian world."[13] Once this was done, the bourgeoisie's fear of the SPD would be "dissipated," and it would be prepared to make "common cause" with the working class against the more reactionary elements in the Prussian absolutist regime.

Thus, Bernstein urged the SPD to put aside its revolutionary fantasies and understand that socialism, liberated from the Hegelian determinism that had disoriented Marx and Engels, was really nothing more than consistent liberalism:

In fact, there is no liberal thought that is not also part of the intellectual equipment of socialism. Even the principle of the economic responsibility of the individual for himself, which appears to be completely Manchesterish, cannot, in my judgment, be denied in theory by socialism, nor are there any conceivable circumstances in which it could be suspended. There is no freedom without responsibility.[14]

---

[11] Ibid., p. 144.

[12] Ibid., p. 157.

[13] Ibid., p. 158.

[14] Ibid., pp. 148–149.

Bernstein went on to dismiss with contempt socialist agitation against bourgeois militarism. He was not opposed, in principle, to colonialism. Under European rule, he wrote, "savages *are without exception better off* than they were before..."[15] This rule applied even to the American Indians: "Whatever wrongs were previously perpetrated on the Indians, nowadays their rights are protected, and it is a known fact that their numbers are no longer declining but are, once again, on the increase."[16]

As for the persistent socialist agitation against the rapacity of German imperialism, Bernstein argued it should not be "a matter of indifference to Social Democracy whether the German nation — which has indeed borne, and is still bearing, its fair share in the civilizing work of nations — be eclipsed in the council of nations."[17] Nor was the SPD correct to urge the replacement of the Kaiser's standing army with a people's militia, for its warnings that the military represented a perpetual threat of violence against the working class were really out of date: "Fortunately," wrote Bernstein, "we are increasingly becoming accustomed to settle political differences in ways other than by the use of firearms."[18]

Nothing is more damaging to the reputation of Bernstein as a political theorist and strategist than the publication of his writings. Even the very careful selections from his writings offered by Steger do not enhance Bernstein's intellectual stature (and the passages that I have quoted do not appear in Steger's biography). If anything comes as a surprise to the contemporary Marxist, it is the pedestrian character of Bernstein's arguments. "This thin gruel," one asks oneself, "actually presented itself as a refutation of Marxism?" One cannot help but be amazed by Bernstein's lack of sensitivity to the serious and disturbing currents of his day. I do not know whether Bernstein was fond of music, but he could have profited from listening to the symphonies of one of his contemporaries, Gustav Mahler. Bernstein might have discovered in the work of Mahler something that was entirely lacking in his own compositions: a presentiment of the tragedy that was overtaking bourgeois civilization. But then again, this Bernstein was Eduard, not Leonard, and I doubt that he would have drawn very much from the work of the anxiety-ridden Austrian composer.

---

[15] Henry Tudor and J.M. Tudor ed., *Marxism and Social Democracy: The Revisionist Debates 1896–1898* (Cambridge: Cambridge University Press, 1988), p. 154.

[16] Ibid.

[17] *The Preconditions of Socialism*, p. 164.

[18] Ibid., p. 162.

When the passages from which I have quoted were written, only fifteen years remained before the outbreak of the very catastrophe that Eduard Bernstein considered to be inconceivable — a catastrophe that was to inaugurate an era of barbarism whose horrors are without equal in history. The tendency of capitalist development led not in the direction of ever-greater democracy and the amelioration of class antagonisms, but toward mass repression and civil war. Looking into the future, the myopic Eduard Bernstein saw only the rainbows of democracy and missed entirely the barbed wire of the trenches and concentration camps.

Opportunism found its most advanced expression in the writings of Bernstein and his contemporaries. In the decades that followed, successive waves of opportunism added nothing of real importance to what had already been said by the Bernsteinians. In our own age, which possesses a far lower level of theoretical self-consciousness, the arguments against Marxism merely reproduce, though with much diminished quality, those advanced by Bernstein. Thus, in examining Bernstein's theoretical conceptions, even after the passage of a century, one is also dealing with the whole gamut of contemporary anti-Marxism.

The style is the man, and the essential content of style is method. When an individual starts to talk about politics, he reveals not merely his opinions on the events of the day, but the theoretical conceptions that underlie those opinions and the intellectual process through which he arrives at them. What is true of individuals holds as well for political tendencies.

The rejection of "scientific socialism"

Political opportunism has certain methodological and epistemological underpinnings. I do not wish to encourage the simplistic conception that all manifestations of opportunism are reducible to a false epistemology, or that an examination of the epistemological underpinnings of revisionism does away with the need to undertake a careful political analysis of disputed issues. But Bernstein did not base his argument only on the claim that one or another element of Marxism had been refuted — though he certainly did believe that contemporary developments had shown Marx and Engels to be wrong in many of their judgments. That, however, was of secondary importance. According to Bernstein, the very concept of a "scientific socialism" was a contradiction in terms. Socialism, he maintained, could not attain the level of science because it was "an engaged movement [that] cannot face science neutrally."[19] "No 'ism' is ever a science," Bernstein stated. "'Isms' are merely perspectives, tendencies, thought systems or demands, but never science."[20] Notwithstanding its scientific pretensions, the socialist mass movement "is nonetheless as little a scientific movement as, for example, the German Peasant Wars, the French Revolution, *or any other historical struggle.* Socialism as a *science* depends on *cognition,* socialism as *movement* is guided by *interest* as its 'noble motivation.'"[21]

There are many things in these statements that need to be answered. Let us begin by examining the claim that to the extent that it, too, is an expression of specific social interests, modern socialism is no more scientific than earlier mass movements. As with so many of Bernstein's arguments, this one was more clever than profound. It is undeniably true that all social movements are motivated by class interests. But the essential difference between the modern socialist and earlier revolutionary mass movements finds expression in the fact that only with the development of Marxism does this motivating element — class interest — become the subject of theoretico-historical analysis.

Marx and Engels were not the first to recognize the class struggle and attribute great significance to it. Traces of this insight were already to be found in the historians of Antiquity, the Renaissance, and, more recently, among the French historians of the post-Napoleonic restoration in the early nineteenth century — especially Guizot. But it was only with Marx and Engels that the underlying foundation of the class struggle was identified and explained. Marx and Engels stressed not only the class struggle and its relation to material, i.e., property, interests, but demonstrated that those interests — and the social struggles to which they give rise — are formed on the basis of the productive forces created by man and the production relations which they necessitate and through which they operate.

This insight into the origins of class society made it possible to elaborate, for the first time, a consistently materialist understanding of history — that is, one which explained not only the formation of economic interests, but also the evolution of social thought. It was especially this second aspect — the derivation of social consciousness from social being — that made it possible for the socialist movement to understand and explain its own origins, existence, development and aspirations in a wholly demystified

---

[19] Manfred Steger, ed., *Selected Writings of Eduard Bernstein 1900–21,* (New Jersey: Humanities Press, 1996), p. 97.

[20] Ibid., p. 99.

[21] Ibid., p. 95.

form — that is, without resort to ideal motivations. Herein lies an essential difference between the Marxian socialist movement and the revolutionary movements that preceded it.

We may safely presume that all social movements — whether of the past, present or future — are somehow the expression of social interests. But the Marxian movement can legitimately assert its scientific foundations to the extent that its principles, program and actions are guided by knowledge of the laws of historical development. Bernstein's distinction between "socialism as science" and "socialism as movement" was, to be blunt, rather silly. To allow that socialism, as a science, cognizes the laws governing the development of social consciousness, and then claim that socialism as a movement is based on "noble motivation" was a crass absurdity. After all, a science which asserts that social consciousness is the product of historical conditions formed on the basis of a given level of productive forces and their corresponding production relations cannot then claim, when it dons the robes of a mass movement, that it is guided by "noble motivation." It would be immediately compelled to explain, if it were to be true to its science, the origins and social basis of the "noble motivation."

Let us now examine Bernstein's claim that "no 'ism' is ever a science." This dictum would seem to place Darwinism in a precarious position. But let us assume that Bernstein merely expressed himself badly — that he intended to argue that the commitment implied by "ism" is incompatible with science. This was an argument to which Bernstein returned again and again: Science is incompatible with any form of partisanship. He declared:

> If socialism were interested in becoming pure science, it would have to forgo being a class doctrine representing the class-based aspirations of workers. At this point, socialism and science must necessarily part.
>
> Let me express my position unambiguously: socialist theory is only science insofar as its propositions are acceptable to any objective, disinterested nonsocialist.[22]

Were this last statement true, it would mean that the only person qualified to render judgment on the scientific credentials of Marxism would be one to whom the fate of humanity was a matter of utter indifference. Invoking the

---

[22] Ibid., p.116.

demands of what he called "pure science," Bernstein insisted that it was incompatible with the presence of "subjective volitional elements."[23] The practice of science could not, he stated, be reconciled with any specific human goal.

But it does not take too much reflection to see that this is hardly true. Science is by no means negated by either partisanship or volition. The biologist who is studying the HIV virus is not, we may assume, disinterested in the consequences of AIDS. The surgeon, let us hope, desires to save the life of the patient under his scalpel. Both are driven by specific "subjective" motivations: the former wishes to annihilate the HIV virus; the latter seeks to save his patient's life. This does not mean that they are incapable of adopting a scientific attitude toward their work.

In his own time, Bernstein was confronted with this very objection. At a lecture delivered in May 1901, in which he argued that socialism could not be scientific because it sought to achieve a special goal, Bernstein was asked if he would deny that medicine was a science because it had a specific aim, i.e., healing. Bernstein answered by reaching deep down into his bag of sophisms: "I replied," he wrote,

> that I consider healing to be the "art of medicine," which is based upon the thorough mastery of the science of medicine. As such the latter is not directed at healing but at the knowledge of the conditions and means that will lead to a cure. If we accept this conceptual distinction as a typical example, then it will not be too difficult, even in more complex cases, to find out where science ends and "art" or "doctrine" begins.[24]

To which Plekhanov replied: "Socialism as a *science* studies the means and conditions of the socialist revolution, while socialism as a 'doctrine,' or as a *political art*, tries to bring about this revolution with the help of acquired knowledge."[25]

Bernstein conceived of science as the mere cataloguing of facts, with scientists little more than learned clerks who collect, weigh, assort and then place them in the proper cubbyholes. Such a conception not only deprived science of its creative impulse and function; it was also ahistorical. The

---

[23] Ibid., p. 118.

[24] Ibid., p. 104.

[25] Georgi Plekhanov, *Selected Philosophical Works*, Volume 3 (Moscow: Progress Publishers, 1976), p. 34.

development of science has proceeded over the last 2,500 years through the struggle of tendencies — in which the divisions have been related not only to abstract conceptions but quite directly to material interests. It seems almost platitudinous to point out that science, as exemplified by the fate of Giordano Bruno and Galileo Galilei, not infrequently encountered the resistance of social classes who perceived in its development a threat to their social position. When Bernstein spoke of "scientific impartiality," he had in mind a very definite conception of the cognitive process — one in which the reflection of the material world in men's minds and the accumulation of knowledge were conceived as a contemplative and passive process. That is, his materialism was of a mechanical, non-dialectical character, in which there existed an abyss between the object of cognition and the thinking subject.

It was not only the scientific legitimacy of Marxism that was called into question by Bernstein. His conception of "pure science" placed in doubt the very possibility of a scientific study of society. In essence, he maintained that the domain of scientific thought is limited to those areas in which the human knowing subject and the object of cognition confront each other as completely alien and separate entities — that is, presumably — in the natural and theoretical sciences. "Pure science," he asserted, demands that its practice not be in any way contaminated by the interpenetration of subject and object in the cognitive process. Each must remain firmly in its place. Science becomes 'impure" and thus loses its scientific validity the moment the absolute boundary that must exist between the knowing subject and the object of cognition is violated.

Thus, virtually by definition, the scientific study of human society, whether by Marxists or anyone else, was technically impossible. For, if Bernstein was right, how could there be any genuine science of society when the human observers and researchers are themselves a part of the organism that they seek to study. As Kautsky noted when he replied to Bernstein on this very point:

> Every science has its peculiar difficulties. Among those of the social sciences is that the observer and researcher are themselves a part of the organism which they have to examine; that they are not outside that organism but inside of it; that everyone has his specific place in it, from which he alone can conduct observations of it, its specific functions, its dependence upon other parts of the organism; and that the specific parts of this organism stand in contradiction to each other. These are certainly serious obstacles, but if they were really so great that they precluded science, then they

would rule out not only scientific socialism but also every other type of social science. Then the same thing Bernstein says about the socialists would also apply to the bourgeois economists.[26]

The metaphysics of objectivity

All of Bernstein's arguments revolve around the same metaphysical, simplistic and vulgar formulae: "Objective" processes are those which operate completely independently of human action and volition. Nothing that is either desired or achieved through activity in which a conscious impulse is to be found is truly objective. The "objective" is only that which is entirely outside of mankind and its consciousness and accomplishes itself spontaneously. Thus, all human behavior, to the extent that it passes through consciousness, is subjective. Therefore, according to Bernstein, the term "objective necessity" could not be properly ascribed to any human social behavior in which more than an instinctual consciousness was present.

From this standpoint, the class struggle itself was not an expression of objective historical necessity, but merely the manifestation of subjective human will imposing itself on the objective course of events. "The desire for improved conditions for a specific social group," stated Bernstein, "can never be 'objective.' One could even say that the explanation of economic transformations never warrant the word 'objective' because these never occur without the mediation of human activity." Attempting to clarify the boundary, within the realm of human behavior, between the objective and subjective, between that which can or cannot be discussed in terms of science and necessity, Bernstein offered the following example:

> The universal need for food is an objective power, but the wish for a varied diet is a subjective factor. Anything that supersedes ongoing life necessities for the realization of an idea or a deliberate goal is not based on objective necessity.[27]

Bernstein's argument does not withstand even a cursory consideration. He tells us that the need for food is objective, but that "the wish for a varied

---

[26] Karl Kautsky, "Problematischer gegen wissenschaftlichen Sozialismus," in: *Die Neue Zeit*, Jg. 19 (1900–1901), Bd. 2 (1901), H. 38, S. 357 (translation by D. North).
[27] *Selected Writings of Eduard Bernstein 1900–21*, p. 36.

diet" is merely subjective. It did not seem to occur to him that a particular "wish" may be the subjective expression of an objectively-grounded need; or, to put it somewhat differently, that the subjective wish may develop on the basis of a conscious insight into objective necessity. The need for food is, of course, an objective necessity. But how man responds to hunger pangs is not merely a raw subjective impulse. The science of nutrition and the concept of a "balanced diet" low in saturated fats represent the refinement, adaptation and direction of the subjective impulse in accordance with a scientific understanding of the needs of the human organism. Indeed, the presence of consciousness is the prerequisite for the progressive harmonization of subjective desire and objective need.

Moving from cuisine to politics, without any improvement in his mode of argument, Bernstein insisted that socialism definitively forfeited any claim to science because it aspired to something — in this case, a form of socioeconomic organization — that did not exist. "But how," asked Bernstein with exasperation, "can something for which we strive ever be pure science?"[28] Science can do no more than observe and comment on what exists. "Because collectivism as an economic system assumes the form of an ideal," Bernstein declared, "it cannot simultaneously be viewed as scientific."[29]

Though Bernstein may have thought that he was puncturing only the scientific pretensions of Marxian socialism, when he asserted that man's aspirations fall outside the domain of science, he was actually denying the very possibility of science. For scientific inquiry is, itself, a social practice whose creative impulse is to be found in man's subjective response to the conditions with which he is confronted. Science arises as the expression of man's conscious appropriation from nature of that which he requires to live and reproduce. Far from assuming the absolute separation of subject and object, a premise of scientific thought is the dialectical relationship of man and nature.

Here it is useful to consult Marx:

> Labor is, in the first place, a process in which both man and Nature participate, and in which man of his own accord starts, regulates and controls the material reactions between himself and Nature. He opposes himself to Nature as one of her own forces, setting in motion arms and legs, head and hands, the natural forces of

---

28 Ibid., 106.
29 Ibid., p. 108.

his body, in order to appropriate Nature's productions in a form adapted to his own wants. By thus acting on the external world and changing it, he at the same time changes his own nature. He develops his slumbering powers and compels them to act in obedience to his sway. ... A spider conducts operations that resemble those of a weaver, and a bee puts to shame many an architect in the construction of her cells. But what distinguishes the worst architect from the best of bees is this, that the architect raises his structure in imagination before he erects it in reality. At the end of every labor-process, we get a result that already existed in the imagination of the laborer at its commencement.[30]

Science does not limit itself, in the manner of a clerk taking inventory, to a description of the material world as it exists outside human consciousness and practice. It does, indeed, concern itself with what does not exist. Science seeks to discover within nature the possibility of translating man's dreams into reality. The myth of Icarus is more than 2,000 years old. The dream of flying eventually translated itself into the drawings of Leonardo, the biplane of the Wright brothers, and, more recently, the space shuttle. "Man's consciousness not only reflects the objective world, but creates it."[31]

Just as man's insight into the laws of nature enables him to utilize and even alter in his own interests its spontaneously given conditions, the scientific insight achieved by Marxism into the laws regulating man's historical development provides the possibility of organizing socioeconomic life on the basis of consciously-understood human needs. Bernstein, while denying in general the possibility of such an insight, misrepresented the crucial distinction between Marxism and the various forms of utopian socialist thought that preceded it. He claimed that the "innermost core" of Marxism was "a theory of a future social order." This was false in two fundamental respects:

First, the "innermost core" of Marxism is not a theory of the future or even a theory of history, but a materialist world outlook, proceeding from the primacy of being over consciousness, grounded upon a dialectical method.

Second, Marx and Engels did not offer a theory of a future social order. Rather, they provided a consistently materialist explanation of the general laws of historical development and, upon that basis, the nature of the

---

[30] Karl Marx, *Capital*, Volume 1 (London: Lawrence & Wishart, 1974), pp. 173–174.
[31] V.I. Lenin, *Collected Works*, Volume 38 (Moscow: Progress Publishers, 1976), p. 212.

capitalist mode of production. In contrast to utopian socialism, which built up its conception of the society of the future upon abstract principles, Marxism revealed the historical necessity and possibility of socialism through the analysis of the contradictions of the existing society. Marx did not set out to devise a new social system. He did not "invent" socialism.

As is well known, Marx made no attempt to draw a blueprint of a future social order. Nothing comparable to the Phalansteries of Fourier will be found in the writings of Marx. Rather, Marx demonstrated that the economic development of bourgeois society, independently of the will of socialists, lays the foundations for the socialization of the means of production; and that the contradictions of the capitalist mode of production, which is based objectively on the exploitation of the working class, tend toward crisis, breakdown and social revolution. Socialism is, therefore, a necessary (though not, in a formal sense, inevitable) outcome of the socioeconomic structure of the existing society, and, in a still more profound sense, the entire historical evolution of man.

Even after recognizing the hollowness of Bernstein's theoretical conceptions, one still feels compelled to ask: how was it possible for Bernstein to have been so utterly blind to the social contradictions that were accumulating and driving European civilization toward a catastrophe? At least part of the answer might be found by posing the question to our contemporaries. Why are so many supposedly intelligent people so completely blind to the contradictions that are driving our own civilization toward the abyss? Why has the collapse of the "Five Tigers of Asia" taken so many supposedly well-informed people by surprise? The life of Eduard Bernstein should be studied not as a model, but, at the least, as a cautionary tale. Especially in our own age of almost universal historical ignorance and political blindness, there is something to be learned from the errors of an Eduard Bernstein who, for all his limitations, would hardly come out badly in comparison to the political figures currently active on the world stage. Moreover, in Bernstein's defense, let us acknowledge that it was not so easy to see, in 1898, amidst the wealth and power of late nineteenth century European capitalism, the signs of impending disaster. What was required was not merely a keen eye, but what Marx had once referred to as "the force of abstraction."

Bernstein's empiricism

It was precisely this intellectual capacity that Bernstein lacked. An empiricist, his political horizons were determined by the "facts" as he derived them from either casual observation or from his reading of the newspapers and his study of economic statistics. Bernstein sincerely believed himself to be a man of science, and his chief reproach against Marx was that his Hegelian methodology and revolutionary aims made it impossible for him to adopt an objective approach to the "facts" of socioeconomic life.

Bernstein was laboring under the common illusion of the empiricist: that "facts" are the elementary, "pure," "value-free" and intellectually uncontaminated particles of absolutely objective data that constitute the organic structure of truth. The accumulation of a sufficient number of these particles of politically-neutral data will provide the social scientist with a truly objective picture of social reality upon which a reasonable course of action can be decided.

What the empiricist denies, or fails to recognize, is that the "facts" of social reality are themselves the products of history, and that the manner in which facts are isolated and placed within a conceptual framework is socially conditioned. Every social fact is the child of historical conditions and exists as part of a complex network of socioeconomic relations. Moreover, these "facts" are cognized — indeed, they only come to be recognized as "facts" — through the operation of cognitive concepts and categories that are also the product and reflection of an historical process.

The empiricist who insists that his selection and study of social facts is entirely neutral is unaware of the historically conditioned character of the concepts with which he is working; that he is, in other words, adopting an uncritical attitude toward the forms of his own thinking.

The uncritical attitude of Bernstein toward his own theoretical conceptions emerged most clearly in his famous statement that the final goal was nothing; that he was concerned only with the here and now. What were the implications of this outlook? Like the facts themselves, the practice of the socialist movement was thus torn out of its historical context. On this basis, political activity was to be formulated without any sense that it was part of a historical process to which it was accountable.

Bernstein rejected the revolutionary perspective at precisely the point at which the contradictions were about to break through to the surface of political life. It is not always a very knowledgeable owl that takes flight at dusk. The appearance of stability is often greatest at the very moment when the sun is just about to set on a given social order. The empirical data testifying to the strength of the existing system has attained, in terms of quantity, its apogee. It seems pointless, to the empiricist, to persist in questioning a social order whose viability is substantiated by such an impressive array of data. But those pieces of data have already been superseded and are, at any rate, no more than contradictory indices of a situation that is, by its very nature, not only inconclusive, but in the process of changing direction. The political empiricist, seizing on the given data to justify capitulation to the existing order, makes the mistake of imposing upon an on-going process an arbitrary conclusion. Thus, he mistakes a moment of historical transition for the final outcome. That is why Bernstein could not see, in 1898, the approaching shadow of 1914, let alone that of 1933.

6

Why are Trade Unions Hostile to Socialism?[1]

Two vexed questions

In the history of the Marxist movement, there are two political issues, or "questions," that have been the source of exceptionally persistent controversy, spanning more than a century. One is the "national question" and the other is the "trade union" question.

What is the reason for the persistence of these questions and what is the relation, if any, between the two? I suggest that the answer is to be found in a study of the historical conditions within which the modern workers movement emerged. The bourgeois nation state, as it arose out of the revolutionary-democratic struggles of the eighteenth and nineteenth centuries, provided the economic impulse and political framework for the development of the European and American working class. The process of national consolidation was, though in many different forms and in different degrees, linked to general democratic issues of great importance to the working class.

The attitude of the working class to the nation could not but be of a highly complex, contradictory and ambivalent character. On the one hand,

---

[1] Lecture delivered on January 10, 1998, at the International School on Marxism and the Fundamental Problems of the Twentieth Century, held in Sydney Australia.

the growth of the working class in numbers and power, and the improvement of its standard of living, were generally linked to the consolidation of the national state and the expansion of its economic-industrial might. At the same time, the development of the economic and social struggles of the working class placed it in a position of hostility to the national state, which, in the final analysis, served the class interests of the bourgeoisie.

The vexed character of the national question within the Marxist movement arose precisely from the complexity of the relation of the workers to the bourgeois nation-state. Nowhere in the world have we seen a painless and organic transcendence by the masses from national to international socialist consciousness. In the life of a human being, the experiences of his or her youth remain powerful influences throughout the rest of their years. An analogous phenomenon is to be observed in the historical evolution of the social consciousness of classes. The historical allegiance of the working class to nationalism is to be explained by the conditions of its origins and the struggles of its formative stages. Social consciousness lags behind — or, to put it more precisely, does not directly and immediately reflect in scientific form a highly complex and contradictory — social being. In the same way, the influence of nationalism over the workers movement does not decline in direct proportion to, and with a speed commensurate with, the growth of the preponderance of world economy over the national state and the increasingly international character of the class struggle.

The persistence of national oppression in the twentieth century — even though its essential cause is of a socioeconomic character — has fortified forms of national consciousness. But despite the power of national influences, it is the responsibility of Marxists to base their program not upon the appeal of old prejudices and obsolete conceptions, but upon a scientific analysis of social reality. The adaptation of its political program to prevailing prejudices, for the sake of short-term tactical advantages, is one of the most common features of opportunism. It proceeds from practical and conjunctural estimates, rather than from considerations of a principled, historical and scientific character.

Denying the political and economic consequences of the globalization of production upon the national state, the opportunists generally attribute to this historically outmoded political form a progressive potential that it altogether lacks. Thus, they persist in glorifying the demand for national self-determination, notwithstanding the fact that this has become the watchword of every reactionary chauvinist movement in the world.

Marxists do not consider the nation-state irrelevant. Though the nation-state form constitutes, from the standpoint of the global development and integration of the productive forces, a barrier to human progress, it remains a mighty factor in world politics. The socialist movement does not ignore this political reality in the elaboration of its tactics. To the extent that the nation-state persists as a basic unit of political and economic organization of bourgeois society, the national question — which, at this point in history, would be more aptly called the "national problem" — persists. But Marxist tactics flow from a scientific understanding of the historical obsolescence of the national state. Through its tactics, the Trotskyist movement strives to implement the guiding strategy of the Fourth International as the World Party of Socialist Revolution. It is this insistence upon the supremacy of international strategy that distinguishes the International Committee of the Fourth International from every national-reformist and opportunist group.

These principled considerations are posed no less urgently in relation to the trade union question, which concerns the role of this very old form of proletarian organization in the development of the revolutionary struggles of the working class for socialism. The emergence of the modern proletariat occurred within the context of the historical development of the nation-state. Its organizations, and their activities, took shape within the framework of the national state. This was especially the case in relation to the trade unions, whose advances and prosperity were, to a great extent, dependent upon the industrial and commercial successes of "their" national state. Just as there exist historical reasons for the ambivalent attitude of the working class toward the national state, there are also deeply rooted objective reasons for the ambivalence, even hostility, of the trade unions toward socialism. This is a problem over which the socialist movement has shed a great many tears for well over a century.

Of course, the seriousness of the problems that were to haunt the relations between revolutionary Marxist parties and the trade unions could not have been fully anticipated in the earliest years of their existence. The attitude adopted by Marxists to the trade unions has, inevitably, reflected the conditions and circumstances of the time. The trade union question is not posed in 1998 as it was in 1847. There has been a fair amount of history over the last 151 years, and the socialist movement has had ample opportunity to acquaint itself with trade unionism. It has learned a great deal about the nature of trade unions, though not a trace of this accumulated knowledge is to be found in the pages of the "left" radical press.

Through much of its history, the socialist movement has ardently pursued the trade unions. Yet, despite much courting and wooing, this romance has been largely unsuccessful. Despite innumerable professions of affection and concern, the socialist suitors have been repeatedly kicked in the teeth and even stabbed in the back by the objects of their desire. Even when the socialists have sought to create trade unions of their own and provide them with an impeccable Marxist education, their offspring have repaid them with the blackest ingratitude. As soon as the opportunity has presented itself, they have tended to spurn the lofty ideals of their socialist elders and find pleasure in the fleshpots of capitalism.

Must socialists submit to the authority of the trade unions?

One would think that there is something to be learned from so many ill-fated experiences. But like the old fools found in the tales of Boccaccio, the aging and toothless radicals today are only too eager to play the cuckold again and again. Thus, the present-day "left" organizations still insist that the socialist movement is duty-bound to minister loyally to the needs and whims of the trade unions. Socialists, they insist, must acknowledge the trade unions as the workers organization *par excellence*, the form most representative of the social interests of the working class. The trade unions, they argue, constitute the authentic and unchallengeable leadership of the working class — the principal and ultimate arbiters of its historical destiny. To challenge the authority of the trade unions over the working class, to question in any way the supposedly "natural" right of the trade unions to speak in the name of the working class, is tantamount to political sacrilege. It is impossible, the radicals claim, to conceive of any genuine workers movement which is not dominated, if not formally led, by the trade unions. Only on the basis of the trade unions can the class struggle be effectively waged. And, finally, whatever hope there exists for the development of a mass socialist movement depends upon "winning" the trade unions, or at least a significant section of them, to a socialist perspective.

To put the matter bluntly, the International Committee rejects every one of these assertions, which are refuted both by theoretical analysis and historical experience. In the eyes of our political opponents, our refusal to bow before the authority of the trade unions is the equivalent of *lèse-majesté*. This does not trouble us greatly, for not only have we become accustomed, over the decades, to being in opposition to "left-wing" — or to be more accurate — petty-bourgeois public opinion; we consider its embittered antipathy the surest sign that the International Committee is, politically speaking, on the correct path.

The radicals' position rests on one crucial premise: by virtue of their mass memberships, the trade unions are "workers organizations." Thus, he who challenges the authority of the trade unions is, by definition, setting himself in opposition to the working class. The problem with this premise is that it reduces the trade unions to empty, ahistorical abstractions. That the trade unions have a large working class membership is undoubtedly true. But so do many other organizations, such as, in the United States, the Elks, the Masons, the Veterans of Foreign Wars and the Catholic Church.

Moreover, a reference to the large working class membership of the trade unions is not an adequate substitute for a more careful analysis of the social composition of these organizations, especially their leading strata — that is, their ruling bureaucracies. It does not automatically flow from the mass working class membership of the trade unions that these organizations act in its interests. Indeed, one is compelled to examine whether there exists, within the trade unions, an objective conflict between the interests of the mass membership and those of the governing bureaucracy, and the extent to which the policies of the unions reflect, not the interests of the former, but the latter.

Even if one were to concede that the trade unions are "workers organizations," very little is added to the sum total of political knowledge by the use of this definition. After all, we could then continue to play the definition game by simply asking, "And precisely what is meant by workers organization?" It would hardly do to reply, "An organization of workers!" In seeking to understand the nature of the trade unions, the real question is, "What is the relation of these organizations to the class struggle in general, and to the liberation of the workers from capitalist exploitation in particular?"

At this point, we must move beyond empty terminology and toward the construction of a more profound definition, based upon a careful historical analysis of the role played by the trade unions in the struggles of the working class and the socialist movement. The purpose of such an analysis is not merely to produce examples of crimes or achievements, depending upon what one is looking for. Rather, it is to uncover the essence of this social phenomenon, that is, the underlying laws of which the actions and policies of the trade unions are the operative and practical expression.

Why do trade unions betray the working class?

Our radical opponents never even attempt such an analysis, and therefore cannot even begin to offer a serious answer to the most elementary and obvious question: "Why have the trade unions failed so miserably to defend the living standards of the working class, let alone raise them?" Not only in the United States, but all over the world, the last quarter-century has witnessed a precipitous decline in the social position of the working class. The trade unions have been incapable of defending the working class against the onslaught of capital. Inasmuch as this failure has been demonstrated over several decades on an international scale, one is led inescapably to search for its underlying causes — both in the socioeconomic environment within which the trade unions now exist and, even more fundamentally, in the nature of the trade unions themselves. In other words, assuming that the environment turned suddenly hostile after 1973, what was it about the trade unions that rendered them so vulnerable to this change and so incapable of adapting to the new conditions?

Let us consider the response of the Spartacist League to this problem. In the course of a furious denunciation of the Socialist Equality Party — spanning four issues of their newspaper and thousands of words, of which an extraordinarily large percentage are abusive adjectives and adverbs — the Spartacists strenuously deny there are any reasons of an objective character for the failure of the trade unions. Rather, everything is to be explained by "the defeatist and treacherous policies of the AFL-CIO misleaders." A more banal explanation could hardly be imagined. A paleontologist might just as well declare that the dinosaurs became extinct because they no longer wished to live! The Spartacists fail to explain why the dinosaurs in the leadership of the AFL-CIO decided to pursue "defeatist and treacherous policies." Was it simply because they were bad people? And if they were bad people, why were so many of them to be found in the leadership of the trade unions, not only in America, but throughout the world? Is there anything in the nature of the trade unions that leads them to attract so many bad people, who then pursue "defeatist and treacherous policies?" We might also ask yet another question, "What is it about the Spartacist League that induces it to support, so enthusiastically, organizations that attract great numbers of bad people who devote themselves to betraying and defeating the workers they supposedly represent?"

The problem with a subjective approach is not only that it avoids grappling with all the really difficult problems; it permits the Spartacist League, and the other radical groups, notwithstanding their verbal assault upon the "misleaders," to hold open the possibility of their eventual redemption and, on that basis, endorse the continuing subordination of the working class to the trade unions and, ultimately, the very same misleaders.

This perspective is spelled out in an article written by Peter Taaffe, the main leader of the British Socialist Party, formerly known as the Militant Tendency.[2] Mr. Taaffe's attempts to dress up his subservience to the labor bureaucracy with radical phraseology produces an effect that is more comical than convincing. He begins by offering a short list of countries in which the trade union officials have been involved in particularly egregious betrayals of the working class. Like the police chief Louis in *Casablanca*, Taaffe is deeply, deeply shocked by the corruption that he observes all about him, even as the political payoffs from the bureaucracy are slipped into his pocket. The role of the Swedish union officials, Taaffe tells us, has been "scandalous." The behavior of Belgian bureaucrats is "brazen and open." Irish leaders are also engaged in a "scandalous spectacle" of betrayal. In Britain, Taaffe states that workers "have paid a heavy price for the impotence of the right-wing leaders." He also notes sorrowfully the capitulation of the union leaders in Brazil, Greece and the United States.

But as far as Taaffe is concerned, the problem of the trade unions is merely one of inadequate leaders who suffer from a false ideology: acceptance of the capitalist market. The organizations themselves are basically healthy. On the basis of this subjective evaluation, Taaffe criticizes "small left groups" — by which he means the sections of the International Committee — who, basing themselves on Trotsky, insist that the betrayals of the unions are the expression of a fundamental tendency of development. This "one-sided" approach, according to Taaffe, fails to recognize the possibility that right wing trade union leaders, "under the pressure of the base, an aroused and embattled working class," can "be forced to separate themselves from the state and head up an opposition movement of the working class."[3]

Therefore, writes Taaffe, the "main tendency in the next period," in Britain and elsewhere, will be that of workers "compelling the unions to fight on their behalf." The fate of the working class depends upon "the regeneration of the unions."[4]

---

[2] Peter Taaffe, "Trade Unions in the Epoch of Neo-Liberalism," *Socialism Today.*

[3] Ibid.

[4] Ibid.

A similar argument is advanced by a faction of the now defunct Workers Revolutionary Party. What must be avoided at all costs, it insists, is any struggle to develop new forms of working class organization opposed to the domination of the trade unions. "Any simplistic rank and fileism which starts from the abstract proposition that the union leaders are in bed with the state and that alternative organizations must be built and linked up will be completely inadequate to grasp the new situation."[5]

I have no special information relating to the nocturnal trysts of union officials in Britain or anywhere else, but their opportunism is anything but a merely "abstract proposition." Rather, the treacherous services of the union officials are propositioned on a daily basis by the employers and the state, and these propositioners are very rarely disappointed.

The prospects for an eventual redemption of the trade unions appear far less likely when one grasps that the characteristics and qualities of the ruling bureaucracies are the subjective manifestations of objective social properties and processes. Denunciations of trade union leaders are permissible and even necessary, but only to the extent that they do not serve as a substitute for an analysis of the nature of trade unionism.

Therefore, our aim is to initiate an analysis of trade unionism, based upon a historical review of critical stages in the development of this specific form of the workers movement. The socialist movement has accumulated, over a period of not less than 150 years, immense historical experience. This experience justifies its claim to be the world's greatest and saddest expert on the subject of trade unionism.

We do not claim that trade unionism represents some sort of historical mistake that should never have occurred. It would be ridiculous to deny that a phenomenon as universal as trade unionism lacked deep roots in the socio-economic structure of capitalist society. There is, to be sure, a definite link between trade unionism and the class struggle; but only in the sense that the organization of workers within trade unions derives its impulse from the existence of a definite conflict between the material interests of employers and workers. It by no means follows from this objective fact that trade unions, as a specific socially-determined organizational form, identify themselves with, or seek to prosecute, the class struggle (to which, in a historical sense, they owe their existence). Rather, history provides overwhelming evidence that they are far more devoted to its suppression.

---

[5] *Workers International Press*, Number 1, February 1997, p. 21.

The trade unions' tendency to suppress the class struggle has found its most intense and developed expression in their attitude toward the social-ist movement. There has been no illusion more tragic, especially for social-ists, than that which imagined the unions as dependable, let alone inevitable, allies in the struggle against capitalism. The organic development of trade unionism proceeds, not in the direction of socialism, but in opposition to it. Notwithstanding the circumstances of their origins — that is, even when the trade unions in one or another country owed their existence directly to the impulse and leadership provided by the revolutionary socialists — the devel-opment and consolidation of the trade unions has invariably led to a resent-ment of socialist tutelage and determined efforts to break free from it. Only through an explanation of this tendency is it possible to arrive at a scientific understanding of trade unionism.

The trade unions as social form

It must be kept in mind that when we set out to study trade unionism, we are dealing with a definite social form. By this, we mean not some sort of casual, accidental and amorphous collection of individuals, but rather a his-torically-evolved connection between people organized in classes and rooted in certain specific relations of production. It is also important to reflect upon the nature of form itself. We all know that a relation exists between form and content, but this relationship is generally conceived as if the form were merely the expression of content. From this standpoint, the social form might be conceptualized as merely an outward, plastic and infinitely malleable expres-sion of the relations upon which it is based. But social forms are more pro-foundly understood as dynamic elements in the historical process. To say that "content is formed" means that form imparts to the content of which it is the expression definite qualities and characteristics. It is through form that content exists and develops.

Perhaps it will be possible to clarify the purpose of this detour into the realm of philosophical categories and abstractions, by referring to the famous section in the first chapter of the first volume of *Capital*, in which Marx asks: "Whence, then, arises the enigmatical character of the product of labor, so soon as it assumes the form of commodities? Clearly from this form itself."[6] That is, when a product of labor assumes the form of a commodity — a

---

[6] Karl Marx, *Capital*, Volume 1 (New York: International Publishers, 1967), p. 76.

transformation that occurs only at a certain stage of society — it acquires a peculiar, fetishistic quality that it did not previously possess. Once products are exchanged on the market, real social relations between people, of which commodities are themselves the outcome, necessarily assume the appearance of a relation between things. A product of labor is a product of labor; and yet, once it assumes, within the framework of new productive relations, the form of a commodity, it acquires new social properties.

Similarly, a group of workers is a group of workers. And yet, when that group assumes the form of a trade union, it acquires, through that form, new and quite distinct social properties to which the workers are inevitably subordinated. What, precisely, is meant by this? The trade unions represent the working class in a very distinct socioeconomic role: as the seller of a commodity, labor-power. Arising on the basis of the productive relations and property forms of capitalism, the trade unions seek to secure for this commodity the best price that can be obtained under prevailing market conditions.

Of course, there is a world of difference between what I have described in theoretical terms as the "essential purpose" of trade unions and their real-life activities. The practical reality — the everyday sell-out of the most immediate interests of the working class — corresponds very little to the theoretically conceived "norm." This divergence does not contradict the theoretical conception, but is itself the outcome of the socioeconomic function of the trade union. Standing on the basis of capitalist production relations, the trade unions are, by their very nature, compelled to adopt a hostile attitude toward the class struggle. Directing their efforts toward securing agreements with employers that fix the price of labor-power and determine the general conditions in which surplus-value will be pumped out of the workers, the trade unions are obligated to guarantee that their members supply their labor-power in accordance with the terms of the negotiated contracts. As Gramsci noted, "The union represents legality, and must aim to make its members respect that legality."

The defense of legality means the suppression of the class struggle. That is why the trade unions ultimately undermine their ability to achieve even the limited aims to which they are officially dedicated. Herein lies the contradiction upon which trade unionism flounders. The conflict between the trade unions and the revolutionary movement arises not, in any fundamental sense, from the faults and failings of the trade union leaders — though both are to be found in abundant supply — but from the nature of the trade unions themselves. At the heart of this conflict lies the organic opposition of the trade unions to the development and extension of the class struggle. That opposition becomes all the more determined, bitter and deadly at the point where the class struggle appears to threaten the production relations of capitalism, that is, the socioeconomic foundations of trade unionism itself.

That opposition, moreover, is focused on the socialist movement, which represents the working class, not in its limited role as a seller of labor-power, but in its historic capacity as the revolutionary antithesis of the production relations of capitalism.

These two critical aspects of trade unionism — its tendency to seek the suppression of the class struggle and its hostility to the socialist movement — are decisively substantiated by the historical record. In this regard, the history of the trade union movement in two countries, England and Germany, yields important lessons and insights.

Trade unionism in England

England is commonly regarded as the great home of modern trade unionism, where, through this form of organization, the working class realized remarkable achievements. Indeed, this was the impression the trade unions made upon Eduard Bernstein, during his extended sojourn in England during the late 1880s and 1890s. The supposed successes of British trade unionism convinced Bernstein that it was the economic struggles of these organizations, not the political efforts of the revolutionary movement, that would be the decisive factor in the advance of the working class and the gradual transformation of society along socialist lines.

Everything said today by the petty-bourgeois radicals was anticipated a century ago, by the founder of modern revisionism. The fact that their arguments are 100 years old does not, in itself, render them invalid. After all, I freely admit that some of the arguments I am using are also 100 years old — for example, the arguments employed by Rosa Luxemburg against Bernstein. These, however, have the advantage of having been substantiated in the course of the last century, while those of the neo-Bernsteinites have been refuted. As a matter of fact, contemporary critics of Bernstein noted that his estimate of the economic achievements of British trade unionism was grossly exaggerated. Indeed, the ascendancy of trade unionism, whose rise to a dominant role in the workers movement had begun in the 1850s, was an expression of the political degeneration and intellectual stagnation that followed in the wake of the defeat of the great revolutionary political movement of the British working class, Chartism.

The Chartist movement represented the culmination of a political, cultural and intellectual ferment that affected broad sections of the working class in the decades that followed the French Revolution. Years after the final defeat of Chartism in 1848–49, Thomas Cooper, one of its most respected leaders, contrasted the revolutionary spirit of the old movement to the dull, petty-bourgeois outlook cultivated by the trade unions. He wrote in his autobiography:

> In our old Chartist time, it is true, Lancashire workmen were in rags by thousands; and many of them often lacked food. But their intelligence was demonstrated wherever you went. You would see them in groups, discussing the great doctrine of political justice — that every grown up, sane man ought to have a vote in the election of the men who were to make the laws by which he was to be governed; or they were in earnest dispute respecting the teachings of Socialism. Now, you will see no groups in Lancashire. But you will hear well-dressed working men talk, with their hands in their pockets, of co-ops, and their shares in them, or in building societies.[7]

A new type of labor leader emerged with the trade unions: timid gentlemen who craved middle-class respectability and preached the new gospel of class compromise took the place of the old revolutionary Chartists. As Theodore Rothstein, a socialist historian of Chartism, wrote:

> Men of great talent, great temperament, of great and profound erudition, who but a few years previously had shaken the very foundations of capitalist society and had been followed by hundreds of thousands of factory workers, were now lonely figures moving in obscurity, misunderstood by the majority, understood only by small groups of the selected few, while their place was taken by new men who did not possess a fraction of their intellect, talent and character, and who attracted similar hundreds of thousands of workers by the shallow gospel of "look after the pennies" and the need of coming to an agreement with the employers on this subject, even at the price of class independence.[8]

---

[7] Quoted in Theodore Rothstein, *From Chartism to Labourism* (London: Lawrence and Wishart, 1983), pp. 183–184.

[8] Ibid., p. 195.

As for trade unionism, Rothstein offered the following assessment:

> The distinguishing feature of this mental outlook was acceptance of capitalist society, which acceptance found its expression in the rejection of political action, and in the recognition of the teachings of vulgar political economy of the harmony of interests as between the employing and the working class.[9]

The apologists of trade unionism have argued that the British workers' retreat from political action was necessary in order to allow the class to concentrate its energy on the more promising opportunities provided by the economic struggle. This theory is disproved by the fact that the rise of trade unionism was not associated with the intensification of economic struggles, but, rather, with their general repudiation by the new leaders of the working class. Between the early 1870s and mid-1890s, the hey-day of trade unionism in England, the wages of workers stagnated. That trade unionism was not discredited during this period is to be explained by the fact that there was a massive drop in the prices of staple goods such as flour, potatoes, bread, meat, tea, sugar and butter took place.

In the early decades of the nineteenth century, when revolutionary sentiments were widespread among the workers, the English bourgeoisie had bitterly resisted all tendencies toward combination. But, by the end of the century, the bourgeoisie had come to appreciate the service rendered by the trade unions to the stability of capitalism — especially by serving as a barrier to the re-emergence of socialist tendencies within the working class. As the German bourgeois economist, Brentano, wrote: If the trade unions were to fail in England, it would

> by no means mean the triumph of the employers. It would mean the strengthening of the revolutionary tendencies all over the world. England, which hitherto boasted of the absence of a revolutionary labor party of any serious importance, would henceforth rival in this with the Continent.[10]

Marx and Engels lived as revolutionary exiles in England during the period of the rise of trade unionism. Even before they had arrived in England,

---

[9] Ibid., p. 197.
[10] Ibid., p. 273.

they had recognized the significance of trade unionism as the response of the working class to the efforts of the employers to lower their wages. In opposition to the petty-bourgeois theoretician Pierre-Joseph Proudhon, who denied the utility of both trade unions and strikes — on the grounds that increases in wages achieved through their efforts led only to increases in prices — Marx insisted that both formed necessary components of the struggle of the working class to defend its standard of living.

Marx was certainly correct in his criticism of the views of Proudhon, but it is necessary to bear in mind that these early writings were produced at a time when the trade unions themselves were still in their swaddling clothes. The experience of the working class with this new organizational form was extremely limited. The possibility could not be foreclosed, at that time, that the trade unions could yet evolve into potent instruments of revolutionary struggle, or at least as the direct forerunners of such instruments. This hope was expressed in Marx's observation in 1866 that as "centers of organization" the trade unions were playing for the working class the same role "as the medieval municipalities and communes did for the middle class."[11]

Even by then, however, Marx was concerned that "the Trades' Unions have not yet fully understood their power of acting against the system of wages slavery itself." But it was in this direction that they had to evolve:

> Apart from their original purposes, they must now learn to act deliberately as organizing centers of the working class in the broad interest of its *complete emancipation*. They must aid every social and political movement tending in that direction. Considering themselves and acting as the champions and representatives of the whole working class, they cannot fail to enlist the non-society men into their ranks. They must look carefully after the interests of the worst paid trades, such as the agricultural laborers, rendered powerless by exceptional circumstances. They must convince the world at large that their efforts, far from being narrow and selfish, aim at the emancipation of the downtrodden millions.[12]

---

[11] Karl Marx and Frederick Engels, *Collected Works*, Volume 20 (New York: International Publishers, 1985), p. 191.

[12] Ibid., p. 192.

Marx sought to impart to the trade unions a socialist orientation. He warned the workers "not to exaggerate to themselves" the significance of the struggles engaged in by the trade unions. At most, the unions were "fighting with effects, but not with the causes of those effects; that they are retarding the downward movement; that they are applying palliatives, not curing the malady." It was necessary for the unions to undertake a struggle against the system that was the cause of the workers' miseries; and, therefore, Marx proposed to the trade unions that they abandon their conservative slogan, "*A fair day's wage for a fair day's work*," and replace it with the revolutionary demand, "*Abolition of the wages system*."[13]

But Marx's advice made little impression, and by the late 1870s, the observations of Marx and Engels on the subject of trade unionism had assumed a far more critical character. Now that bourgeois economists were expressing greater sympathy toward the trade unions, Marx and Engels took pains to qualify their earlier endorsement. They distinguished their views from those of bourgeois thinkers like Lujo Brentano, whose enthusiasm for the trade unions was dictated, according to Marx and Engels, by his desire "to make the wage-slaves into *contented* wage-slaves."[14]

By 1879, it was possible to detect in Engels' writings on the subject of trade unionism an unmistakable tone of disgust. He noted that the trade unions had introduced organizational statutes that prohibited political action, thus barring "any participation in any general activity on the part of the working class as a class." In a letter to Bernstein, dated June 17, 1879, Engels complained that the trade unions had led the working class into a dead end:

> No attempt should be made to conceal the fact that at this moment a genuine workers movement in the continental sense is non-existent here, and hence I don't believe you will miss much if, for the time being, you don't get any reports on the doings of the TRADES UNIONS here.[15]

In an article written six years later, in which he contrasted the England of 1885 to that of 1845, Engels made no attempt to conceal his contempt for the

---

[13] Ibid., p. 149.

[14] Karl Marx and Frederick Engels, *Collected Works*, Volume 27 (New York: International Publishers, 1992), p. 98.

[15] Karl Marx and Frederick Engels, *Collected Works*, Volume 45 (Moscow: Progress Publishers, 1991), p. 361.

conservative role played by the trade unions. Forming an aristocracy within the working class, they cultivated the friendliest relations with the employers, in order to secure for themselves a comfortable position. The trade unionists, Engels wrote with scathing sarcasm, "are very nice people indeed nowadays to deal with, for any sensible capitalist in particular and for the whole capitalist class in general."[16]

The trade unions had all but ignored the great mass of the working class, for whom

> the state of misery and insecurity in which they live now is as low as ever, if not lower. The East-end of London is an ever-spreading pool of stagnant misery and desolation, of starvation when out of work, and degradation, physical and moral, when in work.[17]

Engels' hopes were aroused, toward the end of the 1880s, by the development of a new and militant trade union movement among more exploited sections of the working class. Socialists, including Eleanor Marx, were active in this new movement. Engels responded to these developments with enthusiasm, and noted with great satisfaction:

> These new Trades Unions of unskilled men and women are totally different from the old organizations of the working-class aristocracy and cannot fall into the same conservative ways. ... And they are organized under quite different circumstances — all the leading men and women are Socialists, and socialist agitators too. In them I see the *real* beginning of the movement here.[18]

But it was not too long before these "new" unions began to exhibit the same conservative tendencies as the old ones. This was an early verification of the theoretical conception we consider critical to the analysis of the trade unions — i.e., that the character of these organizations is not determined by the social position and status of the particular sections of workers organized within them. These are factors which, at most, only influence certain secondary aspects of trade

[16] Ibid., Volume 26 (Moscow: Progress Publishers, 1990), p. 299.
[17] Ibid.
[18] Quoted in Hal Draper, *Karl Marx's Theory of Revolution*, Volume 2: "The Politics of Social Classes" (New York: Monthly Review Press, 1978), p. 111.

union policy—perhaps making some unions more or less militant than the average. Yet, in the final analysis, the trade union form, whose structure is drawn from, and embedded in, the social and production relations of capitalism, and, we must add, the nation-state framework, exercises the decisive influence that determines the orientation of its "content" — the working class membership.

German social democracy and the trade unions

On the continent, especially in Germany, theoretical lessons were being drawn from these early experiences with trade unionism. The German socialists viewed the English trade unions, not as the forerunners of socialism, but as the organizational expression of the political and ideological domination of the working class by the bourgeoisie. This critical attitude arose, not only on the basis of theoretical insights, but also reflected a very different relation of forces within the workers movement, between the Marxist political party and the trade unions. In Germany, the impulse for the development of a mass workers movement had been provided not by the trade unions, but by the Social Democratic Party, which had succeeded, between 1878 and 1890—the period of Bismarck's Anti-Socialist Laws—in establishing its political authority as the leadership of the working class. It was at the initiative of the SPD that the so-called "Free" trade unions were established, mainly to serve as recruiting agencies for the socialist movement.

The influence of the trade unions—assisted by the SPD, from which they drew their leading cadre and political insights—began to expand in the 1890s. But the lingering effects of the protracted industrial depression held down their membership, and as late as 1893, the ratio of Social Democratic voters to trade union members was eight to one. Still, concern was expressed within the SPD that the trade unions might seek to compete with the party for influence in the working class. This was strenuously denied by the trade unions, whose leader, Carl Legien, defined them, at the Köln party congress of 1893, as "recruiting schools of the party."

However, with the end of the industrial depression in 1895, the German trade unions began to grow rapidly; and the changing relation of forces increased tensions between the party and the trade unions. By 1900, the membership of the trade unions had grown to 600,000. Four years later, the figure had risen to one million. As the ratio of SPD voters to trade union members declined, the dependence of the SPD upon the votes of trade unionists increased significantly.

Though the trade union leaders themselves refrained from offering any political support to Bernstein when he first unfurled the banner of revisionism, it was widely understood in party circles that his theories could only lead to a reorientation of the German socialist movement along English lines, in which reformist trade unions would replace the revolutionary political party as the axis of the workers movement.

In opposing Bernstein, the principal theoreticians of the Social Democracy paid particular attention to his effort to portray the trade unions as the indispensable bastion of the socialist movement. It was, of course, Rosa Luxemburg who took the lead in this struggle. Her most important work, in this regard, was *Reform or Revolution*, where she made mincemeat of Bernstein's claim that the efforts of the trade unions effectively counteracted the exploitative mechanisms of capitalism and led, however gradually, to the socialization of society. Luxemburg insisted that this was utterly untrue: that trade unionism did not lead to the abolition of class exploitation. Rather, it sought to ensure that the proletariat, within the framework of the exploitative structure of capitalism, received, in the form of wages, the best price that the market would allow.

What could be achieved by the efforts of the trade unions, in terms of raising workers' wages, was limited by the fluctuations of the market and the general dynamic of capitalist expansion. Capitalist society, she warned, was not moving "toward an epoch marked by a victorious development of trade unions, but rather toward a time when the hardships of labor unions will increase."[19] Thus, whatever the temporary gains achieved by the unions, they were engaged, to the extent that their work remained rooted within the boundaries set by the capitalist system, in "the labor of Sisyphus." The trade union leaders never forgave Luxemburg for making use of this winged metaphor, which provided such a devastatingly apt and prescient assessment of the activities of the trade unions.

This summary hardly does justice to Luxemburg's analysis of the reasons for the inability of the trade unions to do more than mitigate, and then only temporarily, the exploitation of the working class under capitalism. Another aspect of her criticism of Bernsteinism that is especially relevant: her denial that there is anything inherently or implicitly socialistic in the activities of the trade unions, or that their work contributes necessarily to the victory of the socialist cause. Luxemburg did not deny that the trade unions, to the extent that they were led by socialists, could render important service to the

---

[19] Rosa Luxemburg, *Reform or Revolution* (New York: Pathfinder Press, 1976), p. 36.

revolutionary movement. Indeed, she hoped, through her criticism, to work for such a development. (It is another matter, which we will consider later, whether that aim was achievable.) But she warned against any illusion in the existence of organic socialistic tendencies in trade unionism as such.

"It is precisely the English trade unions," Luxemburg wrote:

> as the classic representatives of complacent, correct, narrow-mindedness, that bear witness to the fact that the trade union movement, in and for itself, is utterly non-socialist; indeed, it can be, under certain circumstances, a direct obstacle for the expansion of socialist consciousness; just as, in the opposite case, socialist consciousness can be an obstacle for the achievement of purely trade union successes.[20]

This passage remains a stunning rebuke to all those who slavishly adapt themselves to the trade unions and their bureaucracies, and who cannot conceive of a workers movement in anything other than a trade unionist form. As it makes so very clear, there exist no organic and unbreakable links between trade unionism and socialism. They are not, of necessity, moving along parallel trajectories toward the same general destination. Rather, trade unionism, which by its nature is, as Luxemburg stated, "utterly non-socialist," undermines the development of socialist consciousness. And, furthermore, the political principles of the socialists, which require that they base their activities upon the historical interests of the working class, run counter to the practical aims of the trade unions.

In England, the trade unions developed upon the ruins of Chartism and independently of the socialist movement. In Germany, on the other hand, the trade unions emerged under the direct tutelage of the socialist movement. Its leaders were diligently schooled in the teachings of Marx and Engels. And yet, in essence, the German trade unions were no more devoted to socialism than those in England. By the turn of the century, having become more self-confident by the influx of hundreds of thousands of new members, the trade unions were indicating their discomfort with the political influence of the party and their subordination to its political aims. This discomfort found expression in a new platform: that of political neutrality. A growing section of trade union

---

[20] "Die englische Brille," in *Rosa Luxemburg Gesammelte Werke*, Volume 1/1 (Berlin: Dietz Verlag, 1990), p. 481, (translation by D. North).

leaders began to argue that there was no reason why their organizations owed any special loyalty to the campaigns of the SPD. In fact, the domination of the SPD, they argued, cost the trade unions the possibility of winning members among workers who were disinterested in, or opposed to, socialist politics. Among the foremost representatives of this trend was Otto Hué, who insisted that the trade unions could only serve the "professional (not class) interests" of its members if they adopted a position of political neutrality. "Where workers," Hué wrote, "wind up politically under conditions of trade union neutrality is and must be a matter of indifference to the trade union leaders."

Trade unions and the "mass strike"

Between 1900 and 1905 tension mounted between the party and the trade unions. The union leaders, in their capacity as delegates to the congresses of the SPD, continued to cast their votes in favor of socialist orthodoxy. Their innate hostility to socialism as a revolutionary movement had not yet reached the point where they were ready to directly challenge the SPD's political commitment to the struggle for state power. This was changed by the events of 1905, both within Germany and beyond its borders.

The explosion of revolution throughout Russia affected the German working class. Workers followed with intense interest the detailed coverage of the revolutionary struggles in the socialist press. Russian events, moreover, coincided with, and apparently inspired, the eruption of a wave of bitter strikes throughout Germany, but especially in the Ruhr among miners. Despite the militancy of the workers, the strikes encountered stiff resistance from the mine owners. The trade unions were taken aback by the owners' intransigence, to which they had no effective response. The strikes were called off, thus shaking the confidence of the workers in the efficacy of traditional union tactics.

In this new situation, Luxemburg, supported by Kautsky, argued that the events in Russia were of all-European significance and had revealed to the German workers the potential of a new form of mass struggle: the political strike. The idea of a political mass strike found widespread support in the working class. But the trade union leaders were horrified by the implications of Luxemburg's arguments. Were the workers to act on Luxemburg's theories, the unions would find themselves caught up in "revolutionary adventures" that the officials thought were none of their concern. Mass strikes would cost the unions enormous amounts of money and could empty their bank accounts of the cash reserves of which the leaders were so very proud.

To prevent such a catastrophe, the union leaders decided to launch a preemptive strike against Luxemburg and other SPD radicals. At the trade union congress held in Köln in May 1905, a special commission was established to prepare a resolution that would define the attitude of the trade unions to the question of the mass strike. The spokesman of the commission, Theodore Bömelburg, declared:

> To develop our organizations further, we need peace in the labor movement. We must see to it that the discussion of the mass strike disappears, and that the solutions of [the problems of] the future are left open until the appropriate time arrives.[21]

In what amounted to a declaration of war upon the SPD left wing, the trade union congress adopted a resolution that declared discussion on the question of a political mass strike was impermissible within the trade unions. It warned workers "not to let themselves be distracted by the reception and propagation of such ideas from the small day-to-day tasks of building up the organization of labor."[22]

The SPD was shaken by the rebellion of the trade union leaders against the party. Kautsky declared that the congress had revealed the depth of the alienation of the trade unions from the party, and noted, with a sense of irony, that it struck him as absurd that the "desire of the trade unions for peace and quiet" had been proclaimed in a year "that has been the most revolutionary in all human history." It was evident to Kautsky that the trade union leaders were more concerned with the fate of the organization's bank accounts than with the "moral quality of the masses."

For the union leaders, hatred of the SPD left wing assumed pathological dimensions. Rosa Luxemburg, in particular, was the perennial target of vitriolic denunciations. Otto Hué, who edited the miners' journal, urged those who had such a surfeit of revolutionary energy to go to Russia "instead of propagating general strike discussion from their summer resorts."[23] The attacks on Luxemburg intensified, even as she languished in a Polish jail after being arrested for her revolutionary activities. Sickened by the vicious personal attacks on Luxemburg, who was still his friend and ally, Kautsky

---

[21] Carl E. Schorske, *German Social Democracy: 1905–1917; the Development of the Great Schism* (Cambridge, MA: Harvard University Press, 1983), pp. 39–40.

[22] Ibid., p. 40.

[23] Ibid., p. 41.

denounced the persecution of "a leader of the proletarian class struggle." It was not Luxemburg, he wrote, who endangered the relations between party and trade unions, but rather the trade union officials, who felt a "narrow-minded hatred of these elements against any form of the labour movement that sets itself a higher goal than five pennies more per hour..."[24]

For a time, the SPD leadership fought back against the trade union officials, but did so as cautiously as possible. At the Jena party congress of September 1905, Bebel introduced a skillfully worded resolution that partially acknowledged the validity of the political mass strike — but only as a defensive weapon. In return, the trade unions acquiesced to Bebel's formulation, but only briefly. At the party congress in Mannheim in September 1906, the trade union leaders demanded, and obtained from the SPD, passage of a resolution that established the principle of "equality" between the trade unions and the party. This meant that on all issues touching on matters that were of direct concern to the trade unions, the party had to work out a position that was acceptable to them. Over strenuous objections, party leaders collaborated with trade union officials to bureaucratically shut down discussion and ram through the resolution.

From this point on, the SPD was effectively ruled by the general commission of the trade unions. The relation of the trade unions to the party was, as Luxemburg noted, like that of the shrew peasant wife, who told her husband, "Whenever questions arise between us, we shall use the following procedure : When we agree, you will decide. When we disagree, I will decide."

In their disputes with Luxemburg and the revolutionary forces within the SPD, the trade union officials claimed that they had a far better idea of what the average worker really wanted than the revolutionary theorists. Preoccupied with their abstractions and utopian visions, Luxemburg, and revolutionists of her ilk, did not really have practical answers for the problems workers faced in the mines or on the factory floor. It was well and good for the theorists to dream about a future revolutionary cataclysm, and the socialist utopia that would emerge from it, but in the here and now the workers were much more concerned with a few extra marks in their weekly paychecks.

It was probably true that the arguments of the union officials reflected the outlook of substantial sections of workers during the years when the debate on the mass strike first erupted. It is even possible that, had the issue been put to a vote in 1905 or 1906, more workers would have cast their votes for the position of Legien than for that of Luxemburg. However, in considering the attitude of the workers to the dispute between the Marxists and the reformist union leaders, it is important to keep the following in mind: The officials were, so to speak, institutionally and constitutionally "committed" to policies that proceeded from their unions' organic dependence upon capitalist production relations and the national-state setup. The working class, as a revolutionary social force, was not similarly committed to the gradualist program of reformist adaptation.

The development of the underlying contradictions of the capitalist system frayed the fabric of social compromise in Germany. As class tensions increased, the workers adopted a more aggressive and hostile attitude toward the employers and the state. By 1910–11, there were clear signs that Luxemburg's arguments had begun to resonate among broader sections of the working class. Especially in the aftermath of the strikes of 1912–13, which failed in the face of the employers' bitter resistance, the dissatisfaction of the workers with the official unions increased noticeably.

The outbreak of the World War in August 1914 temporarily halted the process of radicalization. But by 1915–16, the social discontent of the working class, exacerbated by the war, surged over the barriers erected by the official unions. The old bureaucratic arguments against the political mass strike finally received their decisive answer in October–November 1918 with the outbreak of the German Revolution. The revolutionary character of the mass movement expressed itself, as had been anticipated theoretically by Luxemburg and foreshadowed practically in the Russian Revolution, in new forms of organization — rank-and-file committees and especially workers councils — that had emerged in opposition to the official unions.

The experiences of the German and English working class represented the greatest historical test of trade unionism. We could, if we had sufficient time, supplement and substantiate our analysis of the conflict between socialism and trade unionism with innumerable examples, drawn from many more countries and spanning all the decades of this century, right up until our own time.

The necessity of socialist consciousness

The purpose of this lecture has not been to provide as many examples as possible of the treachery of the trade unions. Rather, it is to substantiate the necessity of socialist consciousness and the fight for its development in the working class. Herein lies the significance of the revolutionary Marxist party.

Even if a renaissance of spontaneous militancy of a syndicalist character were to occur — and such a development would be unthinkable without explosive rank-and-file rebellions against the old bureaucratic organizations — the development of such a promising movement along revolutionary lines would depend upon the independent work of the Marxist party, fighting to bring socialist consciousness into the working class.

All those who insist upon the incontestable authority of the trade unions, oppose the struggle for Marxism in the working class. Cliff Slaughter[25], for example, denounces those Marxists [of the International Committee] "who persist in thinking that they have the mission of 'consciousness-raising,' 'politically-intervening,' and 'politicizing,' in the spontaneously arising struggles of the working class..."[26]

This statement substantiates Slaughter's repudiation of Marxism and embrace of middle-class anarchism. We are now approaching the conclusion of a century that has witnessed the most terrible of historical tragedies. The price paid in blood for the failures and betrayals of the many revolutionary struggles of this century is incalculable. The victims claimed by the political consequences of revolutions betrayed number in the hundreds of millions. In this decade we have seen the results of the disorientation of the working class in the former Soviet Union. And yet, in the midst of this universal political disorientation, Slaughter denounces those who seek to overcome that disorientation on the basis of socialist science.

The interests of the working class are not served by glorifying its spontaneity — that is, the prevailing level of consciousness and the given forms of organization. In the case of Slaughter and similar ex-Marxists, such testimonials to spontaneity serve merely as a cover for their own collaboration with the labor and trade union bureaucracies. We make no apologies for our insistence that the future of the working class depends on the strength of our political interventions and the success of our efforts to raise its consciousness.

We stand on the foundations laid down by the great founders and representatives of scientific socialism. We reject Slaughter's statement as a repudiation of the essential principles that have constituted the historic *raison d'être* of the Marxist movement from its earliest days. The proletariat is the active historical subject of the socialist project. But socialism did not, and could

---

[25] Cliff Slaughter is a former leader of the British Workers Revolutionary Party who broke politically with the International Committee of the Fourth International in 1986.

[26] Cliff Slaughter, "Review of Istvan Mezsaros' 'Beyond Capital,'" *Workers International Press*, Number 3, (London, June 1997).

not, arise directly out of the working class. It has its own intellectual history. Marx never claimed that his conception of the historical tasks of the proletariat conformed to whatever might be the general "public opinion" of the vast majority of workers at any given moment in their development. It is absurd even to suggest that Marx devoted his entire life to formulating ideas that merely reproduced what the average worker was likely to think on his own.

If socialist consciousness were generated by the spontaneous development of the class struggle, there would have been no reason to organize this international school. What need would there be for lectures on history, philosophy, political economy, revolutionary strategy and culture if the working class, with its existing mass organizations and prevailing level of political and historical consciousness, could automatically rise to the level of the tasks that are being posed to it by the development of the world crisis of capitalism?

Let us consider the political backdrop against which this school is being held. Even as we meet, the economies of Southeast Asia are in turmoil. Almost overnight, the existence of hundreds of millions of people is being placed in peril. In Indonesia, the value of the currency fell by 22 percent the day before yesterday. In the course of six months, the Indonesian rupee has lost nearly 80 percent of its value. The IMF is demanding a regime of brutal austerity, and under these conditions the eruption of massive social struggles is inevitable.

However, does not the outcome of these struggles depend on the assimilation by the Indonesian working class of the tragic lessons of its own history, which constitute yet another nightmarish chapter in the history of the twentieth century? Is it not necessary to review with Indonesian workers, students and intellectuals the events of 1965–66 — that is, how the largest Communist Party in the world outside the USSR and China, with a membership of more than a million people, proved powerless in the face of Suharto's coup? More than a half-million people were slaughtered in that counterrevolution. The rivers of Sumatra and Bali were clogged with the corpses of the murdered. The executions of prisoners arrested in the aftermath of Suharto's coup continued into the 1990s. But how many questions and problems remain unanswered and unclarified! The strategic lessons of that period constitute the basis for the historic revenge that the Indonesian workers must exact for the crimes committed by the Indonesian bourgeoisie, abetted by American and, I might add, Australian imperialism.

At issue here is not an Indonesian problem, but a world-historical task. Thus, we end this school as we began it, by stressing that the future of humanity in the twenty-first century depends on its assimilation of the lessons of the strategic historical experiences of the twentieth. And if I were compelled to state, in just a few words, the principal conclusion at which we have arrived at the end of our examination of this troubled century, it is that the destiny of mankind is inescapably intertwined with the struggle for the development of socialist consciousness and culture within the international working class, a struggle which finds its political expression in the building of the World Party of Socialist Revolution.

7

Postmodernism's Twentieth Century: Political Demoralization and the Flight from Historical Truth[1]

Understanding the twentieth century

Today we are beginning a week-long series of lectures on the subject of "Marxism, the October Revolution and the Historical Foundations of the Fourth International." In the course of these lectures we intend to examine the historical events, theoretical controversies and political struggles out of which the Fourth International emerged. The central focus of these lectures will be the first forty years of the twentieth century. This limitation is determined partially by the amount of time we have at our disposal. There is only so much that can be accomplished in one week, and to work through the first four decades of the last century in just seven days is an ambitious undertaking. And yet there is a certain historical logic in our concentration on the period between 1900 and 1940.

By the time Leon Trotsky was assassinated in August 1940, all the major events that determined the political characteristics of the twentieth century

---

[1] Lecture delivered August 14, 2005, at the summer school of the Socialist Equality Party (US) in Ann Arbor, Michigan.

had already occurred: The outbreak of World War I in August 1914; the conquest of political power by the Bolshevik Party in October 1917 and the subsequent establishment of the Soviet Union as the first socialist workers state; the emergence, in the aftermath of World War I, of the United States as the most powerful imperialist state; the failure of the German Revolution in 1923; the bureaucratic degeneration of the Soviet Union; the defeat of the Left Opposition and the expulsion of Trotsky from the Communist Party and the Third International in 1927; the betrayal of the Chinese Revolution in 1926–27; the Wall Street crash of October 1929 and the beginning of the world capitalist depression; Hitler's rise to power and the victory of fascism in Germany in January 1933; the Moscow Trials of 1936–38 and the campaign of political genocide against the socialist intelligentsia and working class in the USSR; the betrayal and defeat of the Spanish Revolution in 1937–39 under the aegis of the Stalinist-led Popular Front; the outbreak of World War II in September 1939; and the beginning of the extermination of European Jewry.

During these four decades the political characteristics of the twentieth century were defined. All the major political problems that were to confront the international working class during the post-World War II period could be understood only when examined through the prism of the strategic lessons of the major revolutionary and counterrevolutionary experiences of the pre-World War II era.

The analysis of the policies of social democratic parties after World War II required an understanding of the historical implications of the collapse of the Second International in August 1914. The nature of the Soviet Union, of the regimes established in eastern Europe in the aftermath of World War II, and of the Maoist regime established in China in October 1949, could be comprehended only by studying the October Revolution, and the protracted degeneration of the first workers state. Answers to the problems of the great wave of anti-colonial and anti-imperialist revolutions that swept Asia, the Middle East, Africa and Latin America after 1945 could be found only on the basis of a painstaking study of the political and theoretical controversies surrounding Trotsky's theory of permanent revolution, which he had initially formulated in 1905.

The relation between historical knowledge and political analysis and orientation found its most profound expression in the last decade of the Soviet Union. By the time Mikhail Gorbachev came to power in March 1985, the Stalinist regime was in desperate crisis. The deterioration of the

Soviet economy could no longer be concealed once oil prices, whose rapid rise during the 1970s had provided a short-term windfall, began to fall sharply. What measures would the Kremlin take to reverse the decline? Issues of policy immediately became entangled with unanswered questions of Soviet history.

For more than sixty years the Stalinist regime had been engaged in an unrelenting campaign of historical falsification. The citizens of the Soviet Union were largely ignorant of the facts of their own revolutionary history. The works of Trotsky and his co-thinkers had been censored and suppressed for decades. There existed not a single credible work of Soviet history. Each new edition of the official Soviet encyclopedia revised history in accordance with the political interests and instructions of the Kremlin. In the Soviet Union, as our late comrade Vadim Rogovin once noted, the past was as unpredictable as the future!

For those factions within the bureaucracy and privileged *nomenklatura* which favored the dismantling of nationalized industry, the revival of private property, and the restoration of capitalism, the Soviet economic crisis was "proof" that socialism had failed and that the October Revolution was a catastrophic mistake from which all subsequent Soviet tragedies flowed. The economic prescriptions advanced by these pro-market forces were based on an interpretation of Soviet history that claimed that Stalinism was the inevitable outcome of the October Revolution.

The answer to the advocates of capitalist restoration could not be given simply on the basis of economics. Rather, the refutation of the pro-capitalist arguments demanded an examination of Soviet history, proving that Stalinism was neither the necessary nor inevitable outcome of the October Revolution. It had to be shown that an alternative to Stalinism was not only theoretically conceivable, but also that such an alternative had actually existed in the form of the Left Opposition led by Leon Trotsky.

What I am saying today is more or less what I told an audience of students and teachers in the Soviet Union, at the Historical Archival Institute of Moscow University, in November 1989. I began my lecture on "The Future of Socialism" by noting that "in order to discuss the future, it is necessary to dwell at considerable length on the past. Because how can one discuss socialism today without dealing with the many controversies that confront the socialist movement? And, of course, when we discuss the future of socialism, we are discussing the fate of the October Revolution — an event which is of world significance and which has had a profound effect on the working class of every country. Much of this past, particularly in the Soviet Union, is still shrouded in mystery and falsification."[2]

There was at that time in the Soviet Union a growing interest in historical questions. My own lecture, which was organized with less than twenty-four hours preparation in response to an impromptu invitation by the director of the Historical Archival Institute, attracted an audience of several hundred people. The publicity for the meeting was confined almost entirely to word of mouth. The news quickly got around that an American Trotskyist would be speaking at the Institute, and a large number of people turned up.

Though in the brief era of *glasnost* it was not a complete novelty for a Trotskyist to speak publicly, a lecture by an *American* Trotskyist was still something of a sensation. The intellectual climate for such a lecture was extremely favorable. There was a hunger for historical truth. As Comrade Fred Williams recently noted in his review of Robert Service's miserable Stalin biography, the Soviet journal *Argumenti i Fakty* (*Arguments and Facts*) which had been a minor publication in the pre-*glasnost* era, saw its circulation climb exponentially, to thirty-three million, on the basis of its publication of essays and long-suppressed documents related to Soviet history.[3]

The working class and history

Frightened by the widespread interest in Marxism and Trotskyism, the bureaucracy sought to preempt this intellectual process of *historical* clarification, which would tend to encourage a resurgence of socialist consciousness, by accelerating its movement toward the breakup of the USSR. The manner in which the bureaucracy orchestrated the dissolution of the USSR in December 1991—the culmination of the Stalinist betrayal of the October Revolution foreseen by Trotsky more than a half-century earlier — is a subject that remains to be examined with the necessary detail. But it is undeniable that a major factor that undermined popular resistance to the dissolution of the USSR — whose catastrophic consequences have become all too clear — was *ignorance of history*. The burden of decades of historical falsification could not be overcome in time for the Soviet working class to orient itself politically,

---

[2] *The USSR and Socialism: The Trotskyist Perspective* (Detroit: Labor Publications, 1990), pp. 1–2.

[3] Available: http://www.wsws.org/en/articles/2005/06/stal-j02.html and http://www.wsws.org/en/articles/2005/06/stal-j03.html

uphold its independent social interests, and oppose the dissolution of the Soviet Union and the restoration of capitalism.

There is a lesson in this historical tragedy. Without a thorough knowledge of the historical experiences through which it has passed, the working class cannot defend even its most elementary social interests, let alone conduct a politically conscious struggle against the capitalist system.

Historical consciousness is an essential component of class consciousness. The words of Rosa Luxemburg are as relevant today as they were when written in early 1915, less than a year after the outbreak of World War I and the capitulation of the German Social Democratic Party to Prussian militarism and imperialism:

> Historical experience is [the working class'] only teacher. His Via Dolorosa to freedom is covered not only with unspeakable suffering, but with countless mistakes. The goal of his journey, his final liberation, depends entirely upon the proletariat, on whether *it* understands to learn from *its* own mistakes. Self-criticism, cruel, unsparing criticism that goes to the very root of the evil is life and breath for the proletarian movement. The catastrophe into which the world has thrust the socialist proletariat is an unexampled misfortune for humanity. But socialism is lost only if the international proletariat is unable to measure the depths of the catastrophe and refuses to understand the lesson that it teaches.[4]

The conception of history that we uphold, which assigns to the knowledge and theoretical assimilation of historical experience such a critical role in the struggle for human liberation, is hostile to all prevailing trends of bourgeois thought. The political, economic and social decay of bourgeois society is mirrored in its intellectual degradation. In a period of political reaction, Trotsky once noted, ignorance bares its teeth.

The specific form of ignorance championed today by the most skilled and cynical academic representatives of bourgeois thought, the postmodernists, is *ignorance of and contempt for history.* The postmodernists' rejection of the validity of history, and the central role assigned to it by all genuine progressive

---

[4] Rosa Luxemburg, *The Junius Pamphlet* (Colombo: Young Socialist Publication, undated), p. 7.

trends of social thought, is inextricably linked with another element of their theoretical conceptions — the denial and explicit repudiation of objective truth as a goal of philosophical inquiry.

The postmodern rejection of history

What, then, is postmodernity? Professor Keith Jenkins, an exponent of this trend, explains:

> Today we live within the general condition of *postmodernity*. We do not have a choice about this. For postmodernity is not an "ideology" or a position we can choose to subscribe to or not; postmodernity is precisely our condition: it is our fate. And this condition has arguably been caused by the general failure — a general failure which can now be picked out very clearly as the dust settles over the twentieth century — of that experiment in social living which we call *modernity*. It is a general failure, as measured in its own terms, of the attempt, from around the eighteenth century in Europe, to bring about through the application of reason, science and technology, a level of personal and social wellbeing within social formations which, legislating for an increasingly generous emancipation of their citizens/subjects, we might characterize by saying that they were trying, at best, to become "human rights communities."
>
> ...[T]here are not — and nor have there ever been — any "real" foundations of the kind alleged to underpin the experiment of the modern...[5]

Allow me to "deconstruct" this passage. For more than two hundred years, stretching back into the eighteenth century, there were people, inspired by the science and philosophy of the Enlightenment, who believed in progress, in the possibility of human perfectibility, and who sought the revolutionary transformation of society on the basis of what they believed to be a scientific insight into the laws of history. There were Marxists who believed

---

[5] Keith Jenkins, *On "What Is History?": From Carr and Elton to Rorty and White* (London and New York: Routledge, 1995), pp. 6–7.

that History (with a capital H) is a law-governed process, determined by socioeconomic forces existing independently of the subjective consciousness of individuals, but which man could discover, understand and act upon in the interest of human progress.

But all such conceptions, declare the postmodernists, have been shown to be naïve illusions. We now know better: there is no History with a capital H. There is not even history with a small h, understood as an objective process. There are only subjective "narratives," or "discourses," with shifting vocabularies employed to achieve one or another subjectively-determined purpose, whatever that purpose might be.

From this standpoint, the very idea of deriving "lessons" from "history" is a futile project. There is nothing to be studied and nothing to be learned. As Jenkins insists:

> [W]e now just have to understand that we live amidst social formations which have no legitimizing ontological or episte-mological or ethical grounds for our beliefs or actions beyond the status of an ultimately self-referencing (rhetorical) conversation... Consequently, we recognize today that there never has been, and that there never will be, any such thing as a past which is expressive of some sort of essence. [6]

Translated into comprehensible English, Jenkins is saying 1) the functioning of human societies, either past or present, cannot be understood in terms of laws that can be or are waiting to be discovered; and 2) there is no objective foundation underlying what people may think, say, or do about the society in which they live. People who call themselves historians may advance one or another interpretation of the past, but replacement of one interpretation with another does not express an advance toward something more objectively true than what was previously written — for there is no objective truth to get closer to. It is merely the replacement of one way of talking about the past with another way of talking about the past — for reasons suited to the subjectively-perceived uses of the historian.

The proponents of this outlook assert the demise of modernity, but refuse to examine the underlying historical and political judgments upon which their conclusions are premised. They do, of course, hold political positions

---

[6] Ibid, pp. 7–9.

that find expression in their theoretical views. Professor Hayden White, one of the leading exponents of postmodernism, has written:

> Now I am against revolutions, whether launched from "above" or "below" in the social hierarchy and whether directed by leaders who profess to possess a science of society and history or be celebrators of political "spontaneity."[7]

The legitimacy of a given philosophical conception is not automatically refuted by the politics of the individual by whom it is advanced. But the anti-Marxist and anti-socialist trajectory of postmodernism is so evident that it is impossible to disentangle its theoretical conceptions from its political perspective.

Jean-François Lyotard

This connection finds expression in the writings of the French philosopher Jean-François Lyotard and the American philosopher Richard Rorty. I will begin with the former. Lyotard was directly involved in socialist politics. In 1954, he joined *Socialisme ou Barbarie*, an organization that had emerged in 1949 out of a split with the PCI (Parti Communiste Internationaliste), the French section of the Fourth International. The basis of that split was the group's rejection of Trotsky's definition of the USSR as a degenerated workers state. The *Socialisme ou Barbarie* group, whose leading theoreticians were Cornelius Castoriadis and Claude Lefort, developed the position that the bureaucracy was not a parasitic social stratum, but a new exploiting social class. Lyotard remained in this group until the mid-1960s, by which time he had broken completely with Marxism.

Lyotard is principally identified with the repudiation of the "grand narratives" of human emancipation, whose legitimacy, he claims, had been refuted by the events of the twentieth century. He argues that

> the very basis of each of the great narratives of emancipation has, so to speak, been invalidated over the last fifty years. All that is real is rational, all that is rational is real: "Auschwitz" refutes speculative doctrine. At least that crime, which was real, was not rational. All

---

[7] Hayden V. White, *The Content of the Form: Narrative Discourse and Historical Representation* (Baltimore: Johns Hopkins University Press, 1990), p. 63.

that is proletarian is communist, all that is communist is proletarian: "Berlin 1953, Budapest 1956, Czechoslovakia 1968, Poland 1980" (to mention only the most obvious examples) refute the doctrine of historical materialism: the workers rise up against the Party. All that is democratic exists through and for the people, and vice versa: "May 1968" refutes the doctrine of parliamentary liberalism. If left to themselves, the laws of supply and demand will result in universal prosperity, and vice versa: "The crises of 1911 and 1929" refute the doctrine of economic liberalism. [8]

The combination of disorientation, demoralization, pessimism and confusion that underlies the entire theoretical project of Lyotard's postmodernism is summed up in this passage. The argument that Auschwitz refutes all attempts at a scientific understanding of history is by no means original to Lyotard. A similar idea forms the basis of the post-World War II writings of Adorno and Horkheimer, the fathers of the Frankfurt School. Lyotard's declaration that Auschwitz was both real and irrational is a simplistic distortion of Hegel's dialectical revolutionary conception. Lyotard's supposed refutation is based on a vulgar identification of the *real*, as a philosophical concept, with what at any given moment exists. But as Engels explained, reality, as understood by Hegel, is "in no way an attribute predictable of any given state of affairs, social or political, in all circumstances and at all times."[9] That which exists can be so utterly in conflict with the development of human society as to be socially and historically irrational, and therefore unreal, unviable and doomed. In this profound sense, German imperialism — out of which Nazism and Auschwitz arose — demonstrated the truth of Hegel's philosophical dictum.

The working class uprisings against Stalinism did not refute historical materialism. Rather, they refuted the politics of *Socialisme ou Barbarie* which Lyotard had espoused. Trotsky had predicted such uprisings. The *Socialisme ou Barbarie* group had attributed to the Stalinist bureaucracies a degree of power and stability that they, as a parasitic caste, lacked. Moreover, Lyotard implies an identity between communism as a revolutionary movement and the Communist parties, which were, in fact, the political organizations of the Stalinist bureaucracies.

---

[8] Quoted in Simon Malpas, *Jean-François Lyotard* (London and New York: Routledge, 2003), pp. 75–76.

[9] Karl Marx and Frederick Engels, *Collected Works*, Volume 26 (Moscow: Progress Publishers, 1990), p. 358.

As for the refutation of economic and parliamentary liberalism, this was accomplished by Marxists long before the events cited by Lyotard. His reference to May 1968 as the downfall of parliamentary liberalism is particularly grotesque. What about the Spanish Civil War? The collapse of the Weimar Republic? The betrayal of the French Popular Front? All these events occurred more than thirty years before May–June 1968. What Lyotard presents as great philosophical innovations are little more than the expression of the pessimism and cynicism of the disappointed ex-left (or rightward-moving) academic petty bourgeoisie.

Richard Rorty

Richard Rorty is unabashed in connecting his rejection of the concept of objective truth with the repudiation of revolutionary socialist politics. For Rorty, the collapse of the Stalinist regimes in eastern Europe and the dissolution of the Soviet Union provided leftish intellectuals with the long-awaited opportunity to renounce, for once and for all, any sort of intellectual (or even emotional) commitment to a revolutionary socialist perspective. In his essay "The End of Leninism, Havel and Social Hope," Rorty declared:

> I hope that intellectuals will use the death of Leninism as an occasion to rid themselves of the idea that they know, or ought to know, something about deep, underlying forces — forces that determine the fates of human communities.
>
> We intellectuals have been making claims to such knowledge ever since we set up shop. Once we claimed to know that justice could not reign until kings became philosophers or philosophers kings; we claimed to know this on the basis of a searching inspection of the human soul. More recently, we claimed to know that it will not reign until capitalism is overthrown and culture decommodified; we claimed to know this on the basis of a grasp of the shape and movement of History. I would hope that we have reached a time at which we can finally get rid of the conviction common to Plato and Marx that there *must* be large theoretical ways of finding out how to end injustice, as opposed to small experimental ways.[10]

---

[10] Richard Rorty, *Truth and Progress* (Cambridge: Cambridge University Press, 1998) p. 228.

What would follow from such a theoretical renunciation? Rorty offers his proposals for the reorientation of "left" politics:

> I think the time has come to drop the terms "capitalism" and "socialism" from the political vocabulary of the Left. It would be a good idea to stop talking about "the anticapitalist struggle" and to substitute something banal and untheoretical — something like "the struggle against avoidable human misery." More generally, I hope that we can banalize the entire vocabulary of leftist political deliberation. I suggest we start talking about greed and selfishness rather than about bourgeois ideology, about starvation wages and layoffs rather than about the commodification of labor, and about differential per-pupil expenditure on schools and differential access to health care rather than about the division of society into classes.[11]

And this is to be taken seriously as political philosophy? What Rorty calls "banalization" would be better described as intellectual and political castration. He proposes to banish from discussion the achievements of more than 200 years of theoretical thought. Underlying this proposal is the conception that the development of thought is an arbitrary subjective process. Words, theoretical concepts, logical categories and philosophical systems are merely verbal constructs, pragmatically conjured up in the interest of various subjective ends. The claim that the development of theoretical thought is an objective process, expressing man's evolving, deepening, and ever more complex and precise understanding of nature and society is, as far as Rorty is concerned, nothing more than a Hegelian-Marxian shibboleth. As he asserts in another passage, "There is no activity called 'knowing' which has a nature to be discovered, and at which natural scientists are particularly skilled. There is simply the process of justifying beliefs to audiences."[12]

And so, terms such as "capitalism," "working class," "socialist," "surplus value," "wage-labor," "exploitation" and "imperialism" are not concepts which express and denote an objective reality. Rorty suggests that we talk about "the struggle against avoidable human misery." Let us, for a moment, accept this brilliant suggestion. But we are almost immediately confronted with a

---

[11] Ibid, p. 229.

[12] Richard Rorty, *Philosophy and Social Hope* (London and New York: Penguin, 1999), p. 36.

problem. How is one to define misery? How should we determine what form of human misery is avoidable? On what basis are we to claim that misery is avoidable, or even that it should be avoided? What response should be given to those who argue that misery is man's lot, the consequence of the fall from grace? And even if we somehow evade the arguments of theologians, and conceive of misery in secular terms, as a socioeconomic problem, we would still confront the problem of analyzing the causes of misery.

Therefore, a program for abolishing "avoidable human misery" would be compelled to analyze the economic structure of society. To the extent that such an investigation was carried out with any notable degree of honesty, the crusaders against "avoidable human misery" would encounter the phenomena and relations of "ownership," "property," "profit" and "class." They could use euphemisms to describe these social phenomena, but that would not negate their objective existence.

Rorty's theoretical conceptions abound with the most blatant inconsistencies and contradictions. He categorically insists that there is no "truth" to be discovered and known. Presumably, he holds his discovery of the non-existence of truth to be "true," as it forms the foundation of his philosophy. But if he is asked to explain this gross inconsistency, Rorty evades the problem by proclaiming that he will not submit to the terms of the question, which is rooted in traditional philosophical discourse, dating all the way back to Plato. Truth, Rorty insists, is one of those old issues which are now out of date and about which one simply cannot have an interesting philosophical discussion. When the issue arises, Rorty, as he has noted rather cynically, "would simply like to change the subject."[13]

The key to an understanding of the philosophical conceptions of Rorty is to be found in his political positions. While Rorty has sought on various occasions to downplay the link between philosophy and politics, it would be hard to find another contemporary philosopher whose theoretical conceptions are so directly embedded in a political position — that is, in his rejection of and opposition to Marxist revolutionary politics. Rorty does not attempt a systematic analysis and refutation of Marxism. The socialist project (which Rorty largely identifies with the fate of the Soviet Union) failed, and there is, as far as Rorty is concerned, little hope for it to be successful in the future. From the wreckage of the Old Marxian Left, there is nothing to be salvaged. Rather than engaging in new doctrinal struggles over history,

---

[13] Cited in Jenkins, p. 105.

principles, programs, and, worst of all, objective truth, it is better to retreat to a much more modest politics of the lowest common denominator. This is what Rorty's philosophy — and, indeed, much of American academic post-modernist discourse — is really all about.

For Rorty (and, as we shall see, so many others) the "events of 1989 have convinced those who were still trying to hold on to Marxism that we need a way of holding our time in thought, and a plan for making the future better than the present, which drops reference to capitalism, bourgeois ways of life, bourgeois ideology, and the working class."[14] The time has come, he argues, to

> stop using "History" as the name of an object around which to weave our fantasies of diminished misery. We should con-cede Francis Fukuyama's point (in his celebrated essay, *The End of History*) that if you still long for total revolution, for the Radically Other on a world-historical scale, the events of 1989 show that you are out of luck.[15]

The impact of 1989

This sort of cynical irony is expressive of the prostration and demoraliza-tion that swept over the milieu of left academics and radicals in the face of the political reaction that followed the collapse of the Stalinist regimes. Rather than attempting a serious analysis of the historical, political, economic and social roots of the break-up of the Stalinist regimes, these tendencies quickly adapted themselves to the prevailing climate of reaction, confusion and pessimism.

Explaining the political capitulation to the wave of Stalinist and fascist reaction during the 1930s, Trotsky observed that force not only conquers, it also convinces. The sudden collapse of the Stalinist regimes, which came as a complete surprise to so many radicals and left-inclined intellectuals, left them theoretically, politically and even morally disarmed before the onslaught of bourgeois and imperialist triumphalism that followed the dismantling of the Berlin Wall. The myriad tendencies of petty-bourgeois left politics were bewildered by the sudden disappearance of the bureaucratic regimes, and sub-sequently claimed that their demise represented the failure of Marxism.

---

[14] *Truth and Progress*, p. 233.
[15] Ibid., p. 229.

There was, aside from cowardice, a substantial degree of intellectual dishonesty involved in their claims that Marxism had been discredited by the dissolution of the USSR. Professor Bryan Turner wrote, for example, that "the authority of Marxist theory has been severely challenged, not least for the failure of Marxism to anticipate the total collapse of east European communism and the Soviet Union."[16] Such statements cannot be explained by ignorance. The left academics who wrote this and similar statements were not completely unaware of the Trotskyist analysis of the nature of the Stalinist regime, which warned that the policies of the bureaucracy would lead ultimately to the collapse of the Soviet Union.

The International Committee published many statements that foresaw the catastrophic trajectory of Stalinism. Prior to the demise of the USSR, the petty-bourgeois radicals considered such warnings nothing less than sectarian lunacy. After the collapse of the Soviet Union, they found it easier to blame Marxism for the failure of "real existing socialism" than to undertake a critical examination of their own political outlook. Angry and disappointed, they now looked upon their political, intellectual and emotional commitment to socialism as a bad investment that they deeply regretted. Their outlook has been summed up by the historian Eric Hobsbawm, long-time member of the British Communist Party who served for decades as an apologist for Stalinism. He has written in his autobiography:

> Communism is now dead. The USSR and most of the states and
> societies built on its model, children of the October Revolution
> of 1917 which inspired us, have collapsed so completely, leaving
> behind a landscape of material and moral ruin, that it must now be
> obvious that failure was built into this enterprise from the start.[17]

Hobsbawm's claim that the October Revolution was a doomed enterprise is a capitulation to the arguments of the unabashed right-wing opponents of socialism. The ideologists of bourgeois reaction assert that the collapse of the USSR is irrefutable proof that socialism is an insane utopian vision.

Robert Conquest, in his inquisitorial *Reflections on a Ravaged Century,* condemns "the archaic idea that utopia can be constructed on earth" and "the

---

[16] Bryan S. Turner, Preface, *Max Weber and Karl Marx,* by Karl Löwith (New York and London: Routledge, 1993), p. 5.

[17] E.J. Hobsbawm, *Interesting Times: A Twentieth-Century Life* (New York: Pantheon Books, 2002), p. 127.

offer of a millenarian solution to all human problems."[18] The Polish-American historian Andrzej Walicki has proclaimed that "The fate of communism world-wide indicates ... that the vision itself was inherently unrealizable. Hence, the enormous energy put into its implementation was doomed to be wasted."[19] The recently deceased American historian, Martin Malia, elaborated upon this theme in his 1994 book, *The Soviet Tragedy*, in which he declared that "...the failure of integral socialism stems not from its having been tried out first in the wrong place, Russia, but from the socialist idea per se. And the reason for this failure is that socialism as full noncapitalism is intrinsically impossible."[20]

Richard Pipes and property

An explanation of why socialism is "intrinsically impossible" is to be found in a book by the dean of American anti-Marxist Cold War historians, Richard Pipes of Harvard University. In a book entitled *Property and Freedom*, Pipes establishes a zoological foundation for his theory of property:

> One of the constants of human nature, impervious to legislative and pedagogic manipulation, is acquisitiveness. ... Acquisitiveness is common to all living things, being universal among animals and children as well as adults at every level of civilization, for which reason it is not a proper subject of moralizing. On the most elementary level, it is an expression of the instinct of survival. But beyond this, it constitutes a basic trait of the human personality, for which achievements and acquisitions are means of self-fulfillment. And inasmuch as fulfillment of the self is the essence of liberty, liberty cannot flourish when property and the inequality to which it gives rise are forcibly eliminated.[21]

The forms of property and their legal conceptualization have evolved historically. The exclusive identification of property with personal ownership dates back only to the seventeenth century. In earlier historical periods,

[18] Robert Conquest, *Reflections on a Ravaged Century* (New York: Norton, 2000), p. 3.

[19] Andrzej Walicki, *Marxism and the Leap to the Kingdom of Freedom: The Rise and Fall of the Communist Utopia* (Stanford, California: Stanford University Press, 1995), p. 278.

[20] Martin E. Malia, *The Soviet Tragedy: A History of Socialism in Russia, 1917–1991* (New York: Free Press, 1994), p. 225.

[21] Richard Pipes, *Property and Freedom* (New York: Alfred A. Knopf, 1999), p. 286.

property was generally defined in a far broader and even communal sense. Pipes employs a definition of property that came into usage only when market relations became predominant in economic life. At that point, property came to be understood principally as the right of an individual "to exclude others from some use or enjoyment of something. ..."[22]

This form of property, whose prominent role is of relatively recent vintage among human beings, is — I think it's safe to say — more or less unknown in the rest of the animal kingdom! At any rate, for those of you who worry about what will become of your iPods, homes, cars and other treasured pieces of personal property under socialism, allow me to assure you that the form of property that socialism seeks to abolish is private ownership of the means of production.

The one positive feature of Professor Pipes' most recent works — those written in the aftermath of the dissolution of the Soviet Union — is that the connection between his earlier tendentious volumes on Soviet history and his right-wing political agenda is made explicit. For Pipes, the October Revolution and the creation of the Soviet Union represented an assault on the prerogatives of ownership and property. It was the apex of a worldwide and mass movement for social equality, the terrible fruit of the ideals of the Enlightenment. But that chapter of history has now come to an end.

"The rights of ownership," Pipes proclaims, "need to be restored to their proper place in the scale of values instead of being sacrificed to the unattainable ideal of social equality and all-embracing economic security."[23] What would the restoration of property rights demanded by Pipes entail?

> The entire concept of the welfare state as it has evolved in the second half of the twentieth century is incompatible with individual liberty ... Abolishing welfare with its sundry "entitlements" and spurious "rights" and returning the responsibilities for social assistance to the family or private charity, which shouldered them prior to the twentieth century, would go a long way toward resolving this predicament.[24]

For the ruling elites, the end of the Soviet Union is seen as the beginning of a global restoration of the capitalist *ancien regime*, the reestablishment of a

---

[22] C.B. Macpherson, *The Rise and Fall of Economic Justice and Other Essays* (Oxford: Oxford University Press, 1987), p. 77.

[23] *Property and Freedom*, p. 287.

[24] Ibid. p. 284

social order in which all restraints on the rights of property, the exploitation of labor, and the accumulation of personal wealth are removed. It is by no means a coincidence that during the nearly fifteen years that have followed the dissolution of the Soviet Union, there has been a staggering growth in social inequality and in the scale of wealth concentration within the richest 1 percent (and especially the top 0.1 percent) of the world's population. The world-wide assault on Marxism and socialism is, in essence, the ideological reflection of this reactionary and historically retrograde social process.

The demoralization of the middle class intellectuals

This process finds expression not only in the anti-Marxist diatribes of the extreme right. The intellectual decomposition of bourgeois society is also manifested in the demoralized capitulation of the remnants of the petty-bourgeois left to the ideological offensive of the extreme right. The bookstores of the world are well stocked with volumes produced by mournful ex-radicals, proclaiming to one and all the shipwreck of their hopes and dreams. They seem to derive perverse satisfaction from proclaiming their despair, discouragement and impotence to all who will listen. Of course, they do not hold themselves responsible for their failures. No, they were the victims of Marxism, which promised them a socialist revolution and then failed to deliver.

Their memoirs of confession are not only pathetic, but also somewhat comical. Attempting to invest their personal catastrophes with a sort of world-historical significance, they wind up making themselves look ridiculous. For example, Professor Ronald Aronson, a philosopher manqué, begins his volume *After Marxism* with the following existential dirge:

> Marxism is over, and we are on our own. Until recently, for so many on the Left, being on our own has been an unthinkable affliction — an utter loss of bearings, an orphan's state. ... As Marxism's last generation, we have been assigned by history the unenviable task of burying it.[25]

A theme common to so many of these would-be undertakers is that the dissolution of the Soviet Union shattered not only their political but

---

[25] Ronald Aronson, *After Marxism* (New York: Guilford Press, 1995), p. 1.

also their emotional equilibrium. Whatever their political criticisms of the Kremlin bureaucracy, they never imagined that its policies would lead to the destruction of the USSR — that is, they never accepted Trotsky's analysis of Stalinism as counterrevolutionary. Thus, Aronson confesses:

> The very immobility and ponderousness of the Soviet Union counted for something positive in our collective psychic space, allowing us to keep hope alive that a successful socialism might still emerge. It provided a backdrop against which alternatives could be thought about and discussed, including, for some, the hope that other versions of Marxism remained viable. But now, no longer. Try as we may to rescue its theoretical possibility from Communism's demise, the great world-historical project of struggle and transformation identified with the name of Karl Marx seems to have ended. And, as the postmodernists know, an entire world view has crashed along with Marxism. Not only Marxists and socialists, but other radicals, as well as those regarding themselves as progressives and liberals, have lost their sense of direction.[26]

Unintentionally, Aronson reveals the dirty little secret of so much of post-war radical politics — that is, the depth of its dependence upon the Stalinist and reformist labor bureaucracies. This dependence had a concrete social basis in the class and political relationships of the post-World War II era. In seeking to redress the political and social grievances of their own class milieu, significant sections of the petty bourgeoisie relied upon the resources commanded by the powerful labor bureaucracies. As part of, or in alliance with, these bureaucracies, the disgruntled middle class radicals could shake their fists at the ruling class and extract concessions. The collapse of the Soviet regime, followed almost immediately by the disintegration of reformist labor organizations all over the world, deprived the radicals of the bureaucratic patronage upon which they relied. Suddenly, these unhappy Willy Lomans of radical politics were on their own.

It is more or less taken for granted among these tendencies that the historical role assigned by classical Marxism to the working class was a fatal error. At most, they may be prepared to accept that there was once, at some point

---

[26] Ibid., pp. vii–viii.

safely in the past, a time when it might have been justified. But certainly not now. Aronson declares:

> There is in fact much evidence in support of the argument that the Marxian project is over, because of structural transformations in capitalism and even in the working class itself. The centrality of Marxism's cardinal category, labor, has been placed in question by capitalism's own evolution, as has the primacy of class.[27]

This is written at a time when the exploitation of the working class proceeds on a world scale at a level that neither Marx nor Engels could have imagined. The process of extracting surplus value from human labor-power has been vastly intensified by the revolution in information and communication technology. Labor continues to occupy the decisive role in the capitalist mode of production. The relentless and increasingly brutal drive to lower wages, slash and eliminate social benefits, and rationalize production proceeds ferociously.

Utopian myths and irrationalism

"There are none so blind as those who would not see." If there exists no real social force capable of waging a revolutionary struggle against capitalism, how can one even conceptualize an alternative to the existing order? This dilemma underlies another form of contemporary political pessimism, neo-Utopianism. Seeking to revive the pre-Marxian and utopian stages of socialist thought, the neo-Utopians lament and denounce the efforts of Marx and Engels to place socialism on a scientific basis.

For the neo-Utopians, classical Marxism absorbed too much of the nineteenth century's preoccupation with the discovery of objective forces. This outlook underlay the socialist movement's preoccupation with the working class and its political education. The Marxists, claim the neo-Utopians, placed exaggerated and unwarranted confidence in the objective force of capitalist contradictions, not to mention the revolutionary potential of the working class. Moreover, they failed to appreciate the power and persuasive force of the irrational.

---

[27] Ibid., p. 56.

The way out of this dilemma, claim the neo-Utopians, is by embracing and propagating "myths" that can inspire and excite. Whether or not such myths correspond to any objective reality is of no real importance. A leading exponent of neo-Utopian mythologizing, Vincent Geoghegan, criticizes Marx and Engels for having "failed to develop a psychology. They left a very poor legacy on the complexities of human motivation and most of their immediate successors felt little need to overcome this deficiency."[28] Unlike the socialists, complains Geoghegan, it was the extreme right, especially the Nazis, who understood the power of myths and their imagery.

> It was the National Socialists who managed to create a vision of a thousand-year reich out of romantic conceptions of Teutonic Knights, Saxon kings, and the mysterious promptings of "the Blood." The left all too often abandoned the field, muttering about reaction appealing to reaction.[29]

This appeal to irrationalism, with its reactionary political implications, flows with a sort of perverse logic from the view that there exists no objective basis for socialist revolution. What cannot be found in the jeremiads about the failure of Marxism, of socialism and, of course, the working class, is any attempt to uncover, based on a precise study of events, of parties, and of programs, the causes for the victories and defeats of the revolutionary movement in the twentieth century. In its edition for the year 2000, which was devoted to the theme of utopianism, the *Socialist Register* informed us that it was necessary to add "a new conceptual layer to Marxism, a dimension formerly missing or undeveloped."[30] That is the last thing that is needed. What is required, rather, is the use of the dialectical and historical materialist method in the study and analysis of the twentieth century.

The record of the Fourth International

The International Committee of the Fourth International has never denied that the dissolution of the Soviet Union signified a major defeat for the working class. But that event, the product of decades of Stalinist betrayals,

---

[28] Vincent Geoghegan, *Utopianism and Marxism* (London, New York: Methuen, 1987), p. 68.

[29] Ibid., p. 72.

[30] Leo Panitch and Sam Gindin, "Transcending Pessimism: Rekindling Socialist Imagination," *Necessary and Unnecessary Utopias: Socialist Register 2000* (Suffolk: Merlin Press, 1999), p. 22.

did not invalidate either the Marxist method or the perspective of socialism. Neither the latter nor the former were in any way implicated in the collapse of the USSR. The Marxist opposition to the Stalinist bureaucracy emerged in 1923 with the formation of the Left Opposition. Trotsky's decision to found the Fourth International, together with his call for a political revolution within the Soviet Union, was based on his conclusion that the defense of the social gains of the October Revolution and the very survival of the USSR as a workers state depended upon the violent overthrow of the bureaucracy.

The International Committee emerged in 1953 out of the struggle within the Fourth International against the tendency, led by Ernest Mandel and Michel Pablo, which argued that the Soviet bureaucracy, in the aftermath of Stalin's death, was undergoing a process of political self-reform, a gradual return to the principles of Marxism and Bolshevism, which invalidated Trotsky's call for a political revolution.

The history of the Fourth International and the International Committee testifies to the political perspicacity of the analysis of Stalinism developed on the basis of the Marxist method. No one has demonstrated to us how Marxism has been refuted by the betrayals and crimes of the Stalinist bureaucracy. We are told by one representative of the leftish academic fraternity that:

> To argue that the collapse of organized communism as a political force and the destruction of state socialism as a form of society have no bearing on the intellectual credibility of Marxism would be rather like arguing that the discovery of the bones of Christ in an Israeli grave-yard, the abdication of the Pope, and the closure of Christendom would have no relevance to the intellectual coherence of Christian theology.[31]

This metaphor is poorly chosen, for the Marxist opponents of Stalinism, i.e., the Trotskyists, did not view the Kremlin as the Vatican of the socialist movement. The doctrine of Stalin's infallibility, if my memory serves me correctly, was never adhered to by the Fourth International — though the same cannot be said of the many left petty-bourgeois and radical opponents of the Trotskyist movement.

It is difficult to satisfy the skeptics. Even if Marxism cannot be held responsible for the crimes of Stalinism, they ask, does not the dissolution of

---

[31] Turner, in *Max Weber and Karl Marx*, p. 5. Since Mr. Turner wrote this passage, a sitting Pope — Benedict XVI — has abdicated, with little noticable effect, positive or negative, on the "intellectual coherence of Christian theology."

the Soviet Union testify to the failure of the revolutionary socialist project? What this question betrays is the absence of 1) a broad historical perspective, 2) knowledge of the contradictions and achievements of Soviet society, and 3) a theoretically-informed understanding of the international political context within which the Russian Revolution unfolded.

The Russian Revolution itself was but one episode in the transition from capitalism to socialism. What precedents do we have that might indicate the appropriate time frame for the completion of such a vast historical process? The social and political upheavals that accompanied the transition from an agricultural-feudal form of social organization to an industrial-capitalist society spanned several centuries. Though the dynamic of the modern world — with its complex economic, technological and social interconnectedness — excludes such a prolonged time frame in the transition from capitalism to socialism, the analysis of historical processes that involve the most fundamental, complex and far-reaching social and economic transformations demands a time frame substantially longer than that which can be used for the study of more conventional events.

Still, the lifespan of the USSR was not insignificant. When the Bolsheviks seized power in 1917, few observers outside Russia expected the new regime to survive even one month. The state that emerged from the October Revolution lasted seventy-four years, nearly three-quarters of a century. In the course of that time, the regime underwent a terrible political degeneration. But that degeneration, which culminated in the dissolution of the Soviet Union by Gorbachev and Yeltsin in December 1991, does not mean that the conquest of power by Lenin and Trotsky in October 1917 was a doomed and futile project. It violates historical law to deduce the final chapter of Soviet history directly, and without the necessary mediating processes, from the Bolshevik seizure of power. A serious study of the history of the USSR does not permit such a facile conflation of events. The outcome of Soviet history was not preordained. The development of the Soviet Union could have taken another direction. The mistakes and crimes of its political leadership, concentrated on defending the interests of the parasitic bureaucratic caste, played the decisive role in the ultimate destruction of the USSR.

The Soviet Union's dissolution in 1991 does not invalidate the historical significance of the Russian Revolution and its aftermath. It was the greatest event of the twentieth century, and among the very greatest of world history. Its impact on the lives of billions of people — including the American working class — was of an immensely progressive character. Our opposition

to Stalinism is not lessened by acknowledging the colossal social achievements of the Soviet Union. The country underwent, as a consequence of the
Revolution, an economic, social and cultural transformation unprecedented
in human history. Moreover, the impact of the October Revolution on the
consciousness of the oppressed masses throughout the world cannot be overstated. It set into motion all the revolutionary movements of the twentieth
century.

The Soviet Union was not, we emphasize, a socialist society. The level
of planning remained rudimentary. The program of building socialism in
one country initiated by Stalin and Bukharin in 1924 — a project that had
no foundation in Marxist theory — repudiated the international perspective
that inspired the October Revolution. Still, the Soviet Union represented the
birth of a new social formation, established on the basis of a working class
revolution. The potential of nationalized industry was clearly demonstrated.
The Soviet Union could not escape the legacy of Russian backwardness — not
to mention that of its Central Asian republics — but its advances in the
sphere of science, education, social welfare and the arts were real and substantial. If the Marxist-Trotskyist warnings of the catastrophic implications
of Stalinism seemed so implausible even to those on the left who were critical
of the Stalinist regime, it was because the achievements of Soviet society were
so substantial.

The place of the October Revolution in world history

The nature and significance of the October Revolution can be understood only if it is placed within the global political context within which it
emerged. If the October Revolution were merely a historical aberration, then
the same must of be said of the twentieth century as a whole. The legitimacy
of the October Revolution can be denied only if it can be plausibly claimed
that the Bolshevik seizure of power lacked a substantial foundation in the
deeper currents and contradictions of early twentieth century European and
international capitalism.

But this claim is refuted by the fact that the historical setting of the
Russian Revolution and the Bolshevik seizure of power was World War I.
The two events are inextricably linked, not merely in the sense that the
war weakened the tsarist regime and created the conditions for revolution.
The October Revolution was a different manifestation of the same crisis of
the international capitalist order out of which the war had emerged. The

contradictions of world imperialism brought the conflict between international economy and the capitalist nation-state system to the point of explosion in August 1914. The same contradictions underlay the eruption of the Russian Revolution. The leaders of bourgeois Europe had sought to resolve the chaos of world capitalism in one way. The leaders of the revolutionary working class, the Bolsheviks, attempted to find a way out of that same chaos in another.

In order to evade the historical and political implications of this deeper link between the world war and the Russian Revolution, academicians tend to emphasize the accidental and contingent aspects of the First World War. They argue that the war need not have broken out in August 1914, and that the crisis unleashed by the assassination of Archduke Franz Ferdinand in Sarajevo could have been settled peacefully. Two points must be made in response to those arguments.

First: while other solutions were conceivable, war was the resolution that was consciously and deliberately chosen by the governments of Austro-Hungary, Russia, Germany, France, and, finally, Great Britain. It is not necessarily the case that all these powers desired war, but in the end they all decided that war was preferable to a negotiated settlement that might require the surrender of one or another strategic interest. The leaders of bourgeois Europe continued the war even as the cost in human lives mounted into the millions. No serious negotiations to restore peace were conducted among the belligerent powers until the outbreak of social revolution, first in Russia and then in Germany, created a change in class relations that forced an end to the war.

The second point is that the outbreak of a disastrous world war had long been foreseen by the socialist leaders of the working class. As early as the 1880s, Engels had warned of a war in which the clash of industrialized capitalist powers would lay waste to much of Europe. A war, wrote Engels to Adolf Sorge in January 1888, "would mean devastation like that of the Thirty Years War. And it wouldn't be over quickly, despite the colossal military forces engaged. ... If the war were fought to a finish without internal disorder, the state of prostration would be unlike anything Europe has experienced in the past 200 years."[32]

A year later, in March 1889, Engels wrote to Lafargue that war is

---

[32] Karl Marx and Frederick Engels, *Collected Works*, Volume 48 (London: Lawrence and Wishart, 2001), p. 139.

the most terrible of eventualities ... there will be 10 to 15 million combatants, unparalleled devastation simply to keep them fed, universal and forcible suppression of our movement, a recrudescence of chauvinism in all countries and, ultimately, enfeeblement ten times worse than after 1815, a period of reaction based on the inanition of all the peoples by then bled white — and, withal, only a slender hope that the bitter war may result in revolution — it fills me with horror.[33]

For the next twenty-five years, the European socialist movement placed at the center of its political agitation the struggle against capitalist and imperialist militarism. The analysis of the link between capitalism, imperialism and militarism by the finest theoreticians of the socialist movement, and their innumerable warnings that an imperialist war was all but inevitable, refute the claim that the events of August 1914 were accidental, unforeseen and unrelated to the inescapable contradictions of the world capitalist order.

In March 1913, less than eighteen months before the outbreak of the world war, the following analysis was made of the implications of the crisis in the Balkans:

[T]he Balkan War has not only destroyed the old frontiers in the Balkans, and not only fanned to white heat the mutual hatred and envy between the Balkan states, it has also lastingly disturbed the equilibrium between the capitalist states of Europe.

... European equilibrium, which was highly unstable already, has now been completely upset. It is hard to foresee whether those in charge of Europe's fate will decide this time to carry matters to the limit and start an all-European war.[34]

The author of these lines was Leon Trotsky.

From the supposedly accidental and contingent character of World War I, the academic apologists of capitalism deduce the coincidental nature of every other unpleasant episode in the history of twentieth century capitalism: the Great Depression, the rise of fascism, and the outbreak of World

---

[33] Ibid., p. 283.

[34] Leon Trotsky, *The Balkan Wars, 1912–13* (New York: Monad Press, 1980), pp. 382–383.

War II. It was all a matter of misjudgments, unforeseeable accidents and various bad guys. As we have been told by the French historian, the late François Furet:

> A true understanding of our time is possible only when we free ourselves from the illusion of necessity: the only way to explain the twentieth century, to the extent an explanation is possible, is to reassert its unpredictable character...

Furet declares that "the history of the twentieth century, like that of the eighteenth and nineteenth, could have taken a different course: we need only imagine it without Lenin, Hitler, or Stalin."[35]

In a similar vein, Professor Henry Ashby Turner, Jr. of Yale University devoted an entire book to demonstrating that the coming to power of Hitler was largely the outcome of accidents. Yes, there were certain long-standing problems in German history, not to mention a few unfortunate events like the world war, the Versailles Peace and the world depression. But, far more importantly, "Luck — that most capricious of contingencies — was clearly on Hitler's side."[36] There were also "personal affinities and aversions, injured feelings, soured friendships, and desire for revenge" — all combining to influence German politics in unforeseeable ways. And yes, there was also "the chance encounter between Papen and Baron von Schröder at the Gentlemen's Club" that ultimately worked to Hitler's advantage.[37]

One wonders: if only von Papen had caught a cold and stayed in bed, rather than go to the Gentlemen's Club, the course of the twentieth century might have been changed! It is equally possible that we owe the entire development of modern physics to the glorious apple that just happened to fall on Newton's head.

If history is merely "a tale told by an idiot, full of sound and fury, signifying nothing," what is the point of studying it? The solution to the problems of the world in which we live — problems that threaten mankind with catastrophe — require not only an exhaustive factual knowledge of the history of the twentieth century, but also a thoughtful assimilation of the lessons of the

---

[35] François Furet, *The Passing of an Illusion: The Idea of Communism in the Twentieth Century* (Chicago: University of Chicago Press, 1999), p. 2.

[36] Henry Ashby Turner, *Hitler's Thirty Days to Power: January 1933* (Reading, Mass.: Addison-Wesley, 1996), p. 168.

[37] Ibid.

many tragic events through which the working class has passed during the past 100 years.

As the year 2000 approached, many volumes devoted to a study of the departing century were released onto the book market. One of the characterizations of the period that obtained a notable degree of popularity was that of the "short twentieth century." It was promoted particularly by Eric Hobsbawm, who argued that the characteristics that defined the century began with the outbreak of the World War in 1914 and ended with the demise of the USSR in 1991. Whatever Hobsbawm's intentions may have been, this approach tended to support the argument that the decisive events of the twentieth century were a surrealistic departure from normal history, rather than the outcome of objective social, economic and political contradictions created by capitalism.

Rejecting this definition, I think that the epoch would be far better characterized as the *unfinished century*. Of course, the calendar tells us that the twentieth century has run its course. But all the horrors that confronted the working class during the last century — war, fascism, even the possibility of the extinction of all human civilization — threaten us today. We are not speaking, in the manner of existentialists, of dangers and dilemmas that are immanent in the inescapable hopelessness of the human condition. No, we are dealing with the contradictions of the capitalist mode of production, with which the greatest revolutionary Marxists of the twentieth century — Lenin, Luxemburg and Trotsky — grappled at a far earlier stage of their development. What could not be solved in the last century must be solved in this one. Otherwise, there is a real danger that this century will be mankind's last. That is why the study of the history of the twentieth century and the assimilation of its lessons are a matter of life and death.

8

Lenin's Theory of Socialist Consciousness: The Origins of Bolshevism and *What Is To Be Done?*[1]

Today's lecture will be devoted to an analysis of one of the most important works of socialist political theory, Lenin's *What Is To Be Done?* Few works have been subjected to such a degree of misrepresentation and falsification. To the innumerable Lenin-haters of the bourgeois academy — some of whom professed until 1991 to admire Lenin — this is the book that is ultimately responsible for many, if not all, of the evils of the twentieth century. I intend to reply to these denunciations, and also explain why this work — written in 1902 for a small socialist movement in tsarist Russia — retains such an exceptional degree of theoretical and practical relevance for the socialist movement in the first decade of the twenty-first century.

Many years later, after the Bolshevik Party had come to power, Lenin wrote that Russia "achieved Marxism — the only correct revolutionary theory — virtually through the *agony* she experienced in half a century of unparalleled torment and sacrifice, of unparalleled revolutionary heroism,

---

[1] Lecture delivered August 15, 2005, at the summer school of the Socialist Equality Party (US) in Ann Arbor, Michigan.

incredible energy, devoted searching, study, practical trial, disappointment, verification, and comparison with European experience."[2]

That experience spanned nearly an entire century. Beginning in 1825, with the unsuccessful attempt by a group of high-ranking officers in the imperial army to overthrow the tsarist autocracy, a tradition of self-sacrifice, incorruptibility and fearless passion emerged within a small section of the Russian intelligentsia. It sought to transform the terrible and degrading reality of the poverty and social backwardness over which the brutal tsarist regime presided. In the course of the nineteenth century a revolutionary movement devoted to the overthrow of the autocratic regime, slowly took shape. In a very fine passage in his biography *The Young Trotsky*, Max Eastman (in what were still his socialist years) gave us this description of the Russian revolutionary personality:

> A wonderful generation of men and women was born to fulfill this revolution in Russia. You may be traveling in any remote part of that country, and you will see some quiet, strong, thoughtful face in your coach or omnibus — a middle-aged man with white, philosophic forehead and soft brown beard, or an elderly woman with sharply arching eyebrows and a stern motherliness about her mouth, or perhaps a middle-aged man, or a younger woman who is still sensuously beautiful, but carries herself as though she had walked up to a cannon — you will inquire, and you will find out that they are the "old party workers." Reared in the tradition of the Terrorist movement, a stern and sublime heritage of martyr-faith, taught in infancy to love mankind, and to think without sentimentality, and to be masters of themselves, and to admit death into their company, they learned in youth a new thing — to think practically. And they were tempered in the fires of gaol and exile. They became almost a noble order, a selected stock of men and women who could be relied upon to be heroic, like the Knights of the Round Table or the Samurai, but with the patents of their nobility in the future, not the past.[3]

---

[2] V.I. Lenin, *Collected Works*, Volume 31 (Moscow: Progress Publishers, 1966), pp. 25–26.
[3] Max Eastman, *The Young Trotsky* (London: New Park Publications, 1980), pp. 53–54.

The Russian revolutionary movement did not, in its initial stages, direct itself to the working class. Rather, it was oriented to the peasantry, of which the overwhelming majority of the population was comprised. The formal liberation of the peasants from serfdom, proclaimed by Tsar Alexander II in 1861, intensified the contradictions of the socio-political structure of the Russian Empire. The 1870s saw the beginning of a movement of student youth, who went out among the peasants to educate and draw them into conscious political activity. The major political influence in these movements came from the theorists of anarchism, principally Lavrov and Bakunin. The latter envisaged the revolutionary transformation of Russia emerging out of an uprising of the peasant masses. The combination of peasant indifference and state repression drove the movement to adopt conspiratorial and terrorist methods of struggle. The most significant of the terrorist organizations was *Narodnaia Volya*, the People's Will.

G.V. Plekhanov: The father of Russian Marxism

The theoretical and political foundations for the Marxist movement in Russia were laid in the 1880s in the struggle waged by G.V. Plekhanov (1856–1918) against populism and its terrorist orientation. Basic questions of historical perspective underlay the conflict between the populists and the new Marxist tendency. Was Russia's path to socialism to be realized through a peasant revolution, in which traditional communal forms of peasant property would provide the basis for socialism? Or would the overthrow of tsarism, the establishment of a democratic republic and the beginning of the transition to socialism follow the development of Russian capitalism and the emergence of a modern industrial proletariat?

In arguing against terrorism and the populist characterization of the peasantry as the decisive revolutionary force, Plekhanov — who had himself been a leading member of the populist movement — insisted that Russia was developing along capitalist lines. He argued that the growth of an industrial proletariat would be an inevitable consequence of this process. Moreover, the new social class would be the decisive force in the overthrow of the autocracy, the democratization of Russia, the wiping away of all the political and economic remnants of feudalism, and the beginning of the transition to socialism.

Plekhanov's founding of the Emancipation of Labor Group in 1883, the year of Marx's death, required political foresight, not to mention intellectual and physical courage. The arguments advanced by Plekhanov against the

Russian populists of his day not only established the programmatic foundations upon which the Russian Social Democratic Labor Party would later be
based; Plekhanov also anticipated many of the critical issues of class orientation and revolutionary strategy that would continue to bedevil the socialist
movement throughout the twentieth century and, indeed, up to the present
day.

Today, Plekhanov is remembered principally — but without sufficient
appreciation — as one of the most important interpreters of Marxist philosophy in the era of the Second International (1889–1914). In this capacity, much of his work is subjected to generally ignorant criticism — especially
from those who claim that Plekhanov failed to appreciate the significance
of Hegel and the dialectical method. One can only wish, when reading
such polemical rants, that their authors would take the time to actually read
Plekhanov's works before proceeding to denounce them.[4]

There is another aspect of Plekhanov's contribution to revolutionary
strategy that is underestimated, if not ignored: his insistence on the development of the proletariat's independent political struggle against the bourgeoisie as a critical element in the formation of socialist consciousness.

In his early work, *Socialism and the Political Struggle*, written not long
after he had founded the Emancipation of Labor movement, Plekhanov
opposed the views of the Russian anarchists, who rejected the importance of
politics and went so far as to insist that the workers should not contaminate
themselves with political interests. Plekhanov noted that "not a single class
which has achieved political domination has had cause to regret its interest
in 'politics,' but on the contrary ... each of them attained the highest, the culminating point of its development only after it had acquired political domination ... we must admit that the political struggle is an instrument of social
reconstruction whose effectiveness is proved by history."

Plekhanov then traced the main stages in the development of class consciousness. A lengthy citation is justified by the enduring relevance of this
passage:

> Only gradually does the oppressed class become clear about
> the connection between its *economic* position and its *political*
> role in the state. For a long time it does not understand even its

---

[4] Among Plekhanov's most important works on Marxist philosophy are *The Development of
the Monist View of History, Essays on the History of Materialism, Materialism or Kantianism* and
For the Sixtieth Anniversary of Hegel's Death.

economic task to the full. The individuals composing it wage a hard struggle for their daily subsistence without even thinking which aspects of the social organisation they owe their wretched condition to. They try to avoid the blows aimed at them without asking where they come from or by whom, in the final analysis, they are aimed. As yet they have no class consciousness and there is no guiding idea in their struggle against individual oppressors. The oppressed class does not yet exist *for itself*; in time it *will be* the advanced class in society, but it is not yet *becoming* such. Facing the consciously organized power of the ruling class are separate individual strivings of isolated individuals or isolated groups of individuals. Even now, for example, we frequently enough meet a worker who hates the particularly intensive exploiter but does not yet suspect that the whole class of exploiters must be fought and the very possibility of exploitation of man by man removed.

Little by little, however, the process of generalisation takes effect, and the oppressed begin to be conscious of themselves as a class. But their understanding of the specific features of their class position still remains too one-sided: the springs and motive forces of the social mechanism as a whole are still hidden from their mind's eye. The class of exploiters appears to them as the simple sum of individual employers, not connected by the threads of political *organisation*. At this stage of development it is not yet clear in the minds of the oppressed ... what connection exists between "society" and "state." State power is presumed to stand above the antagonisms of the classes; its representatives appear to be the natural judges and conciliators of the hostile sides. The oppressed class has complete trust in them and is extremely surprised when its requests for help remain unanswered by them. ...

Only in the next and last stage of development does the oppressed class come to a thorough realisation of its position. It now realises the connection between society and state, and it does not appeal for the curbing of its exploiters to those who constitute the political organ of that exploitation. It knows that the state is a fortress serving as the bulwark and defence of its oppressors, a fortress which the oppressed can and must capture and reorganise for their own defence and which they cannot bypass, counting on its neutrality. ... For a long time they fight only for concessions, demand only such reforms as would give them not domination, but merely the possibility to develop and mature for future domination; reforms which would satisfy the most urgent and immediate of their demands and extend, if only slightly, the sphere of their influence over the country's social life. Only by going through the hard school of the struggle for separate little pieces of enemy territory does the oppressed class acquire the persistence, the daring, and the development necessary for the decisive battle. But once it has acquired those qualities it can look at its opponents as at a class finally condemned by history; it need have no doubt about its victory. What is called the revolution is only the last act in the long drama of revolutionary class struggle which becomes conscious only insofar as it becomes a *political* struggle.[5]

The struggle waged by Plekhanov defined the responsibilities of those who would call themselves socialists — *to concentrate all their efforts on the development of the political class consciousness of the working class and to prepare it for its historical role as the leader of the socialist revolution.* Implicit in this definition is the historical significance of the party itself, which is the instrument through which this consciousness is aroused and developed and organized on the basis of a definite political program.

The writings of Plekhanov threw the populists into crisis. By the late 1880s they were clearly on the defensive before the blows of the man they had just a decade earlier denounced as a renegade from the "people's" cause. The political bankruptcy of terrorism was becoming increasingly evident. Showing that the aim of terrorism was to frighten the tsarist regime and persuade it to change its ways, Plekhanov and the growing legion of Marxists dubbed the terrorists "liberals with bombs" — a description which is as apt today as it was a century ago. Plekhanov argued that terrorism shunned the difficult struggle to raise the consciousness of the working class. Instead, by attempting to electrify the masses with the avenging blows of heroic individuals, the terrorists served only to stupefy and demoralize them.

The pioneering work of Plekhanov influenced an entire generation of intellectuals and youth who entered into revolutionary struggle during the late 1880s and early 1890s. The impact of his polemics was all the greater as

---

[5] Georgi Plekhanov, *Selected Philosophical Works*, Volume 1 (Moscow: Progress Publishers, 1976), pp. 78–79.

the social transformations in the city and the countryside more and more corresponded to Plekhanov's analysis.

The emergence of Lenin

By the 1890s Russia was undergoing a rapid economic development, with the growth of industry producing an increasingly powerful working class. These were the conditions under which Vladimir Ilyich Ulyanov, the younger brother of a martyred revolutionary terrorist, entered into the revolutionary movement. In 1893 he established his reputation as a theoretician with a critique of the populist movement, which he entitled *What the "Friends of the People" Are and How They Fight the Social Democrats*. Ulyanov-Lenin devoted a large portion of his work to attacking what he termed the "subjective sociology" of Mikhailovsky, demonstrating that the politics of the Narodnik (populist) movement was not based on a scientific study of the social relations that existed in Russia. He showed that the Narodniks refused to confront the fact that commodity production had become highly developed, and that large-scale industry had been established and concentrated in the hands of individuals who bought and exploited the labor-power of a mass of workers who were without any property. But even more important than the economic analysis — which was much further developed in his next major work, *The Development of Capitalism in Russia* — was Lenin's characterization of the class nature of the Narodnik movement. He explained that the Narodniks, in essence, were petty-bourgeois democrats whose views reflected the social position of the peasantry.

While Lenin insisted on the importance of the democratic questions — i.e., those related to the abolition of the tsarist autocracy, the destruction of the remnants of feudalism in the countryside, the nationalization of the land — he held no less passionately that it was fundamentally wrong to ignore the distinction between the democratic and socialist movements. The greatest hindrance to the development of the class consciousness of the proletariat was the tendency to subordinate the proletariat to the bourgeois and petty-bourgeois democratic opponents of the autocracy.

In his attack upon the views of Mikhailovsky, Lenin argued that the so-called "socialism" of the petty-bourgeois democrat had nothing in common with the socialism of the proletariat. At best, the "socialism" of the petty bourgeoisie reflects its frustration in the face of the powerful growth of capital and its concentration in the hands of the magnates of banking and industry. Petty-bourgeois socialism is incapable of making a scientific and historical analysis of the development of capitalism. Such an analysis would demonstrate the hopeless position of the petty bourgeoisie itself, which, far from being a rising class, represented the surviving fragments of the economic past.

The conclusion that Lenin drew for the revolutionary socialist movement is that it must fight against the influence of petty-bourgeois democratic ideology within the workers movement. It had to understand the difference between socialist and bourgeois-democratic demands. The abolition of the autocracy and the destruction of feudal estates, while historically progressive, did not secure the end of the exploitation of the working class. In fact, the outcome of the realization of these demands would, in itself, facilitate the development of capitalism and the intensified exploitation of wage-labor. This did not mean that the working class should not support the democratic struggle. Quite the opposite: the working class must be in the vanguard of the democratic struggle. But under no conditions should it wage that struggle under the banner of the bourgeoisie or petty bourgeoisie. Rather, it must wage the struggle for democracy only in order to facilitate the struggle against the bourgeoisie itself.

Lenin denounced the "amalgamators" and "alliance advocates" who proposed that the workers should, in the name of fighting against tsarism, play down their independent class aims and, without concerning themselves with programmatic issues, form alliances with all the political opponents of the regime. Marxists advanced the democratic struggle not by adapting to the liberals and petty-bourgeois democrats, but by organizing the workers into an independent political party of their own, based on a revolutionary socialist program. Summing up the nature of Russian populism, Lenin wrote:

> If you refuse to believe the flowery talk about the "interests of the people" and try to delve deeper, you will find that you are dealing with the out-and-out ideologists of the petty bourgeoisie...[6]

In bringing his work to a conclusion, Lenin stressed that the work of the revolutionary party had to be directed toward making the worker understand the political and economic structure of the system that oppressed him, and the necessity and inevitability of class antagonisms under this system.

> When its advanced representatives have mastered the ideas of scientific socialism, the idea of the historical role of the Russian

---

[6] V.I. Lenin, *Collected Works*, Volume 1 (Moscow, Progress Publishers, 1963), p. 295–296.

worker, when these ideas become widespread, and when stable organisations are formed among the workers to transform the workers' present sporadic economic war into conscious class struggle — then the Russian WORKER, rising at the head of all the democratic elements, will overthrow absolutism and lead the RUSSIAN PROLETARIAT (side by side with the proletariat of ALL COUNTRIES) *along the straight road of open political struggle to* THE VICTORIOUS COMMUNIST REVOLUTION.[7]

In this seminal work, Lenin developed the conceptions that were to guide the construction of the Bolshevik Party. He did not invent the concept of the party or of the independent political organization of the working class. But he endowed these concepts with a political concreteness of unequalled intensity. He was convinced that the political organization of the working class required an intense struggle against theories and programs which reflected the political interests of the bourgeoisie. In 1900, in his article, "The Urgent Tasks of Our Movement," Lenin wrote:

Social-Democracy is the combination of the working-class movement and socialism. Its task is not to serve the working-class movement passively at each of its separate stages, but to represent the interests of the movement as a whole, to point out to this movement its ultimate aim and its political tasks, and to safeguard its political and ideological independence. Isolated from Social-Democracy, the working-class movement becomes petty and inevitably becomes bourgeois. In waging only the economic struggle, the working class loses its political independence; it becomes the tail of other parties and betrays the great principle: "The emancipation of the working classes must be conquered by the working classes themselves." In every country there has been a period in which the working-class movement existed apart from socialism, each going its own way; and in every country this isolation has weakened both socialism and the working-class movement. Only the fusion of socialism with the working-class-movement has in all countries created a durable basis for both.[8]

---

[7] Ibid., p. 300.

[8] V.I. Lenin, *Collected Works*, Volume 4 (Moscow: Progress Publishers, 1964), p. 368.

The fight against Economism

A new tendency had emerged inside Russian Social Democracy, known as Economism, whose existence was bound up with the growth of Bernsteinite revisionism in Germany. The Economists belittled the revolutionary political struggle. Adapting themselves to the spontaneous working class movement in the mid-1890s, they proposed that the social democratic movement concentrate on the development of strike struggles and other aspects of the economic struggle of the working class. The implication of this outlook was that the labor movement should renounce its revolutionary socialist aims. Pride of place in the political struggle against the autocracy was to be conceded to the liberal democratic bourgeois opposition. The independent revolutionary program that had been proclaimed by Plekhanov and Lenin was to be abandoned in favor of trade union activity aimed at improving the economic conditions of the working class within the framework of capitalist society. Or, as E.D. Kuskova proposed in the *Credo* published in 1899:

> Intolerant Marxism, negative Marxism, primitive Marxism (which holds to too schematic a concept of the class division of society) will give way to democratic Marxism, and the social position of the party in the midst of contemporary society will have to change drastically. The party will *recognise* society: its narrow corporative and, in the majority of cases, sectarian tasks will broaden into social tasks and its striving to seize power will be transformed into a desire for change, for the reform of contemporary society along democratic lines that are adapted to the present state of affairs, with the object of protecting, in the most complete and effective way, (all) the rights of the labouring classes.[9]

That was not all: the *Credo* declared that "Talk of an independent workers' political party is nothing but the result of transplanting alien aims and alien achievements on to our soil."[10]

---

[9] Neil Harding, ed., *Marxism in Russia, Key Documents, 1879–1906*, (Cambridge: Cambridge University Press, 1983), p. 251.

[10] Ibid., p. 252.

Economism was an international phenomenon: under conditions in which Marxism had become the dominant political and ideological force in the labor movement of Western Europe, there developed within that labor movement what amounted to a bourgeois opposition to Marxism. The growth of revisionism reflected the attempt by the petty-bourgeois ideologists of capitalism to counteract and undermine the expansion of Marxist influence inside the workers movement. By 1899, the implications of this revisionism had become fairly clear, when the French socialist Millerand entered a bourgeois government.

The eruption of opportunism provoked a crisis inside international social democracy. The first to come out against it was Plekhanov. Later, Rosa Luxemburg contributed to the struggle with her magnificent pamphlet, *Reform or Revolution?* Reluctantly, the German social democrats were drawn into the fray. But nowhere was the struggle against opportunism so fully developed as it was in Russia under the leadership of Lenin.

At the turn of the twentieth century, the Russian socialist movement was not a unified political organization. There were numerous tendencies and groups which identified themselves as socialist, even Marxist, but they conducted their political and practical work on a local basis, or as the representative of a specific ethnic or religious group within the working class. The Jewish Bund was the most famous of the latter type of organization.

As the Russian workers movement gathered strength in the second half of the 1890s, the need for programmatic and organizational coherence became evident and urgent. The first attempt to hold a congress of all Russian social democrats, in Minsk in 1898, was aborted as a result of police repression and the arrests of delegates. In the aftermath of this setback, plans for the convening of a congress were complicated by the increasingly heterogeneous character of the Russian socialist movement, of which the emergence of the Economist tendency was a significant expression.

Iskra

Although Plekhanov was still the revered theoretical leader of Russian socialism, Ulyanov-Lenin emerged as the major figure in the course of the preparatory work for the convening of a unifying congress of Russian social democrats. The basis of his influence was his leading role in the publication of the new political newspaper of the Russian Social Democratic Labor Party, *Iskra* (*The Spark*). Within the émigré movement and among Marxists engaged in practical revolutionary activity in Russia, *Iskra* gained stature as it provided theoretical, political and organizational coherence, on an all-Russia basis, for what would have remained, in its absence, a disparate movement.

The first issue of *Iskra* was published in December 1900. Lenin explained, in a major statement published on its front page:

> Our principal and fundamental task is to facilitate the political development and the political organisation of the working class. Those who push this task into the background, who refuse to subordinate to it all the special tasks and particular methods of struggle, are following a false path and causing serious harm to the movement.[11]

In words which remain, even after the passage of a century, relevant to contemporary conditions, Lenin harshly criticized those "who think it fit and proper to treat the workers to 'politics' only at exceptional moments in their lives, only on festive occasions…" Excoriating the representatives of the Economist tendency, for whom militant trade unionism and agitation over economic demands represented the alpha and omega of radical activity in the working class, Lenin insisted that the decisive task that confronted socialists was the political education of the working class and the formation of its independent socialist political party.

"Not a single class in history," Lenin wrote, "has achieved power without producing its political leaders, its prominent representatives able to organise a movement and lead it." In conclusion, Lenin proposed, somewhat laconically, "to devote a series of articles in forthcoming issues to questions of organisation, which are among the most burning problems confronting us."[12]

What Is To Be Done?

What emerged from this proposal was perhaps the most influential and controversial political tract of the twentieth century, Lenin's *What Is To Be Done?* Given the controversy provoked by this book, especially in the aftermath of the Bolshevik Revolution of 1917, it is a remarkable fact that *What Is To Be Done?*, when it was first published in 1902, was accepted by leading Russian social democrats — most importantly, by Plekhanov — as an authoritative

---

[11] V.I. Lenin, *Collected Works*, Volume 4, p. 369.

[12] Ibid., p. 370.

statement of party principles on questions of political tasks and organization. This is of some political significance, insofar as many of the denunciations of Lenin's pamphlet assert that *What Is To Be Done?* introduced a conspiratorial and totalitarian element into socialism that had no basis in classical Marxism.

Lenin's pamphlet begins by examining the demand raised by the Economist tendency — that is, the Russian followers of Eduard Bernstein — for "Freedom of Criticism." He places this slogan — which, at first hearing, seems eminently democratic and appealing — within the context of the dispute raging within the ranks of international Social Democracy between the defenders of orthodox Marxism and the revisionists, who had undertaken a systematic theoretical and political attack on that orthodoxy.

Noting that Bernstein's theoretical revisions of the programmatic foundations of the German Social Democratic Party found their political expression in the entrance of the French socialist Alexandre Millerand into the government of President Waldeck-Rousseau, Lenin states that the slogan "'freedom of criticism'"

> means freedom for an opportunist trend in Social-Democracy, freedom to convert Social-Democracy into a democratic party of reform, freedom to introduce bourgeois ideas and bourgeois elements into socialism.[13]

To this demand Lenin replies that no one denied the right of the revisionists to criticize. But Marxists, he insists, have no less right to reject their criticisms and to fight the attempt to convert revolutionary Social Democracy into a reformist movement.

After briefly reviewing the origins of the Economist tendency in Russia, Lenin notes its general indifference to theory. He states that the Economists' "much vaunted freedom of criticism does not imply substitution of one theory for another, but freedom from all integral and pondered theory; it implies eclecticism and lack of principle."[14] He observes that this indifference is justified by revisionists who quote, out of context, Marx's statement that the real practical advances of the socialist movement are more important than a dozen programs. "To repeat these words in a period of theoretical confusion," Lenin replies, "is like wishing mourners at a funeral many happy returns of the day."

---

[13] V.I. Lenin, *Collected Works*, Volume 5 (Moscow: Foreign Language Publishing House, 1961), p. 355.

[14] Ibid., p. 369.

He then declares, in words that cannot be quoted too frequently, "Without revolutionary theory there can be no revolutionary movement. This idea cannot be insisted upon too strongly at a time when the fashionable preaching of opportunism goes hand in hand with an infatuation for the narrowest forms of practical activity."[15] He argues that only *"a party that is guided by the most advanced theory"* will be able to provide the working class with revolutionary leadership, and recalls that Frederick Engels had recognized *"not two* forms of the great struggle of Social-Democracy (political and economic), as is the fashion among us, *but three, placing the theoretical struggle on a par with the first two."*[16] Lenin quotes Engels' statement that "Without German philosophy, which preceded it, particularly that of Hegel, German scientific socialism — the only scientific socialism that has ever existed — would never have come into being. Without a sense of theory among the workers, this scientific socialism would never have entered their flesh and blood as much as is the case."[17]

The second section of *What Is To Be Done?* is entitled "The Spontaneity of the Masses and the Consciousness of the Social Democrats." This is, undoubtedly, the most important section of Lenin's pamphlet, and, inevitably, the section that has been subjected to the most unrelenting attacks and misrepresentation. It is in this section, we have been frequently told, that Lenin exposes himself as an arrogant elitist, contemptuous of the mass of workers, disdainful of their aspirations, hostile to their daily struggles, lusting for personal power and dreaming only of the day when he and his accursed party will impose their iron-fisted totalitarian dictatorship over the unsuspecting Russian working class. It is worth our while to examine this section with special care.

The critical issue analyzed by Lenin is the nature of the relationship between Marxism and the revolutionary party on the one side and, on the other, the spontaneous movement of the working class and the forms of social consciousness that develop among workers in the course of that movement. He traces the evolution of the forms of consciousness among Russian workers, beginning with the initial manifestations of class conflict in the 1860s and 1870s.

Those struggles were of an extremely primitive character, involving the destruction of machinery by workers. Driven by desperation, lacking any awareness of the social and class nature of their revolt, these spontaneous

---

[15] Ibid.
[16] Ibid., p. 370.
[17] Ibid., p. 371.

eruptions manifested class consciousness only in an "embryonic" form. The situation that developed three decades later was significantly more advanced. Compared to the early struggles, the strikes of the 1890s manifested a significantly higher level of consciousness among the workers. The strikes were far more organized and even advanced quite detailed demands. But the consciousness exhibited by workers in these struggles was of a trade unionist rather than social democratic character. That is, the strikes did not raise demands of a political character, nor did they express an awareness of the deeper and irreconcilable nature of the conflict between the workers and the existing socioeconomic and political order. The workers, rather, sought only to improve their situation within the framework of the existing social system.

This limitation was inevitable, in the sense that the spontaneous movement of the working class could not develop on its own, "spontaneously," social democratic, i.e., revolutionary, consciousness. It is at this point that Lenin introduces the argument that has provoked so many denunciations. He writes:

> We have said that *there could not have been* Social-Democratic consciousness among the workers. It would have to be brought to them from without. The history of all countries shows that the working class, exclusively by its own effort, is able to develop only trade-union consciousness, i.e., the conviction that it is necessary to combine in unions, fight the employers, and strive to compel the government to pass necessary labour legislation, etc. The theory of socialism, however, grew out of the philosophic, historical, and economic theories elaborated by educated representatives of the propertied classes, by intellectuals. By their social status, the founders of modern scientific socialism, Marx and Engels, themselves belonged to the bourgeois intelligentsia. In the very same way, in Russia, the theoretical doctrine of Social-Democracy arose altogether independently of the spontaneous growth of the working-class movement; it arose as a natural and inevitable outcome of the development of thought among the revolutionary socialist intelligentsia.[18]

In support of his interpretation of the relationship between Marxism and the spontaneously developing trade unionist, i.e., bourgeois, consciousness

---

[18] Ibid., pp. 375–376.

of the working class, Lenin cites — along with approving comments by Karl Kautsky — the draft program of the Austrian Social Democratic Party:

> The more capitalist development increases the numbers of the proletariat, the more the proletariat is compelled and becomes fit to fight against capitalism. The proletariat becomes conscious of the possibility and of the necessity for socialism. In this connection socialist consciousness appears to be a necessary and direct result of the proletarian class struggle. But this is absolutely untrue. Of course, socialism, as a doctrine, has its roots in modern economic relationships just as the class struggle of the proletariat has, and, like the latter, emerges from the struggle against the capitalist-created poverty and misery of the masses. But socialism and the class struggle arise side by side and not one out of the other; each arises under different conditions. Modern socialist consciousness can arise only on the basis of profound scientific knowledge. Indeed, modern economic science is as much a condition for socialist production as, say, modern technology, and the proletariat can create neither the one nor the other, no matter how much it may desire to do so; both arise out of the modern social process. The vehicle of science is not the proletariat, but the *bourgeois intelligentsia* [K.K.'s italics]: it was in the minds of individual members of this stratum that modern socialism originated, and it was they who communicated it to the more intellectually developed proletarians who, in their turn, introduce it into the proletarian class struggle where conditions allow that to be done. Thus, socialist consciousness is something introduced into the proletarian class struggle from without [*von Aussen Hineingretagenes*] and not something that arose within it spontaneously [*urwuchsig*]. Accordingly, the old Hainfeld program quite rightly stated that the task of Social-Democracy is to imbue the proletariat [literally: saturate the proletariat] with the *consciousness* of its position and the consciousness of its task. There would be no need for this if consciousness arose of itself from the class struggle.[19]

Lenin draws from this passage the following conclusion:

---

[19] Ibid., pp. 384–385.

Since there can be no talk of an independent ideology formulated by the working masses themselves in the process of their movement, the *only* choice is — either bourgeois or socialist ideology. There is no middle course (for mankind has not created a "third" ideology, and, moreover, in a society torn by class antagonisms there can never be a non-class or above-class ideology). Hence, to belittle the socialist ideology *in any way, to turn aside from it in the slightest degree* means to strengthen bourgeois ideology. There is much talk of spontaneity. But the *spontaneous* development of the working-class movement leads to its subordination to bourgeois ideology, *to its development along the lines of the Credo programme*; for the spontaneous working-class movement is trade-unionism, is *Nur-Gewerkschaftlerei*, and trade-unionism means the ideological enslavement of the workers by the bourgeoisie. Hence, our task, the task of Social-Democracy, is *to combat spontaneity, to divert* the working-class from this spontaneous, trade-unionist striving to come under the wing of the bourgeoisie, and to bring it under the wing of revolutionary Social-Democracy.[20]

These passages have been denounced again and again as the quintessential expression of Bolshevik "elitism" wherein, moreover, lie the germs of its future totalitarian evolution.[21] In a book entitled *The Seeds of Evil*, Robin Blick refers to the last sentence quoted above (in which Lenin speaks of the "trade unionist striving to come under the wing of the bourgeoisie") as "an absolutely extraordinary formulation for someone usually so concerned to

---

[20] Ibid., pp. 384-385.

[21] In 2006, one year after this lecture was given, the independent scholar Lars Lih published an 867-page study and new translation of *What Is to Be Done?* Entitled *Lenin Rediscovered*, the book claims that the sections of *What Is To Be Done?* in which Lenin insists that socialist consciousness must be brought into the working class are "scandalous passages" which really do not belong in the book, and that their inclusion by Lenin was something of an accident. The passage that explains that socialist consciousness must be introduced into the working class, Lih informs us, "was a last-minute addition inspired by some remarks of Kautsky published after Lenin had already started serious work on *WITBD*." [*Lenin Rediscovered* (Boston: Brill, 2006), p. 655] Lih claims that Lenin included the passage only because he "sought for a place in his draft where he could invoke Kautsky's authority." [Ibid., p. 637] Anticipating the objections of those who would point out that the text of *What Is To Be Done?* does not support his eccentric thesis, Lih insists that "Lenin cannot be understood just by reading Lenin." [Ibid., p. 21] It is remarkable that Lih has written his massive door-stopper just to prove that the most important passages in *What Is To Be Done?* do not belong in Lenin's book!

be seen defending Marxist 'orthodoxy', and certainly equalling in its audacity any of the revisions of Marxism then being undertaken by the German Social-Democrat Eduard Bernstein ... what Marx and Engels never did was to expound in their writings a worked-out doctrine of political *élitism* and organisational manipulation."[22]

Kolakowski's attack on *What Is To Be Done?*

This argument is developed more substantially in the very well known work by the academic philosopher, Leszek Kolakowski, entitled *Main Currents of Marxism*, a three-volume work originally published in 1978. He dismisses as a "novelty" Lenin's assertion that the spontaneous workers movement cannot develop a socialist ideology, and that it must therefore have a bourgeois ideology. Even more disturbing, according to Kolakowski, is the inference that the workers movement must assume a bourgeois character if it is not led by a socialist party:

> This is supplemented by a second inference: the working-class movement in the true sense of the term, i.e. a political revolutionary movement, is defined not by being a movement of workers but by possessing the right ideology, i.e. the Marxist one, which is "proletarian" by definition. In other words, the class composition of a revolutionary party has no significance in determining its class character.[23]

Kolakowski continues with a few snide comments, mocking the claim that the party "knows what is in the 'historical' interest of the proletariat and what the latter's authentic consciousness ought to be at any particular moment, although its empirical consciousness will generally be found lagging behind."[24] Remarks of this sort are supposed by their author to be incredibly clever, exposing the absurd conceit of a small political party that its program articulates the interests of the working class, even if the mass of workers do not agree with, or even understand that program. But arguments of this sort

[22] Robin Blick, *The Seeds of Evil: Lenin and the Origins of Bolshevik Elitism* (London: Steyne Publications, 1995), p. 17.
[23] Leszek Kolakowski, *The Main Currents of Marxism,* Volume 2, "The Golden Age" (Oxford: Oxford University Press, 1978), pp. 389–390.
[24] Ibid., p. 390.

appear clever only as long as one does not bother to think too carefully about them.

If Kolakowski's argument is correct, what need is there for any political party, whether of the working class or, for that matter, the bourgeoisie? After all, is it not the case that all political parties and their leaders claim to speak in the name of and articulate the interests of broader social communities? If one takes the history of the bourgeoisie, its interests as a class have been identified, defined, and articulated by political parties — whose leaders were not infrequently compelled to work in opposition, as a small minority faction and even in illegality, until they won over their class, or at least the most critical elements within it, to the perspective and program for which they fought.

Puritanism existed as a religious-political tendency in England for a half-century before it emerged as the dominant tendency within the rising bourgeoisie and secured, under the leadership of Cromwell, the victory of the Revolution over the Stuart monarchy. One hundred and fifty years later, the Jacobin Party of politicized Rousseauists emerged out of the bitter factional fights within the bourgeoisie and petty bourgeoisie, between 1789 and 1792, as the leadership of the French Revolution. No less pertinent examples could be given from American history, from the pre-Revolutionary period up until the present time.

Policies which express the "objective" interests of a class — that is, which identify and programmatically formulate the means of establishing the conditions required for the advancement of the political, social and economic interests of a particular class — may not be recognized by a majority, or even any substantial section of a class at any given point. The abolition of slavery, as history was to conclusively demonstrate, led to the consolidation of the American national state and a vast acceleration of the industrial and economic growth of capitalism. And yet, the political vanguard of the fight against slavery, the abolitionists, were compelled to wage a bitter struggle that spanned decades against powerful resistance within the bourgeoisie of the Northern states, which opposed and feared a confrontation with the South. The small number of abolitionists understood far better than the vast majority of Northern businessmen, merchants, farmers, and, for that matter, urban workers what was in the best interests of the long-term development of the American national state and Northern capitalism. Of course, the abolitionists of the early nineteenth century did not explain their program and actions in such explicit class terms. But this does not change the fact that they expressed, in the language appropriate to their times, the interests of the rising Northern bourgeoisie as perceived by the most politically far-sighted sections of that class.

A more recent example of a political party defining and fighting for the objective interests of the bourgeoisie in opposition to large portions of that class is the Democratic Party under Roosevelt. He represented that faction within the American bourgeoisie — most definitely a minority — that became convinced that the salvation of capitalism in the United States was not possible without major social reforms, which entailed considerable concessions to the working class.

Let me also point out that the ruling elites employ the services of hundreds of thousands of specialists in politics, sociology, economics, international affairs, etc., to help them understand what their interests are. Even though it is, for reasons I will explain, far easier for the average bourgeois to perceive where his true interests lie than for the average worker, the formulation of ruling class policy can never be merely a direct reflection of what the "average" American businessman, or even the "average" multi-millionaire corporate executive, thinks.

Kolakowski's claim that Lenin's conception of the relation between the socialist party and the development of consciousness had no foundation in Marxism requires that he simply ignore what Marx and Engels actually wrote on this subject. In *The Holy Family*, written in 1844, they explained that in the formulation of the socialist program:

> It is not a question of what this or that proletarian, or even the whole proletariat, at the moment *regards* as its aim. It is a question of *what the proletariat is*, and what, in accordance with this *being*, it will historically be compelled to do. Its aim and historical action is visibly and irrevocably foreshadowed in its own life situation as well as in the whole organisation of bourgeois society today.[25]

A postmodernist critique of Lenin

In another book attacking *What Is To Be Done?*, the above-quoted passage is cited — but not, as in the case of Kolakowski, to discredit only Lenin. The position of British historian Neil Harding is that Lenin was, in fact, an orthodox Marxist. The conceptions advanced in *What Is To Be Done?* were

---

[25] Karl Marx and Frederick Engels, *Collected Works,* Volume 4 (New York: International Publishers, 1975), p. 37.

based on what Marx himself had written in *The Holy Family*. Therefore, according to Harding:

> The privileged role allotted to the socialist intelligentsia in organising and articulating the grievances of the proletariat and leading their political struggle, far from being a Leninist deviation from Marxism, is central to the arrogance of Marxism as a whole. Marx (and all subsequent Marxists) had to assert that he had a more profound awareness of the long-term interests and objectives of the proletariat than any proletarian, or group of proletarians could themselves possess.[26]

While Kolakowski maintains that Lenin revised Marx, and Harding insists that Lenin based himself on Marx, their denunciation of *What Is To Be Done?* proceeds from a rejection of the claim that socialist class consciousness needs to be brought into the working class by a political party, and that any party can claim that its program represents the interests of the working class. The Marxist affirmation of objective truth is derived from an infatuation with science, the belief that the world is, in an objective sense, both knowable and law-governed, "and that the systematic, generalised (or 'objective') knowledge of science was privileged over the 'subjective' knowledge conveyed by immediate experience."[27] Harding attacks the Marxist conception that objective truth is something that should be considered apart from, and even opposed to, the results derived from a canvass of public opinion. Harding writes:

> Leninism is wholly a child of Marxism in respect to the basic foundations of its theory of the party. It bases itself on a similar claim to a special sort of knowledge and a similar arrogant contention that the proletarian cause cannot be discovered merely by taking a poll among workers.[28]

Armed with the fashionable postmodernist jargon so beloved by contemporary ex-leftist academics — in which scientific knowledge is redefined as merely a "privileged" mode of discourse which has managed, for reasons

---

[26] Neil Harding, *Leninism* (Durham, NC: Duke University Press, 1996), p. 34.
[27] Ibid., p. 173.
[28] Ibid., p. 174.

wholly unrelated to the intrinsic quality of its content, to assert its pre-eminence over other less culturally-favored forms of expression — Harding rejects what he refers to as "the shadowy notion of historical immanence" to which both Marx and Lenin subscribed; that is, the notion "that thorough study of the development of society would disclose certain general tendencies which, once established and dominant, propelled men to act in given ways."[29]

The philosophical conceptions underlying *What Is To Be Done?*

This bring us to the central theoretical and philosophical issue that underlies not only Lenin's conception of the role of the party, but the whole Marxist project. If, as Harding maintains, the perceptions and opinions generated in the minds of workers on the basis of their immediate experience are no less valid and legitimate than knowledge developed on the basis of an insight into the laws of social development, then workers have no need for a political party that strives to bring their practice into alignment with the law-governed tendencies disclosed by science. Let me point out that one can, based on Harding's arguments, deny that there is any need for science in any form. Science proceeds from the distinction between reality as it manifests itself in immediate sense perception, and reality as it emerges through a complex and protracted process of analysis and theoretical abstraction.

The principal question which we confront is: Can *objective* social reality — assuming the existence of such a reality (which, for academics, is a big *if*) — be understood by the individual workers, or by the working class as a whole, on the basis of immediate experience? This is a question to which Lenin devoted so much time, especially when he was engaged, several years later, in the writing of the theoretical tract *Materialism and Empirio-Criticism*. Lenin wrote:

> In all social formations of any complexity — and in the capitalist social formation in particular — people in their intercourse are *not conscious* of what kind of social relations are being formed, in accordance with what laws they develop, etc. For instance, a peasant when he sells his grain enters into "intercourse" with the world producers of grain in the world market, but he is not conscious of it; nor is he conscious of the kind of social relations

---

[29] Ibid., p. 172.

that are formed on the basis of exchange. Social consciousness *reflects* social being — that is Marx's teaching. A reflection may be an approximately true copy of the reflected, but to speak of identity is absurd.[30]

... Every individual producer in the world economic system realises that he is introducing this or that change into the technique of production; every owner realises that he exchanges certain products for others; but these producers and these owners do not realise that in doing so they are thereby changing *social being*. The sum-total of these changes in all their ramifications in the capitalist world economy could not be grasped even by seventy Marxes. The most important thing is that the *laws* of these changes have been discovered, that the *objective* logic of these changes and of their historical development has in its chief and basic features been disclosed — objective, not in the sense that a society of conscious beings, of people, could exist and develop independently of the existence of conscious beings (and it is only such trifles that Bogdanov *stresses* by his "theory"), but in the sense that social being is *independent* of *the social consciousness* of people. The fact that you live and conduct your business, beget children, produce products and exchange them, gives rise to an objectively necessary chain of events, a chain of development, which is independent of your *social* consciousness, and is never grasped by the latter completely. The highest task of humanity is to comprehend this objective logic of economic evolution (the evolution of social life) in its general and fundamental features, so that it may be possible to adapt *to it* one's social consciousness and the consciousness of the advanced classes of all capitalist countries in as definite, clear and critical a fashion as possible.[31]

When people go to work, to what extent are they aware of the vast network of global economic interconnections of which their own job is a minute element? One can reasonably assume that even the most intelligent worker would have only the vaguest sense of the relationship of his job, or his company, to the complex processes of modern transnational production and

---

[30] V.I. Lenin, *Collected Works*, Volume 14 (Progress Publishers, 1977), p. 323.
[31] Ibid., p. 325.

exchange of goods and services. Nor is the individual worker in a position to penetrate the mysteries of international capitalist finance, the role of global hedge funds, and the secret and often impenetrable ways (even to experts in the field) that tens of billions of dollars in financial assets are moved across international borders every day. The realities of modern capitalist production, trade and finance are so complex that corporate and political leaders are dependent upon the analyses and advice of major academic institutions, which, more often than not, are divided among themselves as to the meaning of the data at their disposal. But the problem of class consciousness goes beyond the obvious difficulty of assimilating and mastering the complex phenomena of modern economic life. At a more basic level, the precise nature of the social relationship between an individual worker and his employer, let alone between the entire working class and the bourgeoisie, is not and cannot be grasped at the level of sense perception and immediate experience.

Even a worker who is convinced that he or she is being exploited cannot, on the basis of his or her own bitter personal experience, perceive the underlying socioeconomic mechanism of that exploitation. Moreover, the concept of exploitation is not one that is easily understood, let alone derived directly from the instinctive sense that one is not being paid enough. The worker who fills out an application form upon applying for a job does not perceive that she is offering to sell her labor-power, or that the unique quality of that labor-power is its capacity to produce a sum of value greater than the price (the wage) at which it has been purchased; and that profit is derived from this differential between the cost of labor-power and the value that it creates.

Nor is a worker aware that when he purchases a commodity for a definite sum of money, the essence of that exchange is a relation not between things (a coat or some other commodity for a definite amount of money) but between people. Indeed, he does not understand the nature of money, how it emerged historically as the expression of the value form, and how it serves to mask, in a society in which the production and exchange of commodities have been universalized, the underlying social relations of capitalist society.

This last point might serve as a general introduction to the theoretical-epistemological foundation of Marx's most important work, *Capital*. In the concluding section of the first chapter of volume one, Marx introduces his theory of commodity fetishism, which explains the source of the mystification of social relations within capitalist society — that is, the reason why, in this particular economic system, social relations between people necessarily appear as relations between things. It is not, and cannot be apparent to workers, on the basis of sense perception and immediate experience, that any given commodity's value is the crystallized expression of the sum of abstract human labor expended in its production. The discovery of the essence of the value form represented a historical milestone in scientific thought. Without this discovery, neither the objective socioeconomic foundations of the class struggle nor their revolutionary implications could have been understood.

However the worker may dislike the social consequences of the system in which he lives, he is not in a position to grasp, on the basis of immediate experience, either its origins, its internal contradictions or the historically-limited character of its existence. The understanding of the contradictions of the capitalist mode of production, of the exploitative relationship between capital and wage-labor, of the inevitability of class struggle and its revolutionary consequences, arose on the basis of real scientific work, with which the name of Marx will be forever linked. The knowledge obtained through this science, and the method of analysis involved in the achievement and extension of this knowledge, must be introduced into the working class. That is the task of the revolutionary party.

If Lenin were an elitist, then the same label must be affixed to all those who have fought under the banner of scientific truth against innumerable forms of obscurantism. Did not Thomas Jefferson write that he had sworn eternal opposition to every form of ignorance and tyranny over the minds of men? The charge of elitism could justly be leveled against those who denigrate and oppose the political and cultural enlightenment of the working class, and thereby leave it at the mercy of its exploiters.

Finally, let us deal with the charge that Lenin's insistence on the necessity of a struggle against the forms of working class consciousness generated spontaneously within capitalist society, and his hostility to vulgar public opinion, as it takes shape under the bombardment of the propaganda organs of the mass media, was "undemocratic," even "totalitarian." Underlying this accusation is a form of social bitterness, deeply embedded in class interests and social prejudices, evoked by the effort of the socialist movement to create a different, non-bourgeois form of public opinion, in which the real political and historical interests of the working class find expression.

There is no more profoundly democratic project than the effort of the Marxist movement to develop the class consciousness of the working class. Lenin did not "impose" his scientifically-grounded program on the working class. Rather, all his political work over more than a quarter-century prior to the events of 1917 sought to raise the social thought of the advanced sections of the Russian working class to the level of science. And, in that, he and the Bolshevik Party succeeded. In the achievement of this task Lenin represented, as John Reed noted, "A strange popular leader — a leader purely by virtue of intellect ... with the power of explaining profound ideas in simple terms, of analysing a concrete situation. And combined with shrewdness, the greatest intellectual audacity."[32]

It was not Lenin who first proclaimed the necessity of bringing socialist consciousness into the working class. His denunciations of the Economists' glorification of the "spontaneous element" were certainly informed by a profound reading of Marx's *Capital* and an understanding of the manner in which capitalism, as a system of production relations established among people, conceals the real socially-rooted mechanisms of exploitation. Lenin's originality as a political thinker found expression not in his insistence upon the need to introduce consciousness into the working class — this was widely accepted by Marxists throughout Europe — but in the consistency and persistence with which he applied this precept and in the far-reaching political and organizational conclusions he drew from it.

"Political exposures" and class consciousness

How, then, was the political consciousness of the working class to be developed? The answer given by Lenin to this question bears careful study. For the Economists, agitation related to economic "bread and butter" issues and immediate problems encountered in the factory served as the principal means of developing class consciousness. Lenin explicitly rejected the conception that genuine class consciousness could be developed on such a narrow economic basis. Agitation on immediate economic concerns was sufficient only for the development of trade union consciousness, i.e., the bourgeois consciousness of the working class. The development of revolutionary class consciousness, Lenin insisted, required that socialists concentrate their agitation on what he referred to as *political exposures*.

> *In no way* except by means of such exposures *can* the masses be trained in political consciousness and revolutionary activity. Hence, activity of this kind is one of the most important functions of international Social-Democracy as a whole, for even

---

[32] John Reed, *Ten Days That Shook the World* (London: Penguin Books, 1977), p. 128.

political freedom does not in any way eliminate exposures; it merely shifts somewhat their sphere of direction.[33]

In words that have lost none of their relevance — or which, due to the staggering decline in our own period of the nature and significance of socialist consciousness, have actually grown in significance — Lenin wrote:

> Working-class consciousness cannot be genuine political con-
> sciousness unless the workers are trained to respond to *all* cases
> of tyranny, oppression, violence, and abuse, no matter *what class*
> is affected — unless they are trained, moreover, to respond from
> a Social-Democratic [i.e., revolutionary] point of view and no
> other. The consciousness of the working masses cannot be genu-
> ine class-consciousness, unless the workers learn, from concrete,
> and above all from topical, political facts and events to observe
> *every* other social class in *all* the manifestations of its intellectual,
> ethical, and political life; unless they learn to apply in practice the
> materialist analysis and the materialist estimate of *all* aspects of
> the life and activity of *all* classes, strata, and groups of the popula-
> tion. Those who concentrate the attention, observation, and con-
> sciousness of the working class exclusively, or even mainly, upon
> itself alone are not Social-Democrats; for the self-knowledge of
> the working class is indissolubly bound up, not solely with a fully
> clear theoretical understanding — it would be even truer to say,
> not so much with the theoretical, as with the practical, under-
> standing — of the relationships between *all* the various classes
> of modern society, acquired through the experience of political
> life. For this reason the conception of the economic struggle as
> the most widely applicable means of drawing the masses into
> the political movement, which our Economists preach, is so
> extremely harmful and reactionary in its practical significance.[34]

Lenin stressed that the revisionists who insisted that the fastest and easiest way to attract the attention of workers and win their support was to concentrate on economic and "shop-floor" issues — and that the principal

---

[33] Lenin, *Collected Works,* Volume 5, p. 412.
[34] Ibid., pp. 412–413.

activity of socialists should be in the day-to-day economic struggles of work-ers — were really contributing nothing of importance, in terms of the devel-opment of socialist consciousness, to the spontaneous workers movement. In fact, they were acting not as revolutionary socialists but as *mere* trade union-ists. The task of socialists was not to talk to workers about what they already know — day-to-day factory and on-the-job issues — but, rather, about what they cannot acquire from their immediate economic experience — political knowledge.

"You intellectuals can acquire this knowledge," wrote Lenin, affecting the voice of a worker, "and it is your *duty* to bring it to us in a hundred- and a thousand-fold greater measure than you have done up to now; and you must bring it to us, not only in the form of discussions, pamphlets, and articles (which very often — pardon our frankness — are rather dull), but precisely in the form of vivid *exposures* of what our government and our governing classes are doing at this very moment in all spheres of life."[35]

Lenin did not counsel indifference, let alone abstention, from the eco-nomic struggles of the working class. But he opposed the harmful fixation of socialists on such struggles, their tendency to limit their agitation and practical activity to economic issues and trade unionist struggles, and their neglect of the critical political issues that confront the working class as the revolutionary force within society. Moreover, when socialists intervened in trade union struggles, their real responsibility was, as Lenin wrote, "*to uti-lise* the sparks of political consciousness which the economic struggle gener-ates among the workers, for the purpose of *raising* the workers to the level of *Social-Democratic* political consciousness."[36]

I have devoted such a great deal of time to this review of *What Is To Be Done?* because what we have been examining is not only a book written more than a century ago, but also the theoretical conception of the development of socialist consciousness in the working class upon which the *World Socialist Web Site* is based.

[35] Ibid., p. 417.
[36] Ibid., p. 416.

9

The Revolutions of 1848 and the Historical Foundations of Marxist Strategy[1]

We will devote this week to a study of the theory of permanent revolution. It is not difficult to justify our concentration on this subject. The events of the past half year — above all, the revolution in Egypt — impart an intense relevance to this theory. The social dynamic of events in Egypt can be understood only on the basis of this theory. As always, the various bourgeois and petty-bourgeois "left" organizations respond to these events by mouthing the emptiest democratic rhetoric.

The French NPA [New Anticapitalist Party] last January affixed its signature to a joint communiqué, also signed by the Greens, the Unitary Left, the French Communist Party, the Left Party, and the Socialist Party. It stated: "We demand that the French government and the European Union cease their explicit or implicit support for the Tunisian regime and support a *true democratic transition*." At the same time, the social interests that motivated the Pabloite[2] call for a "true democratic transition" (with the assistance of Sarkozy and the EU) found expression in a statement of the Tunisian League

---

[1] Lecture delivered at the summer school held by the Socialist Equality Party (US) in Ann Arbor, Michigan, July 2011.

[2] Pabloism is a petty-bourgeois opportunist tendency that emerged in the early 1950s. It provoked a split in the Fourth International in 1953. A review of the history of this grouping is provided in Chapter 11, pp. 274-275.

for Human Rights, which declared, in the midst of the mass demonstrations: "The question for us now is, 'How can we stop this explosion of pillage, which is becoming intolerable?' These kids are not only attacking the property of the Trabelsi family, but police stations, and everyone's property."

An NPA statement, titled "Tunisia: The Social and Democratic Revolution is Underway," declared:

> Only through the constitution of a provisional government, without any representative of the Destourian regime, in charge of preparing free and democratic elections under a new Election Code for a Constituent Assembly can Tunisians regain control of their destiny and enforce just and fair order in their country. If the people strive for a better life, destiny must acquiesce![3]

In the midst of mass demonstrations in Cairo in January, the ISO featured an interview with Mostafa Omar, a leader of the opposition, who praised ElBaradei because of his "new movement for democracy," and his National Association for Change (NAC).

On February 1, the Revolutionary Socialists sought to encourage illusions in the army, declaring that: "A people's army is the army that protects the revolution." It continued: "Everyone asks: 'Is the army with the people or against them?' The army is not a single bloc. The interests of soldiers and junior officers are the same as the interests of the masses."[4]

Among the defining characteristics of the petty-bourgeois parties is a contemptuous disregard for history. They are aware that a review of great historical experiences would disrupt their opportunist and reactionary politics. But without a thoroughgoing knowledge of the history of revolutionary struggles, it is not possible to comprehend the present world situation and to develop a strategy for socialist revolution in the twenty-first century.

Trotsky: A man of history

The twentieth century can be legitimately described as the Age of Permanent Revolution. This is appropriate both as a definition of the social

---

[3] Available: http://www.attac.org/en/tags/tunisia/
tunisia-social-and-democratic-revolution-underway

[4] Available: http://socialistworker.org/2011/02/07/call-from-egyptian-socialists

logic of the great revolutionary upheavals of the last century and as the central theoretical and strategic issue underlying all the political struggles over revolutionary strategy in the international workers movement. In an essay recalling his encounters with Trotsky during the hearings of the Dewey Commission in April 1937 in Coyóacan, on the outskirts of Mexico City, the American novelist James T. Farrell described the great revolutionary as "a man of history in the sense that most of us are not, and cannot be." This description — or, more correctly, definition — of Trotsky expressed a profound insight.

In what sense was Trotsky "a man of history"? Of course, he was a major figure in many of the greatest events of the twentieth century. Trotsky was the principal strategist and organizer of the 1917 October Revolution that brought the Bolshevik Party to power and led to the establishment of the Soviet Union, the first workers state in history. He became in 1918 the commander of the Red Army, which he led to victory over the forces of counterrevolution in the course of a three-year-long civil war. In 1923, Trotsky initiated the political struggle within the Communist Party of the Soviet Union that led first to the formation of the Left Opposition and, later, to the Fourth International. Trotsky was one of the towering figures of the last century. I would argue that he was the greatest political figure of the twentieth century, and that his influence on history will prove to be the most enduring. The new mass socialist movement of the working class that will develop in this century will be based, to a great extent, on the theoretical and political conceptions of Leon Trotsky.

When Farrell defined Trotsky as a "man of history," he did not only mean that Trotsky was a major historical figure. He was also calling attention to Trotsky's conscious engagement with history as an objective and law-governed process; of the place occupied by history in Trotsky's thought and actions, and even in the constitution of his personality. Trotsky made history; but, in so doing, he lived with a high degree of self-conscious awareness of the place and significance of his own activity — and that of his comrades and the revolutionary workers movement to which he was utterly devoted — in a vast historical process of social transformation. Like an astronomer who looks up at the evening sky, knowing that his own planet occupies a place within the galaxy that he is observing, Trotsky was intensely aware of the broader historical continuum, spanning decades, and even centuries, within which the work of the revolutionary socialist movement unfolds.

History lived in Trotsky. Judging from his writings, I believe that he almost felt as if he *had been* in Paris in 1793, in 1848 and in 1871. His reading of history was not passive. In his mind he debated with Danton and Robespierre as if they were contemporaries. It is true, as Lunacharsky noted, that Trotsky observed his own actions in the mirror of history. But there was not a trace of subjectivism or self-aggrandizement in his historically-oriented self-consciousness. Passionately engaged in the struggles of his time, he continuously related contemporary developments to historical experiences. Trotsky sought to understand the impact and implications of the program and policies for which he fought on the future evolution of the revolutionary struggle. As he stated upon the founding of the Fourth International, a revolutionist "carries on his shoulders a particle of the fate of mankind." It was this unceasing dynamic interaction in his thought of the present, past and future that made Trotsky a "man of history."

Trotsky was part of a generation of revolutionaries for whom the endless reworking of historical experience was a critical component of theoretical and political work. With the recent publication of *Witnesses to Permanent Revolution*, the valuable collection of documents assembled and translated by historians Richard Day and Daniel Gaido, we are able to understand more completely the evolution of revolutionary Marxist thought that led to Trotsky's analysis of the driving forces of the Russian Revolution and his conclusion, more than a decade before the victory of the Bolsheviks, that the overthrow of the Russian autocracy would lead, more or less directly, to the seizure of power by the working class in a socialist revolution. The volume contains important essays, not only by Trotsky, but also by Plekhanov, Ryazanov, Mehring, Luxemburg, Parvus and Kautsky.[5]

Among the most striking features of these essays is the manner in which they seek to relate their analysis of the unfolding Russian Revolution, in the early years of the first decade of the twentieth century, to the antecedent revolutionary events — the Great French Revolution of 1789–94, the revolutions of 1848, and the Paris Commune of 1871. Of course, to the generation that was to pass through the experience of 1905, neither the Paris Commune nor the revolutions of 1848 belonged to an all that distant past. In terms of time span, the Paris Commune was no more distant to the year 1905 than 1977 — the year of Tom Henehan's assassination[6] — is to today. And even 1848 was not particularly remote. Only fifty-seven years separated the revolutionary upheavals of that *annus mirabilis* ("Year of Wonders") from 1905. A similar stretch

---

[5] See Chapter 10 of this volume.

[6] Tom Henehan, a leading member of the Workers League (predecessor of the Socialist Equality Party), was shot to death in New York City on October 16, 1977. He was twenty-six years old.

of time would take us back no further than the early years of the Eisenhower administration. In the European socialist movement at the turn of the twentieth century, there remained not only veterans of the Paris Commune, but also participants in the Revolution of 1848. Wilhelm Liebknecht, Bebel's older cofounder of the Social Democratic Party of Germany and a participant in the struggles of 1848, lived until 1900. Adolf Sorge, the close friend of Marx and Engels who participated in the Baden uprising in Germany, lived until 1906.

The French Revolution

The veterans of the French Revolution of 1789–94 had long before departed from the scene. But the impact of that event — economic, social, political and ideological — was so overwhelming that its shadow still loomed over Europe (and looms to this day!). The modern political world was forged in the Great French Revolution. All of the great struggles of that titanic event, which its participants fought with such passion, prepared the ground for the revolutionary struggles of the future. It was in the cauldron of that revolution that even the most widely accepted terminology of modern social struggles emerged. The advocates of radical social change — the so-called "Mountain" — sat to the left of the presiding officer in the Estates General; the conservatives and reactionaries sat on the right. But in addition to the terms "left" and "right," the phrase "permanent revolution" owes its origin to the French Revolution. As pointed out by Richard Day and Daniel Gaido in their introduction to *Witnesses to Permanent Revolution*, the concept of *"revolution en permanence"* derived from the famous oath, taken on a Versailles tennis court by representatives of the Third Estate in June 1789, which pledged that the National Assembly would exist, wherever its members were assembled, regardless of attempts by the monarch to dissolve it. In other words, the National Assembly of the Third Estate declared its permanence!

More important than its contribution to the terminology of modern politics, the French Revolution destroyed the social and economic foundations of feudalism, cleared a path for the establishment of a bourgeois state and the development of capitalism that led, inevitably, to the emergence of the working class and the class struggle in its modern form. Indeed, it was in the aftermath of the overthrow of the Jacobin dictatorship in July 1794 that the first premonition of the revolutions of the future found expression — in the "Conspiracy of Equals" led by Gracchus Babeuf, which was the first attempt to realize social equality through conscious revolutionary action.

The revolution not only led to the socioeconomic transformation of France; it provided the impulse for an enormous advance toward a scientific understanding of the driving forces of historical development, from which Marxism eventually emerged. After the French Revolution, the significance of material interests, property and class conflict in the background of political life became increasingly clear to the more advanced thinkers.

The impact of economic changes, including industrialization, led to new forms of social conflict that transformed the premonitions of revolution into something far more substantial. As early as 1806, a strike by building workers took place in Paris. In 1817, hat makers in Lyons went on strike to protest the lowering of wages. There were significant strikes by Parisian artisans and manufactory workers between 1825 and 1827. In 1830 popular protests in Paris led to the fall of King Charles X. However, the beneficiaries of this "revolution" were the financiers. The conditions of the developing working class, especially weavers, deteriorated. Taxes on the common people were raised and wages lowered. The growing anger finally exploded in November 1831 in the form of an armed uprising by the workers of Lyons. For several days, government soldiers were driven out of the city. Even though the government was able, after several days, to reestablish control, the bourgeoisie was traumatized by the emergence of class struggle, arising from the resistance of a newly formed proletariat, which threatened capitalist property interests.

The regime of Louis Philippe

The regime that ruled in France was a bourgeois monarchy, presided over by Louis Philippe, whose official title was King of the French — a veiled acknowledgment that the French Revolution and the decapitation of Louis XVI, and later removal of his younger brother, Charles X, had not been entirely in vain. Louis Philippe's father, the ill-fated Philippe Egalité, was a cousin of Louis XVI who broke with the royal family during the revolution and actually voted for the king's execution. However, this did not save him from suspicions that he was, or might become, an instrument of royalist counterrevolution, and Philippe Egalité was guillotined in November 1793. At any rate, his son eventually ascended to the monarchy, but under political and social conditions vastly different to those that had existed prior to 1793.

Louis Philippe sought to emphasize the bourgeois character of his regime by wearing a frock coat and sporting an umbrella. But his "bourgeois" regime served faithfully the interests of only one section of the bourgeoisie, the powerful financial elite. This left other sections of the bourgeoisie, particularly those connected with industry and manufacturing, dissatisfied with the state of affairs. The corruption of the financial elite knew no bounds, to the extent that it undermined the industrial development of France. There exists no greater description of French society under Louis Philippe than that provided by Karl Marx in *The Class Struggles in France*:

> Since the finance aristocracy made the laws, was at the head of the administration of the state, had command of all the organized public authorities, dominated public opinion through the actual state of affairs and through the press, the same prostitution, the same shameless cheating, the same mania to get rich was repeated in every sphere, from the Court to the Café Borgne, to get rich not by production, but by pocketing the already available wealth of others. Clashing every moment with the bourgeois laws themselves, an unbridled assertion of unhealthy and dissolute appetites manifested itself, particularly at the top of bourgeois society — lusts wherein wealth derived from gambling naturally seeks its satisfaction, where pleasure becomes *crapuleux*, where money, filth and blood commingle. The finance aristocracy, in its mode of acquisition as well as in its pleasures, is nothing but the *rebirth of the lumpenproletariat on the heights of bourgeois society*.[7]

But beyond the Court and the Bourse, opposition to the regime was growing — and not only in France but throughout Europe. Since the final defeat of Napoleon in 1815, political reaction had prevailed throughout the continent. The architect of the system of reaction was the Austrian nobleman, Prince Metternich. A critic told Metternich that his means of preserving the status quo "consist of a forest of bayonets and fixed adherence to things as they are. To my mind, by following these lines we are playing into the hands of the revolutionaries."[8] But Metternich knew of no other means to defend a decayed and dying social order.

There were signs of an approaching revolution. In May 1839 the "Society of Seasons," with 900 members led by Auguste Blanqui and Armand Barbès,

---

[7] Karl Marx and Frederick Engels, *Collected Works*, Volume 10 (New York: International Publishers, 1978), pp. 50–51.

[8] Cited in Mike Rapport, *1848: Year of Revolution* (New York, Basic Books, 2008), p. 13.

attempted an insurrection in Paris. They managed to seize the Town Hall and proclaim a provisional government. But the uprising that they had hoped to inspire failed to materialize. Its leaders were captured and sent to prison. But more enduring in their impact than these early experiments in direct action by small numbers of committed militants was the intellectual revolution in the sphere of economic theory and philosophy. Mention should be made in particular of Pierre-Joseph Proudhon's 1840 book, whose title posed the question *What Is Property?* He gave the succinct, provocative, and unforgettable answer: "Property is Theft."

The origins of Marxism

Another path-breaking work was a lengthy essay entitled *Outlines of a Critique of Political Economy*, written in 1843, which began by noting that "Political economy came into being as a natural result of the expansion of trade, and with its appearance elementary, unscientific huckstering was replaced by a developed system of licensed fraud, an entire science of enrichment."[9] Its author was the twenty-three-year-old Frederick Engels. He was soon to write an even greater work, *The Condition of the Working Class in England*.

But the most important of the intellectual developments of the 1840s occurred in the sphere of philosophy, where the critique of the idealist philosophy of Hegel by the young Karl Marx initiated a revolution in thought that would, in time, provide the intellectual substance for the mass revolutionary movement of the international working class. As his own writings show, Marx was aware, at a very early stage of his work, of the explosive implications of his abstract theoretical labors. "The weapon of criticism cannot, of course, replace criticism by weapons, material force must be overthrown by material force," he wrote in early 1844, "but theory also becomes a material force as soon as it has gripped the masses."[10] Marx further declared, a few pages later, "The *emancipation of the German* is the *emancipation of the human being*. The *head* of this emancipation is *philosophy*, its *heart* is the *proletariat*."[11]

By 1845 Marx and Engels had developed the materialist conception of history, which established that revolutions are not the product of well-organized conspiracies carried out by determined leaders and their followers. They

---

[9] Karl Marx and Frederick Engels, *Collected Works*, Volume 3 (New York: International Publishers, 1975), p. 418.

[10] Ibid., p. 182.

[11] Ibid., p. 187.

are the necessary outcome of a complex socioeconomic process, in which the development of the productive forces comes into irrepressible conflict with the existing social relations within which they had heretofore developed. Thus, the source of revolution was to be found not in the movement of ideas, but in the socioeconomic organization of society, conditioned by a certain level of development of the productive forces. The contradiction between the growth of the productive forces and the existing social relationships finds political expression in the class struggle, which in modern society assumes the principal form of the conflict between the bourgeoisie, which owns the means of production, and the proletariat, the working class, which possesses only its ability to work.

In 1847, Marx and Engels joined the League for the Just, which soon became the Communist League. They were assigned by the League to write a program in late 1847, in the form of a Manifesto, which, as we all know, came to exercise a not inconsiderable influence on the course of world history.

By the time the *Communist Manifesto* was published, Europe was on the verge of a political explosion. Independent of the labor of socialist theoreticians, capitalism was in the throes of a major economic crisis that had a devastating impact on broad sections of the working population. The years 1846–47 witnessed human suffering on a scale greater than during any previous period in the nineteenth century. The economic crisis was compounded by a crop failure that produced widespread famine. In Ireland more than 21,000 people died of starvation, and hundreds of thousands fell victim to such diseases as typhus and cholera. People were reduced to living off the carcasses of dead animals. In Belgium, 700,000 people lived on public relief, and there were thousands more who were dependent on charity. In Berlin and Vienna the desperate conditions led to clashes between the people and the armed authorities. In France, bread prices rose dramatically and those of potatoes doubled. The unemployment rate skyrocketed.

The approach of revolution

The popular unrest in France intensified political tensions between the regime of Louis Philippe and a growing opposition movement consisting of various bourgeois political tendencies, including liberals who resented the dictatorship of financial interests and the exclusion of industrial interests from positions of power, and more democratic tendencies that favored, with greater or lesser degrees of fervor, the formation of a republic. Among the better-known and more radical representatives of these tendencies was Alexandre-Auguste Ledru-Rollin (1807–1874), who acquired support among French workers due to the ferocity of his oratorical attacks on the regime prior to 1848. He founded a newspaper, *La Réforme*, which developed a substantial readership. Another figure with a large popular following was Louis Blanc (1811–1882), who was known as a socialist — though his concept of socialism reflected the influence of utopian thinkers such as Robert Owen, Saint-Simon and Étienne Cabet. He believed that progress flowed naturally from the perfectibility of man. Socialism would be achieved not through violent revolution, which he opposed, but through the impeccable logic and persuasive power of his oratory. Prior to the outbreak of revolution, Blanc met from time to time with Engels, who found it difficult to take him and his hodge-podge of ideas entirely seriously. For example, in a letter to Marx in March 1847, Engels makes the following comment about Blanc's *History of the French Revolution*:

> A wild mixture of correct hunches and unbounded craziness. I only read half of the first volume while at Sarcelles *Ça fait un drôle d'effet* [It makes a curious impression]. Hardly has he surprised one with some nice observation when he falls head over heels into the most dreadful lunacy.[12]

During the autumn and winter of 1847–48, bourgeois oppositional tendencies organized what were called "banquets" — an early form of $10 a plate dinners — to attract popular support. Prices were steadily lowered to increase attendance. The radical Ledru-Rollin and socialist Louis Blanc organized their own joint banquets to attract broader middle class and working class participation. The wealthy and conservative bourgeois opposition was not altogether comfortable with the banquet campaign. They did not relish the prospect of an open clash with the regime of Louis Philippe, and they especially feared that the banquets were encouraging, against their better sense, mass struggles outside the control of the propertied interests. Adolph Thiers, who would eventually go down in history as the implacable enemy of the Paris Commune, warned that he sensed the

---

[12] Karl Marx and Frederick Engels, *Collected Works,* Volume 38 (New York: International Publishers, 1982), p. 115.

presence of the red flag of revolution under the tablecloths of the banquet tables! The bourgeoisie, even as it urged one or another form of democratic reform, feared the intervention of the working class into political struggle.

This fear within sections of the bourgeoisie was an expression of the profound changes in the structure of French (and, more broadly, European) society since the Great Revolution of 1789–94. When the representatives of the Third Estate assembled in Versailles in 1789, the class divisions within the popular opposition to the feudal regime remained undeveloped. In its confrontation with Louis XVI, the bourgeoisie did not have to contend with the specter of a socialist opposition based on the working class — an opposition that threatened not only feudal property, but capitalist property as well. This enabled the bourgeoisie to adopt a far more determined revolutionary attitude toward the Old Regime in the 1790s than it would a half-century later. The extreme radicalism of the Great Revolution was derived not from the bourgeoisie — which generally sought to work out a political compromise with Louis XVI — but, rather, from the mass of the urban population, the so-called *sans culottes*, from whom the Jacobin leaders obtained their principal support. It was their repeated insurrectionary uprisings that drove the revolution further and further to the left.

By 1848 the political conflict between the bourgeois opposition and the regime of Louis Philippe was complicated by the emergence of the working class. This change in French and European society would prove to be of decisive significance in the revolutions of 1848. Even though the bourgeois liberals found themselves in opposition to the existing regimes, the depth of their opposition and of their commitment to democracy was circumscribed by their greater fear of the socialist aspirations of the working class. These contradictions — between the democratic pretensions of the bourgeoisie and their material interests, between a bourgeoisie committed to the defense of capitalist property and a working class without property — determined the outcome of the revolutions of 1848.

The political crisis of the regime of Louis Philippe had been long in the making. De Tocqueville issued a prescient warning in January 1848 that the regime was courting revolution. However, few could have imagined that it would take only three days of insurrectionary violence to bring about the collapse of the whole rotten structure. The king himself brushed off de Tocqueville's warning with a flippant jest: "The Parisians won't start a revolution in winter," he said. "They storm things in hot weather. They stormed the Bastille in July, the Bourbon throne in June. But in January and February, no."[13]

February 1848 in Paris

The trouble began with the government's attempt to prevent the holding of a huge opposition banquet, which was scheduled to take place on February 22, 1848. Prices had been cut to attract a large turnout. The government then retreated, and agreed that the banquet could be held in a wealthy neighborhood near the Champs-Elysées, but on the condition that it disband itself almost immediately. Many of the bourgeois organizers were willing to accept this humiliating condition, not simply because they feared the regime, but also because they were fearful of stirring huge crowds into action. However, Ledru-Rollin and his supporters in the *Réforme* group refused to back down. They issued a call to Parisians, urging them to assemble at the Place de la Madeleine on the morning of February 22 and march *en masse* up the Champs-Elysées to the banquet venue. This appeal was opposed by virtually all the newspapers identified with the bourgeois opposition, which regarded the entire enterprise as an adventure that would lead to a clash with the regime and end in a bloody rout of the protesters.

A confrontation did take place. Unruly crowds overturned omnibuses and destroyed street lamps. But the police and National Guard seemed capable of handling the situation. On the evening of the 22nd, Louis Philippe was confident that the situation was under control. But the crowds were even larger the next day. There were growing signs of mutiny in the National Guard, especially within the regiments from poorer districts. Then, on the evening of February 23rd, the workers of Paris went into revolt. They gathered more than eight million paving stones and cut down more than 400,000 trees. By the morning of February 24, approximately 1,500 barricades had been erected all over the city. Louis Philippe had hoped that he could contain the protests by dismissing his prime minister, François Guizot. But the gesture came too late. Surveying the situation in Paris, and recalling the fate of his illustrious family in the last revolution, Louis Philippe abdicated and fled the country. The revolution had been victorious, and it had cost less than 500 lives!

---

[13] Boris Nicolaevsky and Otto Maenchen-Helfen, *Karl Marx: Man and Fighter* (Penguin Books, 1973), p. 149.

But who and what would take the place of the deposed monarch? The bourgeoisie and the better off sections of the middle class were not entirely certain that they welcomed victory. The bourgeois opposition had sought to apply pressure on Louis Philippe and compel him to grant some sort of electoral reform. But now they had a revolution on their hands, with the expectations and aspirations of masses of workers aroused by their successful overthrow of Louis Philippe. Most of the well-established representatives of the liberal bourgeois opposition were shocked and confused by the rapid turn of events. One of the few who managed to retain his political equilibrium was Alphonse de Lamartine, a well-known Romantic poet, who made use of his literary skills to express, with exalted rhetoric, the prosaic and egotistical aspirations of the French bourgeoisie.

The early stages of every revolution witness the ascendancy of such figures, masters of grandiloquent rhetoric that lend to platitudes an air of profundity. Seventy years later, that role would be played in the Russian Revolution by Alexander Kerensky. In the immediate aftermath of the abdication and flight of Louis Philippe, amidst great confusion and under pressure from the populace, Lamartine proclaimed, from a balcony of the Hôtel de Ville, the establishment of the Second Republic. Lamartine actually opposed the proclamation of a republic. But the Parisian masses, who were well aware that they had gained nothing from the overthrow of Charles X in 1830, were determined not to be cheated again of the fruits of victory.

The new Provisional Government, which was to hold power pending elections, consisted almost entirely of conservative representatives of the bourgeoisie. The only figure with a radical identity was Alexandre Ledru-Rollin. Louis Blanc demanded that Ledru-Rollin be included in the government, but only managed to secure the appointment of himself and a worker, known as Albert, as secretaries of the Provisional Government.

For the bourgeoisie, the new republic was seen as a political structure that would continue to defend its class interests. But the working class demanded that the government assume the characteristics of a *social republic* that would restructure society in the interests of the working people. At first, the Provisional Government sought to encourage hope — or, as it turned out, illusions — that the new republic would strive to improve the conditions of the working people. On February 25, the new government pledged "to guarantee a living wage for the workers. It pledges itself to guarantee every man the right to work." This announcement was greeted with enthusiasm. Proudhon wrote: "What are you called, Revolution of 1848?" The answer? "My name is the Right to Work."

A week later, on March 2, the government enacted another law that established a ten-hour workday in Paris and eleven hours in the rest of the country. Still another law abolished "sweated labor," which was the widespread practice in which a labor contractor would accept a job at an agreed upon price and then hire laborers on a temporary basis to do the actual work at a much lower wage. The contractor realized, thereby, an exorbitant profit off the labor of others. As we can see, 175 years ago, a practice that has now become a widespread method of doing business, and has led to the establishment of innumerable profitable businesses known as "temp agencies," was considered intolerable.

These reform measures were very popular, but, as it soon emerged, the Provisional Government established no effective means of enforcing them. Louis Blanc had originally called for the establishment of a Ministry of Labor and Progress. This was rejected by the Provisional Government. Instead, as a compromise, it created a Commission of Labor, which met in the Luxembourg Palace (hence the name by which it was commonly known, the Luxembourg Commission) under the direction of Louis Blanc. It possessed only the authority to investigate and consult on the condition of labor. As weeks passed, the workers became increasingly frustrated with the impotence of the Commission.

It was the issue of jobs that emerged as a central source of conflict between the Provisional Government and the workers. Louis Blanc had urged the creation of "Social Workshops" that he originally conceived as a sort of cooperative structure that would provide meaningful jobs. The National Workshops provided nothing really but useless "make work," if anything at all. They paid a minimum wage of two francs daily for make work when it was available, or one-and-a-half francs when there was no work. While failing to address the problem of jobs in a manner that satisfied the workers, the scheme was unpopular outside Paris, particularly among the vast rural population, which came to believe that its taxes were subsidizing the idleness of Parisian workers. This, as weeks passed, played into the hands of reactionary bourgeois politicians, who were seeking to incite the rural masses against the urban working class.

As the first flush of enthusiasm faded, the political situation turned more and more against the workers. Lamartine and other bourgeois politicians, who had been terrified by the social forces released by the February Revolution, schemed incessantly against the workers. As one historian has written, Lamartine (the bourgeois leader):

had plunged into the first battles with a mixture of confidence and amateurishness, but it was not long before he began to regard the poor, wretched proletariat as a serious enemy, and directed his efforts more to charming than to convincing it. ... He acquired a horror of the masses...[14]

Initially, the workers had looked toward elections as a means of securing sympathetic representation in the national assembly. However, they soon realized that if the elections were held too soon, before the revolution had time to influence the consciousness of the rural masses, the results would be highly unfavorable. The bourgeoisie made the same calculation, and it came to the conclusion that the elections should be held as soon as possible. A mass demonstration was held by workers on March 17, with the aim of pressuring the Provisional Government to delay the elections. They only secured the agreement of the Provisional Government for a delay of two weeks. And when they were held, the elections produced, as the workers had feared, an overwhelmingly conservative result. The mass of peasants who went to the polls on April 23 voted largely as they were instructed to do by local dignitaries and priests.

The political climate turned sharply to the right. The mood of the bourgeoisie, angered by the demands of the workers and their socialist slogans, was captured by Gustave Flaubert in his novel, *Sentimental Education*.

Arnoux was trying to prove that there were two sorts of Socialism, a good and a bad. The industrialist could not see any difference between them, for the word "property" sent him into a fury of indignation.

"It's a right consecrated by Nature. Children cling to their toys; every people, every animal on earth shares my opinion; the lion itself, if it had the power of speech, would call itself a landowner! Take my case, gentlemen: I started with a capital of fifteen thousand francs. Well, you know, I got up regularly at four o'clock in the morning every day for thirty years! I had the very devil of a job to make my fortune. And now they come and tell me that I can't do what I like with it, that my money isn't my money, that property is theft!"

---

[14] Georges Duveau, *1848: The Making of a Revolution*, (New York: Random House, 1967), p. 85.

"But Proudhon..."

"Oh, don't talk to me about Proudhon! If he was here I do believe I'd strangle him!"

He would indeed have strangled him. After the liqueurs especially, there was no holding Fumichon; and his apoplectic face looked as if it were on the point of exploding like a shell.[15]

The newly elected National Assembly set out to provoke the workers with ever more hostile measures. The National Workshops became the focus of right-wing agitation. All the economic problems confronting France, the public was led to believe, were caused by the National Workshops and the pandering to workers' demands. By June, the phrase "This can't go on" was on the lips of countless capitalists and petty bourgeois. The government prepared for a showdown with the workers. Lamartine's confidence that he could deal with the workers had been fortified by the assurances of Ledru-Rollin that he would stand on the side of the government in a confrontation with the working class.

The counterrevolution of June 1848

On June 21, the government announced that workers between the ages of eighteen and twenty-five who were in the National Workshops would be compelled to join the army. Other workers, who had been resident in Paris for less than six months, were to be dropped from the rolls of the National Workshops and sent out of the city. These measures threatened the workers with starvation. On June 23, open hostilities erupted in Paris. Barricades were set up all over the city, much of which fell under the control of the insurgents. The fighters lacked any sort of clearly articulated socialist perspective. They were driven to struggle by the desperation of their situation. The battle raged for four days. The National Guard, with recruits drawn from all parts of France, and who were brought to the city by train, was under the command of General Cavaignac. He was a supporter of the republic, who did not consider himself a reactionary. But he did not flinch from turning his artillery on the barricades. Nearly five hundred insurgents were killed in the fighting. As many as 1,000 National Guardsmen fell in the battle. But the worst came after the insurrection had been suppressed. The insurgents were hunted down and as many as 3,000 were slaughtered in cold blood. Another 12,000 people

---

[15] Gustave Flaubert, *Sentimental Education* (London: Penguin Books, 1975), pp. 342–343.

were arrested, and many hundreds of them were eventually deported to labor camps in Algeria.

Alexander Herzen, one of the early Russian socialists, who observed the carnage in Paris, wrote of the events in June: "Murder in those terrible days became a duty; the man who had not dipped his hands in proletarian blood became suspect in the eyes of the bourgeoisie."[16] With evident horror at what he had observed, Herzen declared: "Moments like these make one hate for a whole decade, seek revenge all one's life. *Woe to those who forgive such moments!*"[17]

The terrible June Days exposed the real state of social relations in the era of capitalism and the class struggle between bourgeois and worker. The events of 1848 in France revealed the brutal reality of class conflict that lay concealed behind the fine bourgeois slogans of democracy, republic and liberty. As Herzen, examining the social psychology of the bourgeois liberals, wrote in 1849:

> For a long time the liberals played happily with the idea of revolution, and the end of their play was February 24th. The popular hurricane swept them up to the top of a high steeple from which they could see where they were going and where they were leading others. Glancing down at the abyss that opened before their eyes, they grew pale. They saw that what was crumbling was not only what they had considered prejudice, but also everything else — what they had considered true and eternal. They were so terrified that some clutched at the falling walls, while others stopped half-way, repentant, and began to swear to all passers-by that this was not at all what they had wanted. This is why the men who proclaimed the republic became the assassins of freedom; this is why the liberal names that had resounded in our ears for a score of years or so, are today those of reactionary deputies, traitors, inquisitors. They want freedom and even a republic provided that it is confined to their own cultivated circle...
>
> Since the Restoration, liberals in all countries have called the people to the destruction of the monarchic and feudal order, in the name of equality, of the tears of the unfortunate, of the suffering of the oppressed, of the hunger of the

---

[16] Alexander Herzen, *From the Other Shore* (Oxford: Oxford University Press, 1979), p. 53.
[17] Ibid., p. 47.

poor. They have enjoyed hounding down various ministers with a series of impossible demands; they rejoiced when one feudal prop collapsed after another, and in the end became so excited that they outstripped their own desires. They came to their senses when, from behind the half-demolished walls, there emerged the proletarian, the worker with his axe and his blackened hands, hungry and half-naked in rags — not as he appears in books or in parliamentary chatter or in philanthropic verbiage, but in reality. This "unfortunate brother" about whom so much has been said, on whom so much pity has been lavished, finally asked what was to be his share in all these blessings, where were *his* freedom, *his* equality, *his* fraternity? The liberals were aghast at the impudence and ingratitude of the worker. They took the streets of Paris by assault, they littered them with corpses, and then they hid from their *brother* behind the bayonets of martial law in their effort to save *civilization and order* ![18]

The lessons of 1848

For Marx, the crushing of the working class in Paris was an event of world historical significance. This confrontation between the two great classes in modern society arose from the irreconcilable character of their interests. The *social republic* was a fantasy. "The bourgeoisie had to refute, arms in hand, the demands of the proletariat," Marx wrote. "And the real birthplace of the bourgeois republic is not the *February victory*; it is the *June defeat*."[19] The demands of the working class had forced the bourgeois republic, Marx continued "to come out forthwith in its pure form as the state whose admitted object it is to perpetuate the rule of capital, the slavery of labor. Having constantly before its eyes the scarred, irreconcilable, invincible enemy — invincible because his existence is the condition of its own life — bourgeois rule, freed from all fetters, was bound to turn immediately into *bourgeois terrorism*."[20]

The events in France marked a great historical turning point. Before February 1848, revolution had simply meant the overthrow of the form of

---

[18] Ibid., pp. 59–60.
[19] Karl Marx and Frederick Engels, *Collected Works*, Volume 10, p. 67.
[20] Ibid., p. 69.

government. But after June, Marx declared, revolution meant the *"overthrow of bourgeois society."*[21]

The revolution in France would have provided sufficient political drama for any normal year. But 1848 was anything but normal. The February Revolution electrified restive populations throughout Europe, and set into motion an unprecedented wave of mass struggles — in Italy, Germany, Austria and Hungary. There was also significant unrest in Switzerland, Denmark, Rumania, Poland and Ireland. Even in England, the bastion of bourgeois rule, the radical movement of the Chartists reached its climax.

All of these struggles are of great historical significance, and their outcomes were to have far-reaching consequences for the political and social evolution of Europe. But, from the standpoint of the origins and development of the theory of permanent revolution, the events in Germany are of the greatest significance.

For reasons of time, it is possible to present today nothing more than the briefest of outlines of the German Revolution. The February Revolution in Paris undoubtedly provided the political and moral impulse for the March uprising in Berlin, which, let us briefly note, occurred only a few days after an uprising in Vienna. The Hohenzollern dynasty in Prussia was deeply shaken. If the pattern of the Great French Revolution of 1789–94 was to be followed, the German bourgeoisie would prosecute its struggle against the dynastic regime to carry out the main tasks of its *bourgeois* revolution: the overthrow of the monarchy and all the political remnants of feudalism, the liquidation of the old principalities and unification of the German people in a large national state; and the establishment of a democratic republic.

But, as it turned out, the German bourgeoisie proved incapable and unwilling to carry out any of these tasks. The story of 1848 in Germany was the betrayal of the bourgeois revolution by the German bourgeoisie. What underlay this betrayal? A noted historian, William Langer, has written:

> Marx and Engels, reflecting on the German situation in January, 1848, asked themselves whether the *bourgeoisie* of any country had ever been in a more splendid position to carry on its struggle against the existing government. They were referring, of course, to the widespread distress and unrest and to the apparent failure of the liberals to take advantage of their opportunity. But these

---

[21] Ibid., p. 71.

liberals — progressive officials, the upper stratum of the intellectuals and professional man, and especially the new business class — were as reluctant in Germany as they were elsewhere to provoke a revolution. Remembering the excesses of the 1793 Terror in France, they dreaded a major upheaval almost as much as did the princes and the aristocrats.[22]

It was not only the example of the events of 1793–94 that terrified the German bourgeoisie. The contemporary developments in France raised all too clearly the specter of a socialist revolution, which threatened capitalist property and the foundations of bourgeois rule. All the actions of the political representatives of the German bourgeoisie, as well as the more radical representatives of the German petty bourgeoisie, were constrained by their fear of the proletariat. A determined struggle against all the remnants of feudalism in the economy and political structure, directed toward the national unification of the German states on a democratic basis, would have required the revolutionary mobilization by the bourgeoisie of the working class and peasantry. Given the development of capitalism and an industrial working class during the previous half-century, such a mobilization posed too great a danger to the bourgeoisie's class interests. It preferred to seek a compromise with the aristocracy at the expense of the working class.

The epitome of bourgeois liberal cowardice was the Frankfurt Parliament, which met in the Church of St. Paul. Its delegates — consisting of innumerable professors and lawyers — talked endlessly and accomplished nothing of significance. The Parliament willingly surrendered the initiative to the Prussian aristocracy and rejected the utilization of revolutionary measures to achieve the unification of Germany. It left this task to the reactionary Prussian regime, which later carried it out under the leadership of Bismarck.

In the bourgeois betrayal of its "own" bourgeois revolution, Marx and Engels excoriated the role played by the left-talking petty-bourgeois radicals, who, at every critical point in the struggle, turned against the working class. Engels characterized their role in the events of 1848–49 with unsparing accuracy:

The history of all political movements since 1830 in Germany, as in France and England, shows that this class is invariably

---

[22] William L. Langer, *The Rise of Modern Europe: Political and Social Upheaval, 1832–1852* (New York: Harper Torchbooks, 1969), p. 387.

full of bluster and loud protestations, at times even extreme as far as talking goes, as long as it perceives no danger; faint-hearted, cautious and calculating as soon as the slightest danger approaches; aghast, alarmed and wavering as soon as the movement it provoked is seized upon and taken up seriously by other classes; treacherous to the whole movement for the sake of its petty-bourgeois existence as soon as there is any question of a struggle with weapons in hand — and in the end, as a result of its indecisiveness, more often than not cheated and ill-treated as soon as the reactionary side has achieved victory.[23]

In March 1850, Marx and Engels summed up the political lessons of the 1848 Revolution in a document known as the "Address of the Central Authority to the League." This document sought to establish, on the basis of the revolutionary experiences of the previous two years, the independent interests and historic role of the working class in the democratic revolution. Marx and Engels insisted that the working class must, under all conditions, maintain its political independence from not only the bourgeois parties, but also the parties and organizations of the democratic petty bourgeoisie. They stressed the underlying social conflict that placed the working class at odds with the middle class democrats:

> Far from desiring to transform the whole of society for the revolutionary proletarians, the democratic petty bourgeois strive for a change in social conditions by means of which the existing society will be made as tolerable and comfortable as possible for them...
>
> While the democratic petty bourgeois wish to bring the revolution to a conclusion as quickly as possible ... it is our interest and our task to make the revolution permanent, until all more or less possessing classes have been forced out of their position of dominance, the proletariat has conquered state power, and the association of proletarians, not only in one country but in all the dominant countries of the world, has advanced so far that competition among the proletarians in these countries has ceased

---

[23] Karl Marx and Frederick Engels, *Collected Works*, Volume 10, p. 150.

and that at least the decisive productive forces are concentrated in the hands of the proletarians.[24]

Marx and Engels concluded their address with the declaration that the "battle cry" of the proletariat must be: "The Revolution in Permanence."[25] More than a half-century later, the experiences and lessons of 1848 would be analyzed and reworked by the great theoreticians of the Russian Social Democratic Party and the Second International, as they sought to understand the political dynamics and historical tasks of the Russian Revolution.

---

[24] Ibid., pp. 280–281.
[25] Ibid., p. 287.

10

Witnesses to Permanent Revolution: A Significant Contribution to the Study of Marxist Political Strategy[1]

Witnesses to Permanent Revolution: The Documentary Record edited and translated by Richard B. Day and Daniel Gaido (Brill, 2009)

The publication of *Witnesses to Permanent Revolution: The Documentary Record* is a major event in the study of the theoretical foundations of the 1917 October Revolution. The documents presented in this substantial volume (677 pages) — compiled, translated and introduced by historians Richard B. Day and Daniel Gaido — provide a comprehensive review of the controversies and polemics from which the theory of permanent revolution emerged. Day and Gaido have produced a book that is indispensable for those who wish to understand the development of Marxist theory and revolutionary strategy in the twentieth century.

Richard Day, who has taught for many years at the University of Toronto in Mississauga, is respected as an authority on Soviet history, economics

---

[1] Published 19 April, 2010 on the *World Socialist Web Site*.

and politics. His best known work, *Leon Trotsky and the Politics of Economic Isolation* (1973), remains an important exposition of the critical theoretical issues that underlay the struggle over economic policy in the Soviet Union in the 1920s. Day's work on the life and ideas of E.A. Preobrazhensky, including a translation of the latter's *Decline of Capitalism* (1985), rescued from historical oblivion this important figure in the Trotskyist Left Opposition, who was eventually murdered by Stalin in 1937. Professor Day has written essays on a wide range of subjects, including Marxist philosophy. He is presently preparing the publication of a new volume of previously unknown writings of Preobrazhensky.

Daniel Gaido, who was born in Argentina, lived and studied in Israel for more than a decade. He was actively involved in the struggle to defend the democratic rights of Palestinians. Gaido recently has returned to Argentina. His published work includes a book, *The Formative Period of American Capitalism: A Materialist Explanation* (2006). American history, as the volume under review demonstrates, is not his only area of research. Gaido has written extensively on the history of the German socialist movement, and is currently preparing a history of the German Social Democratic Party during the period of the Second International.

The central aim of *Witnesses to Permanent Revolution* is the reconstruction of the impressive intellectual scope of the discussion out of which the theory of permanent revolution emerged. While not contesting the decisive role played by Trotsky in its elaboration and, most significantly, its strategic and practical application in the struggles of the Russian working class, Day and Gaido seek to acquaint the reader with the contributions made by other important socialist thinkers, such as Franz Mehring, Rosa Luxemburg, Alexander Helphand (Parvus), Karl Kautsky, and the much less well-known David Ryazanov. Trotsky would not have objected to a detailed account of the origins of the theory with which he had become so intensely and personally identified.

In 1923 the factional attacks on Leon Trotsky, launched by the Politburo troika of Zinoviev, Kamenev and Stalin, developed rapidly into a campaign against the theory of permanent revolution. All of Trotsky's alleged personal failings and political errors, his so-called "underestimation of the peasantry" and his inveterate "anti-Bolshevism" had their source, it was proclaimed over and over, in this pernicious doctrine. Between April and October 1917, the theory of permanent revolution provided the strategic foundation of the Bolshevik Party's struggle against the bourgeois Provisional Government and its Menshevik allies. But only six years later, it was being denounced as a heretical deviation from Marxist principles. As he witnessed not only the distortion of his own ideas but also the falsification of the history of socialist theory, Trotsky wrote with evident exasperation:

> The expression *"permanent revolution"* is an expression of Marx, which he applied to the revolution of 1848. In Marxist litera-ture, naturally not in revisionist but in revolutionary Marxist literature, this term has always had citizenship rights. Franz Mehring employed it for the revolution of 1905–07. The per-manent revolution, in an exact translation, is the continuous revolution, the uninterrupted revolution.[2]

Marx, Engels and "permanent revolution"

Day and Gaido substantiate Trotsky's insistence upon the Marxist pedi-gree of the theory of permanent revolution. As they note, as early as 1843, Marx had written in his essay on *The Jewish Question* that the state could achieve abolition of religion "only by coming into *violent* contradiction with its own conditions of life, only by declaring the revolution to be permanent."[3] More significantly, in March 1850, in their "Address of the Central Authority to the League," Marx and Engels wrote, in opposition to the democratic petty bourgeoisie, that the workers' task was

> to make the revolution permanent until all the more or less propertied classes have been driven from their ruling positions, until the proletariat has conquered state power and ... has pro-gressed sufficiently far — not only in one country but in all the leading countries of the world — that competition between the proletarians of these countries ceases and at least the decisive forces of production are concentrated in the hands of the work-ers. *Our concern cannot simply be to modify private property, but to abolish it, not to hush up class antagonisms but to abolish classes, not to improve the existing society but to found a new one.*[4]

---

[2] Leon Trotsky, "The New Course," *The Challenge of the Left Opposition 1923–25* (New York: Pathfinder Press, 1975), p. 113.

[3] Richard B. Day and Daniel Gaido, ed. and trans., *Witnesses to Permanent Revolution* (Leiden, The Netherlands: Brill Academic Publishers, 2009), p. 3.

[4] Ibid., pp. 9–10.

The concept of the revolution's permanence developed out of the experience of the class struggles that swept across Europe in 1848. Just over a half-century had passed since the Jacobins, representing the most radical wing of the democratic petty bourgeoisie, had shattered, with the aid of revolutionary terror, the feudal ancien regime and laid the foundation for the establishment of a bourgeois state in France. In the intervening period, the social structure of Europe had grown more complex. The nature and political implications of the on-going political conflict between the bourgeois and the old aristocratic elites were altered by the emergence of a new social force, the proletariat — a class without property. The bourgeoisie became fearful that a popular uprising against the old aristocracy, into which the new proletarian masses were being drawn, might assume dimensions that threatened not only the remnants of feudal privilege but also capitalist property.

In the struggles of 1848 and their immediate aftermath, the bourgeoisie sought to contain the revolutionary struggle — at the expense of the working class. In France, the old center of revolution and the most politically advanced of European states, the new class relations found brutal expression in the slaughter of the Parisian proletariat in June 1848 by the military force under the command of General Cavaignac. Beyond the borders of France, the bourgeoisie was willing to compromise with the old aristocracy, even to the extent of abandoning the demand for the establishment of a democratic republic and accepting the continuation of aristocratic domination of the state. This was the fate of the German revolution, in which the bourgeoisie — terrified by popular insurrections and the "specter of communism" — capitulated politically to the Prussian aristocracy.

The betrayal by the bourgeoisie of its "own" bourgeois revolution was facilitated by the representatives of the "left" petty bourgeoisie — which at every critical juncture proved itself to be a completely untrustworthy ally of the working class. As Marx and Engels explained in the "Address of the Central Authority":

> Far from desiring to transform the whole of society for the revolutionary proletarians, the democratic petty bourgeois strive for a change in social conditions by means of which the existing society will be made as tolerable and comfortable as possible for them.[5]

---

[5] Karl Marx and Frederick Engels, *Collected Works*, Volume 10 (London: Lawrence & Wishart, 1978), p. 280.

The working class, Marx and Engels concluded, should not allow its struggles and interests to be limited and betrayed. Rather, the workers

> must do the utmost for their final victory by making it clear
> to themselves what their class interests are, by taking up their
> position as an independent party as soon as possible and by
> not allowing themselves to be misled for a single moment by
> the hypocritical phrases of the democratic petty bourgeois
> into refraining from the independent organisation of the party
> of the proletariat. Their battle cry must be: The Revolution in
> Permanence.[6]

Fifty years later, at the turn of the twentieth century, the political significance and implications of this battle cry were to become the subject of intense debate within the rapidly growing Russian socialist movement. It was beyond dispute that the country was moving inexorably toward a democratic revolution that would sweep away a 300-year-old autocratic regime. But beyond that common premise, sharply divergent views developed regarding the class dynamics, political aims and, finally, the socioeconomic consequences of the revolutionary movement. Would the Russian revolution follow the pattern of the "classical" French Revolution of 1789–1794, in which the overthrow of the feudal autocracy led eventually to bourgeois political rule, grounded in capitalist economic relations? Or would the democratic revolution in Russia, developing more than a century later and under vastly changed socioeconomic conditions, necessarily take a profoundly different form? Did there exist in the Russia of 1900, as there had in the France of 1790, a revolutionary bourgeoisie? Was the Russian bourgeoisie really prepared to conduct, or even support, a revolutionary struggle against the autocracy?

Above all, how would the development of the democratic revolution be affected by the fact that the most active and dynamic social force in Russia as it entered the twentieth century was the industrial working class? The strikes of the 1890s had already revealed the power of a working class that was growing rapidly as the flow of foreign capital into Russia financed large-scale industrialization. What role would the industrial proletariat play in the democratic revolution? There could be no doubt that its strength would be decisive in the overthrow of the autocracy. But would the working class then

---

[6] Ibid., p. 287.

accept the transfer of political power to its class enemy, the Russian bourgeoisie? Or would the workers proceed beyond the limits of the "classical" democratic revolution, seek to take power into their own hands, and undertake a far-reaching economic restructuring of society that violated the sanctity of capitalist property?

The posing of these questions led to a reconsideration and further elaboration of the Marx-Engels concept of permanent revolution. The documents that have been included in this volume testify to the intellectual depth of the discussion that unfolded in the Russian and German socialist movement between 1903 and 1907. Against the backdrop of a deepening political crisis of the autocracy, there was a growing dissatisfaction with the political perspective that had guided the Russian Social Democratic Labor Party since its founding. Theoretical and political objections emerged to a conception of the democratic revolution that accepted, all too readily, that the overthrow of the tsar would inevitably and necessarily place political power in the hands of the Russian bourgeoisie.

Plekhanov's contribution

This perspective was identified principally with the work of G.V. Plekhanov, the "Father of Russian Marxism." Plekhanov maintained that in the struggle against tsarism, the working class was to be allied with the liberal bourgeoisie. Once the autocracy was overthrown, a Russian version of a parliamentary democracy would be established. The party of the working class was to enter the Russian parliament as the socialist opposition, seeking to drive the liberal democratic regime as far to the left as possible. But the country would continue to develop, for the indefinite future, on a capitalist basis. Eventually, but no one knew precisely when, Russia would become sufficiently mature, politically and economically, for socialism. At that point, the working class would proceed to the overthrow of the bourgeois regime.

The central problem in this perspective was that it sought to interpret the nature and tasks of the democratic revolution in accordance with a formula that had been overtaken by history. Indeed, Plekhanov had insisted, as far back as 1889, that the democratic revolution in Russia could only succeed as a workers revolution. But if, as Plekhanov continuously emphasized, the working class was to be the decisive force in the overthrow of the autocracy, why would political power necessarily pass into the hands of the liberal bourgeoisie? The only answer that Plekhanov could advance in an effort to silence such questions was that Russian economic development had not sufficiently matured to permit the assumption of political power by the working class and the implementation of measures of a socialist character.

Kautsky's contribution

Karl Kautsky was the first important theoretician to suggest that Russian development might take a path quite different from that foreseen in the traditional model of the bourgeois democratic revolution. Between 1902 and 1907, Kautsky wrote a series of documents, reproduced in this volume, that gravely undermined the authority of Plekhanov's doctrinaire perspective, contributed to the development of a critical attitude toward out-dated precedents, and encouraged the path-breaking work of a younger generation of Russian and Polish social democratic theoreticians, including Leon Trotsky and Rosa Luxemburg.

In a 1902 article entitled "The Slavs and Revolution," Kautsky questioned the assumption that the Russian bourgeoisie would play a revolutionary role in the struggle against tsarism. The dynamic of class relations had changed profoundly since the era of the earlier democratic revolutions. "After 1870," Kautsky wrote, "the bourgeoisie in all countries began to lose its final remnants of revolutionary ambition. From that time onwards, to be a revolutionary also meant to be a socialist."[7]

In another influential essay, provocatively titled "To What Extent is the *Communist Manifesto* Obsolete?" first written in 1903 and revised in 1906, Kautsky stated that

> insofar as we may speak of a "mistake" in the *Manifesto* and consider criticism to be necessary, this must begin precisely with the "dogma" that the bourgeoisie is revolutionary in political terms. The very displacement of revolution by evolution during the last fifty years grows out of the fact that a *revolutionary bourgeoisie* no longer exists.[8]

Among the most important achievements of the Day-Gaido anthology is its recollection, in accordance with the real historical record, of the important

---

[7] *Witnesses to Permanent Revolution*, p. 63.
[8] Ibid., p. 181.

role played by Kautsky, prior to World War I, in the development of the perspective of permanent revolution. Day and Gaido state that they hope that the publication of Kautsky's writings on the Russian Revolution will help "to overcome the stereotypical and mistaken view of Kautsky as an apostle of quietism and a reformist cloaked in revolutionary phraseology."[9] They add:

> This view — an over-generalization drawn from Kautsky's anti-Bolshevik polemics after 1917 — was first developed by the ultra-left philosopher Karl Korsch in his reply to Kautsky's work *Die materialistische Geschichtsauffassung* (1927) and became established in academic circles after the publication of Erich Matthias' book, *Kautsky and Kautskyanism*. Kautsky's main biographer, Marek Waldenberg, provides abundant material to refute this thesis, which was shared by neither Lenin nor Trotsky, both of whom always recommended the writings of Kautsky's revolutionary period to communist workers.[10]

Kautsky's subsequent betrayal of socialism was a repudiation of his own work. When Lenin used the phrase, "How well Kautsky once wrote," he expressed his own dismay and anger over the political and intellectual collapse of the man who had been his teacher. This volume makes clear why Kautsky's betrayal in August 1914 was so shocking to an entire generation of revolutionaries. The anthology includes so many truly splendid passages from Kautsky's revolutionary writings that it is difficult to resist the temptation to overburden this review with citations that reveal the Second International's "Pope of Marxism" to have been a remarkably perceptive, far-sighted and tough-minded polemicist. In retrospect, it is possible to detect (as we will later note) political weaknesses in certain conceptions advanced by Kautsky, especially when he wrote on the implications of a direct clash between the working class and the state. But the contrast between the stereotyped image of Kautsky as an absent-minded professorial fuddy-duddy, complacently waiting for the revolution's arrival as a gift provided by historical necessity, and the real man emerges. In a document published in February 1904, entitled "Revolutionary Questions," Kautsky argues against the political fatalism that was, according to so many academic critics, supposedly his stock-in-trade:

---

[9] Ibid., p. 569.
[10] Ibid.

The world is not so purposely organized as to lead always to the triumph of the revolution where it is essential for the interest of society. When we speak of the necessity of the proletariat's victory and of socialism following from it, we do not mean that victory is inevitable or even, as many of our critics think, that it will take place automatically and with fatalistic certainty even when the revolutionary class remains idle. Necessity must be understood here in the sense of the revolution being the only possibility of further development. Where the proletariat does not succeed in defeating its opponents, society will not be able to develop further; it must either stagnate or rot.[11]

Another essay, "The *Sans-Culottes* of the French Revolution," written originally in 1889 and republished in 1905, contains a panegyric to revolutionary terrorism. According to Kautsky, the terrorism of the Jacobin regime "was more than a weapon of war to unnerve and intimidate the stealthy internal enemy; it also served to inspire confidence in the defenders of the revolution to continue their struggle against external enemies."[12]

The impact of the 1905 revolution

What about the claim that Kautsky, as an incorrigible "vulgar" materialist, had no sense whatever of the role of the subjective element in politics? Or that Kautsky recognized only dry and impersonal economic impulses, and that he failed to allow that emotions and ideals played any significant role in the political activity of the working class? Those who have accepted this stereotyped portrait of Kautsky will be surprised to discover that he considered the absence of "revolutionary 'romanticism'" among American workers and the prevalence among intellectuals of "the most unscrupulous capitalism of the soul" to be significant factors in the weakness of socialism in the United States.[13]

As the anthology makes clear, Kautsky's active involvement in Russian matters was not merely the expression of a kind-hearted avuncular concern for the travails of his young comrades engaged in a life and death battle against

---

[11] Ibid., p. 223.

[12] Ibid., p. 541.

[13] Ibid., pp. 642–643.

the savagely reactionary police state over which the tsar presided. Events in Russia, particularly in the aftermath of the Russo-Japanese War and the outbreak of the revolution of 1905, were seen by Kautsky and his then close ally, Rosa Luxemburg, as critical to the fate of the socialist movement in Germany.

Kautsky, like Luxemburg, was concerned over the growing authority of the trade unions in determining the political line of the SPD (German Social Democratic Party). Despite the formal victory of the orthodox Marxists over the revisionism of Eduard Bernstein at the Dresden Party Congress in September 1903, the pressure exerted by the trade unions represented an even greater danger to the existence of the SPD as a revolutionary movement. The eruption of the 1905 Revolution intensified political conflict within the party.

The mass strikes in Russia were seen by the leaders of left-wing forces within the SPD as the herald of a new spirit of revolutionary struggle and self-sacrifice in Germany. Even Rudolf Hilferding, later an arch-reformist, drew inspiration from the Russian upheaval. He wrote to Kautsky on November 14, 1905 that:

> the collapse of Czarism is the beginning of our revolution, of our victory, that is now drawing near. The expectation, which Marx had mistakenly expressed about the movement of history in 1848, will now, we hope, be fulfilled.[14]

Kautsky was even more enthusiastic over the mass struggles. He wrote in July 1905: "The Revolution in Permanence is ... precisely what the workers of Russia need."[15] Kautsky declared that

> an era of revolutionary developments has begun. The age of slow, painful, almost imperceptible advances will give way to an epoch of revolutions, of sudden leaps forward, perhaps of occasional great defeats, but also — we must have such confidence in the cause of the proletariat — eventually of great victories.[16]

But the revolution that lifted the spirits of militant tendencies within the SPD filled the trade union leadership with dread and revulsion. Fearful of the

---

[14] Ibid., p. 36.

[15] Ibid., p. 376.

[16] Ibid., p. 407.

impact of the Russian example, the Fifth Congress of the Social Democratic Free Trade Unions, held in May 1905 in Köln, rejected the mass strike and prohibited agitation that promoted it. The SPD chairman, August Bebel, attacked "pure and simple" trade unionism and supported a resolution, passed by the party congress held in Jena in September 1905, endorsing the mass strike in the fight for democratic rights.

However, the balance of power between the SPD and the trade unions had drastically changed, to the disadvantage of the party, over the previous decade. Though they had been founded under the leadership of the party, the trade unions, as their membership grew and their bank accounts swelled, acquired distinct and decidedly anti-revolutionary interests. As Theodore Bömelburg, a spokesman of the unions, bluntly declared, what they wanted above all was "peace and quiet."[17]

By 1905 the annual income of the trade unions was roughly fifty times greater than that of the SPD. To the extent that the SPD grew increasingly dependent on subsidies from the trade unions, it became subject to their demands. Moreover, experienced SPD leaders like Bebel must have recognized the possibility that the trade unions might break with the SPD and create, in alliance with sections of the revisionists, an avowedly anti-revolutionary "workers" party. This would create conditions for a violent attack by the state on the SPD. The pressure on SPD leaders to placate the trade unions was enormous. Thus, despite the passage of the mass strike resolution at the Jena congress, the SPD executive met secretly with the Trade Union General Commission. Bebel capitulated to the trade unions' demand for a pledge that the SPD would "try to prevent a mass strike as much as possible."[18] The General Commission warned the SPD that in the event of a political strike, the trade unions would withhold support. The single concession made by the trade unions was that they would not work openly to sabotage the strike. Given the bitter hostility of the trade union leadership to anything that threatened to radicalize class relations, it is doubtful that the SPD placed much faith in this concession.

This period was the high point of Kautsky's long revolutionary career. As he defended Luxemburg against the bitter attacks of the trade union leaders, she referred to him, affectionately and with admiration, as "Karolus Magnus" (Karl the Great). The terrible disappointment and bitterness felt by

---

[17] Ibid., p. 374.
[18] Ibid., p. 375.

Luxemburg over Kautsky's subsequent drift to the right (which Kautsky justified in private correspondence as an attempt to placate the unions) can only be understood against the background of their long relationship.

Ryazanov's contribution

The anthology includes important but little-known documents that were written by theorists of the Russian Social Democratic Labour Party (RSDLP). Among these are two documents written by David Borisovich Gol'dendakh, whose party name was Ryazanov. Born in Odessa in 1870, he would later become best known as an indefatigable historian and archivist of the literary legacy of Marx and Engels. After the Bolshevik Revolution, he headed the State Archive Association and helped establish the Socialist Academy and the Marx-Engels Institute. He traveled to Western Europe, negotiated with various Social Democratic officials, and acquired a vast quantity of documents related to Marx and Engels.

This brilliant Marxist scholar also had a significant career as a revolutionary theoretician. Like Trotsky, he stood outside the Bolshevik and Menshevik factions. In 1917, he was, again like Trotsky, a member of the Inter-District Organization (*Mezhraionka*) before entering the Bolshevik Party in the summer of that year. Ryazanov's role in the aftermath of the Bolshevik seizure of power, in which he attempted to find common ground with a section of the Mensheviks, has received serious scholarly attention in Alexander Rabinowitch's *The Bolsheviks in Power*. Ryazanov's long revolutionary career, his profound knowledge of Marxist theory and the history of the socialist movement, and his broad cultural interests made him an early and inevitable target of Stalin's campaign to destroy the revolutionary Marxist intelligentsia of the USSR. Ryazanov was first arrested in February 1931 and accused of being part of the "Menshevik Center" and of "wrecking activities on the historical front." Ryazanov, wrote Trotsky, "fell victim to his personal honesty."[19] Expelled from the party and exiled to Saratov, Ryazanov was arrested again in 1937. On January 21, 1938, he was sentenced to death by the so-called Military Collegium and shot the same day.

The first document by Ryazanov included in this anthology dates from 1902–03, entitled "The Draft Program of 'Iskra' and the Tasks of Russian

---

[19] Ibid., p. 70.

Social Democrats." Given the length of the original document, which ran 302 pages, Day and Gaido understandably chose to present only representative excerpts. It is an interesting document that reflects the intensity of the factional conflict which, in retrospect, foreshadowed the split that erupted at the Second Congress of the RSDLP in September 1903. Moreover, the document certainly suggests dissatisfaction with the Plekhanovist conception of the necessarily bourgeois character and form of the coming Russian revolution. However, this reviewer believes that Day and Gaido overstate the case in asserting that "Ryazanov's critique of the *Iskra* program is remarkable because it anticipates in almost every detail the theory of *permanent revolution*..."[20]

There are, indeed, certain formulations in which Ryazanov attempts to define the tasks of the working class in a manner that moves beyond the subordination to bourgeois rule envisioned by Plekhanov in the aftermath of the revolution. Ryazanov also expresses a skeptical attitude, which is later developed more forcefully in the writings of Parvus and Trotsky, toward suggestions that the peasantry might play a significant independent role in the revolutionary struggle. However, Ryazanov's formulations on the nature of the coming revolutionary regime remain somewhat tentative: he writes that the revolution "will unquestionably occur on the basis of bourgeois relations of production and in that sense will certainly be 'bourgeois'..." But it "will also, from beginning to end, be *proletarian* in the sense that the proletariat will be its leading element and will make its class imprint on the entire movement."[21] In another part of the document he asserts: "A democratic republic is the form in which the class struggle of the proletariat against the bourgeoisie will freely develop."[22] These formulations fall substantially short of those later employed by Trotsky, who argued that the working class would not only leave its imprint on the revolution, but would also seize state power.

Much of Ryazanov's document — the weakest sections — is devoted to an attack on Lenin's *What Is To Be Done?*, especially the latter's insistence that socialist consciousness does not develop spontaneously within the working class, but that it is brought into the working class from outside. "Comrade Lenin goes too far," writes Ryazanov, as he launches into a forceful polemic against this idea. The commentary of Day and Gaido indicates that they are to some extent sympathetic to Ryazanov's position. However, it is precisely on

---

[20] Ibid.

[21] Ibid., pp. 133–134.

[22] Ibid., pp. 121–122.

this issue — that socialism is brought into the working class from outside the sphere of its spontaneous economic struggles and practical activities — that Kautsky's influence on Lenin was most pronounced. In *What Is To Be Done?* Lenin included a lengthy passage written by Kautsky, in which the latter explained that "socialist consciousness is something introduced into the proletarian class struggle from without [*von Außen hineingetragenes*] and not something that arose within it spontaneously [*urwüchsig*]."[23] Notwithstanding his opposition to reformism, Ryazanov's document advances positions that in certain critical respects, resemble those of the Economists, the principal target of *What Is To Be Done?* Day and Gaido note that a historian, writing in 1970, described Ryazanov's critique of *Iskra* as "revolutionary economism."[24]

The second Ryazanov document, which was written approximately three years later, in the midst of the 1905 Revolution, includes formulations that come much closer to those being developed by Trotsky and Parvus. Emphasizing the centrality of "the question of property," Ryazanov declared:

> In concentrating all its efforts on completing *its own* tasks, it [the working class] simultaneously approaches the moment when the issue will not be *participation* in a provisional government, but rather the seizure of power by the working class and conversion of the "bourgeois" revolution into a direct prologue for the social revolution.[25]

Lenin's contribution

In the evolution of the theory and strategy of the Russian Revolution, Lenin's conception of the "democratic dictatorship of the proletariat and peasantry" emerged in 1905 as a major alternative to the orthodox conception of Plekhanov. Lenin's perspective differed from Plekhanov's in two fundamental respects, both of which had far-reaching political and practical implications. First, although Lenin characterized the coming revolution as bourgeois, he excluded that this revolution could be led, let alone carried through to a decisive conclusion, by the Russian bourgeoisie. In contrast to Plekhanov, Lenin rejected categorically any political alliance with the bourgeois liberals.

---

[23] Lenin, *Collected Works*, Volume 5 (Moscow: Foreign Languages Publishing House, 1961), p. 384.

[24] *Witnesses to Permanent Revolution*, p. 70.

[25] Ibid., p. 473.

Moreover, for Lenin, the essential historical significance of the "bourgeois" revolution lay not in the establishment of democratic parliamentary institutions, but, rather, in the radical destruction of all vestiges of feudal relations in the countryside. This is why Lenin placed the so-called "agrarian question" at the center of the democratic revolution. As Trotsky emphasized in his last major article on the origins of the theory of permanent revolution, "With infinitely greater power and consistency than Plekhanov, Lenin advanced the agrarian question as the central problem of the democratic overturn in Russia."[26]

From this analysis emerged a political strategy fundamentally different from that of Plekhanov. The success of the democratic revolution, which in the countryside entailed the expropriation of the vast estates of the old landowning class, could only be achieved through the massive mobilization of Russia's tens of millions of peasants. The Russian bourgeoisie, hostile to any form of mass action directed against private property, could neither sanction nor lead a revolutionary overturn of existing property relations in the countryside. But only through such a mobilization of the peasantry, which comprised the overwhelming majority of Russia's population, could the tsarist regime be overthrown.

For Lenin, Plekhanov's orientation toward the liberal bourgeoisie meant the doom of the revolution. The main ally of the working class in the revolutionary struggle against the tsarist regime was the peasantry. It was from this assessment of the dynamics of the democratic revolution that Lenin developed his conception of the new form of revolutionary state power that would replace the tsarist autocracy: the democratic dictatorship of the proletariat and peasantry.

Lenin's conception of the democratic revolution placed the Bolshevik faction of the Russian Social Democratic Labor Party (it was not until 1912 that the Bolsheviks declared themselves as an independent party) in irreconcilable political hostility to the bourgeoisie and all the Menshevik tendencies which, in one form or another, insisted that a liberal bourgeois parliamentary republic was the only legitimate outcome of the overthrow of the tsar. However, Lenin clearly distinguished between the democratic and the socialist revolutions. The democratic dictatorship of the proletariat and peasantry as envisaged by Lenin, would be established on the basis of capitalist relations. Writing in 1905 Lenin explained:

---

[26] *Writings of Leon Trotsky 1939–40* (New York: Pathfinder Press, 1973), p. 58.

But of course it will be a democratic, not a socialist dictatorship. It will be unable (without a series of intermediary stages
of revolutionary development) to affect the foundations of
capitalism. At best, it may bring about a radical redistribution
of landed property in favor of the peasantry, establish consistent and full democracy, including the formation of a republic,
eradicate all the oppressive features of Asiatic bondage, not only
in rural but also in factory life, lay the foundation for a thorough improvement in the conditions of the workers and for a
rise in their standard of living, and — last but not least — carry
the revolutionary conflagration into Europe. Such a victory will
not yet by any means transform our bourgeois revolution into a
socialist revolution; the democratic revolution will not immediately overstep the bounds of bourgeois social and economic
relationships; nevertheless, the significance of such a victory for
the future development of Russia and of the whole world will be
immense.[27]

Lenin's program, as Trotsky later wrote, "represented an enormous step
forward" beyond Plekhanov's conception of the bourgeois revolution.[28]
However, it raised theoretical and political questions that revealed the ambi-
guities and limitations of Lenin's formulation. In particular, Lenin's conception foresaw the creation of a new and unprecedented state form in which
power would be shared by two classes, the proletariat and the peasantry. How
would power be distributed between these classes? Moreover, as Lenin clearly
recognized, the destruction of the old landed estates and the redistribution of
the land did not mean the end of the private ownership of land. The peasantry
remained committed to private property, albeit on a more equitable basis.
However, the peasantry would be hostile to the anti-private property, socialistic aspirations and orientation of the proletariat. This basic contradiction in
the social orientation of the two classes called into question the viability of
Lenin's democratic dictatorship.

Despite the limitations of Lenin's program, it marked a milestone in the
development of Russian revolutionary thought. This reviewer is, therefore,
somewhat puzzled by the ill-considered and almost dismissive attitude taken

---

[27] Lenin, *Collected Works*, Volume 9 (Moscow: Progress Publishers, 1972), pp. 56–57.
[28] *Writings of Leon Trotsky 1939–40*, p. 59.

by Day and Gaido toward Lenin's position. In this one instance, one almost hears the grinding of political axes, and it weakens their generally excellent review of the debate on the theory of permanent revolution. They state:

> The problem with Lenin's notion of a "democratic dictatorship of the proletariat and peasantry" was obvious: in Russia, there was no revolutionary petty-bourgeois party with whom to co-operate. Lenin thought such a party must eventually emerge, but this was hardly a practical basis upon which to base political tactics.[29]

One is surprised by this judgment. Whatever the limitations of Lenin's theory, they were certainly not "obvious." If they were, Trotsky's criticisms of the "democratic dictatorship" perspective and his development beyond it, with the theory of permanent revolution, would not have been such an impressive intellectual achievement. Also, Lenin could hardly be faulted for leaving open the possibility of a mass peasant party in Russia. The future development of the Socialist Revolutionary Party, which acquired a mass, albeit unstable, base within the peasantry, proved Lenin correct.

Finally, it must be kept in mind that Lenin belonged to a generation that grew to political maturity in the aftermath of the catastrophe of the Paris Commune. The inability of the workers of Paris to rally the French peasantry to their side was the decisive factor that enabled the bourgeois regime in Versailles to destroy the Commune in May 1871. That was not a political fail-ure that would be quickly forgotten. For Lenin, the fate of the working class in Russia (and, for that matter, any country with a large agrarian population) depended upon its ability to win the support of the peasantry. It is always worthwhile to think about the historical time-frame. Only thirty-four years separated the Paris Commune from the Revolution of 1905. The destruction of the Commune was a less distant event to Lenin's generation in 1905 than the fall of Saigon in May 1975 is to the present day!

There is another aspect of Lenin's formulation of the democratic dicta-torship that is of enduring significance. Lenin's understanding of the con-tradictory nature of the revolutionary peasant movement—above all, his insistence that peasant insurrections and the mass seizure of land did not necessarily lead to the destruction of capitalist relations—was both subtle

---

[29] *Witnesses to Permanent Revolution*, p. 257.

and perceptive. Tackling an issue that would time and again cause political confusion within the left (among the admirers, for example, of Castro, Mao, the Naxalites and even Mexico's "sub-Comandante" Marcos), Lenin argued against the widespread misconception that peasant radicalism — even when it fights for the distribution of land to the rural poor — is socialistic. Lenin insisted that the nationalization of land is a key component of the democratic revolution, and, under certain conditions, critical for the development of capitalism. Explaining that the nationalization of land is a democratic, rather than socialist, measure, Lenin wrote:

> Failure to grasp this truth makes the Socialist-Revolutionaries unconscious ideologists of the petty bourgeoisie. Insistence on this truth is of enormous importance for Social-Democracy not only from the standpoint of theory but also from that of practical politics, for it follows therefrom that complete class independence of the party of the proletariat in the present "general democratic" movement is an indispensable condition.[30]

The military disasters suffered by Russia in its war with Japan led to the eruption of a revolution that was heralded by the massacre of St. Petersburg workers who had marched in protest on January 9, 1905 to the Winter Palace. The social explosion within the Russian Empire provided a powerful impulse for the development of revolutionary theory. The two figures who played the central role in the formulation of the theory of permanent revolution were Parvus and Trotsky.

Parvus' contribution

Eighty-five years after his death in Germany, Parvus (1867–1924) remains an enigmatic, even somewhat mysterious, figure. He is remembered far more for his nefarious commercial activities during World War I, after he had abandoned the revolutionary movement, than for his remarkable work as a Marxist theoretician during the final years of the nineteenth century and the first years of the twentieth. But it is indisputable that Parvus, born Alexander Helphand, played a critical role in the life of the revolutionary movement in Russia and Germany. He first came to the attention of European socialists with

---

[30] Lenin, *Collected Works*, Volume 9, p. 48.

his attacks on the revisionism of Eduard Bernstein. His first anti-Bernstein articles appeared in the German socialist press in January 1898, even before Luxemburg, let alone Kautsky, entered into the fray. It was not merely their timeliness that made Parvus' articles significant; the articles displayed a remarkable grasp of the economics of German and world capitalism that left the impression that Bernstein did not really know what he was talking about.

As Trotsky later acknowledged, his own thoughts on the dynamic of Russian revolutionary development were deeply influenced by Parvus. It was Parvus, Trotsky wrote, who "definitely transformed the conquest of power by the proletariat from an astronomical 'final' goal to a practical task for our own day."[31] Both Parvus and Trotsky recognized that the emergence of the St. Petersburg Soviet in October 1905 opened up enormous possibilities for the working class. Parvus argued that conceptions of the appropriate "tasks" of the revolution that proceeded from abstract calculations of the "objective" development of the national productive forces, while ignoring the no less objective dynamic of the unfolding class forces in a revolutionary situation, were inadequate. The seizure of power by the working class, Parvus argued, had become possible. He rejected the Menshevik argument that the working class, based on a fatalistic calculation of available economic resources, was obligated to stand aside and watch respectfully as the bourgeoisie took power into its hands. In a brilliant exposition of the interaction of politics and economics, Parvus cleared the path for a far more aggressive formulation of proletarian revolutionary strategy:

> If class relations were determined by the historical course of events in some simple and straightforward manner, then there would be no use in racking our brains: all we would have to do is calculate the moment for social revolution in the same way as astronomers plot the movement of a planet, and then we could sit back and observe. In reality, the relation between classes produces political struggle above all else. What is more, the final outcome of that struggle is determined by the development of class forces. The entire historical process, which embraces centuries, depends upon a multitude of secondary economic, political, and national cultural conditions, but above all it depends on the revolutionary energy and political consciousness of the

---

[31] *Witnesses to Permanent Revolution*, p. 252.

struggling combatants — on their tactics and their skill in seizing the political moment.[32]

Parvus did not claim that Russia was ripe for the establishment of socialism. He stated categorically that "Without a social revolution in Western
Europe, it is presently impossible in Russia to realise socialism."[33] But he
believed that the momentum of the class struggle might create conditions in
which the working class could seize power. It would then use that power in
a manner that advanced as far as possible the interests of the working class.

Parvus did not attempt to predict the exact course of revolutionary
development. Politics, in his view, involved a complex interaction of forces,
influences and factors that allowed for innumerable variants of development.
He foresaw a protracted process of struggle, in which the overthrow of the
tsarist autocracy represented only the starting point of the revolution. Parvus
argued:

> Placing the proletariat at the center and the head of the revolu-
> tionary movement of the whole people and the whole of society,
> Social Democracy must simultaneously prepare it for the civil
> war that will follow the overthrow of autocracy — for the time
> when it will be attacked by agrarian and bourgeois liberalism
> and betrayed by the political radicals and the democrats.
>
> The working class must understand that the revolution and
> the collapse of autocracy are not the same thing, and that, in
> order to carry through the political revolution, it will be neces-
> sary to struggle first against the autocracy and then against the
> bourgeoisie.[34]

Parvus' remarkable essay, "What Was Accomplished on the Ninth of
January," contains a wealth of political insights, which reflect the wisdom of
a political age that stood, at least in its understanding of the realities of the
class struggle, on a level incomparably higher than our own. Discussing the
problems that arise in the course of fighting alongside temporary and unstable allies, Parvus advised:

---

[32] Ibid., p. 261.

[33] Ibid.

[34] Ibid., 267.

1) Do not blur the organizational lines. March separately, but strike in unison.

2) Do not waver in our own political demands.

3) Do not hide differences of interest.

4) Keep watch of our allies in the same way as we watch our enemies.

5) Pay more attention to taking advantage of the situation created by the struggle than to the maintenance of an ally.[35]

In late 1905, Trotsky wrote "Up to the Ninth of January." A complete English translation of this work appears for the first time in this anthology. The work is an acute and devastating exposure of the political rottenness of the liberal representatives of the Russian bourgeoisie. Trotsky chronicles their spineless attitude toward the tsarist regime in a period of mounting crisis, caused by the devastating defeats of the Russian army in the war with Japan. He writes with contempt of the manner in which the liberal politicians acquiesced in the war:

> It was not enough for the [liberals] to join in the dirty work of a shameful slaughter and to take upon themselves — that is, to load upon the people — part of the expenses. They were not satisfied with tacit political connivance and acquiescent cover-up of the work of tsarism — no, they publicly declared to everyone their moral solidarity with those responsible for committing the greatest of crimes. ... One after the other they responded to the declaration of war with loyal pronouncements, using the formal rhetoric of seminars to express their political idiocy...
>
> And what about the liberal press? This pitiful, mumbling, groveling, lying, cringing, depraved and corrupting liberal press![36]

One might be forgiven for believing that the young Trotsky was describing the Democratic Party of the United States and today's *New York Times*. But more than a century ago, the foulness of bourgeois liberalism was well understood by socialists.

---

[35] Ibid., pp. 267–268.
[36] Ibid., pp. 282–284.

Trotsky's contribution

This anthology includes the work of brilliant writers. But the works of the young Trotsky stand out from all the others. He presents a new perspective in a distinctive and powerful voice. What is most remarkable in these early writings is their vivid conceptualization and articulation of an emerging mass revolutionary movement of the working class and the elemental force of its struggle for power. In this sense, the contrast to Kautsky's writings is striking. Even in the best work of the latter, when he is formulating and defending a revolutionary perspective, Kautsky's portrayal of the clash of opposing class forces is detached, and seems to reflect the inner doubts of the writer. He left open the possibility, in a not very convincing manner, that the working class might be able, without resorting to violence, to frighten its class enemy into surrendering power! He wrote:

> A rising class must have the necessary instruments of force at its disposal if it wants to dispossess the old ruling class, but it is not unconditionally necessary that it *employ* them. Under certain circumstances, *awareness* of the existence of such instruments can be enough to induce a declining class to come to an agreement peacefully with an opponent that has become overwhelming.[37]

It should, of course, be kept in mind that Kautsky was well aware of the hostility that existed within sections of the SPD, and especially within the trade unions, to any suggestion that the party believed in the inevitability of, let alone advocated, an armed struggle for power. Nor was he unmindful that incautious formulations, even in a theoretical journal, might be seized upon by the Prussian state as a pretext for an assault on the SPD. The fact that there existed influential voices within the upper echelons of the state that were continuously advocating a bloody showdown with the Social Democracy was well known. But still, it is evident that Kautsky had no clear answer to the unavoidable problem that confronted the working class in a modern capitalist state: how to overcome the resistance of the military forces at the disposal of the government? In one essay, Kautsky went so far as to suggest that the defeat of a government prepared to defend itself by mobilizing the military might

---

[37] Ibid., p. 247.

not be possible. "The consciousness of technical military superiority makes it possible for any government that possesses the necessary ruthlessness to look forward calmly to a popular armed uprising. ...."[38]

Trotsky, as Day and Gaido point out, "makes precisely the opposite argument: a mass strike will necessarily lead to armed conflict when the government responds with orders to shoot down strikers."[39] While for Kautsky the issuing of orders to soldiers that they fire on workers might well mean the end of the revolution, for Trotsky such orders could lead to the end of the oppressors' state. Trotsky noted that reactionaries tend to believe that the defeat of revolution requires only the sufficient application of repressive force. "Grand Duke Vladimir," Trotsky observed laconically,

> who spent his time in Paris studying not only the whore-houses but also the administrative-military history of the Great Revolution, concluded that the old order would have been saved in France if Louis's government had crushed every sprout of revolution, without any wavering or hesitation, and if he had cured the people of Paris with a bold and widely organized blood-letting. On 9 January, our most august alcoholic showed exactly how this should be done. ... Guns, rifles and munitions are excellent servants of order, but they have to be put into action. For that purpose, people are needed. And even though these people are called soldiers, they differ from guns because they feel and think, which means they are not reliable. They hesitate, they are infected by the indecision of their commanders, and the result is disarray and panic in the highest ranks of the bureaucracy.[40]

This collection does not include Trotsky's first definitive elaboration of the theory of permanent revolution, the famous *Results and Prospects*, which was published in 1906. But Day and Gaido present a number of documents in which the development of Trotsky's political thought — from the contemptuous exposure of the reactionary character of Russian liberalism to his conclusion that the logic of class struggle will compel the working class to take

---

[38] Ibid., p. 236.
[39] Ibid., p. 334.
[40] Ibid., p. 347.

power — can be traced. These crucial preparatory works include Trotsky's "Introduction to *Ferdinand Lassalle's Speech to the Jury*," "Social Democracy and Revolution," and the "Foreword to Karl Marx, *Parizhskaya Kommuna*." All of these essays date from 1905, the year in which Trotsky became chairman of the St. Petersburg Soviet and emerged as the greatest orator and mass leader of the first Russian revolution.

Trotsky's "Introduction to *Ferdinand Lassalle's Speech to the Jury*" is one of his early masterpieces. Lassalle had played a major role in the 1848 revolution in Germany, as a representative of the extreme left wing of the democratic forces. Arrested for inciting insurrection against Prussia, Lassalle wrote a speech in his own defense. The speech was not delivered in the courtroom, but thousands of copies of the written text were distributed throughout Germany and made a profound impression. Trotsky, as Day and Gaido observe, "obviously admired the grand rhetoric of Lassalle's *Speech to the Jury*," and it certainly influenced the form taken by Trotsky's no less memorable speech when he was placed on trial in 1906 after the defeat of the 1905 revolution.[41]

In his "Introduction," Trotsky drew lessons from the experience of the 1848 revolution to drive home the essential political point that in the contemporary struggle against the tsarist autocracy, the Russian bourgeoisie was the bitter enemy of the working class. The bourgeoisie had learned from the events of 1789–95 that revolution, however critical for the realization of its own interests, raised the danger of unintended consequences. As it succeeded in consolidating its own social and economic position, the more determined it became to resist the demands of the masses. In the ensuing conflict, the previously concealed nature of society emerged into the open. In a memorable passage, Trotsky described a revolutionary epoch as "a school of political materialism."

> It translates all social norms into the language of force. It gives influence to those who rely upon force and are united, disciplined, and ready to take action. Its mighty tremors drive the masses onto the field of struggle and reveal to them the ruling classes — both those who are departing and those who are arriving. For exactly this reason, it is terrifying both for the class that is losing power and for the one acquiring power. Once they have entered upon this road, the masses develop their own logic and

---

[41] Ibid., p. 411.

go much further than necessary from the viewpoint of the new bourgeois arrivals. Every day brings new slogans, each more radical than the previous one, and they spread as rapidly as blood circulates in the human body. If the bourgeoisie accepts revolution as the starting point of a new system, it will deprive itself of any opportunity to appeal to law and order in opposing the revolutionary encroachments of the masses. That is why a deal with reaction, at the expense of the people's rights, is a class imperative for the liberal bourgeoisie.

This applies equally to its position before, during, and after the revolution.[42]

At the end of his careful review of the German bourgeoisie's betrayal of the democratic revolution of 1848, Trotsky drew the political conclusion: a half-century later, there existed even less possibility that the bourgeoisie would play any sort of progressive political role. Moreover, the global development of capitalism during the preceding half-century had drawn the Russian bourgeoisie into a world-wide system of political domination and economic exploitation. It is at this point that Trotsky calls attention to a new and decisive factor in the development of the Russian revolution:

Imposing its own type of economy and its own relations on all countries, capitalism has transformed the entire world into a single economic and political organism. And just as modern credit binds thousands of enterprises together by an invisible thread and imparts astounding mobility to capital, eliminating numerous small and partial crises while at the same time making general economic crises incomparably more serious, so the entire economic and political functioning of capitalism, with its world trade, its system of monstrous state debts and international political alliances, which are drawing all the reactionary forces into a single worldwide joint-stock company, has not only resisted all partial political crises but has also prepared the conditions for a social crisis of unprecedented dimensions. Internalizing all the pathological processes, circumventing all the difficulties, brushing aside all the profound questions of

---

[42] Ibid., p. 416.

domestic and international politics, and hiding all the contradictions, the bourgeoisie has postponed the denouement while simultaneously preparing a radical, worldwide liquidation of its supremacy. It has avidly clung to every reactionary force without questioning its origins...

From the very outset, this fact gives currently unfolding events an international character and opens up majestic prospects. Political emancipation, led by the Russian working class, is raising the latter to heights that are historically unprecedented, providing it with colossal means and resources, and making it the initiator of capitalism's worldwide liquidation, for which history has prepared all the objective preconditions.[43]

These paragraphs mark Trotsky's emergence as a strategist of world socialist revolution!

Beneath the impact of the monumental strike of October 1905 and the creation of the St. Petersburg Soviet, the most advanced socialist thinkers struggled to discover the political formula that would reconcile the ever more glaring contradiction between the economic backwardness of Russia — which was, according to the conventional interpretation of Marxism, unprepared for socialist revolution — and the undeniable reality that the working class was the decisive force in the unfolding revolutionary situation. Where was the revolution going? What could the working class expect to achieve?

Parvus, writing in November 1905, advised that

> The direct revolutionary goal of the Russian proletariat is to achieve the kind of state system in which the demands of workers' democracy will be realised. Workers' democracy includes all of the most extreme demands of bourgeois democracy, but it imparts to some of them a special character and also includes new demands that are strictly proletarian.[44]

The Russian revolution, he explained, "creates a special connection between the minimum program of Social Democracy and its final goal." Parvus then added:

---

[43] Ibid., p. 444–445.
[44] Ibid., p. 493.

This does not imply the dictatorship of the proletariat, whose task is a fundamental change of production relations in the country, yet it already goes beyond bourgeois democracy. We are not yet ready in Russia to assume the task of converting the bourgeois revolution into a socialist revolution, but we are even less ready to subordinate ourselves to a bourgeois revolution. Not only would this contradict the first premises of our entire program, but the class struggle of the proletariat also drives us forward. Our task is to expand the limits of the bourgeois revolution by including within it the interests of the proletariat and by creating, *within the bourgeois constitution itself,* the greatest possible opportunities for social-revolutionary upheaval.[45] (Emphasis added)

Even Parvus seemed to retreat before the problem posed by the backwardness of Russian economic development and the political dynamism of the working class.

One month later, in his foreword to Marx's speech on the Paris Commune, Trotsky asserted that there was a solution to this problem. But to find it required the understanding that there did not exist a formal and mechanical relationship between the level of development of the productive forces of a given country and the capacity of its working class to take power. The calculations of the revolutionary party had to include other critical factors, i.e., "the relations of class struggle, the international situation, and finally, upon a number of subjective factors that include tradition, initiative, and readiness for the fight."[46] What conclusion followed from this insight? Trotsky declared: "In an economically backward country, the proletariat can come to power sooner than in a country of the most advanced capitalism."[47] A half-century of socioeconomic development, decades of theoretical work, and the experience of a revolution was necessary to arrive at this conclusion.

Trotsky had, at this point, worked out the basic outline of his theory of permanent revolution. In fact, passages from his "Introduction" to Lassalle's speech and his "Foreword" to Marx's speech on the Paris Commune were reproduced in *Results and Prospects.* However, even as he prepared the writing

---

[45] Ibid.
[46] Ibid., p. 502.
[47] Ibid.

of this crucial work, Trotsky continued to find encouragement and inspiration in the writings of Kautsky.

Kautsky's analysis of the American class struggle

Among the most important documents included in the Day-Gaido anthology is a virtually unknown work by Kautsky from February 1906, "The American Worker." It was written as a reply to the study of American society by the German sociologist Werner Sombart (1863–1941), which bore the intriguing title, *Why Is There No Socialism in the United States?* The question was an important one. Obviously, from the political standpoint, it had to be addressed. What was the future of socialism if it remained unable to obtain a mass following in the working class within the most advanced capitalist country? Moreover, there was a critical theoretical issue that could not be ignored. How was one to explain, within the framework of Marxist theory, the following paradox: In the United States, the most advanced capitalist country, socialism seemed to be making very little headway. But in Russia, among the countries where capitalism was the least developed, socialism was advancing by leaps and bounds. How was the paradox to be explained? Yet another question was raised. If, as Marx had indicated, the advanced countries revealed the "pattern" of development which less developed countries would necessarily reproduce, what were the implications of the "non-socialist" pattern of development of the most advanced and powerful country in the world? Sombart, drawing the most conservative conclusions, argued that the United States showed Europe its future.

Kautsky raised an objection. Sombart's claim, he wrote, "can be accepted only with great reservations." The sociologist's error was to abstract American conditions in a one-sided manner out of a complex totality of economic, social and political relations formed on the basis of the global development of capitalism. Sombart failed to note that the pattern of development with which Marx was most familiar, that of England, had not been simply reproduced in other countries. The England of Marx's time possessed the most developed industry. But the advance of industrial capitalism generated the opposing tendencies of proletarian resistance and organization. So England saw the emergence of Chartism, and later trade unions and social legislation. But this development, in which there existed interaction of capitalist development and working class counter-action, did not establish a universal "pattern."

Kautsky explained:

> Today, there is a whole series of countries in which capital controls the whole of economic life, but none of them has developed all the aspects of the capitalist mode of production to the same extent. There are, in particular, two states that face each other as extremes, in which one of the two elements of this mode of production is disproportionately strong, i.e., stronger than it should be according to its level of development: *in America, the capitalist class; in Russia, the working class.*[48]

Which country, then, showed Germany its future? Kautsky answered:

> Germany's *economy* is closest to the *American* one; its *politics*, on the other hand, are closest to the *Russian*. In this way, both countries show us our future; it will have a half-American, half-Russian character. The more we study Russia and America, and the better we understand both, the more clearly we will be able to comprehend our own future. The American example alone would be as misleading as the Russian.
>
> It is certainly a peculiar phenomenon that precisely the Russian proletariat should show us our future — as far as the rebellion of the working class, not the organisation of capital, is concerned — because Russia is, of all the great states of the capitalist world, the most backward. This seems to contradict the materialist conception of history, according to which economic development constitutes the basis of politics. But, in fact, it only contradicts that kind of historical materialism of which our opponents and critics accuse us, by which they understand a *ready-made model* and not a *method of inquiry.* They reject the materialist conception of history only because they are unable to understand it and to apply it fruitfully.[49]

It is not possible, without adding substantially to the length of this review, to examine Kautsky's explanation of the peculiarity of America's political

---

[48] Ibid., pp. 620–621.
[49] Ibid., p. 621.

development. Suffice it to say that Kautsky offered an extremely insightful analysis of the economic and social environment that made it exceptionally difficult for socialism to advance in America as it had in Europe. Among the factors to which he pointed was the manner in which the great wealth of American capitalism corrupted a substantial section of the intelligentsia, rendering it indifferent to the political and social needs of the working class. Nevertheless, Kautsky concluded that, despite the many obstacles, socialism would eventually become a substantial political force in the United States.

Kautsky's "The American Worker" exerted a powerful influence on Trotsky, as he explicitly acknowledged in *Results and Prospects*. He included in his work passages from the paragraphs cited above. Trotsky never denied the debt that he and others of his generation owed to Kautsky. Trotsky did not forgive Kautsky's later betrayals, but he saw no need to minimize, let alone deny, his achievements. Trotsky remembered Kautsky, at the time of his death in 1938, "as our former teacher to whom we once owed a great deal, but who separated himself from the proletarian revolution and from whom, consequently, we had to separate ourselves."[50]

If Kautsky's vital contribution to Trotsky's elaboration of the theory of permanent revolution needs to be stressed, it is because so much ink has been wasted by the petty-bourgeois anti-Marxist left on behalf of its efforts to completely discredit the theoretical heritage of socialism, in whose development Kautsky played a major role. The denunciations of the whole corpus of Kautsky's work, promoted by the Frankfurt School and amplified by diverse varieties of petty-bourgeois radicalism, *have been from the right*, directed not at the weaknesses of the pre-1914 social democracy, but rather against its greatest strength: that it was based on and sought to educate, politically and culturally, the working class. The study of Kautsky's writings, written before he succumbed to the political pressures bearing down on the pre-1914 Social Democracy, will make possible a deeper understanding of the development of Marxist thought, including that of Lenin and Trotsky. This reviewer endorses fully the words with which Day and Gaido conclude their introduction to this splendid volume:

> The theory of permanent revolution has been a focus of debate
> for decades, not only between Trotsky's followers and his crit-
> ics but also amongst academic historians. But in the court of

---

[50] Ibid., p. 58.

history, as Trotsky understood very well when judging Kautsky, fairness and decency require that participants be assured every opportunity to speak for themselves.[51]

Between the years 1903 and 1907 Marxist social and political thought underwent a rapid development. To study these documents is to return to an age when political thought stood incomparably higher than it does today. This review, despite its length, has provided only a glimpse of the riches contained in *Witnesses to Permanent Revolution*. It is inevitable that documents as complex and far-ranging as those presented in this anthology lend themselves to diverse interpretations. I have indicated certain areas where I disagree with the judgments of Richard Day and Daniel Gaido. But this does not diminish in the least my very great appreciation, which will be felt by many socialists, for their important contribution to the revival of interest in the development of revolutionary theory in the twentieth century.

---

[51] Ibid.

11

Trotsky's Victory over Stalinism:
Seventy-five Years of the
Fourth International 1938–2013[1]

Seventy-five years ago, on September 3, 1938, the Fourth International was founded at a conference held on the outskirts of Paris. The work of the conference had to be completed within one day due to precarious security conditions. During the twelve months that preceded the conference, the Trotskyist movement had been under relentless attack. Though he lived in exile in Mexico, Leon Trotsky was viewed by the Stalinist regime in the Soviet Union as its most dangerous political opponent. Stalin was determined to destroy the international movement that Trotsky had created during the decade that followed his expulsion from the Soviet Communist Party in 1927 and his deportation from the USSR in 1929.

In September 1937, Erwin Wolf, a political secretary of Trotsky, was murdered in Spain by agents of the Soviet secret police, the GPU. During that same month, Ignace Reiss, who had defected from the GPU and declared his loyalty to the new International being founded by Trotsky, was assassinated in Lausanne, Switzerland. In February 1938, Leon Sedov — Trotsky's eldest son and most important political representative in Europe — was murdered

---

[1] Published 4 September 2013 on the *World Socialist Web Site*.

by the GPU in Paris. And in July 1938, only six weeks before the founding conference, Rudolf Klement — the leader of the movement's International Secretariat — was kidnapped from his apartment in Paris and murdered.

Sedov, Wolf and Klement were elected honorary presidents of the conference, and the French Trotskyist, Pierre Naville, informed the delegates that "Owing to the tragic death of Klement there would be no formal report; Klement had had a detailed, written report in preparation which was to have been circulated, but it had disappeared with the rest of his papers. The present report would be merely a summary."[2]

The hellish conditions in which the conference was held reflected the political situation that confronted the international working class. Fascist regimes held power in Germany and Italy. Europe teetered on the brink of war. The infamous Munich conference at which British and French imperialism surrendered Czechoslovakia to Hitler — with the acquiescence of the capitalist government in Prague — was to be held only several weeks later. The Spanish revolution, having been misled and betrayed by its Stalinist and anarchist leaders, was rapidly approaching defeat after more than two years of civil war. In France, the Popular Front government of 1936–38 had done everything in its power to politically demoralize the working class. In the Soviet Union, the terror that had been unleashed by Stalin in 1936 had annihilated virtually the entire generation of Old Bolsheviks. The betrayals of the Stalinists and social democrats had sabotaged the only means by which the outbreak of a second imperialist world war could have been prevented — that is, the socialist revolution of the working class.

The crisis of leadership

The main task facing the delegates attending the founding conference was the adoption of a document that had been drafted by Leon Trotsky. It was titled "The Death Agony of Capitalism and the Tasks of the Fourth International." Its opening sentence, among the most significant and profound in the annals of political literature, stated: "The world political situation as a whole is chiefly characterized by a historical crisis of the leadership of the proletariat."

With these words Trotsky summed up not only the situation as it existed in 1938, but also the central political problem of modern history. The

---

[2] Will Reissner, ed., *Documents of the Fourth International: The Formative Years 1933–40* (New York: Pathfinder Press, 1973), p. 285.

objective prerequisites — i.e., the international development of the productive forces, the existence of the revolutionary class — for the replacement of capitalism by socialism were present. But revolution was not merely the automatic outcome of objective economic conditions. It required the politically conscious intervention of the working class in the historical process, based on a socialist program and armed with a clearly elaborated strategic plan. The revolutionary politics of the working class could not be *less conscious* than the counterrevolutionary politics of the capitalist class it sought to overthrow. Herein lay the historic significance of the revolutionary party.

But the decisive role of the revolutionary party, which had been positively demonstrated in October 1917 — when the Russian working class, under the leadership of the Bolshevik Party of Lenin and Trotsky, overthrew the capitalist class and established the first workers state in history — was confirmed in the negative by the defeats of the 1920s and 1930s. A series of revolutionary opportunities had been lost by the false policies and deliberate betrayals carried out by the mass social democratic and Communist (Stalinist) parties that commanded the allegiance of the working class.

The political bankruptcy and reactionary role of the social democratic parties of the Second International had been laid bare as early as 1914, when they repudiated their own internationalist programs and supported the war policies of their own national ruling classes. The Communist (or Third) International had been formed in the aftermath of the October Revolution, in opposition to the betrayal of the social democracy.

But the growth of the state bureaucracy within the Soviet Union and the political degeneration of the Russian Communist Party had far-reaching consequences for the Communist International. In 1923, the Left Opposition had been formed under Trotsky's leadership to combat the bureaucratization of the Russian Communist Party. But the bureaucracy, which found in Stalin a dedicated representative of its interests and privileges, fought back savagely against its Marxist opponents. In 1924, Stalin and Bukharin proclaimed the program of "socialism in one country," which repudiated the program of socialist internationalism — that is, of *permanent revolution* — upon which Lenin and Trotsky had based the Bolshevik conquest of power in October 1917. The Stalin-Bukharin program provided an anti-Marxist theoretical justification for the practical subordination of the interests of the international working class to the national interests of the Soviet bureaucracy.

The impact of this fundamental revision of Marxist theory on the practice of the Third International and its affiliated parties was catastrophic. In the course of the 1920s, those leaders of national Communist parties who failed to fall in line with the dictates of Moscow were bureaucratically removed and replaced with compliant and incompetent factotums. Disoriented by the policies formulated by Stalin — who ever more openly viewed the Third International not as a party of world socialist revolution, but rather as an instrument of Soviet foreign policy — the Communist parties staggered from one disaster to another. The defeat of the British General Strike in 1926 and, one year later, the defeat of the Chinese Revolution were critical milestones in the degeneration of the Third International.

In 1928, having been exiled to Alma Ata in Central Asia, Trotsky wrote *The Draft Program of the Communist International: A Criticism of Fundamentals* on the eve of the organization's Sixth Congress. This document was a detailed elaboration of the theoretical and political causes of the defeats suffered by the Communist parties during the preceding five years. The main target of Trotsky's critique was the Stalin-Bukharin theory of "socialism in one country." He wrote:

> In our epoch, which is the epoch of imperialism, i.e., of *world* economy and *world* politics under the hegemony of finance capital, not a single communist party can establish its program by proceeding solely or mainly from conditions and tendencies of developments in its own country. This also holds entirely for the party that wields the state power within the boundaries of the USSR. On August 4, 1914, the death knell sounded for national programs for all time. The revolutionary party of the proletariat can base itself only upon an international program corresponding to the character of the epoch, the epoch of the highest development and collapse of capitalism. An international communist program is in no case the sum total of national programs or an amalgam of their common features. The international program must proceed directly from an analysis of the conditions and tendencies of world economy and of the world political system taken as a whole in all its connections and contradictions, that is, with the mutually antagonistic interdependence of its separate parts. In the present epoch, to a much larger extent than in the past, the national orientation of the proletariat must and can flow only from a world orientation and not vice versa. Herein lies the basic and primary

difference between communist internationalism and all varieties of national socialism.[3]

Trotsky's emphasis on the primacy of a world orientation arose not simply from general theoretical considerations, but from his analysis — which he
developed in 1923–24 — of the global implications of the emergence of the
United States as the principal imperialist power.

Trotsky was barred from attending the sessions of the Communist
International. His writings were already proscribed within all the Communist
parties. However, through some fortuitous bureaucratic mishap, Trotsky's
Criticism was translated into English and came into the possession of James P.
Cannon, who was attending the Sixth Congress as a delegate of the American
Communist Party. Persuaded by Trotsky's *Criticism*, Cannon, with the assistance of a Canadian delegate, Maurice Spector, smuggled the document out
of the Soviet Union. On the basis of the analysis presented in the *Criticism of
Fundamentals*, Cannon — joined by Max Shachtman, Martin Abern and several
other leading members of the Communist Party — began the fight for Trotsky's
ideas outside the Soviet Union. Soon expelled from the Communist Party,
Cannon and Shachtman formed the Communist League of America, which
played a critical role in the emergence of the International Left Opposition.

When it was formed in 1923, the aim of the Left Opposition was the
reform of the Communist Party on the basis of the program of revolutionary internationalism, and the reestablishment of open debate within the
party in accordance with the principles of democratic centralism. With the
establishment of the International Left Opposition, which rapidly gained
adherents throughout the world, Trotsky sought to achieve the reform of the
Communist International. As long as there remained the possibility that the
disastrous policies of Stalin might be reversed through the growth of opposition within the Soviet Communist Party and the Third International, Trotsky
refrained from issuing the call for a new International.

The rise of fascism in Germany

The situation in Germany between 1930 and 1933 weighed heavily
in Trotsky's calculations. With the collapse of the German economy in the

---

[3] Leon Trotsky, *The Third International After Lenin*, (New York: Pathfinder Press, 1996),
pp. 23–24.

aftermath of the Wall Street crash of 1929, Hitler's National Socialist (Nazi) party emerged as a mass force. Whether or not Hitler came to power depended on the policies of the two mass organizations of the German working class, the Social Democratic Party (SPD) and the Communist Party (KPD). These two parties commanded the allegiance of millions of German workers and possessed the power to defeat the Nazis.

Having been exiled in 1929 to the island of Prinkipo, off the coast of Turkey, Trotsky wrote voluminously, analyzing the German crisis and appealing for united action by the two working class parties to stop Hitler's march to power. But the SPD, subservient to the bourgeois state and opposed to any politically independent action by the working class, would not countenance even a defensive struggle against the Nazis. The fate of the German working class was, instead, to be left in the hands of the corrupt and criminal bourgeois politicians of the Weimar regime who were scheming to bring Hitler to power. As for the KPD, it adhered blindly to the Moscow-dictated definition of the Social Democracy as "social fascist" — that is, the political equivalent of the Nazi party. The Stalinists rejected Trotsky's call for a United Front of the KPD and SPD against Hitler. In a political prognosis that must be counted among the most disastrous miscalculations in history, the Stalinists — justifying their own passivity — proclaimed that a Nazi victory would soon be followed by a socialist revolution that would bring the Communist Party to power. "After Hitler, us," was the Stalinist slogan.

The tragic denouement came on January 30, 1933. Appointed chancellor by the aged President von Hindenburg, Hitler came to power legally, without a shot being fired. Both the SPD and KPD, organizations with millions of members between them, did nothing to oppose the Nazis' triumph. Within days, the Nazis, now in control of the state apparatus, set their terror into motion. Within months, the SPD, the KPD, the trade unions and all other mass working class organizations were smashed. The twelve-year nightmare, which would cost the lives of millions, including the vast majority of European Jewry, had begun.

Trotsky waited several months after Hitler's accession to power to see whether the German catastrophe would evoke protests and opposition within either the remnants of the KPD or the Third International. But the opposite occurred. The Stalinist organizations, within Germany and in the International, reaffirmed the correctness of the political line that had been dictated by the Soviet bureaucracy.

The outcome in Germany convinced Trotsky that there existed no possibility for the reform of the Communist International. Therefore, in July 1933, Trotsky issued a public call for the formation of the Fourth International. This fundamental shift in policy in relation to the Third International led Trotsky to a further conclusion. If the possibility of reforming the Communist International did not exist, the perspective of reform was no longer valid for the Communist Party of the Soviet Union. To change the policies of the Stalinist regime would require its overthrow. However, as this overthrow would be aimed at defending, rather than replacing, the nationalized property relations established in the aftermath of October 1917, the revolution advocated by Trotsky would be of a *political* rather than a *social* character.

The events between 1933 and 1938 confirmed the correctness of Trotsky's new course. During the five years that followed Hitler's conquest of power, the Stalinist regime emerged as the most dangerous counterrevolutionary force within the international workers movement. The defeats that were caused by the policies of the Kremlin bureaucracy were not the outcome of mistakes, but, rather, of conscious policies. The Stalinist regime feared that the success of social revolution in any country might inspire a reawakening of the revolutionary fervor of the Soviet working class.

Arguments against the founding of the Fourth International

As Trotsky worked systematically for the formal establishment of the Fourth International, he encountered two major forms of opposition.

The first was that of tendencies and individuals who refused to draw any conclusions of a principled character from the international experience of the class struggle and the betrayals of Stalinism and Social Democracy. While occasionally expressing sympathy and even agreement with one or another aspect of Trotsky's analysis, they refused to commit themselves and their organizations to the fight for a new revolutionary International. In effect, these tendencies — which Trotsky designated "centrist" — sought to find a safe middle ground between revolution and counterrevolution. Underlying their unprincipled political maneuvering were opportunist calculations. They were determined to prevent international principles from impinging on their national tactics. The parties that exemplified this form of national opportunism were the German Socialist Workers Party (SAP), the Spanish Workers Party of Marxist Unification (POUM), and the British Independent Labour Party (ILP). The latter organization, led by Fenner

Brockway (later Lord Brockway), played a major role in the establishment of the so-called London Bureau.

The second argument against the formation of the Fourth International was that its proclamation was premature. An International, it was claimed, could arise only out of "great events," by which was meant a successful revolution. At the founding conference, this position was advanced by a Polish delegate, identified in the minutes as Karl, who argued that a new International could be created only in a period of "revolutionary upsurge." The conditions of "intense reaction and depression" were "circumstances wholly unfavorable for the proclamation of the Fourth." The delegate stated that "the forces constituting the Fourth were disproportionately small in relation to its tasks," and that "It was therefore necessary to wait for a favorable moment and not be premature."[4]

As he drafted the founding document of the Fourth International, Trotsky anticipated the arguments of the Polish delegate:

> Skeptics ask: But has the moment for the creation of the Fourth International yet arrived? It is impossible, they say, to create an International "artificially"; it can arise only out of great events, etc., etc. All of these objections merely show that skeptics are no good for the building of a new International. They are good for scarcely anything at all.
>
> The Fourth International has already arisen out of great events: the greatest defeats of the proletariat in history. The cause for these defeats is to be found in the degeneration and perfidy of the old leadership. The class struggle does not tolerate an interruption. The Third International, following the Second, is dead for purposes of revolution. Long live the Fourth International![5]

In October 1938, Trotsky recorded a speech in which he welcomed, with evident emotion, the founding of the Fourth International.

> Dear friends, we are not a party like other parties. Our ambition is not only to have more members, more papers, more money in the treasury, more deputies. All that is necessary, but only as a

---

[4] *Documents of the Fourth International*, pp. 296–297.

[5] Leon Trotsky, *The Transitional Program for Socialist Revolution* (New York: Pathfinder Press, 1977) p. 184

means. Our aim is the full material and spiritual liberation of the toilers and exploited through the socialist revolution. Nobody will prepare it and nobody will guide it but ourselves. The old Internationals — the Second, the Third, that of Amsterdam, we will add to them also the London Bureau — are rotten through and through.

The great events which rush upon mankind will not leave of these outlived organizations one stone upon another. Only the Fourth International looks with confidence at the future. It is the World Party of Socialist Revolution! There never was a greater task on the earth. Upon every one of us rests a tremendous historical responsibility.[6]

With the perspective afforded by three quarters of a century, it is possible to judge whether history has vindicated Trotsky's appraisal. What remains of the old organizations — Stalinist, social democratic and centrist — whose political shipwreck was foretold by Trotsky? The Second International exists only as a center of anti-working class operations and conspiracies directed by the CIA and various other state intelligence agencies. The Third International was officially dissolved by Stalin in 1943. The Stalinist parties throughout the world continued to orbit around the Kremlin bureaucracy for several more decades, until the dissolution of the USSR in 1991 swept them into the garbage dump of history.

The Russian Communist Party, though much reduced in size, continues to exist. It holds demonstrations in Moscow alongside Russian nationalists and fascists, where placards bearing the portrait of Stalin are waved alongside banners that have the swastika emblazoned upon them. And it is true that the "Communist Party" holds power in China, where it presides over the second largest capitalist economy in the world, whose police state regime guarantees that super-profits extracted from the working class are transferred to the transnational corporations of the United States and Europe.

The political struggle within the Fourth International

The Fourth International, the sole revolutionary organization, has successfully navigated the shoals and rapids of such an extended period of history. Of course, it has passed through intense political struggles and splits.

---

[6] *Writings of Leon Trotsky 1938–39* (New York: Pathfinder Press, 1974), p. 93.

The internal conflicts reflected the vicissitudes of the class struggle under continually changing international socioeconomic conditions and the realignment of social forces — not only within the working class, but also among different layers of the middle class — under the impact of these changes.

Political cynics, who ferment in abundance in the bubbling miasma of ex- and pseudo-left academics, are fond of pointing to the splits within the Fourth International. Such people, who submit in silence to the crimes of the capitalist parties to which they give their vote year after year, understand nothing of the class dynamics of politics. Nor, on a personal level, can they understand why anyone, anywhere, would conduct a determined and uncompromising political struggle over matters of principle.

Fifteen years after the founding of the Fourth International, in November 1953, the emergence of a pro-Stalinist tendency led to a split in which fundamental questions of class orientation, historical perspective, and political strategy were involved. The combined pressure of the post-war restabilization of capitalism, the political influence of the Stalinist bureaucracy, and the increasing political self-consciousness of a growing middle class found expression in the development of a new form of opportunism. This new opportunism, known as Pabloism (derived from its best known exponent, Michel Pablo), rejected Trotsky's characterization of the Soviet bureaucracy and Stalinism as counterrevolutionary. It envisaged the realization of socialism in a process that was to unfold in the course of centuries, through revolutions led by the bureaucracy and its affiliated Stalinist parties. It even suggested that a nuclear world war would create the conditions for the victory of socialist revolution. The Pabloite theory also attributed revolutionary capacities denied by Trotsky to numerous bourgeois national and petty bourgeois radical movements, especially in the colonial and "Third World" countries.

The essential content of Pabloism's revision of Marxist theory and the Trotskyist perspective was its rejection of the central role of the working class in the socialist revolution. The International Committee of the Fourth International was formed in 1953, at the initiative of James P. Cannon, to fight against the influence of Pabloite opportunism, whose political logic and practice would lead, unless opposed, to the liquidation of the Fourth International as a revolutionary working class party.

The political struggle against the influence of Pabloism raged within the Fourth International for more than thirty years. This struggle was brought to a successful conclusion in 1985 when the orthodox Trotskyists of the International Committee regained the political leadership of the Fourth

International. The factors that contributed to this victory were the deepening global crisis of capitalism, the deep crisis of the Stalinist bureaucracy, and the evident bankruptcy of all labor organizations based on a national reformist program.

However, these objective conditions alone would have been insufficient. The defeat of the revisionists and opportunists by the orthodox Trotskyists of the International Committee was achieved because the latter consciously based their work on the vast political and theoretical legacy of Trotsky and the Fourth International. This legacy, which had been developed and built upon over decades, was an inexhaustible source of political strength. In the final analysis, the development of the world crisis of capitalism and the class struggle unfolded in accordance with the perspective developed by Trotsky and the Fourth International.

Seventy-five years — three quarters of a century — is a substantial period of time. Obviously, much has changed since the time of the Founding Congress of the Fourth International. But the basic structures and contradictions of capitalist society persist. For all the technological innovations, the situation that confronts modern capitalism appears no less desperate than it was in 1938. In fact, it is worse. When Trotsky wrote the founding document of the Fourth International, the world bourgeoisie was plagued by an intractable economic crisis, abandoning democracy and racing toward war. Today, as we celebrate seventy-five years since the founding of the Fourth International, global capitalism is... plagued by an intractable economic crisis, abandoning democracy and racing toward war.

The words of Trotsky, written seventy-five years ago, retain an extraordinary immediacy:

> All talk to the effect that historical conditions have not yet "ripened" for socialism is the product of ignorance or conscious deception. The objective prerequisites for the proletarian revolution have not only "ripened"; they have begun to get somewhat rotten. Without a socialist revolution, in the next historical period at that, a catastrophe threatens the whole culture of mankind. It is now the turn of the proletariat, i.e., chiefly of its revolutionary vanguard. The historical crisis of mankind is reduced to the crisis of the revolutionary leadership.[7]

---

[7] *The Transitional Program for Socialist Revolution*, p. 138.

12

The Myth of "Ordinary Germans": A Review of Daniel Goldhagen's *Hitler's Willing Executioners*[1]

A little more than a half-century has passed since the collapse of Hitler's Third Reich, and mankind is still struggling to come to grips with its legacy of horror and bestiality. The scenes of mass murder that were exposed in the spring of 1945 with the opening of the Nazi extermination camps are images that will never be erased from human consciousness. But it is not enough that the crimes against humanity that were committed at Auschwitz, Treblinka, Bergen-Belsen, Buchenwald and Dachau should never be forgotten. It is no less vital that the significance and meaning of those crimes be understood.

Here we encounter a terrible problem: For all that has been said and written about the Holocaust, it remains a strangely obscure event. It is true that a vast amount of empirical data about the Holocaust has been collected. We possess detailed information about how the Nazis organized and executed their "Final Solution," the murder of six million European Jews. And yet the issues that are central to an understanding of the Holocaust — its historical origins, political causes and, finally, its place in the history of the twentieth century — have, with very few exceptions, been dealt with poorly. This

---

[1] Lecture delivered April 17, 1997 at Michigan State University in East Lansing.

is, really, an intolerable state of affairs. The one basic question raised by the Holocaust, "Why did it happen?" is precisely that to which it is most difficult to obtain an answer.

This situation is rationalized too often with the argument that the Holocaust is so terrible an event that it simply defies a rational explanation. If, as Adorno said, it was no longer possible to write poetry after Auschwitz, it was presumably also no longer possible to place much confidence in the historian's ability to comprehend the forces that drive the social — or, more precisely, the antisocial — activity of man. Historical science and political theory were seen to be helpless in the presence of such unfathomable evil.

The Holocaust and despair

Thus, to those who hold this view, there is nothing of great importance to be gained from a study of the economic foundations, class structure and political struggles of European and German society prior to the advent of the Third Reich. At best, such a scientific-materialist approach will offer nothing more than background information about the incidental social setting in which the forces of human evil, lodged deep in man's soul or psyche, gained ascendancy, as they inevitably must, over the restraining moral influences of civilization.

In the 1950s a novel was written that promoted this gloomy vision of the human condition. Most of you are, I am sure, familiar with William Golding's *Lord of the Flies*, which argued that barbarism is the natural condition of mankind. Release a group of ordinary school boys from the normal restraints of civilization and they will, within a few weeks, revert to a state of homicidal savagery. This misanthropic work flowed from the conclusions drawn by Golding from the experiences of the Second World War. "Anyone who moved through those years," he later wrote, "without understanding that man produces evil as a bee produces honey, must have been blind or wrong in the head."[2]

The popularity of *Lord of the Flies* reflected the bewilderment and despair provoked by the horrors of World War II. This mood was strengthened by the political relations that arose in the aftermath of the war. It actually became more difficult to engage in a discussion of the nature of the Third Reich after

---

[2] Andrew Michael Roberts, *The Novel: From Its Origins to the Present Day* (London: Bloomsbury, 1993), p. 173.

1945 than it had been before. In the reactionary political environment of the Cold War, it was no longer considered appropriate, especially in the United States, to dwell too seriously on the relation between fascism and modern capitalism.

In the 1930s, politically-literate and class-conscious people understood that the rise of European fascism after World War I was a direct response by capitalist society to the revolutionary dangers posed by mass socialist workers movements. The examples of Mussolini's Italy, Hitler's Germany and Franco's Spain had shown all too clearly that fascism was, in essence, the counterrevolutionary political mobilization, in the interests of capitalism, of the enraged middle classes, the petty bourgeoisie, against the socialist labor movement. Where fascism came to power, the working class ceased to exist as an organized political and social force.

In the 1930s, it was not only the relationship between capitalism and fascism that was widely understood. Socialists warned over and over that the world capitalist economic crisis, which had ruined the middle classes and driven it into the arms of fascism, threatened the Jews with physical annihilation.

As Leon Trotsky wrote in 1940:

> The period of the wasting away of foreign trade and the decline of domestic trade is at the same time the period of the monstrous intensification of chauvinism and especially of anti-Semitism. In the epoch of its rise, capitalism took the Jewish people out of the ghetto and utilized them as an instrument in its commercial expansion. Today decaying capitalist society is striving to squeeze the Jewish people from all its pores; seventeen million individuals out of the two billion populating the globe, that is, less than 1 percent, can no longer find a place on our planet! Amid the vast expanses of land and the marvels of technology, which has also conquered the skies for man as well as the earth, the bourgeoisie has managed to convert our planet into a foul prison.[3]

To the extent that a frank discussion of the real origins, class bases and political objectives of fascism was circumscribed by the prevailing political

---

[3] Will Reissner, ed., *Documents of the Fourth International: The Formative Years 1933–40* (New York: Pathfinder Press, 1973), p. 312.

interests of the US government, an intellectual vacuum was created which encouraged the infiltration of ahistorical and thoroughly unscientific conceptions of fascism, the Third Reich and the Holocaust. This had far-reaching consequences for popular consciousness. Having been torn out of its historical and political context, the Holocaust was rendered incomprehensible. Public consciousness of the Holocaust was more and more conditioned by exploitative sensationalism, cheap moral platitudes and existential hand-wringing.

If any lesson was to be drawn from the Holocaust, it was that man is capable — if only given half a chance — of unspeakable brutality; and that it is delusionary to believe, after the cold-blooded murder of six million human beings, in progress and the perfectibility of man. In this way, the Holocaust was used to justify the postwar status quo and deprecate the struggle for a better world.

I do not wish to suggest that no works of scientific value have been produced over the last fifty years. There have been a number of historians who have produced outstanding monographs on different aspects of the Nazi regime and the Holocaust. But public consciousness is barely touched by the research of such outstanding historians, whose works are generally followed, especially in the United States, only by specialists in the field.

And, if only to draw attention to the depressed level of modern politico-historical consciousness, permit me to note that it is highly unusual to find in contemporary works of historical scholarship any reference at all to Leon Trotsky's writings on the subject of Nazism between 1930 and 1934, although no other man of his time understood so clearly the danger and destructive potential of German fascism.

Goldhagen and the Germans

The works that attract the greatest attention are precisely those which leave unchallenged, or actually reinforce, the basest prejudices and misconceptions. Daniel Goldhagen's immensely successful and thoroughly deplorable *Hitler's Willing Executioners: Ordinary Germans and the Holocaust* falls within this category.

The principal theme of Goldhagen's book is easily summarized. The cause of the Holocaust is to be found in the mind-set and beliefs of the Germans. A vast national collective, the German people, motivated by a uniquely German anti-Semitic ideology, carried out a Germanic enterprise, the Holocaust. The systematic killing of Jews became a national pastime, in which all Germans who were given the opportunity gladly and enthusiastically participated.

Germans killed Jews because they were consumed, as Germans, by an uncontrollable Germanic anti-Semitism. Hatred of Jews constituted the foundation of the universally accepted *weltanschauung*, world view, of the German people.

The politics of the regime was of only secondary importance. Goldhagen insists that terms such as "Nazis" and "SS men" are "inappropriate labels" that should not be used when referring to the murderers. Goldhagen seems to suggest that the only essential causal relationship between the Third Reich and the extermination of the Jews was that it allowed the Germans to act, without restraint, as Germans, in accordance with German beliefs.

As Goldhagen writes:

> The most appropriate, indeed the only appropriate *general* proper name for the Germans who perpetrated the Holocaust is "Germans." They were Germans acting in the name of Germany and its highly popular leader, Adolf Hitler.[4]

So as not to distract attention from the flow of Goldhagen's astonishing insights, I will not dwell on the fact that Hitler himself was an Austrian, or that his racial theories were plagiarized from the writings of a nineteenth century French count, Gobineau, or that his political hero, Mussolini, was an Italian, or that his chief ideologist, Alfred Rosenberg, hailed from a Baltic province of tsarist Russia, or that Hitler's closest comrade-in-arms, Rudolf Hess, was born in Egypt.

Rather than ponder the implications of such awkward contradictions, let us move quickly to Goldhagen's conclusion:

> that antisemitism moved many thousands of "ordinary" Germans — and would have moved millions more, had they been appropriately positioned — to slaughter Jews. Not economic hardship, not the coercive means of a totalitarian state, not social psychological pressure, not invariable psychological propensities, but ideas about Jews that were pervasive in

---

[4] Daniel Goldhagen, *Hitler's Willing Executioners: Ordinary Germans and the Holocaust*, (New York: Alfred A. Knopf, 1996), p. 6.

Germany, and had been for decades, induced ordinary Germans to kill unarmed, defenseless Jewish men, women, and children by the thousands, systematically and without pity.[5]

Employing a crude version of Kantian epistemology, Goldhagen argues repeatedly that anti-Semitism was an integral, virtually a priori, component of the cognitive apparatus of the Germans: "the antisemitic creed," he writes, "was essentially unchallenged in Germany."[6]

I will examine somewhat later the degree to which Goldhagen's arguments are based on facts. But, first, I would like to make a few observations about his method of thought and analysis.

The most common feature of vulgar thought is its tendency to simplify a complex and multifaceted reality with overly broad, amorphous and one-dimensional definitions. Scientific thought strives to identify and examine in their mutual interaction the diverse and antagonistic elements of which every phenomenon is composed. It attempts to develop concepts that accurately express the complexity, that is, the contradictory nature, of the reality that is being reflected in the mind of the scientist.

Vulgar thinking, on the other hand, resorts to vacuous generalizations that ignore the essential internal contradictions that constitute the structure of the phenomenon it presumes to analyze. Such empty generalizations are known, in philosophy, as abstract identities, that is, identities from which all internal difference is excluded. They are abstract, in the bad sense of the word, because they are inadequate mental representations of reality: the material world simply does not consist of such internally undifferentiated phenomena.

Every "identity" contains difference within itself. Herein lies the basic flaw of vulgar thought: it operates with one-sided concepts of the lowest order, with such abstract identities that are incapable of providing a scientific and truthful representation of reality.

"Ordinary Germans"

The methodological flaw of Professor Goldhagen's book is indicated in its title: *Hitler's Willing Executioners: Ordinary Germans and the Holocaust.* Let us stop right there: What is meant by "ordinary Germans?" For those of

---

[5] Ibid., p. 9.
[6] Ibid., p. 33.

you who would like a textbook example of an "abstract identity," this is it. This is a category that is so broad, it is capable of including virtually everyone, except, presumably, Germans of Jewish parentage. What, after all, makes any particular German an "ordinary" one? Is it a large girth and a fondness for knockwurst and sauerbraten? Is it blond hair, blue eyes and a penchant for sunbathing in the nude? Is it a talent for abstruse philosophizing and a passion for 300-pound Wagnerian sopranos? A concept built upon such foolish and arbitrary stereotypes cannot be of any scientific value in the cognition of objective reality.

But if we should attempt to include in our definition more serious sociological characteristics, the worthlessness of the concept of "ordinariness" becomes immediately apparent. In 1933 German society possessed a complex class structure. Was the "ordinary German" at the time of Hitler's accession to power a factory worker, a ruined shopkeeper, a demoralized member of the lumpenproletariat, a heavily indebted peasant, an East Prussian land-owning Junker or an industrial magnate?

If all these elements of diverse social strata are to be lumped together as "ordinary Germans," it simply means that the concept of "ordinariness" does not reflect the internal antagonisms and conflicts of German society as it existed in 1933. What Goldhagen, therefore, offers his readers is not a scientific examination of German society as it really was constituted in 1933, but rather — and it is unpleasant to say this — an idealized portrait of a homogeneous society that uncritically substantiates the Nazi myth of a unified German Volk, defined by race and blood.

Having chosen this concept of the "ordinary German" as the basis of his entire analysis, Goldhagen is compelled to exclude from his book anything or anyone that might call into question the validity of this stereotype. His reply to the Nazi specter of *der ewige Jude*, the eternal Jew, as the relentless enemy of the German people is the specter of *der ewige Deutsche*, the eternal German, the relentless and unchanging enemy of the Jewish people.

Having posited a nation without any sort of internal differentiation, other than the fixed division between German and Jew, Goldhagen is compelled to posit a nation without any real history. There is virtually no reference to the events and personalities that determined the course of German development in the 100 years that preceded Hitler's accession to power.

In Goldhagen's book, the socialist movement is all but invisible. Not a single reference is to be found, in the course of this 622-page book, to Karl Marx, Frederick Engels, Ferdinand Lassalle, August Bebel or Wilhelm

Liebknecht. Not a word is to be found about the anti-socialist laws of 1878–90 implemented by the regime of Bismarck. The Social Democratic Party, the first mass party in history, which by 1912 held the largest number of seats in the German Reichstag, is mentioned only in passing. There is no reference to the 1918 revolution or the uprising of the Spartacus League.

These omissions cannot be explained as an oversight. Goldhagen simply cannot deal with the German socialist movement because its historical existence represents a refutation of his entire theory. Yet without an examination of the emergence of the German socialist workers movement, it is impossible to understand the nature and significance of modern anti-Semitism.

Political anti-Semitism

Hostility to Jews is certainly not a modern phenomenon, let alone one confined to Germany. But it was only in the last third of the nineteenth century that anti-Semitism emerged as a distinct and powerful political movement, not only in Germany, but in a number of European countries. It is indisputable that the growth of anti-Semitic political movements was rooted in complex social processes related to the development of modern industrial capitalism.

The most important of these was the emergence of a new and immensely powerful social class, the industrial proletariat. By the 1870s, certainly after the Paris Commune of 1871, the existence of a mass working class, increasingly influenced by socialist ideology, was recognized as a potentially revolutionary threat to capitalist interests.

In response to this danger, the privileged classes — the bourgeoisie and still substantial landowning interests — sought to cultivate a mass base for the defense of the existing social order. Paradoxically, the mass base for the defense of capitalism against the socialist labor movement was to emerge out of the elements of the middle class whose social and economic position was being steadily undermined by the processes of modern industrial development.

In Germany, the onset of a severe depression was announced in 1873 with a spectacular stock market crash that took an especially heavy toll on the savings of middle class investors. Mass sentiment against Bismarck's free trade and laissez-faire policies developed fairly rapidly. The unfortunate involvement of a significant number of Jewish speculators in the scandals surrounding the stock market crash provided a focus for the anger of the disoriented middle classes. In this situation, the identification of the Jew with the evils of modern capitalism acquired a new political significance.

To be sure, the susceptibility of the petty-bourgeois masses to such appeals was facilitated by long-standing religious prejudices. But definite conditions, created by capitalist development, directed these old prejudices along extremely reactionary lines and endowed them with a terrible destructive force.

Anti-Semitic writers such as Otto Glagau, Rudolf Meyer and Wilhelm Marr, who depicted the Jews as the embodiment of capitalist rapacity, acquired a substantial audience among the despairing sections of the German *Mittelstand* — petty tradesmen, artisans, the unemployed and nervous professionals.

The effort to direct the confused anticapitalist sentiments of the German *Mittelstand* into anger against the Jews was facilitated by significant improvements in the social position of the German Jews in the course of the nineteenth century. "By the 1870s," writes the historian Robert Wistrich, "the Jews appeared as the bourgeois par excellence in a society that was still not fully embourgeoised, as innovative modernizers in a nation that was not yet modernized."[7]

According to figures provided by Wistrich, 22 percent of the employees working in banks and on the stock exchanges in 1882 were Jews. At a time when Jews accounted for little more than one percent of the German population, they represented 43.25 percent of the proprietors and directors of banking and credit enterprises. Some of the greatest banks in Germany were controlled by Jews, such as that of Bleichröder in Berlin, Warburg in Hamburg, Oppenheim in Köln and Rothschild in Frankfurt. In the early 1900s, the renowned economist Werner Sombart noted that 25 percent of the members of the boards of directors in ten major branches of German industry were Jews.

Another important feature of the success of German Jewry was its prominent position in the skilled professions: by 1882 11.7 percent of all doctors, 8.6 percent of journalists and 7.9 percent of all lawyers were Jews. As these figures indicate, Jewish youth attended colleges in great numbers.

This success provided further grounds for anti-Semitic appeals to the insecurity of the German *Mittelstand*, which resented Jewish competition.

In an earlier age, anti-Jewish sentiments had focused on the supposed exclusivity of the Jews, whose religion and traditions kept them apart from

---

[7] Robert S. Wistrich, *Socialism and the Jews: The Dilemmas of Assimilation in Germany and Austria-Hungary* (London and Toronto: Associated University Presses, 1982), p. 56.

the general population. The new political anti-Semitism now protested the excessive integration of the Jews into national life; and these protests were buttressed with pseudoscientific racial theories that were the rage of the late nineteenth century. The demagogic calls for a struggle against Jewish capital were combined with hysterical appeals for the defense of the Germanic race against the danger of Semitic domination. Wilhelm Marr declared that "the struggle between 'Semitism' and Germandom was an irreversible 'world-historical fate.'"[8]

Political anti-Semitism was not confined to Germany. An analogous phenomenon developed in France. Anti-Semitism was seen by its proponents as the most effective means of mobilizing mass support against not only the emerging socialist proletariat, but all elements of liberal democracy as well. On the basis of anti-Semitism, a new national consensus was to be forged, transcending the class divisions that had been created by the process of capitalist industrialization and upon which the appeal of socialism was based. The reactionary theoretician, Mores, conceived of anti-Semitism as a means of reintegrating the proletariat into the body of the nation. "One must suppress the proletariat," he wrote. "One must give these people something to defend, something to conquer." This national project was to be realized through the anti-Jewish revolution.[9]

The arch-reactionary Charles Maurras declared that an integral national unity could not be achieved without the use of anti-Semitism, which facilitated the suppression of class antagonisms. "Everything seems impossible or terribly difficult without the providential appearance of anti-Semitism. It enables everything to be arranged, smoothed over, and simplified. If one were not an anti-Semite through patriotism, one would become one through a simple sense of opportunity."[10]

This was the ideological background against which the Dreyfus case exploded in France in 1894. The wealthy Jewish army officer falsely accused of espionage on behalf of Germany became the center of vitriolic anti-Semitic agitation. More than seventy towns and cities witnessed anti-Jewish rioting by mobs which screamed, "Death to the Jews!" Synagogues were attacked, Jewish-owned shops were ransacked and Jews were beaten in the streets.

---

[8] Quoted in *Socialism and the Jews*, p. 53.

[9] Quoted in Zeev Sternhell, *Neither Right Nor Left: Fascist Ideology in France*, trans. David Maisel (Princeton: Princeton University Press, 1986), pp. 45–46.

[10] Ibid., p. 46.

As in Germany, the anti-Semitic movement drew its popular support principally from the middle class, especially among shopkeepers and other segments of small and marginal businesses. No references to the Dreyfus affair or to the anti-Semitic movements in France are to be found in Professor Goldhagen's book.

A central premise of *Hitler's Willing Executioners* is that anti-Semitism was universally accepted by all segments of German society. Professor Goldhagen goes so far as to insist that there is no significant or credible documentary evidence that there existed the slightest opposition to anti-Semitism in Germany. That such a statement can be made in a book that purports to be a work of scholarly research is staggering.

Social Democracy's fight against anti-Semitism

The history of the German social democracy, in the years when it represented a revolutionary mass movement of the working class — that is, from the 1870s to the outbreak of the First World War I in 1914 — is one of unrelenting struggle against anti-Semitism. The exigencies of the political struggle in the working class required an intransigent attitude toward all forms of anti-Semitic propaganda. Aside from democratic principles and moral considerations, the Social Democratic Party saw the association of anti-Semitism with demagogic anticapitalist rhetoric as an attempt to disorient the working class and subordinate it to the political representatives of the middle class.

The formation by Adolf Stoecker of his explicitly anti-Semitic Christian Social Workers Party sought to use Jew-baiting as a means of winning the working class away from the increasingly influential, albeit illegal, social democracy. In opposition to Stoecker, the social democracy waged a powerful campaign to educate the working class as to the reactionary nature of anti-Semitism. In the official statement of the SPD for the 1881 election, the party stated:

> The scandal of the anti-Semitic disturbances was first made possible after the anti-socialist law; that they did not assume the extent of a general Jew-bait is solely due to the Social Democrats, who warned the working class against this disgraceful activity, springing from the basest motives...[11]

---

[11] Quoted in *Socialism and the Jews*, p. 94.

The counteroffensive of the SPD exerted significant political and moral influence over the working class. Anti-Semitic rallies were broken up by workers, and Stoecker was jeered. The opposition of the SPD to anti-Semitism found a powerful symbol in its selection of a Jewish socialist businessman, Paul Singer, as its candidate for the Reichstag in an important Berlin district. In the elections of 1887, Singer received more votes than any other candidate in the city.

Wistrich writes:

> Opposition to anti-Semitism had become a badge of honor for the workers movement. ... The fierce campaign undertaken by the German Social Democrats against Adolf Stoecker's Berlin movement did to a large extent immunize the working class against anti-Semitism. It did not eliminate anti-Jewish prejudice in the labor movement but it rendered it politically marginal. ... The struggle against Stoecker was a fight *for* social democracy, an assertion of the democratic rights of the working class itself.[12]

The role played by the SPD in the struggle against anti-Semitism eventually won it broad support from one segment of the German population that had viewed its activities for many years with a marked reserve, the Jewish middle class. Notwithstanding the important role that had been played by a small but significant section of German Jewish intellectuals since the earliest days of the socialist movement, the vast majority of the Jewish middle class and bourgeoisie, for reasons of crass economic self-interest, remained aloof from the social democracy. An additional reason for the antagonistic attitude adopted by many Jews toward the SPD was the desire, born perhaps of an inner insecurity, to demonstrate, as ostentatiously as possible, their loyalty to the regime of Kaiser Wilhelm.

By the turn of the century, however, it had become impossible for German Jews to ignore the fact that the Social Democratic Party was the only one that unequivocally opposed anti-Semitism. Indeed, the SPD was the only party that selected Jews to stand as its candidates for the Reichstag. In the election of 1903, the SPD won, for the first time, a substantial section of the German Jewish vote.

---

[12] Ibid., 94–101.

This is, by the way, another important element of the pre-1933 political history of Germany to which Professor Goldhagen makes no reference.

Anti-Semitism in tsarist Russia

As a result of the struggle of the SPD, the political influence of the anti-Semitic parties declined precipitously between the mid-1890s and the outbreak of World War I. In the first years of the twentieth century, the most violent outbursts of anti-Semitism occurred not in Germany, or even in France, but in Russia.

The bloody pogroms that occurred in Russia were a direct response by the tsarist regime to the growing revolutionary movement of the working class. The government sponsored the formation of right-wing paramilitary squads, known as the Black Hundreds, to terrorize the working class.

Historian Orlando Figes writes:

> As with the Fascist movements of inter-war Europe, most of their support came from those embittered *lumpen* elements who had either lost — or were afraid of losing — their petty status in the social hierarchy as a result of modernization and reform: uprooted peasants forced into the towns as casual laborers; small shopkeepers and artisans squeezed by competition from big business; low-ranking officials and policemen ... and pub patriots of all kinds disturbed by the sight of "upstart" workers, students and Jews challenging the God-given power of the tsar.[13]

The regime of Tsar Nicholas II responded to the revolutionary movement of 1905 by unleashing a wave of terror, of which Jews were a principal target. In the two weeks that followed the issuing of the tsar's Manifesto of October 1905, which pledged to support the establishment of democratic institutions, 690 pogroms occurred. Three thousand Jews were murdered during this period. A pogrom in Odessa cost the lives of 800 Jews. Five hundred were wounded and more than 100,000 were made homeless. It was soon established that the pogroms had been organized with the direct assistance of

---

[13] Orlando Figes, *A People's Tragedy: A History of the Russian Revolution* (New York: Viking Press, 1996), pp. 196–197.

the government. The political mechanics of the pogroms were described in a socialist newspaper of the time:

> The old familiar picture! The police organises the pogrom beforehand. The police instigates it: leaflets are printed in government printing offices calling for a massacre of the Jews. When the pogrom begins, the police is inactive. The troops quietly look on at the exploits of the Black Hundreds. But later this very police go through the farce of prosecution and trial of the pogromists. The investigations and trials conducted by the officials of the old authority always end in the same way: the cases drag on, none of the pogromists are found guilty, sometimes even the battered and mutilated Jews and intellectuals are dragged before the court, months pass — and the old, but ever new story is forgotten, until the next pogrom.[14]

The author of this article, written in June 1906, was Lenin.

Rather than permit his thesis of the uniqueness of German anti-Semitism to be disturbed by the intrusion of historical facts, Goldhagen simply avoids any reference to the worst outbreaks of anti-Jewish violence in Europe prior to the establishment of the Third Reich.

It was following World War I, which had ended with the outbreak of revolution in Germany and the collapse of the Hohenzollern monarchy, that the use of anti-Semitism as an instrument of political organization once again became a serious factor. The potency of anti-Semitism, which played a major role in the propaganda of the Nazis, was in direct proportion to the desperation of the petty bourgeoisie and the political disorientation of the working class.

The petty bourgeoisie was traumatized and ruined by the events which followed the defeat of Germany in the war. The Weimar Republic, founded on the basis of a strangled revolution, staggered from crisis to crisis.

Trotsky wrote:

> The postwar chaos hit the artisans, the peddlers, and the civil employees no less cruelly than the workers. ... In the atmosphere brought to white heat by war, defeat, reparations, inflation, occupation of the Ruhr, crisis, need, and despair, the petty

---

[14] V.I. Lenin, *Collected Works*, Volume 10 (Moscow: Progress Publishers, 1972), p. 509.

bourgeoisie rose up against all the old parties that had bamboo-zled it. The sharp grievances of small proprietors never out of bankruptcy, of their university sons without posts and clients, of their daughters without dowries and suitors, demanded order and an iron hand.[15]

Hitler's anti-Semitism

The desperation, anxieties and traumas of this milieu, forever fearful of being driven down into the ranks of the proletariat, were articulated by Hitler. A product of the lower-middle class, Hitler spent his formative years in Vienna, where his world view was shaped by the cheap right-wing gutter press and where he acquired his life-long hatred of the working class and socialism. Hitler's anti-Semitism was, according to the perceptive antifascist German writer Konrad Heiden, a by-product of his all-consuming hatred of the proletariat.

Hitler, Heiden explained,

> hated the whole great sphere of human existence which is devoted to the regular transference of energy into product; and he hated the men who had let themselves be caught and crushed in this process of production. All his life the workers were for him a picture of horror, a dismal gruesome mass ... everything which he later said from the speaker's platform to flatter the manual worker was pure lies.[16]

Herein lies the key to an understanding of Hitler's demonic obses-sion with the Jews. In *Mein Kampf*, Hitler explained how his conversion to anti-Semitism flowed from his encounters with the labor movement. It was among the workers that Hitler first came into contact with Jews. He then discovered, to his amazement, that many Jews played prominent roles in the labor movement. "The great light dawned on him," wrote Heiden. "Suddenly the 'Jewish question' became clear. ... The labor movement did not repel him because it was led by Jews; the Jews repelled him because they led the labor movement."[17]

---

[15] Leon Trotsky, *The Struggle Against Fascism in Germany* (New York: Pathfinder Press, 1971), pp. 523–524.

[16] Konrad Heiden, *Der Fuehrer*, (Boston: Houghton Mifflin, 1944), p. 58.

[17] Ibid., p. 66.

One thing is certain, Heiden concluded, "It was not Rothschild, the capitalist, but Karl Marx, the Socialist, who kindled Adolf Hitler's anti-Semitism."[18]

Professor Goldhagen could have profited intellectually from a careful study of Heiden's biography of Hitler. But, he might then have written quite a different work, which would probably not have yielded such handsome monetary profits as *Hitler's Willing Executioners*. In life we all make our choices.

Anti-Semitism was, without question, a potent force in post-World War I Germany. And yet, notwithstanding the claims of Goldhagen, hatred of Jews could not, of itself, have provided the political base necessary for Hitler's rise to power. The Nazis did not come to power by riding an irresistible wave of anti-Semitism. Careful studies of the social bases of the Nazi party have established that the appeal of anti-Semitism remained limited prior to 1933. Indeed, the Nazis discovered that anti-Semitism actually limited their appeal in certain areas of Germany, and local leaders were instructed to restrain their anti-Jewish vitriol, and even, at times, to excise from their speeches all anti-Semitic references.

At any rate, measuring the quantity of anti-Semitism that existed in Germany in 1933 will not explain the victory of the Nazis. However disgusting the prevalence of anti-Semitism, it was only one factor — and by no means the most important — in the political life of Germany. A political regime, whether of the right or the left, is not merely the product of the sum total of all the prejudices and hatreds of the population. It is, in the final analysis, the expression of a certain relationship, forged in the course of social and political struggles, between the main classes in society. In the outcome of those struggles the character of the political leadership of the contending classes, and the program upon which they base their struggle, are critical factors.

If it were possible to quantify the precise amount of anti-Semitism in any given country, such a measurement would in all likelihood establish that this poison was no less abundant in the Russia of 1917 than it was in the Germany of 1933. And yet, the political decisiveness and clarity of the Bolsheviks played a crucial role in enabling the working class to establish its political authority over substantial sections of the urban and rural petty bourgeoisie, that very segment of society which was not known for its sympathy toward Jews.

The political struggles of 1917 in Russia concluded not with the victory of the fascists, but with the victory of the socialists.

---

[18] Ibid.

The defeat of the German revolution

The victory of fascism was not the direct and inevitable product of anti-Semitism, but the outcome of a political process shaped by the class struggle. In that process, the critical factor was the crisis of the German socialist movement, which was, it must be pointed out, part of a broader political crisis of international socialism.

Hitler's rise was not irresistible and his victory was not inevitable. The Nazis were able to come to power only after the mass socialist and communist parties had shown themselves, in the course of the entire postwar period, to be politically bankrupt and utterly incapable of providing the distraught masses with a way out of the disaster created by capitalism.

Only a brief review of the crisis of the German workers movement is possible in the framework of this lecture.

In August 1914, upon the outbreak of the Great War, the Social Democracy had abandoned its revolutionary principles and voted in support of war credits for the German government. This betrayal, the product of years of opportunist degeneration, marked the end of the SPD as a revolutionary party. From that point on, the social democracy functioned ever more openly as a pillar of bourgeois rule. The passage of the SPD into the camp of the bourgeoisie was confirmed by the events of 1918–19.

The Social Democratic government that was brought to power by the revolution of November 1918 devoted itself entirely to the political and physical disarming of the working class and the preservation of capitalist rule. In January 1919 it organized the suppression of the Spartacus uprising and sanctioned the murders of Karl Liebknecht and Rosa Luxemburg.

The victory of the Bolshevik Revolution provided the political inspiration for the founding of the Communist Party, the KPD. But, from the beginning, the party was plagued with an unending crisis of political leadership. In a sense, it never recovered from the loss of Rosa Luxemburg. There was no leader of comparable experience and skill available to take her place. The development of revolutionary political leadership, as the experience of the Bolshevik Party had demonstrated, is a protracted and difficult process that requires years, not months.

Thus, the KPD was utterly unprepared for the revolutionary crisis that unfolded in 1923, in the aftermath of the French occupation of the Ruhr. The eruption of hyperinflation ruined the middle classes, undermined the authority of the reformist social democracy and led to a powerful upsurge of support for the KPD.

All the conditions for a social revolution were present in Germany except one — a politically mature and decisive leadership. As the crisis came to a head in October 1923, an attempt by the KPD to organize the overthrow of the Weimar government was widely anticipated. Indeed, plans for an insurrection were formulated, only to be called off at the last minute by the nervous and indecisive leadership of the KPD. In Hamburg, where the Communist workers had not been informed of the change of plans, the insurrection was started. But this isolated action was easily suppressed. The bourgeois government, which only days before had been convinced that its overthrow was all but inevitable, recovered its nerve. The crisis passed, and bourgeois rule was stabilized.

In the years that followed, the political life of the KPD was shaped by the growing influence of the Stalinist bureaucracy in the Soviet Union and the suppression of the Left Opposition led by Leon Trotsky. The victory of Stalinism in the Soviet Union was to have tragic consequences for the German Communist Party and the working class.

The brief period of stability and prosperity that had followed the defeat of the working class in 1923 came to an end with the Wall Street crash in October 1929 and the beginning of the world Depression. German industry collapsed, millions lost their jobs and the middle class was ruined. These were the conditions which enabled the Nazi party very rapidly to acquire mass support.

Hitler's rise to power

But both the SPD and the KPD, that is, the political organizations of the working class, remained gigantic factors in German politics. These two parties commanded the loyalty of millions of workers. Confronting the danger of fascist counterrevolution, the urgent strategic task of the workers movement was to unify its forces in a common struggle against the Nazis.

The Social Democratic leaders, however, committed to the defense of the bourgeois Weimar regime, opposed all political collaboration with the KPD, even for the purpose of organizing a united defense against the attacks of the Brown Shirts. Notwithstanding the obstructionist position of the Social Democrats, the task of the KPD was to call upon the SPD leaders to accept, regardless of political differences, the need for united action by both parties against the Nazi danger.

However, the KPD, following the instructions of Stalin, pursued a political line that played into the hands of the Social Democrats and the fascists. In

1928, one year after the expulsion of Trotsky and the Left Opposition from the Communist Party and Communist International, the Stalinists suddenly announced the beginning of the so-called Third Period of decisive revolutionary battles. This policy was largely introduced to complement and justify collectivization in the USSR. In its practical implementation, the Third Period consisted of denouncing the Social Democrats as nothing more than an appendage of fascism. Thus, in Germany, the Stalinists insisted that a united front with social democracy was impermissible, for the latter was merely the left wing of fascism. The Social Democrats were dubbed "Social fascists."

The consequence of this criminally irresponsible, almost insane, policy is that it all but excluded the possibility of a unified struggle by the massive socialist workers movement against fascism.

In his very brief review of the political events that preceded Hitler's appointment as chancellor in January 1933, Goldhagen points out that the Nazis received almost fourteen million votes in the election of July 1932, *37.4* percent of the voters. The number is placed in italics, in order to emphasize the overwhelming character of pro-Nazi sentiment.

Goldhagen does not give the vote for the Social Democratic Party and Communist Party. In fact, the SPD received 7.95 million (21.6 percent) and the KPD received 5.2 million (14.6 percent). That is, the combined vote of the two socialist parties in Germany was nearly 13.2 million, or 36.2 percent. In other words, the political life of Germany was polarized between socialist revolution and fascist counterrevolution.

The next election, in November 1932, which Goldhagen does not mention, saw the vote of the Nazis fall dramatically by two million. Their total vote was 11.73 million (33.1 percent). The SPD vote fell to 7.24 million (20.4 percent), while that of the KPD rose to 5.98 million (16.9 percent). The combined vote of the two socialist parties was now a half million more than that of the fascists. In percentage terms, the combined SPD-KPD vote was 37.3 percent.

This election was an unmitigated political disaster for the Nazis. It clearly demonstrated that their high tide had passed, and that Hitler's political tactics — an erratic combination of ultimatums and vacillation — had cost the Nazis dearly. The noted American historian, Henry Ashby Turner, in a recent study of the last stage of the Nazi rise to power states:

> The November election dealt a staggering blow to Hitler and his party. After an unbroken succession of dramatic gains over the

previous three years, the Nazi juggernaut faltered. Many voters who had cast their ballots for the Nazis in July in the expectation that they would soon come to power and provide quick, decisive remedies to Germany's plight, defected in frustration at the failure of Hitler's bid for the chancellorship.[19]

In purely electoral terms, even on the eve of Hitler's appointment as chancellor, the socialist workers movement represented a larger force than the fascists. As a social force, occupying decisive positions within industry, the socialist workers movement was, in its potential, infinitely more powerful. As Trotsky wrote in 1931:

> On the scales of election statistics, a thousand Fascist votes weigh as much as a thousand Communist votes. But on the scales of the revolutionary struggle, a thousand workers in one big factory represent a force a hundred times greater than a thousand petty officials, clerks, their wives and their mothers-in-law. The great bulk of the Fascists consists of human dust.[20]

And yet, the working class was politically immobilized by the irresponsible and defeatist policies of its leadership. The Social Democracy clung to the rotting corpse of the Weimar Republic, reassuring itself that the democratic constitution would provide protection for the working class even if Hitler came to power. The KPD refused to alter its disastrous tactics, hiding its growing demoralization behind a mask of demagogic bombast.

The end game was played out in January 1933. Finally convinced that the two workers parties were too paralyzed to offer serious resistance, the German bourgeoisie invited Hitler to take power through constitutional means. Without a single shot being fired, Hitler became chancellor on January 30, 1933.

The working class suffered the greatest defeat in its history, and this defeat cleared the way for the catastrophe that followed.

Toward the end of his book, Goldhagen writes:

---

[19] Henry A. Turner, *Hitler's Thirty Days to Power: January 1933* (New York: Addison-Wesley, 1996), pp. 14–15.
[20] *The Struggle Against Fascism in Germany*, p. 164.

> The Nazi German revolution ... was an unusual revolution in that, domestically, it was being realized — the repression of the political left in the first few years notwithstanding — without massive coercion and violence. ... By and large, it was a peaceful revolution willingly acquiesced to by the German people. Domestically, the Nazi German revolution was, on the whole, consensual.[21]

Until I read those words, I had been inclined to look upon Goldhagen as a rather sad and somewhat pathetic figure, a young man whose study of the fate of European Jewry had left him intellectually, if not emotionally, traumatized. But in this paragraph something very ugly emerges. Except for its treatment of the Jews, the Nazi "revolution" — Goldhagen does not use the word "counterrevolution" — was a rather benign affair. His reference to the "repression of the political left" is inserted between hyphens, suggesting that it was not all too big a deal.

The claim that the Nazi conquest of power was "a peaceful revolution willingly acquiesced to by the German people" is a despicable falsification. What Goldhagen refers to as the "repression of the political left" consisted, in fact, of the physical destruction of mass socialist parties that represented the hopes and aspirations of millions of workers and the best elements of the German intelligentsia for a just and decent world. German socialism was not only a political movement: it was, for all its internal contradictions, both the inspirer and expression of a flowering of human intellect and culture. Its destruction required the barbaric methods in which the Nazis excelled.

The burning of books, the flight of scientists, artists and writers from Germany, the establishment of Dachau concentration camp and the incarceration of thousands of left-wing political opponents, the illegalization of all political parties other than the National Socialists, the liquidation of the trade unions — these were, in the first months of the Nazi regime, the principal achievements of its "peaceful revolution."

Despite the terror unleashed by the Nazis, there was persistent and considerable opposition.

Historian F.L. Carsten writes:

> A sizeable minority of Social Democrats and Communists were not willing to knuckle under and to accept passively whatever

---

[21] *Hitler's Willing Executioners*, p. 456.

the new regime might order them to do. The widespread terror accompanying the "seizure of power" and the mass arrests of the early months told them enough. Large numbers responded by forming underground groups, producing and distributing underground leaflets and papers and disturbing Nazi propaganda as best they could. In 1933 and 1934 hundreds of clandestine groups sprang up all over Germany — and quite often they were equally quickly liquidated by the Gestapo. ... It has been reliably estimated that the KPD between 1933 and 1935 lost about 75,000 members through imprisonment and that several thousands of them were killed. That means that about a quarter of the members registered in 1932 were lost.[22]

The Nazi terror intimidated and cowed millions of Germans. Large sections of the working class, dejected and demoralized by the shameful collapse of their organizations, retreated into apathy. Yet, even in the face of the merciless brutality of the Nazis, there was significant active opposition to the regime among workers.

Carsten explains:

> Even if the majority of the workers had made their peace with the Nazi regime it also remains true that of those who were imprisoned for political reasons the large majority belonged to the working class. Of 21,823 Germans imprisoned at the *Steinwache* in Dortmund for political offenses, the overwhelming majority were workers. Of 629 people from Solingen who were involved in political opposition, over 70 percent were workers and presumably many of the 49 housewives listed also belonged to the working class. In Oberhausen in the Ruhr the number was close to 90 percent. For less industrialized areas the figure would no doubt be lower, but the German working class certainly provided the bulk of those who suffered for their political convictions. In the years 1933 to 1944, 2,162 people were arrested in Essen for leftwing political activity and 1,721 in Düsseldorf, among them 297 women. In the penitentiary of Brandenburg 1,807 people were executed for political reasons

---

[22] F.L. Carsten, *The German Workers and the Nazis* (Aldershot: Scolar Press, 1995), p.180.

during the war and 775 of them were workers or artisans. It was a proud record. They could not overthrow the regime, but that was an impossible task. When it was attempted in 1944 by military and conservative circles they failed equally. It was only after a lost war that the regime finally succumbed and even in its downfall it engulfed many of its opponents. For the dictatorship the disjointed opposition was only an irritant but — like other minorities — it was persecuted without mercy.[23]

Facts such as these are not mentioned in *Hitler's Willing Executioners*. Goldhagen gives the impression of not being particularly concerned with the impact of fascism on anyone other than the Jews. This callousness is derived from his narrow and embittered outlook: conceiving of the Holocaust as a crime committed by "ordinary" Germans against Jews, he is not especially interested in what Germans may have done to each other. At any rate, his thesis does not permit him to recognize the existence of any substantial opposition to Hitler among Germans.

This is not only wrong in a factual sense. The irony of Professor Goldhagen's position is that it renders him incapable of understanding either the cause of the Holocaust or its universal, world historical, significance.

Socialism and the fate of the Jews

The fate of the Jews as a historically oppressed people and that of the working class were inextricably and tragically linked. The downfall of the German socialist movement cleared the way for the destruction of European Jewry. The democratic rights of the Jews, indeed, even their right to exist, depended upon the political strength of the working class. The mass killing of Jews did not begin in 1933. Before a crime of this magnitude could be organized and executed the Nazis had to terrorize and destroy the intellectually vital, progressive and humane elements in German society.

The Holocaust was, in the final analysis, the price which the Jewish people and all humanity paid for the failure of the working class to overthrow capitalism.

That is a lesson that must not be forgotten. We live in a world in which the contradictions of capitalism are once again assuming explosive dimensions.

---

[23] Ibid., p. 182.

Masses of people are being marginalized, if not completely separated from the productive process, by the manic operations of global capitalism. In virtually every European country, unemployment stands at 10 percent or higher. Without the development of a genuine alternative to the social insanity of the world capitalist market, the disoriented victims of capitalism are susceptible to the ranting of right-wing demagogues.

Recently, *The New York Times* carried a report on the resurgence of anti-Semitism in Russia:

> Frustrated with the wrenching economic and social upheaval that followed the collapse of Communism and the Soviet Union, in 1991, and spurred on by politicians willing to tap their resentments, many people are returning to the traditional scapegoat: Jews.[24]

Of what value is the work of Goldhagen in countering the danger posed by such developments?

Under conditions of deepening economic crisis and dislocation, the political lessons of the 1930s will again assume urgent contemporary relevance. That is why it is necessary to study and assimilate the origins and real causes of the Holocaust.

---

[24] Available: http://www.nytimes.com/1997/04/15/world/success-may-be-bad-for-jews-as-old-russian-bias-surfaces.html?pagewanted=all&src=pm

13

The Causes and Consequences
of World War II[1]

The main concern of this lecture is not the specific conflicts and events that triggered World War II, but rather the war's more general causes.

Given the massive scale of the cataclysm that unfolded between 1939 and 1945, it is simplistic, even absurd, to seek the causes of the war primarily in the diplomatic conflicts that led up to the hostilities — such as the dispute over the Danzig Corridor — apart from their broader historical context.

Any consideration of the causes of World War II must proceed from the fact that the development of global military conflict between 1939 and 1945 followed by only twenty-five years the first global military conflict, which occurred between 1914 and 1918. Only twenty-one years passed between the end of World War I and the beginning of World War II. Another way of looking at it is that within the space of just thirty-one years, two catastrophic global wars were fought.

To put this in a contemporary perspective, the time span between 1914 and 1945 is the same as between 1978 — the midpoint of the Carter administration — and 2009. To maintain this sense of historical perspective — making the necessary shift in historical time — let us consider that someone born in 1960 would have been eighteen years old in 1978, that is, old enough to be drafted to fight in a war. If he or she survived, that person would have been

---

[1] Lecture delivered at San Diego State University on October 5, 2009.

only twenty-two at the end of the war. He or she would have been just forty-three when the second war began and only forty-nine when it was over.

What does this mean in very human and personal terms? By the time this individual reached the age of fifty, he or she would have witnessed, directly or indirectly, a staggering level of violence. He would have probably known very many people who were killed in the course of these wars.

Of course, the scale of one's personal acquaintance with death during the two wars depended on where one happened to live. The experience of the average American was not the same as that of the average person in England, France, Germany, Poland, Russia, China or Japan.

The human cost of the world wars

For World War I, estimates of total deaths range from nine million to over sixteen million. Combat-related deaths accounted for 6.8 million of the

Country	Deaths	% of Population Killed
Australia	61,928	1.38
Britain	994,134	2.19
Belgium	120,637	1.63
Canada	66,944	0.93
France	1,697,800	4.29
Greece	176,000	3.67
Italy	1,240,000	3.48
Romania	680,000	9.07
Russia	3,311,000	1.89
Serbia	725,000	16.11
United States	117,465	0.13

Figure 1. Deaths in World War I by country, Allied powers

Country	Deaths	% of Population Killed
Austria-Hungary	1,567,000	3.05
Bulgaria	187,500	3.41
Germany	2,476,897	3.82
Ottoman Empire	2,921,844	13.72

Figure 2. Deaths in World War I by country, Central powers

Country	Deaths	% of Population Killed
China	10,000,000-20,000,000	2 to 4
Dutch East Indies	3,000,000-4,000,000	4.3 to 5.76
French Indochina	1,000,000-1,5000,000	4 to 6
Greece	800,000	11.7
Japan	2,700,000	3.78
Germany	5,600,000-6,500,000	7.8 to 9.4
Poland	5,800,000	16.5
Soviet Union	24,000,000	14
United States	418,000	0.32

Figure 3. Deaths in World War II by country

total number. Another two million military deaths were caused by accidents, disease and the effect of POW camp incarceration.

Figures 1 and 2 give a breakdown of the death toll by country for World War I. These were staggering losses. The millions of deaths that were directly caused by the war were followed almost immediately, after the Armistice, by the deaths of another twenty million people as a result of the influenza epidemic that devastated the physically weakened populations.[2]

The human cost of World War II exceeded by far that of the First World War. Military deaths totaled twenty-two to twenty-five million, including the deaths of five million prisoners of war. Let us examine the death tolls suffered by a number of countries most directly involved in the maelstrom. Poland lost more than 16 percent of its population. The Soviet Union lost approximately 14 percent. Eleven percent of the population of Greece was killed. Other countries that lost at least 10 percent of their populations were Lithuania and Latvia. Other countries that lost at least 3 percent of their people were Estonia, Hungary, the Netherlands, Romania, Singapore and Yugoslavia.

Included in this catalog of death is the genocidal annihilation of European Jewry. Six million Jews were murdered between 1939 and 1945. This includes three million Polish Jews and nearly one million Ukrainian Jews. In terms of percentages, 90 percent of the Jews in Poland, the Baltic countries and Germany were killed. More than 80 percent of Czechoslovak Jews were murdered. More than 70 percent of Dutch, Hungarian and Greek Jews were

---

[2] Exact casualty figures are not available. The totals differ slightly from source to source. The numbers in the tables are drawn from Wikipedia [http://en.wikipedia.org/wiki/World_War_I_casualties] and other books and web sites.

exterminated. Approximately 60 percent of Yugoslav and Belgian Jews were killed. More than 40 percent of Norwegian Jews were exterminated. More than 20 percent of French, Bulgarian and Italian Jews were murdered.

This genocidal campaign was conducted with the substantial support of local authorities. The only Nazi-occupied country in which there was a concerted effort by the local population to save its Jewish citizens was Denmark. In that country, despite the fact that it bordered Germany, out of a pre-war population of 8,000, only fifty-two Jews fell victim to the Nazi terror — that is, less than 1 percent.

The human cost of World War I and II is, according to the best estimates, between eighty and ninety million people. One must add to this the additional hundreds of millions who were, to some degree, physically injured or emotionally scarred by the two wars — those who lost parents, children, siblings and friends; who were displaced, forced to flee their homelands, and who lost irreplaceable and priceless links to their personal and cultural heritage. It is immensely difficult to articulate, let alone comprehend, the horrifying scale of the tragedy that occurred in the thirty-one years between 1914 and 1945.

Please keep in mind that this massive tragedy occurred only a relatively short time ago. There are still tens of millions of people alive today who lived through the Second World War. And for people of my generation, the events of World War I occurred during the lives of our grandparents — who were, in many cases, veterans of that war. World War I and World War II belong to very recent history. The world in which we live is the product of these twin catastrophes. The contradictions — political and economic — out of which these wars emerged have not been resolved. This historical fact alone is sufficient reason to see in the seventieth anniversary of the outbreak of World War II an opportunity for a reexamination of its origins, consequences and lessons.

Of course, within the space of a single lecture, it is possible only to provide a regrettably sparse outline of the principal causes of the war. For the purpose of clarity, but without unnecessary over-simplification, this outline will treat World War I and World War II as inextricably related episodes.

The origins of World War I

The speed with which the crisis unfolded in the summer of 1914 took many by surprise. Few suspected that the assassination of Austrian Archduke Franz Ferdinand in Sarajevo on June 28, 1914 would lead, within only five weeks, to a full-scale European War. Nor did they foresee that it would assume global dimensions with the entry of the United States into the conflict in April 1917. The conditions for a disastrous military conflagration had been maturing during the previous fifteen years, and these conditions were bound up with dramatic changes in world economy and, consequently, world politics.

Prior to the eruption of 1914, there had been no generalized war between the "Great Powers" of Europe since the end of the Napoleonic Wars in 1815. The Congress of Vienna created a relatively stable framework of inter-state relations that was sustained for the rest of the century. This does not mean that the nineteenth century was peaceful. The nation-state system in its modern form emerged out of a series of significant military conflicts, of which the most bloody was the American Civil War. In Europe, the consolidation of the modern German state under the political hegemony of Prussia was achieved by Bismarck with the calculated use of military force against Denmark (1864), Austria (1866) and, finally, France (1870). Earlier, in the 1850s, the British and the French countered the geopolitical ambitions of the Russian Empire in the Crimean conflict. But these military conflicts were relatively contained, and did not lead to a breakdown of the entire framework of European and global politics.

However, by the 1890s the nature of world politics was changing under the impact of the massive expansion of capitalist finance and industry, particularly in Europe and North America, and the growing influence of global economic interests in the calculations of national states. The conflict between major capitalist states — or, to be more precise, the most powerful financial and industrial interests exercising vast influence over the formulation of foreign policy — for dominance within certain "spheres of influence" became the driving force of world politics. This development found its most brutal expression in the struggle for colonies, whose local populations were reduced to a semi-slave status.

The age of imperialism had dawned. It destabilized the equilibrium of global inter-state relations. In the decades that followed the end of the Napoleonic Wars, Britain had enjoyed a position of virtually unchallenged supremacy. Its empire, based on naval power and vast colonial possessions, was the dominant fact of international politics in the nineteenth century. As was commonly said of the British Empire, the sun never set and the wages never rose! France also enjoyed a privileged status in the world system as an old colonial power, but was considerably behind Britain. The emergence of new bourgeois national states, with rapidly expanding capitalist industry and finance, placed the existing geopolitical relations under stress. The two most important "new" capitalist states, which were rapidly acquiring imperialist interests and appetites, were Germany and the United States.

The entry of the United States into the imperialist club occurred in 1898, when the McKinley administration, with unsurpassed cynicism, hypocrisy and dishonesty, concocted a pretext for war against Spain. Within just a few months, Cuba was turned into a semi-colony of the United States. At the same time, the United States, through the occupation of the Philippines, established the foundations for its imperialist domination of the Pacific. Having justified its occupation of the Philippines with the promise of freedom and democracy for its inhabitants, the United States honored its commitments by slaughtering 200,000 local insurgents who opposed American occupation.

The United States was blessed with a precious geographical advantage: a continent that was protected from foreign meddling by two oceans. Most European powers were amazed by the crudeness of McKinley's dishonest war-mongering, but could do absolutely nothing about it.

The growing ambitions of Germany, on the other hand, immediately collided with its imperialist neighbors in Europe — France, Russia, and, above all, Britain. The expanding conflicts of powerful national capitalist states, seeking dominance within an increasingly integrated global economy, formed the real basis for the accumulation of geopolitical tensions that finally exploded in the summer of 1914.

During, and especially after, World War I, there was a great deal of discussion about "who started the war," "who fired the first shot" and, "who was to blame." These questions play a major role in the propaganda of the states involved in war, as their ruling cliques are anxious to absolve themselves of responsibility for the disastrous consequences of their pyromania.

Studied in isolation from broader historical circumstances, there is plenty of evidence that Germany and Austria-Hungary were principally responsible for the outbreak of war in August 1914. Their governments chose, with incredible recklessness, to exploit the assassination of Franz Ferdinand to achieve long-standing geopolitical objectives. They took decisions that set into motion the disastrous chain of events that led to the outbreak of hostilities. But beyond demonstrating the criminality of which capitalist regimes are capable — as we have seen more recently in Washington's launching of the wars in Iraq and Afghanistan on the basis of out-and-out lies — the evidence of German and Austrian premeditation is inadequate as an explanation for the deeper causes of the war.

It is true that France and Britain did not necessarily want war in August 1914. But that is not because they were devoted morally to peace. Britain, it should be remembered, had waged a brutal counter-insurgency war against the Boers in South Africa only a decade earlier. If Britain and France did not necessarily "want" war in 1914, it was because they were more or less satisfied with the geopolitical status quo that favored their global interests. However, when confronted with actions by Germany and Austria-Hungary that threatened the existing set-up and their interests, they accepted war as a political necessity. From the standpoint of the imperialist interests of France and Britain, war was preferable to a peace that changed the balance of power along lines sought by Germany.

In the final analysis, the cause of the war is not to be found in the actions of one or another state that precipitated the shooting, but in the nature of the imperialist system, in the struggle of powerful capitalist national states to maintain — or achieve, depending on the circumstances — a dominant position in an increasingly integrated global economic order.

In the years preceding the war, the international socialist movement had held a series of congresses in which it had warned of the deadly consequences of developing imperialism and the militarism it encouraged. The Second International, which had been founded in 1889, declared again and again its unrelenting opposition to capitalist militarism and pledged to mobilize the working class against war. It warned the European ruling class that if war could not be stopped, the International would use the crisis created by war to hasten the overthrow of capitalism.

But in August 1914 these pledges were betrayed by virtually all the leaders of European socialism. On August 4, 1914, the German Social Democratic Party — the largest socialist party in the world — voted in the Reichstag for credits to finance the war. The same patriotic position was taken by socialist leaders in France, Austria and Britain. Only a handful of major socialist leaders took a clear and unequivocal stand against the war, among whom the most important were Lenin, Trotsky and Rosa Luxemburg.

Trotsky's analysis of the causes of World War I

I would like to focus briefly on the analysis made by Trotsky of the causes of the war. He rejected with contempt the deceitful and hypocritical claims of pro-war socialist leaders that they had sided with their capitalist rulers to defend their countries against foreign aggression. Trotsky exposed the blatant lies with which the warring governments sought to cover up the real political and economic motivations that underlay their decisions to go to war. He insisted that the cause of the war lay deeper, in changes in the structure of world economy and the very nature of the capitalist nation-state system.

Forced to leave Austria with the outbreak of the war, Trotsky first went to Zurich, where, in 1915, he wrote a brilliant pamphlet, *War and the International*, in which he explained the significance of the war.

> The present war is at bottom a revolt of the forces of production against the political form of nation and state. It means the collapse of the national state as an independent economic unit.
>
> The nation must continue to exist as a cultural, ideologic and psychological fact, but its economic foundation has been pulled from under its feet. All talk of the present bloody clash being the work of national defence is either hypocrisy or blindness. On the contrary, the real, objective significance of the War is the breakdown of the present national economic centres, and the substitution of a world economy in its stead. But the way the governments propose to solve this problem of imperialism is not through the intelligent, organized cooperation of all of humanity's producers, but through the exploitation of the world's economic system by the capitalist class of the victorious country; which country is by this War to be transformed from a Great Power into the World Power.
>
> The War proclaims the downfall of the national state. Yet at the same time it proclaims the downfall of the capitalist system of economy. By means of the national state, capitalism has revolutionized the whole economic system of the world. It has divided the whole earth among the oligarchies of the great powers, around which were grouped the satellites, the small nations, who lived off the rivalry between the great ones. The future development of world economy on the capitalistic basis means a ceaseless struggle for new and ever new fields of capitalist exploitation, which must be obtained from one and the same source, the earth. The economic rivalry under the banner of militarism is accompanied by robbery and destruction which violate the elementary principles of human economy. World production revolts not only against the confusion produced by national and state divisions but also

against the capitalist economic organizations, which has now turned into barbarous disorganization and chaos.

The War of 1914 is the most colossal breakdown in history of an economic system destroyed by its own inherent contradictions. ...

Capitalism has created the material conditions of a new Socialist economic system. Imperialism has led the capitalist nations into historic chaos. The War of 1914 shows the way out of this chaos by violently urging the proletariat on to the path of Revolution.[3]

This analysis was vindicated in the eruption of the Russian Revolution, which brought the Bolshevik party, led by Lenin and Trotsky, to power in October 1917.

After four years of unprecedented conflict and bloodshed, the war ended somewhat abruptly in November 1918. What brought the war to an end was related more to changing political conditions within the belligerent countries than to results on the battlefield. The October Revolution led rapidly to Russia's withdrawal from the war. The French army, staggered by soldiers' mutinies in 1917, came close to collapse. Only the infusion of American men and materiel on the side of the allies staved off military defeat and restored, at least to some extent, morale. Anti-war opposition grew rapidly in Germany, especially in the aftermath of the Bolshevik victory in Russia. In October 1918, a naval mutiny in Germany triggered broader revolutionary protests that led to the abdication of Kaiser Wilhelm II. Unable to continue the war, Germany sued for peace.

Despite the defeat of Germany, the war did not produce the results that Britain and France had originally envisioned. In the east, the war had led to socialist revolution in Russia and the radicalization of the working class throughout Europe. In the west, the war created the conditions for the emergence of the United States — which had suffered relatively few losses — as the dominant capitalist power.

The Versailles settlement of 1919 set the stage for the eruption of new conflicts. The vindictive terms insisted upon by French imperialism did little to ensure stable relations on the European continent. The breakup of the Austro-Hungarian Empire resulted in the creation of a new set of unstable

---

[3] Leon Trotsky, *The War and the International 1915*, (Colombo: A Young Socialist Publication, 1971), pp. vii–viii.

national states, torn by sectional rivalries. The Versailles settlement failed to create a foundation for the restoration of the political and economic equilibrium of Europe. Rather, the world capitalist economy, as it emerged from the war, was riven by imbalances that led to the unprecedented collapse that began on Wall Street in October 1929.

The rise of US imperialism

Another major factor in the re-emergence of international tensions that was to lead to a renewal of global war in 1939 was the new role of the United States in world affairs. Wilson was hailed — in the aftermath of the US entry into World War I and the victory of socialist revolution in Russia — as the savior of capitalist Europe. But it soon became clear to the European bourgeoisie that the interests of the United States were in conflict with its own. The American bourgeoisie was not willing to accept European dominance in world affairs. It viewed the privileges enjoyed by Britain within the framework of its Empire as a barrier to the expansion of its own commercial interests.

While the steady expansion of American power gave British diplomats sleepless nights, it thoroughly unnerved the most ruthless representatives of German imperialism. In *Wages of Destruction*, a new study of the origins of World War II, the respected scholar Adam Tooze writes:

> ... America should provide the pivot for our understanding of the Third Reich. In seeking to explain the urgency of Hitler's aggression, historians have underestimated his acute awareness of the threat posed to Germany, along with the rest of the European powers, by the emergence of the United States as the dominant global superpower. On the basis of contemporary economic trends, Hitler predicted already in the 1920s that the European powers had only a few more years to organize themselves against this inevitability. ...
>
> The aggression of Hitler's regime can thus be rationalized as an intelligible response to the tensions stirred up by the uneven development of global capitalism, tensions that are of course still with us today.[4]

---

[4] Adam Tooze, *The Wages of Destruction: The Making and Breaking of the Nazi Economy* (London: Penguin Books, 2006), pp. xxiv–xxv.

The years that followed the conclusion of World War I witnessed the hey-day of pacifism. Wilson had proclaimed upon declaring war on Germany in 1917 that the United States was waging war "to end all wars." The League of Nations — which the US refused to join — was set up by the European victors. In 1927, France and the United States negotiated the Kellogg-Briand Pact, which declared war illegal. And yet, international tensions became increasingly acute, especially after the Wall Street collapse, the onset of the global depression, and the resulting political destabilization of Europe — of which the coming to power in Germany of Hitler's Nazi party in January 1933 was the most ominous expression.

No one grasped the implications of the unfolding crisis of world capitalism with greater foresight and clarity than Leon Trotsky. In June 1934, having been exiled from the Soviet Union by the reactionary bureaucratic regime led by Stalin, Trotsky wrote:

> The same causes, inseparable from modern capitalism, that brought about the last imperialist war have now reached infinitely greater tension than in the middle of 1914. The fear of the consequences of a new war is the only factor that fetters the will of imperialism. But the efficacy of this brake is limited. The stress of the inner contradictions pushes one country after another on the road to fascism, which, in its turn, cannot maintain power except by preparing international explosions. All governments fear war. But none of the governments has any freedom of choice. Without a proletarian revolution, a new world war is inevitable. [5]

Trotsky explained, as he had in 1915, that the principal source of global tensions lay in the contradiction "between the productive forces and the framework of the national state, in conjunction with the principal contradiction — between the productive forces and the private ownership of the means of production..."[6] The defense of the national state served no politically or economically progressive function. "The national state with its borders, passports, monetary system, customs and the army for the protection of customs has become a frightful impediment to the economic and cultural development of humanity."[7]

---

[5] *Writings of Leon Trotsky 1933–34* (New York: Pathfinder Press, 1975), p. 300.
[6] Ibid., p. 304.
[7] Ibid.

With Hitler in power, liberal and reformist apologists for the imperialist bourgeoisie in Britain, France and the United States had begun to argue that a new war would be a fight against dictatorship. This argument would eventually be adopted by the Soviet Stalinist regime. Trotsky emphatically rejected this claim. "A modern war between the great powers," he wrote, "does not signify a conflict between democracy and fascism but a struggle of two imperialisms for the redivision of the world."[8]

Within the context of this political perspective, Trotsky analyzed the global ambitions of the United States:

> U.S. capitalism is up against the same problems that pushed Germany in 1914 on the path of war. The world is divided? It must be redivided. For Germany it was a question of "organizing Europe." The United States must "organize" the world. History is bringing humanity face to face with the volcanic eruption of American imperialism.[9]

These words were to prove extraordinarily prescient. Trotsky insisted that only the revolutionary struggle of the working class, leading to the overthrow of capitalism, could prevent the eruption of a new world war, even bloodier than the first. But the defeats of the working class in Spain and France — the product of the combined treachery of the Stalinist, social democratic and reformist bureaucracies — made war inevitable. It finally began on September 1, 1939.

As in 1914, German imperialism was the principal instigator of the conflict. But the Second World War, like the first, had more profound causes. Trotsky wrote:

> The democratic governments, who in their day hailed Hitler as a crusader against Bolshevism, now make him out to be some kind of Satan unexpectedly loosed from the depths of hell, who violates the sanctity of treaties, boundary lines, rules, and regulations. If it were not for Hitler the capitalist world would blossom like a garden. What a miserable lie! This German epileptic with a calculating machine in his skull and unlimited power in

---

[8] Ibid., p. 307.
[9] Ibid., p. 302.

his hands did not fall from the sky or come up out of hell: he is nothing but the personification of all the destructive forces of imperialism. ... Hitler, rocking the old colonial powers to their foundations, does nothing but give a more finished expression to the imperialist will to power. Through Hitler, world capitalism, driven to desperation by its own impasse, has begun to press a razor-sharp dagger into its own bowels.[10]

Lest one think that Trotsky is here being unjust to the leaders of the wartime opponents of Hitler, it is worth recalling the words of Winston Churchill. In January 1927, sometime before he became British prime minister, Churchill visited Rome, met with the Italian dictator Mussolini, and wrote: "I could not help being charmed by Signor Mussolini's gentle and simple bearing, and by his calm, detached poise in spite of so many burdens and dangers." Italian fascism provided the "necessary antidote to the Russian virus." Churchill told the Italian fascists: "If I had been an Italian I am sure I should have been entirely with you from the beginning to the end of your victorious struggle against the bestial appetites and passions of Leninism."[11]

A historian of the period notes:

> To many Conservatives, and business groups, Hitler's Germany and Mussolini's Italy, dedicated to impeding the spread of communism, were objects of some admiration. As a result, there was strong opposition — especially in Britain — to an alliance with the Soviet Union aimed against the fascist powers.[12]

The outbreak of World War II

Hitler invaded Poland on September 1, 1939, and Britain and France declared war on the Third Reich two days later. After Hitler completed the conquest of Poland within a few weeks, no further military action was taken by Nazi Germany until the spring of 1940, when German armies swept across

[10] *Writings of Leon Trotsky 1939–40* (New York: Pathfinder Press, 1973), p. 233.
[11] Cited in Nicholson Baker, *Human Smoke: The Beginnings of World War II, the End of Civilization* (New York: Simon and Schuster, 2008), p. 16.
[12] Frank McDonough, *Hitler, Chamberlain and Appeasement* (Cambridge: Cambridge University Press, 2002), p. 33.

Western Europe. In June 1940, France — whose ruling class was more concerned with the revolutionary threat posed by its own working class than with the danger of a Nazi takeover of the country — surrendered.

Stalin had hoped that he could avoid war with Germany through his cowardly and treacherous non-aggression pact. But the fascist regime had always viewed the destruction of the Soviet Union as the main component of its plan for domination in Europe. In June 1941, the German invasion of the USSR began. Despite Stalin's disastrous miscalculations and the massive defeats initially suffered by the Red Army, the Nazi forces encountered unyielding resistance.

On December 7, 1941, the Japanese attack on Pearl Harbor brought the United States into the war. Four days later, on December 11, 1941, Germany declared war on the United States, which immediately replied with a declaration of war on Germany. For the next three-and-a-half years, the war was waged with unrelenting ferocity — though it must be stressed that the war in Western Europe, at least until the Allied invasion in June 1944, was, in military terms, a relatively minor side show in comparison to the horrific carnage of the struggle between Nazi Germany and the Soviet Union. The war in Europe finally came to an end on May 8, 1945, with the unconditional capitulation of Nazi Germany, just one week after Hitler's suicide.

The war in Asia continued for another three months, though there was never any doubt of its outcome. There had never existed even a remote possibility that Japan — with its much smaller population, underdeveloped industrial base, and limited access to key raw materials — could prevail against the United States. The Japanese government, as the United States government knew very well, was seeking, from the spring of 1945, acceptable terms for a surrender. But the tragedy was played out to the bloody end. In August 1945, the United States dropped two nuclear devices on the defenseless and militarily insignificant cities of Hiroshima and Nagasaki. The death toll from the two bombs was approximately 150,000 people. As the American historian Gabriel Jackson later observed:

> In the specific circumstances of August 1945, the use of the atom bomb showed that a psychologically very normal and democratically elected chief executive could use the weapon just as the Nazi dictator would have used it. In this way, the United States — for anyone concerned with moral distinctions in the

conduct of different types of government — blurred the difference between fascism and democracy.[13]

Viewing World War I and World War II as interconnected stages in a single historical process, what can we conclude was the source and purpose of the conflict which cost approximately ninety million people their lives?

The eruption of the First World War arose out of inter-imperialist antagonisms generated by the emergence of powerful capitalist states that were dissatisfied with the existing geopolitical relations. Germany resented its inferior position in a world colonial system dominated by Britain and France, and chafed against the restraints placed on the pursuit of its interests by these powerful rivals. At the same time, the United States, whose unsurpassed economic power filled it with confidence and ambition, was unwilling to accept restrictions on the penetration of American capital into foreign markets, including those governed by the protective rules of the British Empire.

The conclusion of World War II brought to a conclusion a distinct period of global conflict that had begun with the dawn of the imperialist epoch in the late 1890s. Germany's bid for its "place in the sun" had suffered a decisive defeat. Similarly, Imperial Japan's dream of establishing its dominance in the Western Pacific, China and Southeast Asia was shattered by its decisive defeat in World War II. The British and the French emerged from the half-century of carnage desperately weakened, lacking sufficient financial resources to sustain their old empires. Whatever illusions they may have had about preserving their status as the premier imperialist powers were given their deathblow within a decade of the end of World War II.

In 1954, the French suffered a devastating military defeat in Dien Bien Phu at the hands of the Vietnamese liberation forces, which forced French withdrawal from Indochina. In 1956, the British government was forced by the United States to call off its invasion of Egypt — a public humiliation that confirmed Britain's subservience to American imperialism. As foreseen by Trotsky decades earlier, the struggle among the main imperialist powers for global dominance, the brutal redivision of the world that cost the lives of tens of millions of human beings, had ended with the victory of American imperialism.

The world that emerged in 1945 from the carnage of two wars was profoundly different from that which existed in 1914. Though the United States

---

[13] Gabriel Jackson, *Civilization and Barbarity in Twentieth Century Europe* (New York: Prometheus Books, 1999), pp. 176–177.

had replaced bankrupt Britain as the pre-eminent imperialist power, it could not re-create, in its own image, the old British Empire. The age of colonial empires, at least in the form they had previously existed, had passed.

In a historical fact pregnant with profound irony, Woodrow Wilson delivered his war message to Congress, in April 1917, just as Vladimir Ilyich Lenin was making his way back to revolutionary Russia. Two great historical lines of development intersected at this critical juncture. Wilson's speech marked the decisive emergence of the United States as the dominant imperialist force on the planet. Lenin's arrival in Russia marked the beginning of a massive wave of socialist and mass anti-imperialist struggles that were to sweep across the globe.

By the time the United States achieved its victory over Germany and Japan in 1945, hundreds of millions of people were already in revolt against imperialist oppression. The task that confronted the United States was to stem the tide of global revolutionary struggle. It is not possible within the framework of this survey to provide even an outline of post-war developments. This would require at least some explanation of the political dynamics of the so-called "Cold War," which defined international politics between 1945 and 1991. However, in bringing this lecture to a conclusion, it is necessary to stress that the United States viewed the dissolution of the Soviet Union in 1991 as an opportunity to finally establish the unchallenged hegemony of American imperialism.

The US doctrine of "preventive war"

In 1992, the US military adopted a strategic doctrine that declared that it would not permit any country to emerge as a challenger to the dominant global position of the United States. In 2002, this expansive military doctrine was supplemented with the promulgation of the doctrine of "preventive war," which declared that the United States reserved the right to attack any country that it believed to pose a *potential* threat to its security. This new doctrine was directed specifically against China, which was warned against building up its own military forces.

It should be pointed out that the new US military doctrine is illegal from the standpoint of international law. The legal precedents established at the Nuremberg war crimes trials held that war is not a legitimate instrument of state policy, and that preventive war is illegal. A military attack by one state upon another is legal only in the presence of a clear and immediate threat. In other words, military action is justified only as an inescapably urgent measure of national self-defense. The attack on Iraq, which followed by only a few months the promulgation of the 2002 doctrine of preventive war, was a war crime. Had the United States been held accountable under the precedents established at Nuremberg in 1946, Bush, Cheney, Rumsfeld, Powell and many others would have been placed on trial.

The critical question that flows inescapably from any examination of World War I and World War II is whether such catastrophes could ever happen again. Were the wars of the twentieth century some sort of horrifying aberration from a "normal" course of historical development? Is it possible to imagine the re-emergence of international disputes and antagonisms that would make the outbreak of World War III possible?

The answer to this question does not require far-fetched speculation. *The real question is less whether a new eruption of global warfare is possible, but how long do we have before such a catastrophe occurs? And, flowing from that second question, the next and most decisive question is whether anything can be done to stop it from happening.*

In weighing the risk of war, bear in mind that the United States has been engaged repeatedly in major military conflicts since 1990, when it first invaded Iraq. During the past decade, since 1999, it has waged major wars in the Balkans, the Persian Gulf and Central Asia. In one way or another, all of these wars have been related to the effort to secure the dominant global position of the United States.

It is highly significant that the increasing use of military force by the United States takes place against the backdrop of its steadily deteriorating global economic position. The weaker the United States becomes from an economic standpoint, the more inclined it is to offset this weakness through the use of military force. There are, in this specific respect, disturbing parallels to the policies of the Nazi regime in the late 1930s.

Moreover, keeping in mind the 2002 Strategic Doctrine, the United States confronts an expanding array of powers whose economic and military development are viewed by State Department and Pentagon strategists as significant threats. As the balance of economic power shifts away from the United States to various global competitors — a process that has been accelerated by an economic crisis that erupted in 2008 and which continues to unfold — there is an ever greater temptation to employ military force to reverse the unfavorable economic trend.

Finally, if we recall that World Wars I and II arose out of the destabilization of the old imperialist order dominated by Britain and France as a result of the emergence of new competitors, it is not unlikely that the present international order — in which the dominant power, the United States, is already riven with internal crisis and hard-pressed to maintain global dominance — will break down beneath the pressure exerted by emerging powers (such as China, India, Russia, Brazil, the EU) which are dissatisfied with existing arrangements.

Add to that the growing intra-regional tensions that threaten at any moment to erupt into military confrontations that could trigger interventions from extra-regional forces and lead to a global conflagration. One need only recall the tense situation which arose in the summer of 2008 as a result of the conflict between Georgia and Russia.

Only socialist revolution can prevent World War III

The world is a powder keg. It is not necessarily the case that the ruling classes want war. But they are not necessarily able to stop it. As Trotsky wrote on the eve of World War II, the capitalist regimes toboggan to disaster with their eyes closed. The insane logic of imperialism and the capitalist nation-state system, of the drive to secure access to markets, raw materials and cheap labor, of the relentless pursuit of profit and personal riches, leads inexorably in the direction of war.

What, then, can stop it? History shows us that the frightful mechanisms of imperialism can be jammed only by the active and conscious intervention of the masses of the world's people — above all, the working class — into the historical process. There is no means of stopping imperialist war except through international socialist revolution.

In 1914, Lenin, opposing the betrayal of the Second International, declared that the imperialist epoch is the epoch of wars and revolution. That is, the global economic, social and political contradictions that gave rise to imperialist war also create the objective foundations for international socialist revolution. In this sense, imperialist war and world socialist revolution are the responses of different and opposed social classes to the historical impasse of capitalism. The correctness of Lenin's assessment of the world situation was confirmed with the eruption of revolution in Russia in 1917.

For all the changes that have occurred since the beginning of World War I ninety-five years ago and World War II seventy years ago, we still live in the imperialist epoch. Thus, the great questions that confront mankind today are: Will the development of political consciousness in the international working class counteract the accumulating destructive tendencies of imperialism? Will the working class develop sufficient political consciousness in time, before capitalism and the imperialist nation-state system lead mankind into the abyss?

These are not questions merely for academic consideration. The very posing of these questions demands an active response. The answers will be provided not in a classroom, but in the real conflict of social forces. Struggle will decide the matter. And the outcome of this struggle will be influenced, to a decisive degree, by the development of revolutionary, that is, socialist consciousness. The struggle against imperialist war finds its highest expression in the fight to develop a new political leadership of the working class.

Only a few months after the outbreak of World War II — a catastrophe made possible by the betrayals of the reactionary Stalinist, social democratic and reformist labor bureaucracies — Trotsky, the supreme political realist, wrote:

> The capitalist world has no way out, unless a prolonged death agony is so considered. It is necessary to prepare for long years, if not decades, of war, uprisings, brief interludes of truce, new wars, and new uprisings. A young revolutionary party must base itself on this perspective. History will provide it with enough opportunities and possibilities to test itself, to accumulate experience, and to mature. The swifter the ranks of the vanguard are fused the more the epoch of bloody convulsions will be shortened, the less destruction will our planet suffer. But the great historical problem will not be solved in any case until a revolutionary party stands at the head of the proletariat. The question of tempos and time intervals is of enormous importance; but it alters neither the general historical perspective nor the direction of our policy. The conclusion is a simple one: it is necessary to carry on the work of educating and organizing the proletarian vanguard with tenfold energy. Precisely in this lies the task of the Fourth International.[14]

This analysis, written at an earlier stage of global imperialist crisis, resonates in the existing situation. The very survival of human civilization is at

---

[14] *Writings of Leon Trotsky 1939–40*, pp. 260–261.

stake. It is, above all, the responsibility of the youth to stop the drive toward war and secure the future of mankind. This is why I must conclude this lecture by appealing to you to join the Socialist Equality Party and contribute to the building of the Fourth International as the World Party of Socialist Revolution.

14

History as Propaganda:
Intellectuals and the Ukrainian Crisis[1]

A group of right-wing academics, journalists, pro-war human-rights activists, and specialists in "discourse" is gathering in Kiev this coming weekend (May 16–19, 2014). The purpose of the meeting — headed by Professor Timothy Snyder of Yale University and Leon Wieseltier, the neo-con literary editor of *The New Republic* — is to bestow political and moral respectability on the Ukrainian regime that came to power in February, through a putsch financed and directed by the United States and Germany.

Promoting themselves as an "international group of intellectuals," the organizers have issued a publicity handout — excuse me, a "Manifesto" — in which the meeting is described as "an encounter between those who care about freedom and a country where freedom is dearly won."[2] There is some truth in this statement, as the overthrow of the Yanukovych government did, in fact, cost the United States a great deal of money.

The meeting is an exercise in imperialist propaganda. Its sponsors include the embassies of Canada, France, Germany, Poland and the United States. Other sponsors include the Ukrainian Foreign Ministry, the European Endowment for Democracy, and *Eurozine*. On the *Eurozine* web site, which

---

[1] Published 16 May 2014 on the *World Socialist Web Site*.
[2] Available: http://www.eurozine.com/UserFiles/docs/Kyiv_2014/Programme_Public_EN.pdf

is heavily promoting the Kiev meeting, there are numerous postings relating to the geostrategic implications of the Ukrainian coup. Prominently featured are articles such as "How to Win Cold War II." Its author, Vladislav Inozemtsev, is presently a visiting fellow at the Center for Strategic and International Studies in Washington, DC.

Back in the 1960s, intellectuals who had participated in the Cold War's anti-communist Congress for Cultural Freedom were somewhat chagrined when the operations of that organization were publicly linked to the machinations of the Central Intelligence Agency. In those days, to be seen collaborating with the CIA and other state intelligence agencies was considered harmful to one's intellectual and moral reputation. *Tempi passati!* The participants of the Kiev assembly are entirely unabashed by the obvious fact that they are part of an event endorsed and stage managed by governments that were heavily involved in the overthrow of the Yanukovych government.

The entire assembly is an exercise in fraud and duplicity. The rhetoric of democratic "discourse" provides a cover for the elaboration of a thoroughly reactionary political agenda. Every phrase must be decrypted.

The Manifesto asserts that the assembly will "carry out a broad public discussion about the meaning of Ukrainian pluralism for the future of Europe, Russia, and the World." What this actually means, when decrypted, is that the assembly will examine how the Ukrainian putsch can serve as a model for further operations aimed at undermining Russia's influence in Europe and Eurasia.

Other questions that will be addressed at the meeting are:

1. "How can human rights be grounded and how are we motivated by the idea of human rights?" [Decrypted: "How can the human rights 'discourse' provide a pretext for political destabilization and the overthrow of opponent regimes?"]

2. "How and when does language provide access to the universal, and how and when does it define political difference?" [Decrypted: "How can democratic jargon be employed to obfuscate the material interests underlying social conflict?"]

3. "How is decency in politics possible amidst international anarchy, domestic corruption, and the general fallibility of individuals?" [Decrypted: "Why the realities of contemporary geopolitics justify the 'transgression of boundaries,' such as the use of torture, targeted assassinations, authoritarianism, war, etc."][3]

---

[3] Ibid.

Dwelling on these questions will allow the discussants to exhale a great deal of hot air while keeping the expenditure of intellectual energy to a minimum. Not listed among the subjects to be raised are questions arising from the Kiev regime's acts of repression against people in southern and eastern Ukraine, which have resulted in scores, if not hundreds, of deaths. Nor do the organizers plan to examine and explain the prominent role played by the neo-fascist forces of Svoboda and Right Sector in February's putsch and the organization of the present government.

The most prominent of the participants are a hastily gathered collection of "usual suspects," i.e., individuals who have a well-established record of promoting imperialist interventions under the false flag of human rights. They specialize in the moral marketing of state policies that are of a criminal character. In one form or another, the invocation of "human rights" has always served as a means of legitimizing imperialism. Even Belgium's King Leopold, as he murdered millions in the Congo in the 1880s, claimed to be acting on behalf of the "moral and material regeneration" of his helpless victims. More than a century ago, John Hobson, one of the first scholars of imperialism, called attention to the insidious role played by the hypocritical use of moral pretenses to conceal the real motives underlying imperialist policy. He wrote:

> It is precisely in this falsification of the real import of motives that the greatest vice and the most signal peril of Imperialism reside. When, out of a medley of mixed motives, the least potent [i.e., "human rights" and/or "democracy"] is selected for public prominence because it is the most presentable, when issues of a policy which was not present at all to the minds of those who formed this policy are treated as chief causes, the moral currency of the nation is debased. The whole policy of Imperialism is riddled with this deception.[4]

The participants include Leon Wieseltier, who served as a leading member of the Committee for the Liberation of Iraq and is closely identified with the Project for the New American Century. Paul Berman, a liberal political theorist, advocated the US bombing of Serbia (in support of Kosovar separatism) and, in the aftermath of 9/11, sought to justify US wars in the Middle

---

[4] J.A. Hobson, *Imperialism: A Study* (Cambridge: Cambridge University Press, 2010), pp. 209–210.

East and Central Asia as a struggle against Islamic fascism. Berman's Sunday evening lecture, entitled "Alexis de Tocqueville and the Idea of Democracy" will, no doubt, be an eye-opener for the fascist Oleh Tyahnybok and his followers in the Svoboda Party.

Bernard Kouchner will be present. Associated many decades ago with Doctors without Borders [*Médecins Sans Frontières*], Kouchner broke with this organization over tactical issues and formed Doctors of the World [*Médecins du Monde*] to advocate a more robust program of "humanitarian interventionism." This platform, as Hobson would have foreseen, sanctioned innumerable pretexts for military intervention in one or another country. Kouchner promoted the intervention in the Balkans. He eventually became foreign minister in the government of French President Sarkozy. In 2011, after having left the cabinet, he supported Sarkozy's attack on Libya, as well as the French invasion of the Ivory Coast. This political reactionary and defender of French imperialism will participate in a panel discussion of the question: "Does Europe Need [a] Ukrainian revolution?"

Kouchner's compatriot, the celebrity philosopher Bernard-Henri Lévy, another supporter of humanitarian interventions, is scheduled to give a speech denouncing Russian President Vladimir Putin. It is entitled "The resistible rise of d'Arturo Poutine." This sophomoric misuse of the title of Berthold Brecht's deadly-serious theatrical allegory [*The Resistible Rise of Arturo Ui*] is characteristic of Lévy's work. Lévy can denounce Putin without fear of retaliation. It would take a good deal more guts — at any rate, more than Lévy has — to denounce the crimes of Obama. Brecht's work was a biting satire on the rise of Hitler to power. Significantly, Brecht set his allegory in Chicago, drawing parallels between the operations of the criminal underworld in a capitalist environment to the workings of the Nazi Party. Among the most chilling lines, which were intended to resonate with an American audience: "Do not rejoice in his defeat, you men. For though the world has stood up and stopped the bastard, the bitch that bore him is in heat again." Old Brecht's warning has acquired a new timeliness.

Lévy's reputation in France as a public intellectual is in tatters. In 2010, he published an essay attacking Kant and the Enlightenment. He based this anti-Kant diatribe on the works of one "Jean-Baptiste Botul," a philosopher whose work had come to Lévy's attention. Unfortunately, Lévy overlooked the fact that "Botul" and his system of thought ("Botulisme") were the wholly fictional creation of a French journalist, Frédéric Pagès. Now an object of derision, one Gallic wit summed up the philosophy of the impressively coifed Lévy with the phrase: "God is dead, but my hair is perfect." For those who wish to learn all they would ever need to know about the thought of BHL, as he is widely known, his *Wikipedia* entry provides a comprehensive two-sentence summary.

Professor Snyder's *Bloodlands*

While Lévy represents the somewhat comic side of the proceedings, Professor Timothy Snyder's presence is of a darker character. His rapid and spectacular rise to public prominence is entirely bound up with his relent-less efforts to provide an ostensibly scholarly justification for US attempts to draw Ukraine into its sphere of influence, *and* to stigmatize Russia as the archenemy of the humane democratic aspirations championed, according to Snyder, by the United States and Europe.

The book that launched Snyder into the stratosphere of academic celeb-rity is entitled *Bloodlands: Europe Between Hitler and Stalin*. Published in late 2010, the book was greeted in the popular media as the work of a mas-ter. There were reviews in countless newspapers, where Snyder was hailed as if he were Thucydides incarnate. Snyder, it seems, enjoyed the attention. In the 2012 paperback edition of his book, the first fourteen pages are devoted entirely to quoting excerpts from reviews that sang his praise.

Why all the fuss? Snyder's book appeared in the aftermath of the 2004–2005 Orange Revolution in Ukraine, which resulted — after mass protests over allegations of vote fraud by supporters of Viktor Yanukovych — in the accession of US-backed Viktor Yushchenko to the Ukrainian presidency. In order to consolidate his hold on power, Yushchenko sought to appeal to right-wing Ukrainian chauvinism. A key element of this campaign, designed to whip up anti-Russian sentiments, was the presentation of Soviet collectiv-ization in the 1930s, which led to catastrophic famine and approximately 3.5 million deaths, as the equivalent of the systematic extermination of European Jewry by the Nazis. The *Holodomor* (death by hunger), he claimed, was a form of genocide planned and carried out by the Soviet Union against Ukrainians, just as the *Holocaust* was the deliberate mass murder of the Jews.

The elevation of the Holodomor into a symbol of Ukraine's victimization by the Soviet Union (and Russia) was politically inflammatory and, therefore, highly useful. The equation of the Ukrainian famine with the Holocaust — two very different events — provided the Ukrainian right with a potent myth, and US imperialism with a propaganda narrative that could be employed to incite anti-Russian sentiment.

Yushchenko was voted out of office in 2010. In one of his final acts, he proclaimed Stepan Bandera (1909–1959) — the notorious Ukrainian nationalist and fascist who had collaborated with the Third Reich and participated in the mass murder of Jews and Poles — a "Hero of Ukraine." This evoked widespread protests, including from the chief rabbi of Ukraine. Curiously, in light of his subsequent writings, Timothy Snyder was among those who issued a protest. In an article published in the February 24, 2010 edition of the *New York Review of Books*, he questioned Yushchenko's action. Snyder provided a concise summary of the crimes of Bandera and the Organization of Ukrainian Nationalists (OUN-B) that he headed:

> The Germans did destroy Poland in 1939, as the Ukrainian nationalists had hoped; and they tried to destroy the Soviet Union in 1941. When the Wehrmacht invaded the Soviet Union that June, they were joined by the armies of Hungary, Romania, Italy, and Slovakia, as well as small contingents of Ukrainian volunteers associated with the OUN-B. Some of these Ukrainian nationalists helped the Germans to organize murderous pogroms of Jews. In so doing, they were advancing a German policy, but one that was consistent with their own program of ethnic purity, and their own identification of Jews with Soviet tyranny.[5]

Snyder described the actions of the Ukrainian Insurgent Army (UPA), which operated under the command of the OUN-B:

> Under their command, the UPA undertook to ethnically cleanse western Ukraine of Poles in 1943 and 1944. UPA partisans murdered tens of thousands of Poles, most of them women and children. Some Jews who had taken shelter with Polish families were also killed. Poles (and a few surviving Jews) fled the countryside, controlled by the UPA, to the towns, controlled by the Germans.[6]

In the aftermath of the Nazi surrender, the Soviet Union and Poland (now ruled by a Stalinist party) were confronted with continued resistance from

---

[5] Available:http://www.nybooks.com/blogs/nyrblog/2010/feb/24/a-fascist-hero-in-democratic-kiev/

[6] Ibid.

the OUN, which received support from the United States. Thousands died in the course of the fighting that continued into the 1950s. The Soviet Union and Poland referred to the OUN as "German-Ukrainian fascists," which, Snyder conceded, was "a characterization accurate enough to serve as enduring and effective propaganda both within and without the Soviet Union." As for Bandera, Snyder noted that: "He remained faithful to the idea of a fascist Ukraine until assassinated by the KGB [Soviet secret police] in 1959."[7]

Commenting on the relationship between the celebration of Bandera and Ukrainian politics, Snyder wrote:

> Yushchenko was soundly defeated in the first round of the presidential elections, *perhaps in some measure because far more Ukrainians identify with the Red Army than with nationalist partisans from western Ukraine.* Bandera was burned in effigy in Odessa after he was named a hero; even his statue in west Ukrainian Lviv, erected by city authorities in 2007, was under guard during the election campaign.[8] (Emphasis added)

Concluding his historical essay, Snyder wrote: "In embracing Bandera as he leaves office, Yushchenko has cast a shadow over his own political legacy."[9]

The OUN disappears

When Snyder published this essay in *early* 2010, he evidently considered Bandera and the OUN to be an important, dangerous and disturbing element of Ukrainian history. However, by the time *Bloodlands* was published in October 2010, *only eight months later*, Snyder's treatment of this subject had undergone a radical change. In his 524-page book, the operations of the Ukrainian nationalists received the most cursory mention. The index of *Bloodlands* does not contain a single entry for either Stepan Bandera or the OUN! The entire book devotes just one sentence, on page 326, to the murderous activities of the UPA, commanded by the OUN.

In the course of 2010, as final preparations were being made for the publication of *Bloodlands*, Snyder decided that references to the crimes of the

---

[7] Ibid.

[8] Ibid.

[9] Ibid.

Ukrainian nationalists should be kept out of the book. None of the facts and issues relating to Ukrainian fascism raised by Snyder in his February 2010 essay in the *New York Review of Books* were raised in *Bloodlands*.

In its published form, *Bloodlands* is an exercise in right-wing historical revisionism. It is an endorsement of the Ukrainian nationalist Holodomor narrative, in which the Soviet Union and Nazi Germany are presented as political and moral equivalents, with the strong implication that the Soviet Union was worse. There is no examination of the historical origins, socioeconomic foundations, and political objectives of the two regimes. The complex historical and political issues that must be addressed in any serious study of collectivization are simply ignored. The catastrophe produced by the reckless implementation of collectivization is "explained" with the assertion that "Stalin chose to kill millions of people in Soviet Ukraine."[10]

In contrast to the popular media, there have been damning reviews of Snyder's book by serious historians. His efforts to minimize the extent of the atrocities carried out by Ukrainian nationalists have raised concerns. Professor Omer Bartov of Brown University notes:

> The vast massacres of Jews by their Ukrainian neighbors throughout eastern Poland at that time [summer 1941] receive scant

---

[10] In serious scholarly analyses of the impact of collectivization, the controversy is not over whether Stalin's policies were responsible for the deaths of over three million Ukrainian peasants. They undoubtedly were, and political decisions that had such monstrous consequences must be judged as criminal. However, the claim that collectivization was conceived as a deliberate plan to exterminate millions of Ukrainian peasants — in the same sense that the Nazi regime planned and implemented the Final Solution in order to exterminate European Jewry — is not supported by historical evidence. Leading historians of Central European and Soviet history have challenged the equation of the Ukrainian famine and the Holocaust and the categorization of the famine as genocide. Canadian-Ukrainian historian John-Paul Himka has recently criticized a "mythicized" presentation of collectivization, which claims that "Stalin unleashed the famine deliberately in order to kill Ukrainians in mass and prevent them from achieving their aspirations to establish a nation state." Himka explains that "the precondition for the famine was the reckless collectivization drive, which almost destroyed Soviet agriculture as a whole." Himka warns:

> The genocide argument is used to buttress the campaign to glorify the anti-Communist resistance of the Ukrainian nationalists during World War II. I do not think that Ukrainians who embrace the heritage of the wartime nationalists should be calling on the world to empathize with the victims of the famine if they are not able to empathize with the victims of the nationalists.

[John-Paul Himka, "Interventions: Challenging the Myths of Twentieth-Century Ukrainian History," in *The Convolutions of Historical Politics,* ed. Alexei Miller and Maria Lipman (Budapest and New York: Central European University Press, 2012), pp. 211–212].

attention and are swiftly related to prior Soviet crimes. Snyder's attempts to explain why Ukrainians butchered their Jewish neighbors, joined the German-controlled police, enrolled in the SS, or served as extermination camp personnel seem quite feeble in view of the violence these men perpetrated.[11]

Bartov objects to Snyder's efforts to equate the violence of Soviet resistance to the violence employed by the Nazi invaders.

> By equating partisans and occupiers, Soviet and Nazi occupation, Wehrmacht and Red Army criminality, and evading interethnic violence, Snyder drains the war of much of its moral content and inadvertently adopts the apologists' argument that where everyone is a criminal no one can be blamed.[12]

The historian Mark Mazower presents a devastating criticism of Snyder's work:

> One can certainly make too much of the importance of East European anti-Semitism — and not a few scholars can be criticized for this — but one can also make too little, and Snyder's treatment here veers in that direction.[13]

In light of Snyder's subsequent evolution, it is difficult to explain *Bloodland's* evasion of the crimes of Ukrainian nationalism as anything other than a politically motivated decision related to the political operations of the United States in Ukraine and Snyder's own increasingly intense involvement in their implementation. During the past several months, Snyder has emerged as one of the most prominent defenders of the Kiev regime. The most striking characteristics of his writings and speeches have been their venomous hostility to Russia and their furious denials of any significant radical right-wing involvement in the February coup and the political physiognomy of the Kiev regime.

In a recent defense of the Kiev regime, published in Wieseltier's *New Republic*, Snyder sinks to new depths. Russia, and even the Soviet Union,

---

[11] Omer Bartov, *Slavic Review,* Summer 2011, p. 426.
[12] Ibid., p. 428.
[13] Mark Mazower, *Contemporary European History,* Volume 21, Issue 02, May 2012, p. 120.

are presented as quasi-fascist regimes. The major role of Svoboda and Right Sector in the political life of Ukraine is ignored. It is in Russia's opposition to the new Ukrainian regime, Snyder claims, that the rising tide of fascism finds expression.

In a bizarre passage, Snyder declares: "Fascism means the celebration of the nude male form, the obsession with homosexuality, simultaneously criminalized and imitated. ... Today, these ideas are on the rise in Russia..." But what about the situation in Ukraine? It is not possible that Snyder is unaware of Svoboda's virulent hostility to homosexuality, and its disruption of a gay rights rally in 2012, which it denounced publicly as "a Sabbath of 50 perverts."[14]

Snyder falsifies history to suit his political agenda. Forgetting what he wrote four years ago, he now states: "The political collaboration and the uprising of Ukrainian nationalists were, all in all, a minor element in the history of the German occupation."[15]

In the work of Timothy Snyder we are confronted with an unhealthy and dangerous tendency: *the obliteration of the distinction between writing history and manufacturing propaganda.*

---

[14] Available: http://en.wikipedia.org/wiki/Svoboda_(political_party)

[15] Available:http://www.newrepublic.com/article/117692/fascism-returns-ukraine

15

It Was All Engels' Fault:
A Review of Tom Rockmore's
Marx After Marxism[1]

Tom Rockmore, who teaches Philosophy at Duquesne University in Pennsylvania, begins his book *Marx After Marxism: The Philosophy of Karl Marx*, with the following statement:

> It is, or at least should be, obvious that as a political approach Marxism has failed as a historical alternative to liberal capitalism. After the rapid demise of the Soviet bloc in 1989, and the break up of the Soviet Union in 1991, the opposition between totalitarian Marxism and liberal capitalism, a major influence in much of the twentieth century, dissolved. As a result, the modern industrialized world entered into an involuntary Pascalian wager firmly based on liberal economic and liberal democratic principles. At the time of writing modern economic liberalism literally has no real rival in the industrialized world.[2]

---

[1] Published 2 May 2006 on the *World Socialist Web Site*.
[2] Tom Rockmore, *Marx After Marxism: The Philosophy of Karl Marx* (Oxford: Blackwell Publishers, 2002), p. xi.

Rockmore's pronouncement of the death of "political Marxism" is typical of the outlook that prevails in academia: that is, the end of the USSR signified the end of Marxism. But what is the basis of this assertion? Nothing more than the premise that the politics of the old Soviet bureaucracy represented Marxism. This premise says far more about the social and political outlook of the professorial fraternity than it does about Marxism. On what basis have academics established equivalence between the reactionary nationalistic politics of the Kremlin and the world scientific outlook of Marxism? Generally, they simply ignore this question entirely. From their lofty heights they look upon the real political struggles waged over many decades by revolutionary Marxists against the Kremlin oligarchy as mere "sectarian squabbles," for which conformist academics have no time. It was enough for them to recognize that the power of the Kremlin bureaucracy was, at least until 1991, real. In other words, the bureaucracy controlled a powerful state, and also had the ability to dispense considerable patronage — some of which was used to finance international symposia which stylishly left academics were always glad to attend.

If defined correctly as the theoretical foundation of revolutionary socialist program and practice, Marxism played no role in the policies of the Soviet regime since the late 1920s — that is, since the formal expulsion of Leon Trotsky and his supporters in the Left Opposition from the Soviet Communist Party. The Kremlin's repudiation of the Marxist origins of the Soviet regime was sealed in blood during the 1930s with the campaign of political genocide that it directed against all remnants of the Marxist and revolutionary intelligentsia and working class within the USSR. The Moscow Trials and the associated purges, which resulted in the murder of hundreds of thousands of revolutionary socialists, spearheaded the program of international counterrevolution directed by Stalin and his associates in the Kremlin.

As early as 1933, following the Stalinist betrayal of the German working class that enabled Hitler's seizure of power, Trotsky called for the overthrow of the Kremlin bureaucracy's regime through a political revolution. The issue for Trotsky was not vengeance, but the preservation of the USSR. He warned repeatedly that unless overthrown by the working class, the policies of the Stalinist regime would lead to the collapse of the Soviet Union. Trotsky's insistence that Stalinism was a regime of crisis, that the nationalist program of the Kremlin bureaucracy was both economically and politically bankrupt, that the autarkic economic policies of the bureaucracy could not, in the long run, shield the USSR from the pressures of a world economy dominated by capitalism, and that the fate of the Soviet Union depended upon the victory of socialist revolution in the advanced capitalist states of Western Europe and North America, were essential components of the Marxist program of the Fourth International.

The collapse of the Soviet Union in 1991 vindicated not only Trotsky but also Marxism as a science of political perspective. It would have been appropriate for scholars claiming to be specialists in the social sciences — who, for the most part, never even imagined that the Soviet Union could disappear overnight — to acknowledge that the Marxist analysis upheld by the Trotskyist movement had proven to be extraordinarily farsighted.

Such manifestations of intellectual humility were not to be found. The demise of the USSR led to an eruption of publications proclaiming the death of Marxism. These works fall into two broad categories. In the first are the products of the unabashed ideological defenders of capitalism from the political right (such as Fukuyama and Pipes), for whom the end of the USSR simply proves the impossibility of any alternative to the existing bourgeois order. In the second are a wide range of works from leftish academics, who still hold open the vague possibility of social change at some point in the distant future — but who insist that it will not be Marxism that provides the theoretical substance for any future social transformation.

Academics search for an alternative to Marxism

What, then, is the alternative to Marxism? A substantial body of new academic literature argues for a revival of various forms of pre-Marxian philosophy and politics. It claims that the emergence of young Dr. Marx in the early 1840s aborted the development of alternative left-progressive philosophies and social movements. Since Marx's work developed on the basis of a withering critique of Hegel, the damage done by Marx's attack must be repaired. Having been stood on his feet by Marx, these writers argue, it is now necessary to turn the old idealist philosopher back on his head. Hegel's work provides sufficient ground for the development, within a contemporary context, of progressive social theory and practice. Some of the works that argue along these lines are explicitly hostile to Marx; others suggest that Marx either added little to Hegel or exaggerated his own originality; and still others make the case for a fusion of Hegelianism and Marxism, generally to the detriment of the latter.

Professor Errol Harris writes in his *Spirit of Hegel* that "it is not Hegel who stands on his head, but Marx and Engels, who cut off the head, and then imagine that the decapitated torso of the dialectic is still capable of life and movement."[3] He adds: "Nobody would wish to suggest that Marx's own doctrines were derisory, but his criticisms of Hegel were often extraordinarily obtuse and blinkered, based as they were on a gross misunderstanding of Hegel's 'Idealism.'"[4]

In *Hegel's Philosophy of Freedom*, Professor Paul Franco argues that it is in Hegel, not Marx, that answers to the problems of the contemporary world will be found:

> For the past thirty years or so, there has been a tremendous revival of interest in Hegel's social and political philosophy. At first largely motivated by the quest for the origins of Marx's project, this revival of interest has begun to focus on Hegel as a thinker in his own right, and one with perhaps something more profound to offer than Marx.[5]

As for the latter, Franco refers to Marx as the "epigone" of Hegel.[6]

The Canadian academic, David MacGregor, has written several books devoted to establishing Hegelianism as the principal theoretical foundation upon which democratic and socially progressive projects must base themselves. In *The Communist Ideal in Hegel and Marx*, MacGregor asserts that

> Marx's misinterpretation of the Hegelian Idea set him against Hegel's theory of the state and may have prevented him from coming fully to grips with the contradictory reality of liberal democracy only now being seriously confronted by his latter-day followers (who have much to learn from Hegel). This book points to an understanding of the liberal democratic state that tempers Marx's critique with the insights of Hegel's political theory.[7]

---

[3] Errol Harris, *The Spirit of Hegel* (New Jersey: Humanities Press, 1993), p. 11.

[4] Ibid., p. 47.

[5] Paul Franco, *Hegel's Philosophy of Freedom* (New Haven and London: Yale University Press, 1999), p. ix.

[6] Ibid., p. 77.

[7] David MacGregor, *The Communist Ideal in Hegel and Marx* (Toronto: University of Toronto Press, 1984), p. 3–4.

MacGregor states frankly that his aim is to "rescue Hegel's thought from the interpretation imposed on it by Marx. I will argue against Marx's claim that the Hegelian dialectic 'must be inverted, in order to discover the rational kernel within the mystical shell.'"[8]

In his later *Hegel, Marx and the English State,* MacGregor expands his criticism of Marx, accusing him of having

> mishandled a major component of the Hegelian legacy. He replaced Hegel's concept of private property, which includes the right of the worker to the product of labor, with the notion of surplus value and the negation of private ownership under communism. This meant that Marx's ideal society lacked not only a state, but also most of the institutions in civil society required to ensure personal freedom and prevent arbitrary rule by a dominant elite.[9]

In yet another work, *Hegel and Marx After the Fall of Communism,* the social-political essence of MacGregor's critique of the well-established Marxian conception of the Hegel-Marx relationship emerges even more clearly:

> The concept of private property forms the controversial nub of the relationship between Hegel and Marx. ... Hegel sought to preserve the institution of private property while Marx urged its overthrow. ... I contend that Hegel would have agreed with Marx's critique of capitalist property. Yet, unlike Hegel, Marx failed to probe the positive side of private rights; instead, he recommended abolition of property in favour of common ownership of the means of production.[10]

For MacGregor, Hegel's political theory provides the intellectual impulse for a viable alternative to the revolutionary socialist aspirations of Marx — that is, the revival of the liberal social welfare state, in which an

---

[8] Ibid., p. 11.

[9] David MacGregor, *Hegel, Marx and the English State* (Toronto, Buffalo and London: Westview Press, 1992), p. 7.

[10] David MacGregor, *Hegel and Marx After the Fall of Communism* (Cardiff: University of Wales Press, 1998), p. 116–118.

eclectic social-market system is directed by a high-minded and public-spirited bureaucracy.

Professor Warren Breckman's *Marx, the Young Hegelians, and the Origins of Radical Social Theory* argues along similar lines. He maintains that the fall of the Soviet Union and associated regimes in Eastern Europe have resulted in the discrediting among academic social theorists of Marx's uncompromising opposition to capitalism and bourgeois "civil society." Breckman writes:

> [T]he one major area of agreement is that Karl Marx's total rejection of the concept of civil society is inadequate to the project of expanding democratic life within complex societies. Here, it is the consensus that is new, not the insight itself. For the shortcomings of Marx's critique of civil society are now openly acknowledged even by those who remain sympathetic to some conception of socialism, retain elements of a Marxian critique of capitalism, or, minimally, as in the case of Jacques Derrida, "take inspiration from a certain spirit of Marxism."[11]

Breckman further notes that

> if the present debate takes for granted the need to go beyond Marxism, one of its characteristic moves has been to look behind Marx for inspiration and theoretical guidance.
>
> This post-Marxist interest in pre-Marxist social theory has significantly enhanced the fortunes and relevance of Hegel, the master thinker whom the young Marx triumphantly claimed to have overcome.[12]

Were its motivation not so politically and intellectually suspect, a revival of interest in Hegel would certainly be a welcome development. However, attempts to develop social and political theory on the basis of Hegel, or any other major figure in the pre-1840 world of German classical idealism, without reference to (or by means of a misrepresentation of) the subsequent intellectual development carried out by Marx and Engels — whose work arose

---

[11] Warren Breckman, *Marx, the Young Hegelians, and the Origins of Radical Social Theory* (Cambridge: Cambridge University Press, 1999), p. 2.
[12] Ibid., p. 3.

historically out of the massive socioeconomic transformation of Europe as well as critical scientific advances that followed Hegel's death in 1831 — represent a major step backward, theoretically and intellectually, and can only serve reactionary political ends.

Rockmore blames Engels

Like the above-cited works, Rockmore's book proposes to discover a new agenda for radical social change by annulling the theoretical impact of Marxism. The approach he takes is somewhat different from the others' works. While they propose to free Hegel from the grip of Marx, Rockmore contends that it is Marx who must be liberated from his ideological imprisonment within Marxism! The real Marx, proclaims Rockmore, was a devout Hegelian idealist. That Marx has been almost universally understood to be a materialist, Rockmore argues, is the product of a grotesque falsification and fraud perpetrated by none other than Frederick Engels, a philosophical simpleton who, lacking the university training necessary for serious theoretical work, removed all the Hegelian subtleties present in the real Marx's thinking and created the ideological monstrosity known as Marxism!

Rockmore writes:

> Marxism, which derives from Engels, turns on its account of the relation of Marx to Hegel, which in turn determines a view of Marx as leaving Hegel behind. I believe the Marxist view of Marx is both substantially inaccurate, and that it impedes a better view of Marx's position, including his philosophical contribution. I will be arguing that to "recover" Marx, we need to free him as much as possible from Marxism, hence from Engels, the first Marxist.[13]

Rockmore is not the first to argue that differences existed between Engels and Marx. At different times, this has been advanced by writers as diverse as Stanisław Brzozowski, Georg Lukács, Lucio Colletti, Jean Hyppolite, George Lichtheim, Leszek Kolakowski, representatives of the Frankfurt School and innumerable postmodernists. The mere fact that Engels outlived Marx by twelve years has been sufficient to give rise to claims that the survivor

---

[13] *Marx After Marxism*, p. 1.

exploited his position as executor of Marx's literary estate to substitute his own views for those of his late associate. The alleged differences between the views of Marx and Engels have assumed by now something of a mythic status. None of the claims advanced by the writers listed above can withstand careful analysis, and Lukács later revised his own position on this question.

Rockmore's thesis is not original. His work is distinguished only by its exceptional sloppiness and intellectual dishonesty. In this sense, it bears the mark of its time. The tone of cynicism that pervades the entire book finds characteristic expression in the manner that Rockmore purports to "answer" those who might assume that Marx and Engels, on the basis of their life-long collaboration, shared a common philosophical-theoretical outlook.

Rockmore writes:

> A main reason to believe that Marx and Engels are the joint authors of a single shared doctrine lies in the close association of the former with the latter. That is a little like saying that people who hang out together must think alike.[14]

"Hang out together"? That may be a fair description of what Professor Rockmore does with his pals in the Philosophy Department of Duquesne University. It is hardly an appropriate way to describe the relationship between Marx and Engels. Their intimate intellectual and political collaboration spanned thirty-nine years, from 1844 until Marx's death in 1883. During that time, they maintained direct contact with each other, either through written correspondence or personal meetings, on virtually a daily basis. The contemporary edition of the *Marx-Engels Collected Works* includes ten volumes (each containing between 500 and 600 pages) of correspondence. These letters, which allow the reader to follow the intellectual development and interaction of these two extraordinary men over four decades, testifies to a degree of philosophical solidarity, moral kinship, and personal friendship for which one can hardly find an equal in history. Where differences arose — whether over theoretical, political or personal matters — there is a documentary record of them.

Aside from their joint authorship of the critical formative philosophical works of Marxism — in particular, *The German Ideology,* which represented the first detailed elaboration of the materialist conception of history — Marx

---

[14] Ibid., p. 8.

provided a full written account of Engels' role in the elaboration of their common theoretical world outlook. Rockmore's attempt to portray Engels as the wicked anti-Hegelian, who covered over Marx's enduring allegiance to German idealism, is shattered by what Marx himself had to say on this very subject in his 1859 Preface to *A Critique of Political Economy*:

> Frederick Engels, with whom I maintained a constant exchange of ideas by correspondence since the publication of his brilliant essay on the critique of economic categories (printed in the *Deutsch-Französische Jahrbücher*), arrived by another road (compare his *Condition of the Working-Class in England*) at the same result as I, and when in the spring of 1845 he too came to live in Brussels, we decided to set forth together our conception as opposed to the ideological one of German philosophy, in fact to settle accounts with our former philosophical conscience. The intention was carried out in the form of a critique of post-Hegelian philosophy. The manuscript, two large octavo volumes [*The German Ideology*], had long ago reached the publishers in Westphalia when we were informed that owing to changed circumstances it could not be printed. We abandoned the manuscript to the gnawing criticism of the mice all the more willingly since we had achieved our main purpose — self-clarification. Of the scattered works in which at that time we presented one or another aspect of our views to the public, I shall mention only the *Manifesto of the Communist Party*, jointly written by Engels and myself, and a *Speech on the Question of Free Trade*, which I myself published. The salient points of our conception were first outlined in an academic, although polemical, form in my *Poverty of Philosophy*...[15]

Marx's reference in just one paragraph to "the same result as I," "our conception," "our former philosophical conscience," "our main purpose — self-clarification," "our views," and, finally, "the salient points of our conception" clearly establishes the very high level of theoretical agreement between himself and Engels.

---

[15] Karl Marx and Frederick Engels, *Collected Works* Volume 29 (New York: International Publishers, 1987), p. 264.

Though Rockmore does refer to Marx's Preface to the *Critique*, he does not cite this crucial passage. This is not the only occasion, as we shall establish, when Rockmore ignores statements by Marx that contradict his own thesis.

Rockmore on Engels' inadequate education

In his zeal to discredit Engels, Rockmore asserts that Marx's lifelong collaborator simply lacked the level of education necessary for a proper understanding of Marx. Engels was a mere "philosophical autodidact" who "was not concerned with philosophical subtleties..."[16] Rockmore reminds his readers that

> Marx studied philosophy, in which he held a doctorate, at the university. Yet Engels did not earn a college degree. He studied philosophy only sporadically, and simply lacked the requisite training, not to mention the philosophical talent, to do high-quality philosophical work of his own. He also lacked the sophisticated appreciation of philosophical doctrines and sheer philosophical inventiveness of Marx. As a philosopher, he was at best a talented amateur with an interest in the topic.[17]

What an unpleasant combination of professorial snobbishness and pompous self-satisfaction! While Professor Rockmore obviously places great weight on academic credentials, it would be very hard to establish, on the basis of the history of philosophical thought, that there exists any correlation between the ability to undertake serious philosophical work and the possession of a university doctorate, let alone a tenured position in a university philosophy department. If Rockmore's standards were to be applied as a basis for determining who may be judged a serious philosopher, quite a few rather well-known names would have to be removed from Western intellectual history — including those of Spinoza and Descartes. As we are informed by Desmond M. Clarke in his excellent new biography of the founder of Cartesian rationalism, "Descartes' formal education had been narrowly scholastic, and it had certainly not provided a basis for the fundamental reform of human knowledge that he eventually undertook."[18] And while Rockmore's

---

[16] *Marx After Marxism*, p. 9.

[17] Ibid., p. 10.

[18] Desmond M. Clarke, *Descartes: A Biography*, (Cambridge: Cambridge University Press, 2006), p. 37.

use of the term "autodidact" (self-taught) is intended pejoratively, one might note that many of the greatest thinkers and writers in history may be included in that category.

In any case, Rockmore's presentation of Engels' intellectual preparation, not to mention the breadth and depth of his knowledge, particularly of philosophy, is utterly false. By the time Engels completed his studies at the Elberfeld *gymnasium*, he had attained a level of education that, if I may hazard a guess, Professor Rockmore rarely encounters among his own doctoral candidates. According to his school report of September 1837 (when he was not quite 17), Engels had achieved such a degree of proficiency in Latin that he "finds no difficulty in understanding the respective writers either of prose or poetry, namely, Livius and Cicero, Virgil and Horace, so that he can easily follow the thread of the longer pieces, grasp the train of thought with clarity and translate the text before him with skill into the mother tongue." As for Greek, the school report stated that Engels "has acquired a satisfactory knowledge of morphology and the rules of syntax, in particular good proficiency and skill in translating the easier Greek prose writers, as also *Homer* and *Euripides*, and could grasp and render the train of thought of a *Platonic* dialogue with skill." The writer of this report also expressed admiration for Engels' work in mathematics, physics, and "*Philosophical propaedeutic*."[19]

For a work that hinges on the claim that Engels lacked either the training or skill required to undertake serious work in the sphere of philosophy, it is shocking that Rockmore makes no reference whatever to the episode in Engels' early career that established him, even before his initial encounter with Marx, as an outstanding figure in German intellectual circles — that is, Engels' refutation of Friedrich Schelling. An aged philosopher by the time he was called to Berlin in 1841 to counter the influence of Hegelianism among radical-democratic students, Schelling's arrival in the Prussian capital caused an uproar. His lectures were viewed as a major philosophical event and drew a large audience that included, among others, the young Kierkegaard, Bakunin and Engels. Schelling, who in his youth had roomed with Hegel and had at one time counted him among his closest friends, repudiated his objective idealist system and turned sharply toward philosophical subjectivism and irrationalism. Moreover, the early renown of Schelling had been eclipsed once Hegel emerged as the dominant figure in German philosophy. In the

---

[19] Karl Marx and Frederick Engels, *Collected Works,* Volume 2, (New York: International Publishers, 1975), pp. 584–585.

aftermath of Hegel's death in 1831, the Prussian state authorities became increasingly troubled by the revolutionary conclusions that students were drawing from the late philosopher's works. Schelling was given the task of stopping the spread of the radical Hegelian contagion.

In the struggle to defend the reputation and legacy of Hegelianism, it was none other than Engels who emerged as the major figure. Three works written by Engels in 1841 — *Schelling and Revelation, Schelling on Hegel,* and *Schelling, Philosopher in Christ* — were hailed by the Left Hegelian youth as the decisive refutation of Schelling from a Hegelian standpoint. That Rockmore chooses to ignore these texts — which would immediately expose the absurdity of his claim that "Engels knew neither philosophy nor Hegel well"[20] — is intellectually indefensible.

Engels the "Positivist"

Rockmore asserts repeatedly that Engels was a "positivist," convinced that philosophy had been entirely superseded by science and had lost all intellectual relevance. Engels, according to Rockmore, "consistently treats Hegel as if the latter's philosophy were pre-scientific nonsense."[21] One has the impression that Rockmore believes that, in the prevailing climate of anti-Marxist reaction, he is freed from all traditional standards of scholarship. Whether a particular statement is true or false, or whether it can be supported on the basis of written texts and the historical record, is of no importance whatever. What he strives for is not intellectual clarification and theoretical precision, but the fulfillment of a preconceived ideological agenda.

It would not be difficult to fill dozens of pages with quotations in which Engels paid tribute to the genius of Hegel, whom he memorably described as "the most encyclopaedic mind of his time."[22] Engels' appreciation of Hegel found its most evocative expression in his brilliant pamphlet on *Ludwig Feuerbach and the End of Classical German Philosophy.* There, Engels referred to Hegel as an "Olympian Zeus" who presented

a wealth of thought which is astounding even today. The phenomenology of the mind (which one may call a parallel to the

[20] *Marx After Marxism,* p. 162.
[21] Ibid., p. 15.
[22] Karl Marx and Frederick Engels, *Collected Works,* Volume 25 (New York: International Publishers, 1987) p. 25.

embryology and palaeontology of the mind, a development of individual consciousness through its different stages, set in the form of an abbreviated reproduction of the stages through which the consciousness of man has passed in the course of history), logic, philosophy of nature, philosophy of the mind, and the latter in turn elaborated in its separate, historical sub-divisions: philosophy of history, of law, of religion, history of philosophy, aesthetics, etc. — in all these different historical fields Hegel worked to discover and demonstrate the pervading thread of development. And as he was not only a creative genius but also a man of encyclopaedic erudition, he played an epoch-making role in every sphere. It is self-evident that owing to the needs of the "system" he very often had to resort to those forced constructions about which his pygmean opponents make such a terrible fuss even today. But these constructions are only the frame and scaffolding of his work. If one does not loiter here needlessly, but presses on farther into the huge edifice, one finds innumerable treasures which still today retain their full value.[23]

How is it possible, given the existence of this and countless other passages authored by Engels, that Rockmore can claim that Engels dismissed Hegel's work as "pre-scientific nonsense"? Rockmore must assume that neither his editors, nor the academic community in which he navigates his career, will be troubled by his fabrications. In works dealing with Marxism, there seems to be no expectation of scholarly rigor. The prevailing motto is, rather, "Anything goes!"

Engels on the relationship between philosophy and science

Rockmore's assertion that Engels was a positivist, who maintained that the development of science rendered philosophy superfluous, is no less false. Engels wrote precisely the opposite. He repeatedly warned that the work of even the most brilliant natural scientists was limited, to the extent that they lacked serious acquaintance with the history of human conceptual thinking as it finds expression in the history of philosophy. The "art" of conceptual thinking, essential for the correct interpretation of the results of empirical research,

---

[23] Karl Marx and Frederick Engels, *Collected Works*, Volume 26 (Moscow: Progress Publishers, 1990), p. 361–362.

Engels insisted, could be acquired only through the painstaking study of the history of philosophy. In a crucial passage, Engels wrote:

> Empirical natural science has accumulated such a tremendous mass of positive material for knowledge that the necessity of classifying it in each separate field of investigation systematically and in accordance with its inner inter-connection has become absolutely imperative. It is becoming equally imperative to bring the individual spheres of knowledge into the correct connection with one another. In doing so, however, natural science enters the field of theory and here the methods of empiricism will not work, here only theoretical thinking can be of assistance. But theoretical thinking is an innate quality only as regards natural capacity. This natural capacity must be developed, improved, and for its improvement there is as yet no other means than the study of previous philosophy.[24]

I cannot resist citing another passage, in which Engels presents a conception of the relevance of philosophy that is the absolute opposite of the position attributed to him by Rockmore:

> Natural scientists believe that they free themselves from philosophy by ignoring it or abusing it. They cannot, however, make any headway without thought, and for thought they need thought determinations. But they take these categories unreflectingly from the common consciousness of so-called educated persons, which is dominated by the relics of long obsolete philosophies, or from the little bit of philosophy compulsorily listened to at the University (which is not only fragmentary, but also a medley of views of people belonging to the most varied and usually the worst schools), or from uncritical and unsystematic reading of philosophical writings of all kinds. Hence they are no less in bondage to philosophy, but unfortunately in most cases to the worst philosophy, and those who abuse philosophy most are slaves to precisely the worst vulgarized relics of the worst philosophies.[25]

---

[24] Karl Marx and Frederick Engels, *Collected Works*, Volume 25, p. 338.
[25] Ibid., p. 490–491.

By now the reader must be asking himself or herself a question: how is it possible, given the extensive record of Engels' writings, that Rockmore can commit to paper statements that are so glaringly false? The answer is, "Welcome to the world of professional academic anti-Marxism, where anything goes!"

The purpose of Rockmore's assault on Engels becomes transparent as soon as he turns his attention to Marx. By claiming that it was the philosophically ignorant Engels who created what is known as "Marxism" by falsifying and distorting the conceptions of his lifelong comrade and friend, Rockmore feels free to unveil a "new" Marx — that is, one without the materialistic "narrative" (to use postmodernist jargon) that supposedly was conjured up by Engels after the former's death. And so, contrary to the claims of Engels and several generations of "Marxists," the real Marx had no substantial differences with the philosophical outlook of Hegel. Rockmore claims that

> it is crucial to go beyond politically motivated Marxist claims for distinctions in kind between Marx and Hegel, or again between Marx and philosophy, or even between philosophy and science; for it is only in this way that one can see that in the final analysis Marx is not only a philosopher, or a German philosopher, but a German Hegelian, hence a German idealist philosopher.[26]

Prior to Rockmore, we are expected to believe, the "Marxists" had denied and obscured the real Marx's allegiance to idealism. The materialist and anti-Hegelian positions they ascribed to Marx were largely a product of their own theoretical incompetence in philosophical matters. "Engels knew neither philosophy nor Hegel well," writes Rockmore. "Since Engels, few Marxists, including Lenin, have been well versed in Hegel. ... Marxist denigration of Hegel retarded awareness of his significance for Marx's position..."[27]

The claim that "few Marxists, including Lenin" have made a careful study of Hegel is another blatant falsehood. Again, Rockmore relies on the intellectual acquiescence of an academic community steeped in cynicism and indifference. He takes for granted that no one, at least in the academic milieu within which he operates, will take him to task for writing things that have absolutely no basis in fact. Has Rockmore ever bothered to review the writings of G.V. Plekhanov, the "Father of Russian Marxism"? Even those who disagree with

---

[26] *Marx After Marxism*, p. 161.
[27] Ibid., p. 162.

Plekhanov's philosophical conceptions could not claim, in good faith, that his familiarity with Hegel was anything less than exhaustive. Is Rockmore unfamiliar with Lenin's *Conspectus on Hegel's Science of Logic*? Composed in 1914–15, the later publication of Lenin's "Philosophical Notebooks" — which includes his extensive annotation of Hegel's *Logic* — had a major impact on the appreciation of the weighty theoretical basis of Lenin's political work. Rockmore seems to be unaware that it was precisely Lenin's *Conspectus* that contributed to a significant revival of theoretical interest in Hegel among Marxist scholars — including, by the way, Lukács, for whom Rockmore professes admiration. What about the writings of Trotsky, which exhibit a mastery of dialectic method?[28] Or the works of early Soviet theoreticians such as Deborin and Akselrod? We might add as well the work of later Soviet philosophers such as Mikhail Lifshits and E.V. Ilyenkov, who made important contributions to the understanding of the Hegel-Marx relationship despite the repressive conditions in the USSR, enforced by a privileged bureaucracy hostile to serious theoretical work (both during and after Stalin's rule).

Was Marx an idealist?

Previously we showed that the greatest obstacle to Rockmore's efforts to portray Engels as a positivist, who simply dismissed the relevance of philosophy, were the words of Engels himself. Similarly, the refutation of Rockmore's claim that Marx was a German idealist is to be found in Marx's own writings. The manner in which Rockmore tiptoes around the works of Marx, citing rather sparingly and highly selectively, indicates that he himself realizes his thesis lacks any substantial foundation. Rockmore gets off to a bad start by stating that Marx "is in part responsible" for the widespread belief that he broke from Hegel. This is because, in an oft-quoted passage in the *Afterword* to the second edition of *Capital*, Marx "obscurely" suggests that his own

---

[28] In his polemical response to Professor James Burnham, a pragmatist and bitter opponent of Hegel (whom he had denounced as the "century-dead, arch-muddler of human thought"), Trotsky paid tribute to the great German philosopher: "Hegel wrote before Darwin and before Marx. Thanks to the powerful impulse given to thought by the French Revolution, Hegel anticipated the general movement of science. But because it was only an *anticipation*, although by a genius, it received from Hegel an idealistic character. Hegel operated with ideological shadows as the ultimate reality. Marx demonstrated that the movement of these ideological shadows reflected nothing but the movement of material bodies." [*In Defense of Marxism* (London: New Park Publications,1971), p. 66] At the conclusion of the faction fight that erupted inside the Trotskyist movement in 1939–40, Burnham repudiated socialist politics and began his rapid political evolution to the extreme right.

position results from the inversion of Hegel's. Since Engels, generations of Marxists have approached Marx's position as the inversion of Hegel's.

Actually, there is nothing that is in the least obscure in the passage to which Rockmore refers. This is what Marx wrote in January 1873:

> My dialectic method is not only different from the Hegelian, but is its direct opposite. To Hegel, the life-process of the human brain, *i.e.,* the process of thinking, which, under the name of "the Idea," he even transforms into an independent subject, is the demiurgos of the real world, and the real world is only the external, phenomenal form of "the Idea." With me, on the contrary, the ideal is nothing else than the material world reflected by the human mind, and translated into forms of thought.[29]

This English translation is a faithful rendition of what Marx wrote in the original German. There is nothing in Marx's words that is obscure, oblique or confused. Marx is saying, as clearly as he possibly can, that his own method is fundamentally different than Hegel's — "its direct opposite." And why? Because Hegel's dialectic is that of an idealist, for whom the real world is a manifestation of thought; whereas for Marx, thought forms are a reflection in the human mind of a real existing material world. Take extra note of the fact that the phrase "*reflected* by the human mind" is used by Marx. On the other hand, Rockmore tells us that "For our purposes, it suffices to point out that the reflection theory of knowledge, which was later adopted by a long line of Marxists, has no basis in Marx's writing."[30] As we have already noted, anything goes!

Rockmore has no end of difficulties with the writings of Marx. Referring to Marx's *Critique of Hegel's Philosophy of Right*, he states that "The text, which Marx did not prepare for publication, is repetitive and somewhat painful to read."[31] No doubt it is — for Rockmore. The cause of his discomfort is that the content of Marx's *Critique* cannot be in any way reconciled with Rockmore's attempt to portray Marx as a Hegelian idealist. With the writing of this *Critique*, Marx initiated the theoretical work (to which Engels contributed significantly) that shattered the idealist framework of Hegel's philosophical system, demystified his dialectical method, and established the

---

[29] Karl Marx, *Capital*, Volume 1 (London: Lawrence & Wishart, 1974), p. 29.

[30] *Marx After Marxism*, p. 6.

[31] Ibid., p. 47.

foundations for the development of a genuinely materialist ontology rooted in the historical study of man as a *social being*. The decisive achievement of Marx's *Critique*, for which the earlier work of Ludwig Feuerbach (who goes virtually unmentioned by Rockmore) provided a critical philosophical impulse, was his demonstration of the basic inadequacy of Hegel's speculative idealism as an instrument of historical and social analysis. For Hegel, the logical categories, which he elaborated as objective moments in the dialectical reconstitution of the Absolute Idea, represented the underlying and inner foundation of material reality itself. He derived the forms of Being from the dialectical process of abstract logical thought. Marx established that Hegel's procedure reversed the real relationship between consciousness and reality, and, by so doing, prevented the genuine cognition of the "civil society" (as Hegel referred to the existing social order) within which man lived. Rather than discovering the material source of real social processes, Hegel deals with them in terms of abstract logical relations. As Marx explains:

> The transition of the family and civil society into the political state is, therefore, this: the mind of these spheres, which is *implicitly* the mind of the state, now also behaves to itself as such and is *actual* for itself as their inner core. The transition is thus derived, not from the *particular* nature of the family, etc., and from the particular nature of the state, but from the *general* relationship of *necessity* to *freedom*. It is exactly the same transition as is effected in logic from the sphere of essence to the sphere of the concept. The same transition is made in the philosophy of nature from inorganic nature to life. It is always the same categories which provide the soul, now for this, now for that sphere. It is only a matter of spotting for the separate concrete attributes the corresponding abstract attributes.[32]

By way of example, Marx examines a characteristically convoluted and obscure passage from Hegel's *Philosophy of Law*, which reads:

> *Necessity* in ideality [writes Hegel] is the *development* of the idea within itself. As *subjective* substantiality it is **political conviction**, as

---

[32] Karl Marx and Frederick Engels, *Collected Works*, Volume 3 (New York: International Publishers, 1976), p. 10.

objective substantiality, in distinction therefrom, it is the *organism* of the state, the strictly *political* state and *its constitution.*[33]

Marx then exposes the analytical poverty, even sophistry, which is concealed in the abstruse Hegelian jargon:

> The *subject* here is "necessity in ideality" — the "idea within itself." The *predicate: political conviction* and the *political constitution.* In plain language *political conviction* is the subjective and the *political constitution* the *objective substance* of the state. The logical development from family and civil society to the state is thus sheer *pretence.* For it is not explained how family sentiment, civic sentiment, the institution of the family and social institutions as such are related to political conviction and to the political constitution, and how they are connected.[34]

In Hegel, writes Marx:

> The sole interest is in rediscovering "the idea" pure and simple, the "logical idea," in every element, whether of the state or of nature, and the actual subjects, in this case the "political constitution," come to be nothing but their mere *names,* so that all that we have is the appearance of real understanding. *They are and remain uncomprehended, because they are not grasped in their specific character.*[35] (Emphasis added)

The main weakness of Hegel's method is that:

> He does not develop his thinking from the object, but expounds the object in accordance with a thinking that is cut and dried — already formed and fixed in the abstract sphere of logic. It is not a question of evolving the specific idea of the political constitution, but of establishing a relationship of the political

---

[33] Ibid.
[34] Ibid., p. 10–11.
[35] Ibid., p. 12.

constitution to the abstract idea, of placing it as a phase in the life-history of the idea, a manifest piece of mystification.[36]

Thus, Marx sums up the fundamental error of the Hegelian approach:

> Philosophical work does not consist in embodying thinking in political definitions, but in evaporating the existing political definitions into abstract thoughts. Not the logic of the matter, but the matter of logic is the philosophical element. The logic does not serve to prove the state, but the state to prove the logic.[37]

Rockmore skips over Marx's critique of Hegel's methodology. He makes a brief and vague reference to Marx's criticism of Hegel's derivation of the state from logic, without acknowledging its far-reaching significance in the theoretical development of Marx himself. In fact, Rockmore tries to dismiss it as a misunderstanding, stating that "we must ask ourselves whether Marx's critique of Hegel does justice to Hegel, or rather rests on an incorrect reading..."[38] This question exposes the dishonesty that underlies Rockmore's project. Marx is, on the one hand proclaimed to be a Hegelian idealist, and the subsequent creation of an anti-idealist "Marxism" is the product of distortions introduced by the materialist usurper, Frederick Engels. Yet, on the other hand, whenever Rockmore is compelled to make reference to works by Marx that criticize Hegel along materialist lines, the professor suggests that Marx simply did not know what he was talking about.

Rockmore proceeds with the same evasiveness when dealing with the series of works that followed the *Critique,* in which Marx (with the increasingly significant collaboration of Engels) carried through his materialist demystification and reworking of the Hegelian dialectic. Rockmore has virtually nothing to say about Marx's lengthy and detailed analysis of the Hegelian method in the *Economic and Philosophic Manuscripts of 1844.* Marx entitled this section, *Critique of the Hegelian Dialectic and Philosophy as a Whole.* Marx gave as his reason for writing this *Critique* the need to distinguish his own work from that of Hegel and his epigones. Marx took such well-known Left Hegelians as Bruno Bauer to task for having failed to adopt a critical

---

[36] Ibid., p. 14.
[37] Ibid., pp. 17–18.
[38] *Marx After Marxism*, p. 48.

attitude to their teacher. Marx, on the other hand, professed the greatest admiration for Feuerbach, whom he praised as "the only one who has a *serious, critical* attitude to the Hegelian dialectic and who has made genuine discoveries in this field. He is in fact the true conqueror of the old philosophy."[39] Why would Marx have paid this tribute to Feuerbach if he had continued to view himself as a Hegelian?

The next great work produced by Marx *with* Engels, *The Holy Family*, is also dismissed by Rockmore, who writes:

> The book contains much arid polemic directed against Bauer and other left-wing Hegelians. When he is at his best [i.e., when Marx agrees with Rockmore], Marx is an insightful writer, attentive and quick to respond to various nuances in the authors he considers, and capable of brilliant insight. This book, on the contrary, is almost wholly polemical, mainly a collection of simplistic views [i.e., which contradict Rockmore], lacking the nuances of previous and later Marxian writings, quicker to denounce than to comprehend, full of sharp oppositions.[40]

The Holy Family

For Rockmore, "nuance" really means obfuscation, a characteristic that is not to be found in Marx's theoretical work. The latter's criticism of Hegel's position is so clearly defined that it is difficult to distort and misrepresent. It is virtually impossible to describe the conceptions advanced by Marx as compatible with the idealist speculation of Hegel. *The Holy Family* represents a decisive advance toward the elaboration of the materialist conception of history and the identification of the proletariat as the revolutionary force in bourgeois society. The material practice of this class, not the self-movement of logical concepts, shall provide the basis for the revolutionary transformation of society. The real foundation of social revolution is lodged not in the thought of any individual worker, but in the objective social being of the proletariat as a class. The historical implications of Marx's critique of German speculative idealism emerges with the discovery by Marx and Engels, that

---

[39] Karl Marx and Frederick Engels, *Collected Works*, Volume 3, p. 328.
[40] *Marx After Marxism*, p. 75.

It is not a question of what this or that proletarian, or even the whole proletariat, at the moment *regards* as its aim. It is a question of *what the proletariat is,* and what, in accordance with this *being,* it will historically be compelled to do. Its aim and historical action is visibly and irrevocably foreshadowed in its own life situation as well as in the whole organisation of bourgeois society today.[41]

It comes as no surprise that this crucial passage, in which the emergence of the proletariat as a new revolutionary class found, in the writings of Marx and Engels, conscious theoretical expression, is not cited by Rockmore. Presumably, he found it too "arid," lacking in "nuance," too "polemical," and too "simplistic" to merit comment.

Another crucial section of *The Holy Family* that Rockmore chooses to ignore is the lengthy outline of the evolution of modern materialism. Having already announced that "Materialism is a doctrine that is clear in Engels, but certainly less clear in Marx,"[42] Rockmore cannot welcome *The Holy Family's* brilliantly concise review, written by Marx himself, of the development of modern materialism since the seventeenth century and its profound contribution to the development of socialist thought:

Just as *Cartesian* materialism passes into the *natural science proper*, the other trend of French materialism leads directly to *socialism* and *communism*.

There is no need for any great penetration to see from the teaching of materialism on the original goodness and equal intellectual endowment of men, the omnipotence of experience, habit and education, and the influence of environment on man, the great significance of industry, the justification of enjoyment, etc., how necessarily materialism is connected with communism and socialism. If man draws all his knowledge, sensation, etc., from the world of the senses and the experience gained in it, then what has to be done is to arrange the empirical world in such a way that man experiences and becomes accustomed to

[41] Karl Marx and Frederick Engels, *Collected Works*, Volume 4, (New York: International Publishers, 1975), p. 37.
[42] *Marx After Marxism*, p. 5.

what is truly human in it and that he becomes aware of himself as man.[43]

As a consequence of his dismissive attitude toward Marx's critique of Hegel's idealism, Rockmore is unable to understand either the foundations of Marx's theory of capitalist society, let alone its most important contributions to the development of scientific political economy. He writes:

> The central idea in his own [Marx's] rival economic theory is not his theory of value, nor his account of commodities, nor again his conception of alienation, nor even his view of the fetishism of commodities. It is rather the decisive insight, based on Adam Smith and developed in part by Hegel, that modern society is a transitory stage arising from the efforts of individuals to meet their needs within the economic framework of the capitalist world.[44]

Here we have a banal platitude that one might encounter in a high school class on Home Economics (that modern society consists of individuals trying to make a living) palmed off as the "decisive insight" gleaned by Marx from his painstaking analyses of the writings of Hegel and Adam Smith (to whom Marx devoted several hundred pages in his *Theories of Surplus Value*)! There is a connection, however, between this vulgar observation and Rockmore's misrepresentation of Marx's theoretical development. He dismisses all the most important elements of Marx's general theory of capitalist society as a whole, whose discovery and elaboration would not have been possible without the critique of speculative idealism and the materialist reworking of the Hegelian dialectic. Indeed, Marx's "economic turn," which began in 1844 flowed necessarily from the critical stance that he had taken toward Hegel's derivation of the world from the movement of logical concepts. The materialist explanation of the real foundations of human society and its necessary reflection in definite forms of social consciousness required that philosophy turn its attention from heaven to earth, away from God in all forms (including the philosophical God of Hegel's Absolute Idea) to man, away from the abstract contemplation of pure thought to the

---

[43] Karl Marx and Frederick Engels, *Collected Works*, Volume 4, p. 130.
[44] *Marx After Marxism*, p. xvi.

study of labor as the real foundation for the creation, reproduction and cultural development of human society.

Notwithstanding the exhaustive and explicit character of Marx's critique, Rockmore attempts to salvage his portrayal of Marx as an idealist philosopher, who did not really break with Hegel, by fooling around with terminology. He writes, "If we understand 'idealism' as referring to the idea that the subject in some sense produces its world and itself, then Marx is clearly an idealist."[45] In other words, anyone who accepts that human beings, endowed with consciousness, act upon the world and, in so doing, change the world and themselves, is an idealist. This definition evades the central issues involved in the collision between idealism and materialism, and would allow an amalgamation of the most diverse and incompatible philosophical outlooks. Rockmore's definition asserts that idealism includes all philosophical tendencies that regard consciousness as an active and creative force in history.

Matter and consciousness

This leaves unanswered two critical and interrelated philosophical issues. The first concerns the relationship of thought and matter, and poses the following questions: Does matter exist independently of consciousness, or does consciousness arise independently of matter? Does matter precede thought, or is it the other way around? Is the existence of a material world an absolute precondition for consciousness, or can consciousness (or spirit) exist either without, or independently of, a material world? Did the creation of the universe precede consciousness, or was consciousness present before the universe came into existence? The second issue, rooted in the first, raises questions relating to the nature and reliability of the cognitive process — that is, to what extent can the mind know what exists outside of it? Is it possible for thinking to give an accurate presentation of reality?

The answers that different philosophers give to these questions determine whether they belong to the camp of idealism or materialism. Those who assert, in one form or another, the primacy of thought over matter, of consciousness over being, are idealists. Those who, in opposition to this position, assert the primacy of matter over consciousness, and insist that consciousness emerged only as the product of the evolution of matter, are materialists.

---

[45] Ibid., p. 70.

Rockmore's definition of idealism is merely a subterfuge aimed at confusing the critical philosophical issues. Moreover, he is hardly the first to find a universal basis for idealism in the undeniable fact that human beings act with consciousness. As Engels pointed out:

> we simply cannot evade the fact that everything which motivates men must pass through their brains — even eating and drinking, which begins as a consequence of the sensation of hunger or thirst transmitted through the brain, and ends as a result of the sensation of satisfaction likewise transmitted through the brain. The influences of the external world upon man express themselves in his brain, are reflected therein as feelings, thoughts, impulses, volitions — in short, as "ideal tendencies," and in this form become "ideal powers." If, then, a man is to be deemed an idealist because he follows "ideal tendencies" and admits that "ideal powers" have an influence over him, then every person who is at all normally developed is a born idealist and how, in that case, can there be any materialists at all?[46]

It is not the recognition of the presence of "ideal powers" or their influence over human beings that is at issue in the dispute between materialism and idealism, but rather how the origins and nature of those "ideal powers" are understood and explained. Is the source of the "ideal" to be found, in the final analysis, outside the mind, in an objectively existing material world, or not?

Rockmore repeatedly attempts to misrepresent the answer Marx gives to this question, which is consistently and unequivocally materialist. For example, in dealing with the method employed in the writing of *Capital*, Rockmore cites from the *Afterword* to the second German edition, where Marx states that "if the life of the subject matter is ideally reflected as in a mirror, then it may appear as if we had before us a mere *a priori* construction." Rockmore then comments:

> Marx's wording here easily creates misunderstanding. He is obviously not espousing the reflection theory of knowledge pioneered for Marxism by Engels. He is also not saying that

---

[46] Karl Marx and Frederick Engels, *Collected Works*, Volume 26 (Moscow: Progress Publishers, 1990), p. 373.

knowledge in fact requires that mind literally reflect an independent world.[47]

The ideal and the real

Once again, Rockmore attempts to deny the materialism of Marx and to
counterpose his views to those of Engels by means of a subterfuge. The use of
the word "literally" is a red herring introduced only to create confusion. The crucial issue is whether the mind reflects an independent world. The ideal forms, in
which the material world is reflected, are complex and contradictory. The ideal
reproduction of the real in the human mind proceeds through a historically and
socially-conditioned process of abstraction. In this specific sense, the mind is not
functioning merely as a "mirror," in which reality is, on the basis of immediate
reflection, reproduced in all its complexity.[48] Nevertheless, in the final analysis,
the images, thoughts and concepts that emerge in the human mind are reflections of an objective reality that exists outside the mind of the cognizing subject.

The very words by Marx quoted by Rockmore appear in the *Afterword*
to *Capital* almost immediately after a lengthy passage in which Marx's philosophical outlook and analytical method were described by a contemporary
reviewer writing for a Russian journal. Marx cited approvingly from the
review, which states in part:

> Marx treats the social movement as a process of natural his-
> tory, governed by laws not only independent of human will,

---

[47] *Marx After Marxism*, p. 131.

[48] Lenin, in his *Conspectus of Hegel's Science of Logic*, wrote: "Logic is the science of cognition.
It is the theory of knowledge. Knowledge is the reflection of nature by man. But this is not a
simple, not an immediate, not a complete reflection, but the process of a series of abstractions,
the formation and development of concepts, laws, etc., and these concepts, laws, etc. (thought,
science = 'the logical Idea') *embrace* conditionally, approximately, the universal law-governed
character of eternally moving and developing nature. Here there are *actually*, objectively, **three**
members: 1) nature; 2) human cognition = the human **brain** (as the highest product of this
same nature), and 3) the form of reflection of nature in human cognition, and this form consists precisely of concepts, laws, categories, etc. Man cannot comprehend = reflect = mirror
nature *as a whole*, in its completeness, its 'immediate totality,' he can only *eternally* come closer
to this, creating abstractions, concepts, laws, a scientific picture of the world, etc., etc." [Lenin,
Collected Works, Volume 38 (Moscow: Progress Publishers, 1972), p. 182].
And in another passage, Lenin noted: "Cognition is the eternal, endless approximation of
thought to the object. The *reflection* of nature in man's thought must be understood not 'life-
lessly,' not 'abstractly,' *not devoid of movement*, **not without contradictions**, but in the eternal
process of movement, the arising of contradictions and their solution." [Ibid., p. 195]

consciousness and intelligence, but rather, on the contrary, determining that will, consciousness and intelligence. ... If in the history of civilization the conscious element plays a part so subordinate, then it is self-evident that a critical inquiry whose subject-matter is civilization, can, less than anything else, have for its basis any form of, or any result of, consciousness. That is to say, that not the idea, but the material phenomenon alone can serve as its starting-point.[49]

Rockmore chooses not to cite this passage.

Instead, he proceeds to conclude his potted analysis of the *Afterword* by claiming that Marx "reaffirms the obvious in declaring himself a Hegelian..." In fact, Marx describes himself not as a Hegelian but, more precisely and correctly, as "the pupil of that mighty thinker" — having already explained in detail precisely what separated the materialist student from the idealist teacher. He concludes the exposition of the relationship of his method to that of Hegel by stating:

The mystification which dialectic suffers in Hegel's hands, by no means prevents him from being the first to present its general form of working in a comprehensive and conscious manner. With him it is standing on its head. It must be turned right side up again, if you would discover the rational kernel within the mystical shell.[50]

It should be clear by now that Rockmore's claim that "Marx is clearly an idealist"[51]; and that "Marx, as distinguished from Marxism, is committed to idealism"[52] misrepresents the philosophical position held by Marx from 1843 until his death in 1883. However, it is appropriate to settle this particular argument by letting Marx, once again, speak for himself. In a letter written to his friend Ludwig Kugelmann on March 6, 1868, Marx sharply criticizes a review of *Capital* that was written by a young professor, Eugen Dühring (later to become the subject of Engels' immortal polemic). Complaining that Dühring "practices deception," Marx writes:

---

[49] Karl Marx, *Capital*, Volume 1, p. 27.
[50] Ibid., p. 29.
[51] *Marx After Marxism*, p. 70.
[52] Ibid., p. 179.

He knows full well that my method of exposition is *not* Hegelian, since I am a materialist, and Hegel an idealist. Hegel's dialectic is the basic form of all dialectic, but only *after* being stripped of its mystical form, and it is precisely this which distinguishes *my* method.[53]

It is hard to believe that Professor Rockmore failed to come across this well-known letter in the course of preparing the writing of his book. Rather, he simply chose to ignore it. Thus, the charge leveled by Marx against Dühring can be placed just as fittingly on Rockmore's doorstep.

Marx the reformist

What, then, is the purpose of Rockmore's tortured efforts to separate Marx from Engels and Marxism, while at the same time reclaiming him as a Hegelian idealist? The answer finally comes near the conclusion of the book, when Rockmore purports to discover a "stunning passage" in Volume 3 of *Capital,* in which Marx repudiates his earlier views on the necessity of social revolution. "According to Marx," writes Rockmore, "freedom, which only begins where forced labor ceases, consists in establishing control over the economic process in conditions favorable to human beings. Although real needs must still, and will always need to be, met through the economic process, that is, within the realm of necessity, beyond it lies what Marx now calls the realm of freedom. In suggesting that its prerequisite lies in shortening the working day, he implies that as the goal of history real freedom lies in free time."[54]

Rockmore then cites at length from Marx:

> In fact, the realm of freedom actually begins only where labor which is determined by necessity and mundane considerations ceases; thus in the very nature of things it lies beyond the sphere of actual material production. Just as the savage must wrestle with Nature to satisfy his wants, to maintain and reproduce life, so must civilized man, and he must do so in all social formations and under all possible modes of production.

[53] Karl Marx and Frederick Engels, *Collected Works*, Volume 42 (New York: International Publishers, 1987), p. 544.
[54] *Marx After Marxism*, pp. 172–173.

With his development this realm of physical necessity expands as a result of his wants; but, at the same time, the forces of production which satisfy these wants also increase. Freedom in this field can only consist in socialized man, the associated producers, rationally regulating their interchange with Nature, bringing it under their common control, instead of being ruled by it as by the blind forces of Nature; and achieving this with the least expenditure of energy and under conditions most favorable to, and worthy of, their human nature. But it none-theless still remains a realm of necessity. Beyond it begins that development of human energy which is an end in itself, the true realm of freedom, which, however, can blossom forth only with this realm of necessity as its basis. The shortening of the working day is its basic prerequisite.[55]

I have reproduced the passage as cited by Rockmore in its entirety, so that the reader may decide for himself or herself whether the conclusion drawn by Rockmore is in the least justified by what Marx actually wrote.

Many things could be said about this remarkable passage. Perhaps the most obvious is that, after many years of fighting for communism, Marx here just as obviously abandons it as a precondition of real human freedom. Freedom no longer lies in a break with a previous stage of society, that is in revolution, but in a basic improvement in the conditions of life, or in reform. In a word, Marx here substitutes reform for revolution.[56]

It is no doubt true that many things could be said about this passage, but nothing that Rockmore says is correct. To find in this passage a rejection of rev-olution in favor of reform requires that one attribute to virtually every sentence its opposite meaning. "Freedom," proclaims Marx, can be realized by "social-ized man, the associated producers, rationally regulating their interchange with Nature, bringing it under their common control, instead of being ruled by it as by the blind forces of Nature..." This, of course, can be achieved only through the overthrow of capitalism, a mode of production where economic

---

[55] Ibid., p. 173. (Original passage appears in *Capital*, Volume 3, p. 820).
[56] Ibid.

anarchy prevails in the form of the all-powerful market. On this basis, free-dom — understood as the development of man's creative capacities, beyond the sphere of work dictated by the necessity to maintain and reproduce life — will expand. Freedom arises out of and remains rooted in necessity, that is, man's need to obtain from nature everything he needs to survive and reproduce. As for the shortening of the working day, that is the basic measurement of the grad-ual encroachment of freedom upon necessity — but not itself the realization of freedom, and certainly not within the framework of capitalism. Nothing in this passage supports the next statement by Rockmore:

> Marxism has traditionally been hostile to mere reform. Yet in this passage Marx seems to hold out hope that modern indus-trial society and real human freedom are in principle compat-ible if and only if human beings can reestablish control over the economic process, which is the real master in capitalist society.[57]

But rational control over economic life is not possible under capital-ism, nor can the drive for profit be subordinated to the realization of purely human needs.

What Rockmore advocates — a Marx without historical materialism, without Engels, without Marxism — proves, in the end, to be a Marx without socialist revolution, a "Marx" that is not simply stood on his head, but also handcuffed and gagged.

Epilogue

It is necessary to attach to this review a brief epilogue. The publication of *Marx After Marxism* has been followed by the release of a volume edited by Professor Rockmore, entitled *The Philosophical Challenge of September 11*. In the introduction to this volume, co-authored by Rockmore and Joseph Margolis (Professor of Philosophy at Temple University), we read the following:

> One wonders whether we are prepared to address 9/11 in accord with the familiar terms and categories of our tradition, or whether they are even adequate to the task. We are no longer

---

[57] Ibid.

certain about our analytic instruments. ... Political philosophy as we have known it now seems outdated, seems unable to help us in our hour of need.

One suspects that the impasse extends to other domains. All of our ready conceptual assurances are confounded by 9/11. The assumption that we have captured the world in our theories has been stalemated by the world itself. The world has changed in ways no one could have foreseen. We cannot diagnose the events of 9/11 by any simple application of the usual tools. They defy our sense of legible order, and we cannot say when our categories will adjust again."[58]

As a confession of theoretical paralysis and intellectual bankruptcy in the face of reality, one can hardly imagine a more embarrassing self-exposure. Professor Rockmore would have us believe that the airplanes seized by the hijackers shattered not only the World Trade Center, but also the cognitive and analytical structures developed in the course of 2,500 years of philosophical thought.

Rockmore does not tell us what it is that imparted to the events of 9/11 their singularly incomprehensible character. After all that happened in the twentieth century — the horrors of two world wars, the Holocaust, the Stalinist purges, the dropping of two atomic bombs, and countless other acts of barbarism which, in their totality, claimed the lives of hundreds of millions of human beings — what sets September 11, 2001 apart from all antecedent tragedies? What new and heretofore unimagined qualities and characteristics did the events of that day reveal?

It now seems fairly obvious that Rockmore's assault on Marxism left him singularly unprepared for the very first political challenge of the twenty-first century. Having proclaimed the death of "Marxism" and the philosophical illegitimacy of the Marxist refutation of Hegelian idealism, Rockmore quite clearly has failed to discover an alternative theoretical structure that would enable him to analyze and understand contemporary reality.

---

[58] Tom Rockmore, Joseph Margolis and Armen T. Marsoobian, ed., *The Philosophical Challenge of September 11* (Malden MA, Oxford, Carlton Victoria: Blackwell Publishing, 2005), p. 3.

Appendix 1

A Letter to *The New York Times Book Review*

The New York Times Book Review chose not to publish the following letter addressed to the editor of its Book Review section.

March 26, 1996

Editor
The New York Times Book Review
229 West 43rd Street
New York, N.Y. 10036

Dear Sir:

The selection of Richard Pipes to review the late Dmitri Volkogonov's biography of Leon Trotsky precluded any critical examination of this book in the pages of *The New York Times*. As the author of several tendentious works on the Russian Revolution, in which the honest treatment of facts is subordinated to his own right-wing ideological obsessions, Professor Pipes could hardly be expected to make an issue of a similar tendency in the writings of General Volkogonov. However, Pipes did not merely overlook the innumerable factual errors that more scrupulous reviewers of Volkogonov's book have noted. It appears, rather, that Pipes conceived of his review as an opportunity to add to Volkogonov's falsehoods and blackguard the historical reputation of Leon Trotsky. The results of this effort are rather shocking. In what might appear at first as a paradox, Pipes, the foremost representative of right-wing Cold War Sovietology, presents a picture of Trotsky that reads as if it were plagiarized from a Soviet text book.

In terms reminiscent of the attacks leveled against Trotsky by his Stalinist opponents from the 1920s on, he is described by Pipes as "inordinately vain, arrogant, often rude" and "constitutionally incapable of the kind of disciplined teamwork that the Bolshevik Party required of its members." Trotsky was portrayed this way in countless Soviet publications by a regime that was determined to obliterate all popular recollection of a man who had been the principal organizer of the October Revolution, a mass leader without equal, and the founder and commander of the Red Army, whose reputation for disciplined work was legendary. One must ask why Pipes recycles these Stalinist-style attacks on Trotsky's personality. After all, what the Stalinists had in mind when they referred to Trotsky's "vanity" and hostility to "teamwork" was his unyielding refusal to subordinate his revolutionary principles to the demands of the ruling bureaucracy. Why does Pipes find this type of inflexibility so unattractive?

Pipes then proceeds to direct misrepresentations of historical facts. Referring to Lenin's attitude toward Trotsky, Pipes asserts that "of his political and administrative abilities he [Lenin] had a very low opinion." This claim is contradicted by Lenin's well-known political testament of December 1922, in which he wrote that Trotsky "is distinguished not only by outstanding ability. He is personally perhaps the most capable man in the present C[entral] C[ommittee]."

Curiously, Pipes writes rather sympathetically of Stalin, whom he refers to as "Lenin's true disciple and legitimate successor." Really? This description would have pleased Stalin, who insisted upon being called "The Lenin of Our Time." Attempting to perpetuate this crude version of an apostolic succession from Lenin to Stalin, the Harvard historian has managed to overlook the well-known fact that the above-cited political testament also included a specific appeal by Lenin for the removal of Stalin from the post of general secretary. Indeed, as the professor of history should recall, among the last actions taken by Lenin, before suffering the stroke that ended his political life, was the dictation of a letter in which the Soviet leader threatened to sever all personal relations with Stalin.

Even worse than these distortions of historical fact is Professor Pipes' gratuitous endorsement of the lie that constituted the basis of the Moscow Trials
and the associated terror of the late 1930s. "Trotsky and Lev Sedov, his son,"
writes Pipes, "frequently said and wrote that Stalin's regime had to be overthrown and Stalin himself assassinated."

It is well known, of course, that Trotsky publicly called for a political revolution in the Soviet Union. But it is a blatant and odious lie, discredited for
decades, that Trotsky and his son advocated, publicly or privately, the assassination of Stalin. This is no small matter. The accusation that Trotsky and
his son had plotted the assassination of Stalin and other leaders of the USSR
provided the legal pretext for the Moscow Trials of 1936–38 and the physical extermination of hundreds of thousands of socialists in the Soviet Union.

In September 1937, the Commission of Inquiry that had been established, under the chairmanship of the philosopher John Dewey, to investigate independently the charges made by the Stalinist regime against Leon
Trotsky issued its findings. On the critical question of whether Trotsky had
plotted the assassination of Stalin, the Commission concluded: "We find
that Trotsky throughout his whole career has always been a consistent opponent of individual terror. The Commission further finds that Trotsky never
instructed any of the defendants or witnesses in the Moscow trials to assassinate any political opponent."

On a purely moral plane, it is unspeakable that a prominent historian
should give credence to a lie that was used to justify the murder of hundreds of
thousands of people. But more is involved here than a careless attitude toward
facts. The question which must be answered is: Why does Professor Pipes,
in his treatment of the socialist opponents of the Stalinist regime, and especially Trotsky, rely upon the lies and misinformation that were peddled for
decades by the Kremlin? Permit me to suggest that the answer is to be found
in the right-wing ideological and political agenda that drives his approach
to history. Socialist opponents of Stalinism have frequently noted the peculiar coincidence between the Stalinist version of Soviet history and that presented by Cold War ideologists in the West. Both proceed from the supposed
identity of Marxism and the policies of the post-Lenin Soviet regime.

This identification of Stalinism and Marxism is the axiomatic foundation
of Pipes' interpretation of Soviet history. Determined to demonstrate that all
the crimes committed by the Stalinist regime flowed necessarily and inexorably from the October Revolution itself, Pipes cannot allow that there existed
a Marxist alternative to Stalinism. Thus, it is necessary for him to insist upon

the essential political continuity between Lenin and Stalin, and to depict the Marxist opponents of Stalin, above all Trotsky, as no less ruthless and murderous than the Kremlin tyrant. As this interpretation of history cannot be sustained by an honest presentation of facts, Professor Pipes must resort to lies. And there is no need for him to invent new ones. Pipes merely takes what he requires from the archives of Stalinism, which constitute an inexhaustible source of anti-Marxist falsehoods and fabrications.

Sincerely,
David North
National Secretary
Socialist Equality Party

Appendix 2

An Exchange with Richard Pipes

David North to Richard Pipes

March 27, 1996

Dear Professor Pipes:

In your review of the late General Dmitri Volkogonov's biography of Leon Trotsky, which appeared in the March 24 issue of *The New York Times Book Review*, you wrote the following: "Trotsky and Lev Sedov, his son and closest aide, frequently said and wrote that Stalin's regime had to be overthrown and Stalin himself assassinated."

This statement contains a glaring and serious error. While it is true that Trotsky advocated the overthrow of the Stalinist regime through a political revolution, he never advocated, publicly or privately, the assassination of Stalin.

As a historian, you certainly know that the allegation that Trotsky sought to assassinate Stalin served as the legal pretext for the Moscow Trials of 1936–38 and the physical extermination of hundreds of thousands of socialists in the Soviet Union. It has long been accepted that all the charges of terrorist activities leveled by the Stalinist regime against Trotsky and his supporters were concoctions of the GPU, and that the Moscow Trials were frame-ups.

The independent Commission of Inquiry established in 1937, under the chairmanship of John Dewey, to investigate the allegations against Trotsky specifically rejected the charge that the former Bolshevik leader had plotted the assassination of Stalin. It wrote: "We find that Trotsky throughout his whole career has always been a consistent opponent of individual terror. The Commission further finds that Trotsky never instructed any of the defendants or witnesses in the Moscow trials to assassinate any political opponent."

More recently, in 1988, the Supreme Court of the Soviet Union finally declared that all the defendants in the Moscow Trials were innocent of the crimes of which they were accused.

Those who are familiar with your historical writings know of your fervent ideological opposition to the 1917 October Revolution and especially bitter hatred of Leon Trotsky for the leading role that he played in that event. You are entitled to your opinion. However, you are not entitled to falsify the historical record. It is ironic, Professor Pipes, that in your zeal to discredit Trotsky, you should draw upon the very lies that were employed by Stalin to justify the mass murder of his socialist political opponents.

If you are prepared to stand by your claim that Trotsky called for the assassination of Stalin, and thereby provide belated legitimacy to the Moscow Trials and the associated purges, then you should publish the historical documents which support this position. If, however, you are unable to produce such documents, then you have a professional and ethical responsibility to retract publicly the false statement that you wrote in *The New York Times*.

Sincerely,
David North
National Secretary
Socialist Equality Party

David North to Richard Pipes

May 13, 1996

Dear Professor Pipes:

In a letter dated March 27, 1996, I called to your attention a serious error of fact that appeared in your review for *The New York Times* of the late General Dmitri Volkogonov's biography of Leon Trotsky. You claimed that

"Trotsky and Lev Sedov, his son and closest aide, frequently said and wrote that Stalin's regime had to be overthrown and Stalin himself assassinated."

As my letter explained, the claim that Trotsky and his son favored and urged the assassination of Stalin was the concocted pretext for the Moscow Trials of 1936–38 and the associated mass terror that resulted in the murder of hundreds of thousands of socialist opponents of the totalitarian regime. Beginning with the Dewey Commission of 1937 and culminating with the official repudiation of the trials by the Soviet government in the late 1980s, the charges of terrorist assassination plots presented at the Moscow Trials have been exposed comprehensively as criminal fabrications.

In concluding my letter of March 27, I placed before you the following challenge: "If you are prepared to stand by your claim that Trotsky called for the assassination of Stalin, and thereby provide belated legitimacy to the Moscow Trials and the associated purges, then you should publish the historical documents which support this position. If, however, you are unable to produce such documents, then you have a professional and ethical responsibility to retract publicly the false statement that you wrote in *The New York Times*."

Nearly six weeks have passed without a reply. I hope this delay does not mean that you intend to ignore the matter. I once again urge you to set the historical record straight and issue a retraction.

Sincerely,
David North
National Secretary
Socialist Equality Party

Richard Pipes to David North

May 20, 1996

Dear Mr. North:

I did not answer your letter of March 27 because I found it offensive. I shall reply to your letter of May 13 because it meets general standards of civility.

If, instead of fulminating against me and my statements concerning Trotsky, you had taken the trouble to look into Volkogonov's biography, the subject of my review, you would have found that Sedov told one of Stalin's secret police agents that Stalin ought to be killed (see pp. 378–79). It is possible that Zborowski, the agent in question, made up the threat: but the important thing is that such sentiments were passed on to Moscow and apparently taken at face value.

Secondly, as you yourself admit, Trotsky as well as Sedov repeatedly urged that Stalin's regime be overthrown. Now can you really imagine overthrowing a totalitarian dictatorship in any other way but by killing its leader? Do you think Stalin, facing defeat, would have graciously resigned and gone into retirement? As Volkogonov remarks: "The call for revolution was tantamount to calling for a coup d'état." (p. 370) From the point of view of the dictator, a call for the "liquidation" of his regime is tantamount of a call for his personal "liquidation."

I nowhere implied that the charges against Zinoviev, Kamenev, Bukharin, and the others were remotely true. They were pure fabrications. What I was saying is that the charges of "Trotskyism" were in some measure inspired by the irresponsible threats made by Trotsky and his son. They served Stalinist purposes.

Yours sincerely,
Richard Pipes

David North to Richard Pipes

June 16, 1996

Dear Professor Pipes:

Thank you for your letter of May 20. I regret that you found my letter of March 27 "offensive." I have reread that letter and cannot accept your claim that it fell short of "general standards of civility." But let us put this matter aside and concentrate, instead, on the important historical issue that is the subject of our difference — that is, whether, as you claimed in your review of Dmitri Volkogonov's biography, "Trotsky and Lev Sedov, his son and closest aide, frequently said and wrote that Stalin's regime had to be overthrown and Stalin himself assassinated."

At issue here is not a matter of interpretation but of facts. I attacked this statement because it is untrue. I pointed out that there existed no historical evidence to support the claim that Trotsky and his son had called for, let alone secretly plotted, the assassination of Stalin. Rather, it is factually indisputable that Stalin fabricated tales of "Trotskyite" murder conspiracies to justify the infamous Moscow show trials of 1936–38 and the physical liquidation of the socialist opposition to his totalitarian regime.

Your response to my criticism is confused and internally inconsistent.

First, you argue that your statement is based upon information provided by Volkogonov. Suggesting that I had failed to read Volkogonov's book with sufficient care, you draw attention to his citation of a report by an NKVD agent, Mark Zborowski, in which the latter claimed that he had been told by Sedov that Stalin should be killed.

Let me assure you that I studied this chapter of Volkogonov's biography with particular care, and it contradicts your categorical assertion that Trotsky and his son favored and called for the assassination of Stalin. Far from accepting the credibility of Zborowski's report, Volkogonov considers it possible that "the report was a fabrication designed to add fuel to the prosecution's arguments at the forthcoming trial" (p. 379). In another passage, citing a similar report from Zborowski, Volkogonov comments: "It may have been fabricated by the NKVD to be used should it be decided to recall Zborowski to Moscow for trial and liquidation. Nor can the possibility be ruled out that Zborowski was simply fantasizing" (p. 380).

It is clear that Volkogonov himself did not consider these reports to be credible evidence of a plan by Trotsky and/or Sedov to assassinate Stalin. Rather, in direct contrast to what you wrote in your review, Volkogonov concluded that "there is not a single shred of evidence that the Trotskyists carried out or prepared for any high-profile act of terrorism" (p. 380).

In what appears to be an attempt to shift attention away from historical facts, your letter introduces a new line of argument. Whether or not Trotsky and Sedov called for the assassination of Stalin is not decisive. "It is possible," you acknowledge, "that Zborowski, the agent in question, made up the threat." However, you then go on to state that "the important thing is that such sentiments [in Zborowski's reports] were passed on to Moscow and apparently taken at face value."

You seem to be suggesting that the Terror was, at least to some extent, motivated by Stalin's legitimate though misinformed belief that he was the target of Trotskyist assassination plots. This argument is as weak in its internal logic as it is in facts. If the incidents referred to by Zborowski were fabrications of the secret police — as Volkogonov more or less concedes — why would they have been taken at face value by Stalin? And even if Zborowski's report accurately reproduced a politically insignificant threat uttered by Sedov in a moment of anger, who can seriously believe that such a remark provided the motivation for the Moscow Trials and their fantastic allegations of sabotage, assassinations and espionage? In fact, the first of the two Zborowski reports cited by Volkogonov was dated February 8, 1937, one week after the executions of the defendants in the second of the three Moscow trials. The second report was dated one year later, on the very eve of the third trial. On this basis alone, what Sedov may or may not have said to Zborowski is utterly irrelevant to an understanding of Stalin's terror.

Unfortunately, you seem determined to place upon Trotsky at least some of the responsibility for the Moscow Trials, even though, as Volkogonov writes, "they were staged so as to destroy Trotsky morally, politically and psychologically..." (p. 381). In pursuit of this effort, you are compelled to resort to arguments that make a mockery of serious historical analysis.

Trotsky and Sedov, you point out triumphantly, urged the overthrow of Stalin. On the basis of this well-known fact, that no one has ever denied, you pose the following rhetorical questions: "Now can you really imagine overthrowing a totalitarian dictatorship in any other way but by killing its leader? Do you think Stalin, facing defeat, would have graciously resigned and gone into retirement?"

At the risk of offending you yet again, permit me to say that these questions are quite beside the point. Let us grant that Stalin, with his policeman's mentality, identified a political revolution with his own physical destruction. After all, no tyrant expects anything positive from a revolution. Stalin's political anxieties and subjective apprehensions were certainly a central factor in the decision to stage show trials and murder his opponents. But the obvious fact that Stalin feared Trotsky adds absolutely nothing to the legal credibility of the charges presented at the trials. Furthermore, the question raised by the Moscow Trials was not whether Trotsky's program of political revolution might lead, if it were accepted and acted upon by the Soviet masses, to the eventual death of Stalin. Rather, the question was whether Trotsky and his associates sought to remove Stalin from power through assassination.

The distinction is not a small one, and it was understood by politically thoughtful people back in the 1930s. As John Dewey put the matter so well in 1937, "Trotsky was not convicted upon charges of theoretical and political opposition to the regime which exists in the Soviet Union. He was convicted upon certain definite charges whose truth or falsity is a matter of objective fact."[1]

---

[1] Jo Ann Boydston, ed., *The Later Works of John Dewey, 1925–1953,* Volume 11 (Carbondale: Southern Illinois University Press, 1987), p. 317.

There is another historical issue posed by your rhetorical questions which deserves attention. You write that it is unimaginable that a totalitarian regime could be overthrown "in any other way but by killing its leader." I suppose that most terrorists would agree with you, but this outlook betrays a limited understanding of history and a simplistic conception of politics.

By way of contrast, I am obliged to offer a brief summary of Trotsky's understanding of the Stalinist totalitarian regime. As a Marxist, Trotsky approached politics from the standpoint of the interaction and struggle of great social forces, and he conceived of revolution as the conscious intervention of the broad masses of the working people in political life. Never did Trotsky reduce the complex phenomenon of the bureaucratic dictatorship in the Soviet Union to the ambitions and crimes of one man. With a degree of clarity that surpassed all his contemporaries, Trotsky explained the economic, social and political roots of postrevolutionary bureaucratic despotism in the Soviet Union. To the end of his days he never considered Stalin to be anything more than an "outstanding mediocrity," whose personal dictatorship was the concentrated expression of the monopolization of political power by the Soviet bureaucracy. The overthrow of Stalinism required, Trotsky insisted, the political reawakening of the working class and its mobilization on the basis of a revolutionary program directed against the privileged status of the bureaucracy and its suppression of the workers' democratic rights. The answer to Stalinism was not to be found in an assassin's bullet, but in the struggle of great masses of people. For this reason, Trotsky occupied himself not with the recruitment of assassins (as Stalin claimed), but with the building of a new international Marxist movement and the political and theoretical education of its cadres.

As for the personal fate of Stalin, this was largely a matter of indifference to Trotsky. It is reasonable to assume that he expected that a victorious revolutionary movement would deal with Stalin and his henchmen as they deserved. But in the voluminous writings of Trotsky published and unpublished, I doubt that the conscientious researcher would find more than a few sentences in which Trotsky dwelled on this question. He simply did not think it was an issue of great importance.

In your concluding paragraph, you finally state: "I nowhere implied that the charges against Zinoviev, Kamenev, Bukharin, and the others were remotely true. They were pure fabrications." In fact, Professor Pipes, your review of Volkogonov's biography not only implied, but directly supported the Stalinist allegations of assassination plots. Still, I am willing to accept this statement as a correction of what you wrote in your review.

However, this correction is tainted and made equivocal by the last two sentences of your letter. You write: "What I was saying is that the charges of 'Trotskyism' were in some measure inspired by the irresponsible threats made by Trotsky and his son. They served Stalinist purposes." What you mean by "charges of 'Trotskyism'" is not quite clear to me. But the reference to "irresponsible threats" and the serving of "Stalinist purposes" represents again an attempt to place upon Trotsky blame for the crimes committed by the Soviet bureaucracy against him and his supporters. You seem to be saying that if Trotsky had not opposed the Soviet regime, Stalin would not have been compelled to murder his political opponents. But this is a tautology that explains nothing at all.

Trotsky's opposition to the Soviet bureaucracy was the irrepressible expression of his Marxist and socialist convictions. The program of this opposition articulated the social interests of a working class whose rights were trampled upon by a privileged bureaucracy. Trotsky's life and death struggle against bureaucratic despotism heroically illustrates the very political fact that you have sought to disprove in so many of your writings, that Marxism and Stalinism stand in irreconcilable opposition to each other. Of all the alternatives open to Trotsky in the 1920s and 1930s, the one which he never contemplated was that of political compromise and accommodation with the Stalinist bureaucracy. Even Dmitri Volkogonov, for all the many failings of his biography of Trotsky, pays tribute to the implacable character of his struggle against Stalinism. "Trotsky was perhaps the first person," writes Volkogonov, "to place on the open agenda the need to liquidate Stalinism as a system, as an ideology, as a mode of operations and as a way of thinking. For Trotsky, Stalinism was the worst form of totalitarianism, comparable only with Fascism. Genuine democratic development could only occur if the Stalinist system was first dismantled. Only then could socialism have a future" (p. 370).

Yours sincerely,
David North
National Secretary
Equality Party

Index